Spring Security

Third Edition

Secure your web applications, RESTful services, and microservice architectures

Mick Knutson
Robert Winch
Peter Mularien

BIRMINGHAM - MUMBAI

Spring Security

Third Edition

Copyright © 2017 Packt Publishing

All rights reserved. No part of this book may be reproduced, stored in a retrieval system, or transmitted in any form or by any means, without the prior written permission of the publisher, except in the case of brief quotations embedded in critical articles or reviews.

Every effort has been made in the preparation of this book to ensure the accuracy of the information presented. However, the information contained in this book is sold without warranty, either express or implied. Neither the author, nor Packt Publishing, and its dealers and distributors will be held liable for any damages caused or alleged to be caused directly or indirectly by this book.

Packt Publishing has endeavored to provide trademark information about all of the companies and products mentioned in this book by the appropriate use of capitals. However, Packt Publishing cannot guarantee the accuracy of this information.

First published: May 2010

Second edition: December 2012

Third edition: November 2017

Production reference: 1241117

Published by Packt Publishing Ltd.
Livery Place
35 Livery Street
Birmingham
B3 2PB, UK.

ISBN 978-1-78712-951-1

www.packtpub.com

Credits

Authors
Mick Knutson
Robert Winch
Peter Mularien

Reviewers
Tejaswini Mandar Jog
Jay Lee

Commissioning Editor
Aaron Lazar

Acquisition Editor
Karan Sadawana

Content Development Editor
Zeeyan Pinheiro

Technical Editor
Vibhuti Gawde

Copy Editors
Pranjali Chury
Safis Editing

Project Coordinator
Vaidehi Sawant

Proofreader
Safis Editing

Indexer
Francy Puthiry

Graphics
Jason Monteiro

Production Coordinator
Shantanu Zagade

About the Authors

Mick Knutson has over 25 years of experience in the IT industry. As a passionate and experienced enterprise technology consultant, Java architect, and software developer, he looks forward to using his unique professional experience to help students learn about software development in an effective, practical, and convenient manner.

Mick's real-world expertise comes from providing individuals and mid-to-large-size businesses with advanced software consulting and training. He has collaborated with many notable clients and partners including VMware, Spring Source, FuseSource, Global Knowledge, and Knowledge United. His technical expertise includes OOA/OOD/OOP, Java, Java EE, Spring Security, Oracle, Enterprise Integration, and Message-Oriented Middleware (MOM).

As a veteran of the IT industry, Mick is determined to help as many people as possible and show that anyone can become a software developer. He has spoken around the world at training seminars, luncheons, book publishing engagements, and white paper engagements. He has authored several technical books and articles on Spring Security, Java EE 6, HTTP, and VisualVM. He is also a featured blogger at DZone, where he is part of the curated Most Valuable Blogger (MVB) group.

Having lived and breathed software development for over two decades, Mick enjoys translating complex technical concepts into plain English for different audiences. Whether he is helping an experienced software professional or someone who is new to the field, he can simplify even the most intricate IT concepts.

Mick's mission is to use his seasoned professional experience to help anyone who wants to learn about software development. As an expert and professional, Mick designs his training courses to make the learning experience as enriching, seamless, and convenient as possible so that you can master software development in the shortest amount of time.

Learn from an expert. Mick warmly looks forward to helping you learn software development in the right way so that you can maximize both your money and your time.

You can also refer to his following books:

- *Spring Security Third Edition*
- *Distributed Configuration with Spring Cloud Config*
- *Java EE6 Cookbook*
- *HTTP Reference Card* (DZone)
- *VisualVM Reference Card* (DZone)

You can also refer to his video on *BASELogic* available on YouTube.

You can also connect with him on the following social media sites:

- LinkedIn (`mickknutson`)
- Twitter (`mickknutson`)
- GitHub (`mickknutson`)
- Bitbucket (`mickknutson`)
- Udemy video series (`MickKnutson`)
- Facebook (`BASELogic`)
- Google+ (`BASElogic`)

I would like to thank all the randomly assembled molecules that I have collided with on my journey through the universe.

Robert Winch is currently a senior software engineer at VMware and is the project lead of the Spring Security framework. In the past, he has worked as a software architect at Cerner, the largest provider of electronic medical systems in the US, securing healthcare applications. Throughout his career, he has developed hands-on experience integrating Spring Security with an array of security standards (that is, LDAP, SAML, CAS, OAuth, and so on). Before he was employed at Cerner, he worked as an independent web contractor in proteomics research at Loyola University Chicago and on the Globus Toolkit at Argonne National Laboratory.

Peter Mularien is an experienced software architect and engineer and the author of the book Spring Security 3, Packt Publishing. Peter currently works for a large financial services company and has over 12 years of consulting and product experience in Java, Spring, Oracle, and many other enterprise technologies. He is also the reviewer of this book.

About the Reviewers

Tejaswini Mandar Jog is a passionate and enthusiastic Java trainer. She has over nine years of experience in the IT training field, specializing in Java, J2EE, Spring, and relevant technologies. She has worked with many renowned corporate companies on training and skill enhancement programs. She is also involved in the development of projects using Java, Spring, and Hibernate.

She is the author of the books *Learning Modular Java Programming, Learning Spring 5.0*, and *Reactive Programming With Java9*.

> *Thank you Mandar and Ojas for being with me as my biggest support.*

Jay Lee currently works at Pivotal as a senior platform architect. His job is to help big enterprise's Cloud Native Journey with Spring, Spring Boot, Spring Cloud, and Cloud Foundry. Before joining Pivotal, he spent ten years at Oracle and worked with big enterprises for their large-scale Java distributed system and Middleware. He is authoring Microservices book (name should be decided) using Spring Boot, and Spring Cloud at the moment.

www.Packtpub.com

For support files and downloads related to your book, please visit www.PacktPub.com.

Did you know that Packt offers eBook versions of every book published, with PDF and ePub files available? You can upgrade to the eBook version at www.PacktPub.com and as a print book customer, you are entitled to a discount on the eBook copy. Get in touch with us at service@packtpub.com for more details.

At www.PacktPub.com, you can also read a collection of free technical articles, sign up for a range of free newsletters and receive exclusive discounts and offers on Packt books and eBooks.

https://www.packtpub.com/mapt

Get the most in-demand software skills with Mapt. Mapt gives you full access to all Packt books and video courses, as well as industry-leading tools to help you plan your personal development and advance your career.

Why subscribe?

- Fully searchable across every book published by Packt
- Copy and paste, print, and bookmark content
- On demand and accessible via a web browser

Customer Feedback

Thanks for purchasing this Packt book. At Packt, quality is at the heart of our editorial process. To help us improve, please leave us an honest review on this book's Amazon page at https://www.amazon.in/dp/1787129519.

If you'd like to join our team of regular reviewers, you can e-mail us at customerreviews@packtpub.com. We award our regular reviewers with free eBooks and videos in exchange for their valuable feedback. Help us be relentless in improving our products!

Table of Contents

Preface

Welcome to the world of Spring Security 4.2! We're certainly pleased that you have acquired the only published book fully devoted to Spring Security 4.2. Before we get started with the book, we would like to give you an overview of how the book is organized and how you can get the most out of it.

Once you have read this book, you should be familiar with key security concepts and understand how to solve the majority of the real-world problems that you will need to solve with Spring Security. Through this discovery, you will gain an in-depth understanding of Spring Security's architecture, which will allow you to handle any unexpected use cases the book does not cover.

The book is divided into the following four main sections:

- The first section (Chapter 1, *Anatomy of an Unsafe Application* and Chapter 2, *Getting Started with Spring Security*) provides an introduction to Spring Security and allows you to get started with Spring Security quickly
- The second section (Chapter 3, *Custom Authentication*, Chapter 4, *JDBC-Based Authentication*, Chapter 5, *Authentication with Spring Data*, Chapter 6, *LDAP Directory Services*, Chapter 7, *Remember-Me Services*, Chapter 8, *Client Certificate Authentication with TLS*, and Chapter 9, *Opening up to OAuth 2*) provides in-depth instructions for integrating with a number of different authentication technologies
- The third section (Chapter 10, *Single Sign-On with the Central Authentication Service*, Chapter 11, *Fine-Grained Access Control*, and Chapter 12, *Access Control Lists*) explains how Spring Security's authorization support works
- Finally, the last section (Chapters 13, *Custom Authorization*, Chapter 14, *Session Management*, Chapter 15, *Additional Spring Security Features*, and Chapter 16, *Migration to Spring Security 4.2*, Chapter 17, *Microservice Security with OAuth 2 and JSON Web Tokens*) provides information specialized topics and guides that help you perform very specific tasks

Security is a very interwoven concept, and so are many of the topics in the book. However, once you have read through the first three chapters, the rest of the chapters are fairly independent. This means that you can easily skip chapters and still understand what is happening. The goal is to provide a cookbook-style guide that when read in its entirety still helps you develop a clear understanding of Spring Security.

The book uses a simple Spring Web MVC-based application to illustrate how to solve real-world problems. The application is intended to be very simple and straightforward, and deliberately contains very little functionality—the goal of this application is to encourage you to focus on Spring Security concepts and not get tied up in the complexities of application development. You will have a much easier time following the book if you take the time to review the sample application source code and try to follow along with the exercises. Some tips on getting started are found in the *Getting started with the JBCP calendar sample code* section in `Appendix`, *Additional Reference Material*.

What this book covers

`Chapter 1`, *Anatomy of an Unsafe Application*, covers a hypothetical security audit of our calendar application, illustrating common issues that can be resolved through the proper application of Spring Security. You will learn about some basic security terminology and review some prerequisites for getting the sample application up and running.

`Chapter 2`, *Getting Started with Spring Security*, demonstrates the "Hello World" installation of Spring Security. After the chapter walks the reader through some of the most common customizations of Spring Security.

`Chapter 3`, *Custom Authentication*, incrementally explains Spring Security's authentication architecture by customizing key pieces of the authentication infrastructure to address real-world problems. Through these customizations, you will gain an understanding of how Spring Security authentication works and how you can integrate with existing and new authentication mechanisms.

`Chapter 4`, *JDBC-Based Authentication*, covers authenticating against a database using Spring Security's built-in JDBC support. We then discuss how we can secure our passwords using Spring Security's new cryptography module.

`Chapter 5`, *Authentication with Spring Data*, covers authenticating against a database using Spring Security's integration with Spring Data JPA and Spring Data MongoDB.

`Chapter 6`, *LDAP Directory Services*, provides a guide to application integration with an LDAP directory server.

`Chapter 7`, *Remember-Me Services*, demonstrates the use of the remember-me feature in Spring Security and how to configure it. We also explore additional considerations to bear in mind when using it.

Chapter 8, *Client Certificate Authentication with TLS*, makes X.509 certificate-based authentication a clear alternative for certain business scenarios, where managed certificates can add an additional layer of security to our application.

Chapter 9, *Opening up to OAuth 2*, covers OAuth 2-enabled login and user attribute exchange, as well as a high-level overview of the logical flow of the OAuth 2 protocol, including Spring OAuth 2 and Spring social integration.

Chapter 10, *Single Sign-on with Central Authentication Service*, shows how integrating with Central Authentication Service (CAS) can provide Single Sign-On and single logout support to your Spring Security-enabled applications. It also demonstrates how you can use CAS proxy ticket support with stateless services.

Chapter 11, *Fine-Grained Access Control*, covers in-page authorization checking (partial page rendering) and business-layer security using Spring Security's method security capabilities.

Chapter 12, *Access Control Lists*, covers the concepts and basic implementation of business object-level security using the Spring Security ACL module—a powerful module with a very flexible applicability to challenging business security problems.

Chapter 13, *Custom Authorization*, explains how Spring Security's authorization works by writing custom implementations of key parts of Spring Security's authorization infrastructure.

Chapter 14, *Session Management*, discusses how Spring Security manages and secures user sessions. The chapter starts by explaining session fixation attacks and how Spring Security defends against them. It then discusses how you can manage logged-in users and restrict the number of concurrent sessions a single user has. Finally, we describe how Spring Security associates a user to HttpSession and how to customize this behavior.

Chapter 15, *Additional Spring Security Features*, covers other Spring Security features, including common security vulnerabilities such as Cross-Site Scripting (XSS), Cross-Site Request Forgery (CSRF), synchronizer tokens, and Clickjacking, and how to protect against them.

Chapter 16, *Migration to Spring Security 4.2*, provides a migration path from Spring Security 3, including notable configuration changes, class and package migrations, and important new features. It also highlights the new features that can be found in Spring Security 4.2 and provides references to examples of the features in the book.

`Chapter 17`, *Microservice Security with OAuth 2 and JSON Web Tokens*, looks at microservice-based architectures and how OAuth 2 with JWT play a role in securing microservices in a Spring-based application.

`Appendix`, *Additional Reference Material*, contains some reference material that is not directly related to Spring Security, but is still relevant to the topics covered in this book. Most importantly, it contains a section that assists in running the sample code included with the book.

What you need for this book

The following list contains the software required in order to run the sample applications included with the book. Some chapters have the following additional requirements that are outlined in the respective chapters:

- Java Development Kit 1.8 can be downloaded from Oracle's website at `http://www.oracle.com/technetwork/java/javase/downloads/index.html`
- IntelliJ IDEA 2017+ can be downloaded from `https://www.jetbrains.com/idea/`
- Spring Tool Suite 3.9.1.RELEASE+ can be downloaded from `https://spring.io/tools/sts`

Who this book is for

If you are a Java Web and/or RESTful web service developer and have a basic understanding of creating Java 8, Java Web and/or RESTful web service applications, XML, and the Spring Framework, this book is for you. You are not expected to have any previous experience with Spring Security.

Conventions

In this book, you will find a number of text styles that distinguish between different kinds of information. Here are some examples of these styles and an explanation of their meaning. Code words in text, database table names, folder names, filenames, file extensions, pathnames, dummy URLs, user input, and Twitter handles are shown as follows: "The next steps involve a series of updates to the `web.xml` file". A block of code is set as follows:

```
//build.gradle:
    dependencies {
        compile "org.springframework.security:spring-security-
        config:${springSecurityVersion}"
```

```
compile "org.springframework.security:spring-security-
core:${springSecurityVersion}"
compile "org.springframework.security:spring-security-
web:${springSecurityVersion}"
...
}
```

When we wish to draw your attention to a particular part of a code block, the relevant lines or items are set in bold:

```
[default]
exten => s,1,Dial(Zap/1|30)
exten => s,2,Voicemail(u100)
exten => s,102,Voicemail(b100)
exten => i,1,Voicemail(s0)
```

Any command-line input or output is written as follows:

```
$ ./gradlew idea
```

New terms and **important words** are shown in bold.

Words that you see on the screen, for example, in menus or dialog boxes, appear in the text like this: "In Microsoft Windows, you can view some of the ACL capabilities of a file by right-clicking on a file and examining its security properties (**Properties** | **Security**), as shown in the following screenshot".

Warnings or important notes appear like this.

Tips and tricks appear like this.

Reader feedback

Feedback from our readers is always welcome. Let us know what you think about this book-what you liked or disliked. Reader feedback is important for us as it helps us develop titles that you will really get the most out of.

To send us general feedback, simply email feedback@packtpub.com, and mention the book's title in the subject of your message.

If there is a topic that you have expertise in and you are interested in either writing or contributing to a book, see our author guide at www.packtpub.com/authors.

Customer support

Now that you are the proud owner of a Packt book, we have a number of things to help you to get the most from your purchase.

Downloading the example code

You can download the example code files for this book from your account at http://www.packtpub.com. If you purchased this book elsewhere, you can visit http://www.packtpub.com/support and register to have the files emailed directly to you. You can download the code files by following these steps:

1. Log in or register to our website using your email address and password.
2. Hover the mouse pointer on the **SUPPORT** tab at the top.
3. Click on **Code Downloads & Errata**.
4. Enter the name of the book in the **Search** box.
5. Select the book for which you're looking to download the code files.
6. Choose from the drop-down menu where you purchased this book from.
7. Click on **Code Download**.

Once the file is downloaded, please make sure that you unzip or extract the folder using the latest version of:

- WinRAR / 7-Zip for Windows
- Zipeg / iZip / UnRarX for Mac
- 7-Zip / PeaZip for Linux

The code bundle for the book is also hosted on GitHub at https://github.com/PacktPublishing/Spring-Security-Third-Edition. We also have other code bundles from our rich catalog of books and videos available at https://github.com/PacktPublishing/. Check them out!

Errata

Although we have taken every care to ensure the accuracy of our content, mistakes do happen. If you find a mistake in one of our books-maybe a mistake in the text or the code-we would be grateful if you could report this to us. By doing so, you can save other readers from frustration and help us improve subsequent versions of this book. If you find any errata, please report them by visiting http://www.packtpub.com/submit-errata, selecting your book, clicking on the **Errata Submission Form** link, and entering the details of your errata. Once your errata are verified, your submission will be accepted and the errata will be uploaded to our website or added to any list of existing errata under the Errata section of that title. To view the previously submitted errata, go to https://www.packtpub.com/books/content/support and enter the name of the book in the search field. The required information will appear under the **Errata** section.

Piracy

Piracy of copyrighted material on the internet is an ongoing problem across all media. At Packt, we take the protection of our copyright and licenses very seriously. If you come across any illegal copies of our works in any form on the internet, please provide us with the location address or website name immediately so that we can pursue a remedy. Please contact us at copyright@packtpub.com with a link to the suspected pirated material. We appreciate your help in protecting our authors and our ability to bring you valuable content.

Questions

If you have a problem with any aspect of this book, you can contact us at questions@packtpub.com, and we will do our best to address the problem.

1
Anatomy of an Unsafe Application

Security is arguably one of the most critical architectural components of any web-based application written in the 21st century. In an era where malware, criminals, and rogue employees are always present and actively testing software for exploits, smart and comprehensive use of security is a key element to any project for which you'll be responsible.

This book is written to follow a pattern of development that, we feel, provides a useful premise for tackling a complex subject—taking a web-based application with a Spring 4.2 foundation, and understanding the core concepts and strategies for securing it with Spring Security 4.2. We complement this approach by providing sample code for each chapter in the form of complete web applications.

Whether you're already using Spring Security or are interested in taking your basic use of the software to the next level of complexity, you'll find something to help you in this book. During the course of this chapter, we will cover the following topics:

- The results of a fictional security audit
- Some common security problems of web-based applications
- Several core software security terms and concepts

If you are already familiar with basic security terminology, you may skip to Chapter 2, *Getting Started with Spring Security*, where we start using the basic functionality of the framework.

Security audit

It's early in the morning at your job as a software developer for the **Jim Bob Circle Pants Online Calendar** (JBCPCalendar.com), and you're halfway through your first cup of coffee when you get the following email from your supervisor:

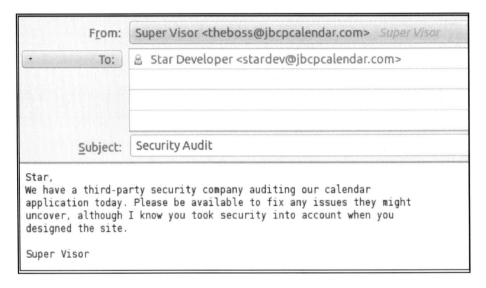

What? You didn't think about security when you designed the application? In fact, at this point, you are not even sure what a security audit is. Sounds like you'll have a lot to learn from the security auditors! Later in this chapter, we will review what an audit is, along with the results of an audit. First, let's spend a bit of time examining the application that's under review.

About the sample application

Although we'll be working through a contrived scenario as we progress through this book, the design of the application and the changes that we'll make to it are drawn from the real-world usage of Spring-based applications. The calendar application allows users to create and view events:

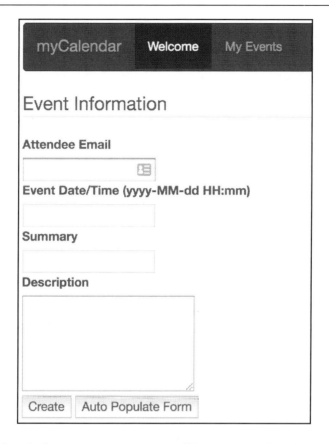

After entering the details for a new event, you will be presented with the following screenshot:

The application is designed to be simplistic, to allow us to focus on the important aspects of security and not get tied up in the details of **object-relational mapping (ORM)** and complex UI techniques. We expect you to refer to other supplementary materials in the Appendix, *Additional Reference Material* (in the *Supplementary Materials* section of this book) to cover some of the baseline functionality that is provided as part of the sample code.

The code is written in Spring and Spring Security 4.2, but it would be relatively easy to adapt many of the examples to other versions of Spring Security. Refer to the discussion about the detailed changes between Spring Security 3 and 4.2 in Chapter 16, *Migration to Spring Security 4.2*, for assistance in translating the examples to the Spring Security 4 syntax.

Please don't use this application as a baseline to build a real online calendar application. It has been purposely structured to be simple and to focus on the concepts and configuration that we illustrate in this book.

The JBCP calendar application architecture

The web application follows a standard three-tier architecture consisting of a web, service, and data access layer, as indicated in the following diagram:

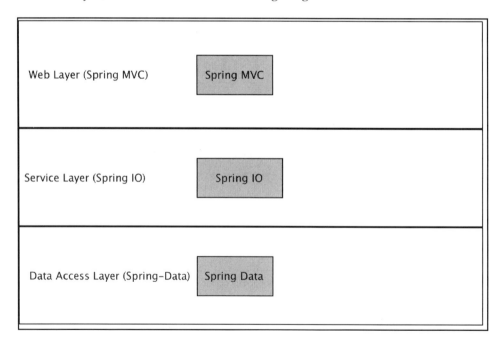

You can find additional material about MVC architectures in the *Supplementary Materials* section of the Appendix, *Additional Reference Material*.

The web layer encapsulates MVC code and functionality. In this sample application, we will use the Spring MVC framework, but we could just as easily use **Spring Web Flow (SWF)**, **Apache Struts**, or even a Spring-friendly web stack, such as **Apache Wicket**.

In a typical web application, leveraging Spring Security, the web layer is where much of the configuration and augmentation of code takes place. For example, the EventsController class is used to transform an HTTP request into persisting an event into the database. If you haven't had a lot of experience with web applications and Spring MVC specifically, it would be wise to review the baseline code closely and make sure you understand it before we move on to more complex subjects. Again, we've tried to make the website as simple as possible, and the construct of a calendar application is used just to provide a sensible title and light structure to the site.

 You can find detailed instructions on setting up the sample application within the *Appendix, Additional Reference Material*.

The service layer encapsulates the business logic for the application. In our sample application, we use DefaultCalendarService as a very light facade over the data access layer, to illustrate particular points about securing application service methods. The service layer is also used to operate on both Spring Security APIs and our Calendar APIs within a single method call. We will discuss this in greater detail in Chapter 3, *Custom Authentication*.

In a typical web application, this layer would incorporate business rule validation, composition and decomposition of business objects, and cross-cutting concerns such as auditing.

The data access layer encapsulates the code responsible for manipulating the contents of database tables. In many Spring applications, this is where you would see the use of ORM, such as Hibernate or JPA. It exposes an object-based API to the service layer. In our sample application, we use basic JDBC functionality to achieve persistence to the in-memory H2 database. For example, JdbcEventDao is used to save event objects to the database.

In a typical web application, a more comprehensive data access solution would be utilized. As ORM, and more generally data access, tends to be confusing for some developers, this is an area we have chosen to simplify as much as possible for the purposes of clarity.

Application technology

We have endeavored to make the application as easy to run as possible by focusing on some basic tools and technologies that almost every Spring developer would have on their development machine. Nevertheless, we have provided the *Getting started* section as supplementary information in the Append, *Getting Started with JBCP Calendar Sample Code*.

The primary method for integrating with the sample code is providing Gradle--compatible projects. Since many IDEs have rich integration with Gradle, users should be able to import the code into any IDE that supports Gradle. As many developers use Gradle, we felt this was the most straightforward method of packaging the examples. Whatever development environment you are familiar with, hopefully, you will find a way to work through the examples in this book.

Many IDEs provide Gradle tooling that can automatically download the Spring and Spring Security 4.2 Javadoc and source code for you. However, there may be times when this is not possible. In such cases, you'll want to download the full releases of both Spring 4.2 and Spring Security 4.2. The Javadoc and source code are top-notch. If you get confused or want more information, the samples can provide an additional level of support or reassurance for your learning. Visit the *Supplementary Materials* section, in `Appendix`, *Additional Reference Material* to find additional information about Gradle, including running the samples, obtaining the source code and Javadoc, and the alternatives for building your projects without Gradle.

Reviewing the audit results

Let's return to our email and see how the audit is progressing. Uh-oh, the results don't look good:

From:	Super Visor <theboss@jbcpcalendar.com> *Super Visor*
To:	🔒 Star Developer <stardev@jbcpcalendar.com>
Subject:	Security Audit

```
Star,
Have a look at the results and come up with a plan to address these
issues.

Super Visor
```

APPLICATION AUDIT RESULTS

This application exhibits the following insecure behavior:

- Inadvertent privilege escalation due to lack of URL protection and general authentication
- Inappropriate or non-existent use of authorization
- Missing database credential security
- Personally-identifiable or sensitive information is easily accessible or unencrypted
- Insecure transport-level protection due to lack of SSL encryption
- Risk level is high

We recommend that this application should be taken offline until these issues can be resolved.

Ouch! This result looks bad for our company. We'd better work to resolve these issues as quickly as possible.

Third-party security specialists are often hired by companies (or their partners or customers) to audit the effectiveness of their software security, through a combination of white hat hacking, source code review, and formal or informal conversations with application developers and architects.

White hat hacking or **ethical hacking** is done by professionals who are hired to instruct companies on how to protect themselves better, rather than with the intent to be malicious.

Typically, the goal of security audits is to provide management or clients with the assurance that basic secure development practices have been followed, to ensure the integrity and safety of the customer's data and system functions. Depending on the industry the software is targeted at, the auditor may also test it using industry-specific standards or compliance metrics.

Two specific security standards that you're likely to run into at some point in your career are the **Payment Card Industry Data Security Standard (PCI DSS)** and the **Health Insurance Privacy and Accountability Act (HIPAA)** privacy rules. Both these standards are intended to ensure the safety of specific sensitive information (such as credit card and medical information) through a combination of process and software controls. Many other industries and countries have similar rules about sensitive or **Personally Identifiable Information (PII)**. Failure to follow these standards is not only bad practice but also something that could expose you or your company to significant liability (not to mention bad press) in the event of a security breach.

Receiving the results of a security audit can be an eye-opening experience. Following through with the required software improvements can be the perfect opportunity for self-education and software improvement, and can allow you to implement practices and policies that lead to secure software.

Let's review the auditor's findings, and come up with a plan to address them in detail.

Authentication

Authentication is one of two key security concepts that you must internalize when developing secure applications (the other being authorization). **Authentication** identifies who is attempting to request a resource. You may be familiar with authentication in your daily online and offline life, in very different contexts, as follows:

- **Credential-based authentication**: When you log in to your web-based email account, you most likely provide your username and password. The email provider matches your username with a known user in its database and verifies that your password matches what they have on record. These credentials are what the email system uses to validate that you are a valid user of the system. First, we'll use this type of authentication to secure sensitive areas of the JBCP calendar application. Technically speaking, the email system can check credentials not only in the database but anywhere, for example, a corporate directory server such as **Microsoft Active Directory**. A number of these types of integrations are covered throughout this book.

- **Two-factor authentication**: When you withdraw money from your bank's automated teller machine, you swipe your ID card and enter your personal identification number before you are allowed to retrieve cash or conduct other transactions. This type of authentication is similar to the username and password authentication, except that the username is encoded on the card's magnetic strip. The combination of the physical card and user-entered PIN allows the bank to ensure that you should have access to the account. The combination of a password and a physical device (your plastic ATM card) is a ubiquitous form of two-factor authentication. In a professional, security-conscious environment, it's common to see these types of devices in regular use for access to highly secure systems, especially dealing with finance or personally identifiable information. A hardware device, such as **RSA SecurID**, combines a time-based hardware device with server-based authentication software, making the environment extremely difficult to compromise.

- **Hardware authentication**: When you start your car in the morning, you slip your metal key into the ignition and turn it to get the car started. Although it may not feel similar to the other two examples, the correct match of the bumps on the key and the tumblers in the ignition switch function as a form of hardware authentication.

There are literally dozens of forms of authentication that can be applied to the problem of software and hardware security, each with their own pros and cons. We'll review some of these methods as they apply to Spring Security throughout the first half of this book. Our application lacks any type of authentication, which is why the audit included the risk of inadvertent privilege escalation.

Typically, a software system will be divided into two high-level realms, such as unauthenticated (or anonymous) and authenticated, as shown in the following screenshot:

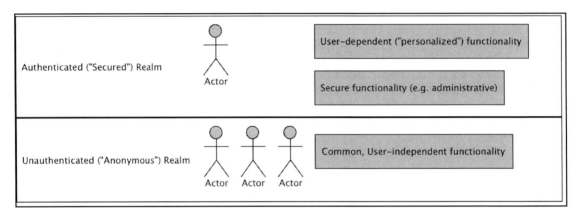

Application functionality in the anonymous realm is the functionality that is independent of a user's identity (think of a welcome page for an online application).

Anonymous areas do not do the following:

- Require a user to log in to the system or otherwise identify themselves to be usable
- Display sensitive information, such as names, addresses, credit cards, and orders
- Provide functionality to manipulate the overall state of the system or its data

Unauthenticated areas of the system are intended for use by everyone, even by users who we haven't specifically identified yet. However, it may be that additional functionality appears to identified users in these areas (for example, the ubiquitous `Welcome {First Name}` text). The selective displaying of content to authenticated users is fully supported through the use of the Spring Security tag library and is covered in `Chapter 11`, *Fine-Grained Access Control*.

We'll resolve this finding and implement form-based authentication using the automatic configuration capability of Spring Security in `Chapter 2`, *Getting Started with Spring Security*. Afterwards, we will explore various other means of performing authentication (which usually revolves around system integration with enterprise or other external authentication stores).

Authorization

Inappropriate or non-existent use of authorization

Authorization is the second of two core security concepts that are crucial in implementing and understanding application security. **Authorization** uses the information that was validated during authentication to determine whether access should be granted to a particular resource. Built around the authorization model for the application, authorization partitions the application functionality and data so that the availability of these items can be controlled by matching the combination of privileges, functionality, and data to users. Our application's failure at this point of the audit indicates that the application's functionality isn't restricted by the user role. Imagine if you were running an e-commerce site and the ability to view, cancel, or modify orders and customer information was available to any user of the site!

Authorization typically involves the following two separate aspects that combine to describe the accessibility of the secured system:

- The first is the mapping of an authenticated principal to one or more authorities (often called **roles**). For example, a casual user of your website might be viewed as having visitor authority, while a site administrator might be assigned administrative authority.
- The second is the assignment of authority checks to secured resources of the system. This is typically done at the time a system is developed, either through an explicit declaration in code or through configuration parameters. For example, the screen that allows for the viewing of other users' events should be made available only to those users with administrative authority.

 A secured resource may be any aspect of the system that should be conditionally available based on the authority of the user.

Secured resources of a web-based application could be individual web pages, entire portions of the website, or portions of individual pages. Conversely, secured business resources might be method calls on classes or individual business objects.

You might imagine an authority check that would examine the principal, look up its user account, and determine whether the principal is, in fact, an administrator. If this authority check determines that the principal who is attempting to access the secured area is, in fact, an administrator, then the request will succeed. If, however, the principal does not have the sufficient authority, the request should be denied.

Let's take a closer look at an example of a particular secured resource, the **All Events** page. The **All Events** page requires administrative access (after all, we don't want regular users viewing other users' events), and as such, looks for a certain level of authority in the principal accessing it.

If we think about how a decision might be made when a site administrator attempts to access the protected resource, we'd imagine that the examination of the actual authority versus the required authority might be expressed concisely in terms of the set theory. We might then choose to represent this decision as a **Venn** diagram for the administrative user:

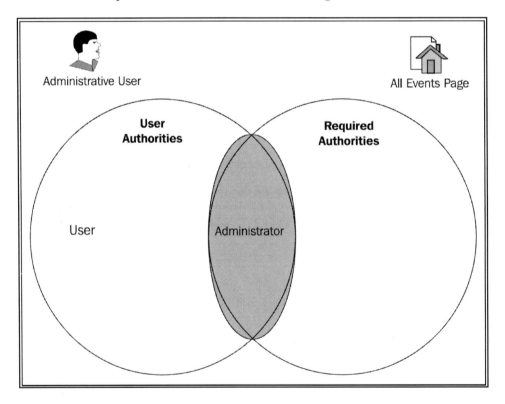

There is an intersection between **User Authorities** (users and administrators) and **Required Authorities** (administrators) for the page, so the user is provided with access.

Contrast this with an unauthorized user, as follows:

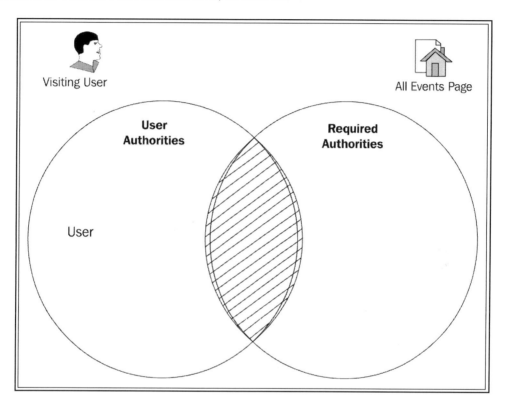

The sets of authorities are disjointed and have no common elements. So, the user is denied access to the page. Thus, we have demonstrated the basic principle of the authorization of access to resources.

In reality, there's real code making this decision, with the consequence that the user is granted or denied access to the requested protected resource. We'll address the basic authorization problem with the authorization infrastructure of Spring Security in Chapter 2, *Getting Started with Spring Security*, followed by more advanced authorization in Chapter 12, *Access Control Lists*, and Chapter 13, *Custom Authorization*.

Database credential security

Database credentials are not secure or easily accessible. Through the examination of the application source code and configuration files, the auditors noted that user passwords were stored in plain text in the configuration files, making it very easy for a malicious user with access to the server to gain access to the application.

As the application contains personal and financial data, a rogue user being able to access any data could expose the company to identity theft or tampering. Protecting access to the credentials used to access the application should be a top priority for us, and an important first step is ensuring that one point of failure in security does not compromise the entire system.

We'll examine the configuration of database access layers in Spring Security for credential storage, which requires JDBC connectivity, in `Chapter 4`, *JDBC-Based Authentication*. In the same chapter, we'll also look at built-in techniques to increase the security of passwords stored in the database.

Sensitive information

Personally identifiable or sensitive information is easily accessible or unencrypted. The auditors noted that some significant and sensitive pieces of data were completely unencrypted or masked anywhere in the system. Fortunately, there are some simple design patterns and tools that allow us to protect this information securely, with annotation-based AOP support in Spring Security.

Transport-level protection

There is insecure transport-level protection due to lack of SSL encryption.

While, in the real world, it's unthinkable that an online application containing private information would operate without SSL protection, unfortunately, the JBCP calendar is in just this situation. SSL protection ensures that communication between the browser client and the web application server are secure against many kinds of tampering and snooping.

In the *HTTPS Setup in Tomcat* section, in `Appendix`, *Additional Reference Material*, we'll review the basic options for using transport-level security as part of the definition of the secured structure of the application.

Using Spring Security 4.2 to address security concerns

Spring Security 4.2 provides a wealth of resources that allow for many common security practices to be declared or configured in a straightforward manner. In the coming chapters, we'll apply a combination of source code and application configuration changes to address all of the concerns raised by the security auditors (and more), to give ourselves the confidence that our calendar application is secure.

With Spring Security 4.2, we'll be able to make the following changes to increase our application's security:

- Segment users of the system into user classes
- Assign levels of authorization to user roles
- Assign user roles to user classes
- Apply authentication rules globally across application resources
- Apply authorization rules at all levels of the application architecture
- Prevent common types of attacks intended to manipulate or steal a user's session

Why Spring Security?

Spring Security exists to fill a gap in the universe of Java third-party libraries, much as the Spring Framework originally did when it was first introduced. Standards such as **Java Authentication and Authorization Service (JAAS)** or **Java EE Security** do offer some ways of performing some of the same authentication and authorization functions, but Spring Security is a winner because it includes everything you need to implement a top-to-bottom application security solution in a concise and sensible way.

Additionally, Spring Security appeals to many, because it offers out-of-the-box integration with many common enterprise authentication systems; so it's adaptable to most situations with little effort (beyond configuration) on the part of the developer.

It's in wide use because there's really no other mainstream framework quite like it!

Summary

In this chapter, we have reviewed the common points of risk in an unsecured web application and the basic architecture of the sample application. We have also discussed the strategies for securing the application.

In the next chapter, we'll explore how to get Spring Security set up quickly and get a basic understanding of how it works.

2
Getting Started with Spring Security

In this chapter, we'll apply a minimal Spring Security configuration to start addressing our first finding—inadvertent privilege escalation due to a lack of URL protection, and general authentication from the security audit discussed in Chapter 1, *Anatomy of an Unsafe Application*. We will then build on the basic configuration to provide a customized experience for our users. This chapter is intended to get you up and running with Spring Security and to provide a foundation for any other security-related tasks you will need to perform.

During the course of this chapter, we will cover the following topics:

- Implementing a basic level of security on the JBCP calendar application, using the automatic configuration option in Spring Security
- Learning how to customize both the login and logout experience
- Configuring Spring Security to restrict access differently, depending on the URL
- Leveraging the expression-based access controls of Spring Security
- Conditionally displaying basic information about the logged-in user using the JSP library in Spring Security
- Determining the user's default location after login, based on their role

Hello Spring Security

Although Spring Security can be extremely difficult to configure, the creators of the product have been thoughtful and have provided us with a very simple mechanism to enable much of the software's functionality with a strong baseline. From this baseline, additional configuration will allow for a fine level of detailed control over the security behavior of the application.

We'll start with our unsecured calendar application from Chapter 1, *Anatomy of an Unsafe Application*, and turn it into a site that's secured with a rudimentary username and password authentication. This authentication serves merely to illustrate the steps involved in enabling Spring Security for our web application; you'll see that there are some obvious flaws in this approach that will lead us to make further configuration refinements.

Importing the sample application

We encourage you to import the chapter02.00-calendar project into your IDE, and follow along by obtaining the source code from this chapter, as described in the *Getting started with JBCP calendar sample code* section in the Appendix, *Additional Reference Material.*

For each chapter, you will find multiple revisions of the code that represent checkpoints within the book. This makes it easy to compare your work to the correct answers as you go. At the beginning of each chapter, we will import the first revision of that chapter as a starting point. For example, in this chapter, we start with chapter02.00-calendar, and the first checkpoint will be chapter02.01-calendar. In Chapter 3, *Custom Authentication*, we will start with chapter03.00-calendar, and the first checkpoint will be chapter03.01-calendar. There are additional details in the *Getting started with JBCP calendar sample code* section in the Appendix, *Additional Reference Material,* so be sure to refer to it for details.

Updating your dependencies

The first step is to update the project's dependencies to include the necessary Spring Security JAR files. Update the Gradle build.gradle file (from the sample application you imported previously) to include the Spring Security JAR files that we will use in the following few sections.

Throughout the book, we will be demonstrating how to provide the required dependencies using Gradle. The build.gradle file is located in the root of the project and represents all that is needed to build the project (including the project's dependencies). Remember that Gradle will download the transitive dependencies for each listed dependency. So, if you are using another mechanism to manage dependencies, ensure that you also include the transitive dependencies. When managing the dependencies manually, it is useful to know that the Spring Security reference includes a list of its transitive dependencies. A link to the Spring Security reference can be found in the *Supplementary Materials* section in the *Supplementary materials* section in the Appendix, *Additional Reference Material*.

Let's take a look at the following code snippet:

```
build.gradle:
dependencies {
    compile "org.springframework.security:spring-security-
    config:${springSecurityVersion}"
    compile "org.springframework.security:spring-security-
    core:${springSecurityVersion}"
    compile "org.springframework.security:spring-security-
    web:${springSecurityVersion}"
    ...
}
```

Using Spring 4.3 and Spring Security 4.2

Spring 4.2 is used consistently. Our sample applications provide an example of the former option, which means that no additional work is required by you.

In the following code, we present an example fragment of what is added to the Gradle build.gradle file to utilize the dependency management feature of Gradle; this ensures that correct Spring version is used throughout the entire application. We are going to leverage the Spring IO **bill of materials (BOM)** dependency, which will ensure that all the dependency versions imported by the BOM will work together correctly:

```
build.gradle
// Spring Security IO with ensures correct Springframework versions
dependencyManagement {
    imports {
        mavenBom 'io.spring.platform:platform-bom:Brussels-
${springIoVersion}'
    }
```

```
    }
    dependencies {
        ...
    }
```

 If you are using Spring Tool Suite, any time you update the
build.gradle file, ensure you right-click on the project and navigate to
Gradle | Refresh Gradle Project... and select **OK** to update all the
dependencies.

For more information about how Gradle handles transitive dependencies, as well as the
BOM, refer to the Gradle documentation, which is listed in the *Supplementary materials*
section, in Appendix, *Additional Reference Material*.

Implementing a Spring Security XML configuration file

The next step in the configuration process is to create a Java configuration file representing
all Spring Security components required to cover standard web requests.

Create a new Java file in the
src/main/java/com/packtpub/springsecurity/configuration/ directory with the
name SecurityConfig.java, and the following content. Among other things, the
following file demonstrates user login requirements for every page in our application,
provides a login page, authenticates the user, and requires the logged-in user to be
associated with a role called USER for every URL element:

```
//src/main/java/com/packtpub/springsecurity/configuration/
SecurityConfig.java

@Configuration
@EnableWebSecurity
public class SecurityConfig extends WebSecurityConfigurerAdapter {
    @Override
    public void configure(final AuthenticationManagerBuilder auth)
throws Exception
    {
        auth.inMemoryAuthentication().withUser("user1@example.com")
        .password("user1").roles("USER");
    }
    @Override
    protected void configure(final HttpSecurity http) throws Exception
    {
```

```
http.authorizeRequests()
        .antMatchers("/**").access("hasRole('USER')")
        // equivalent to <http auto-config="true">
        .and().formLogin()
        .and().httpBasic()
        .and().logout()
        // CSRF is enabled by default (will discuss later)
        .and().csrf().disable();
    }
}
```

 If you are using Spring Tool Suite, you can easily review `WebSecurityConfigurerAdapter` by using *F3*. Remember that the next checkpoint (`chapter02.01-calendar`) has a working solution, so the file can be copied from there as well.

This is the only Spring Security configuration required to get our web application secured with a minimal standard configuration. This style of configuration, using a Spring Security-specific Java configuration, is known as **Java Config**.

Let's take a minute to break this configuration apart so we can get a high-level idea of what is happening. In the `configure(HttpSecurity)` method, the `HttpSecurity` object creates a Servlet Filter, which ensures that the currently logged-in user is associated with the appropriate role. In this instance, the filter will ensure that the user is associated with `ROLE_USER`. It is important to understand that the name of the role is arbitrary. Later, we will create a user with `ROLE_ADMIN` and will allow this user to have access to additional URLs that our current user does not have access to.

In the `configure(AuthenticationManagerBuilder)` method, the `AuthenticationManagerBuilder` object is how Spring Security authenticates the user. In this instance, we utilize an in-memory data store to compare a username and password.

Our example and explanation of what is happening are a bit contrived. An in-memory authentication store would not work in a production environment. However, it allows us to get things up and running quickly. We will incrementally improve our understanding of Spring Security as we update our application to use production quality security throughout this book.

General support for **Java Configuration** was added to Spring Framework in Spring 3.1. Since Spring Security 3.2 release, there has been Spring Security Java Configuration support, which enables users to easily configure Spring Security without the use of any XML. If you are familiar with Chapter 6, *LDAP Directory Services*, and the Spring Security documentation, then you should find quite a few similarities between it and **Security Java Configuration** support.

Updating your web.xml file

The next steps involve a series of updates to the web.xml file. Some of the steps have already been performed because the application was already using Spring MVC. However, we will go over these requirements to ensure that more fundamental Spring requirements are understood, in the event that you are using Spring Security in an application that is not Spring-enabled.

The ContextLoaderListener class

The first step of updating the web.xml file is to remove it and replace it with javax.servlet.ServletContainerInitializer, which is the preferred approach to Servlet 3.0+ initialization. Spring MVC provides the o.s.w.WebApplicationInitializer interface, which leverages this mechanism. In Spring MVC, the preferred approach is to extend o.s.w.servlet.support.AbstractAnnotationConfigDispatcherServletInitializer. The WebApplicationInitializer class is polymorphically o.s.w.context.AbstractContextLoaderInitializer and uses the abstract createRootApplicationContext() method to create a root ApplicationContext, then delegates it to ContextLoaderListener, which is registered in the ServletContext instance, as shown in the following code snippet:

```
//src/main/java/c/p/s/web/configuration/WebAppInitializer

public class WebAppInitializer extends
AbstractAnnotationConfigDispatcherServletInitializer {
    @Override
    protected Class<?>[] getRootConfigClasses() {
        return new Class[] { JavaConfig.class, SecurityConfig.class,
        DataSourceConfig.class };
    }
    ...
}
```

The updated configuration will now load `SecurityConfig.class` from the classpath of the WAR file.

ContextLoaderListener versus DispatcherServlet

The `o.s.web.servlet.DispatcherServlet` interface specifies configuration classes to be loaded on their own using the `getServletConfigClasses()` method:

```
//src/main/java/c/p/s/web/configuration/WebAppInitializer

public class WebAppInitializer extends
AbstractAnnotationConfigDispatcherServletInitializer {
    ...
    @Override
    protected Class<?>[] getServletConfigClasses() {
        return new Class[] { WebMvcConfig.class };
    }
    ...
    @Override
    public void onStartup(final ServletContext servletContext) throws
    ServletException {
        // Registers DispatcherServlet
        super.onStartup(servletContext);
    }
}
```

The `DispatcherServlet` class creates `o.s.context.ApplicationContext`, which is a child of the root `ApplicationContext` interface. Typically, Spring MVC-specific components are initialized in the `ApplicationContext` interface of `DispatcherServlet`, while the rest are loaded by `ContextLoaderListener`. It is important to know that beans in a child `ApplicationContext` (such as those created by `DispatcherServlet`) can reference beans of the parent `ApplicationContext` (such as those created by `ContextLoaderListener`). However, the parent `ApplicationContext` interface cannot refer to beans of the child `ApplicationContext`.

This is illustrated in the following diagram, in which **Child Beans** can refer to **Root Beans**, but **Root Beans** cannot refer to **Child Beans**:

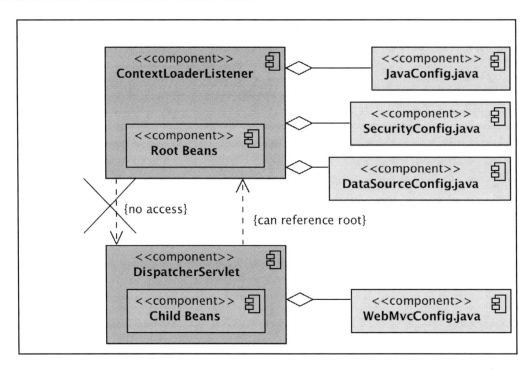

As in most use cases of Spring Security, we do not need Spring Security to refer to any of the MVC-declared beans. Therefore, we have decided to have `ContextLoaderListener` initialize all configurations of Spring Security.

The springSecurityFilterChain filter

The next step is to configure `springSecurityFilterChain` to intercept all requests by creating an implementation of `AbstractSecurityWebApplicationInitializer`. It is critical for `springSecurityFilterChain` to be declared first, to ensure the request is secured prior to any other logic being invoked. To ensure `springSecurityFilterChain` gets loaded first, we can use `@Order(1)` as shown in the following configuration:

```
//src/main/java/c/p/s/web/configuration/SecurityWebAppInitializer

@Order(1)
public class SecurityWebAppInitializer extends
AbstractSecurityWebApplicationInitializer {
```

```
        public SecurityWebAppInitializer() {
            super();
        }
    }
```

The `SecurityWebAppInitializer` class will automatically register
the `springSecurityFilterChain` filter for every URL in your application and will
add `ContextLoaderListener`, which loads `SecurityConfig`.

The DelegatingFilterProxy class

The `o.s.web.filter.DelegatingFilterProxy` class is a Servlet Filter provided by
Spring Web that will delegate all work to a Spring bean from
the `ApplicationContext` root, which must implement `javax.servlet.Filter`. Since by
default the bean is looked up by name, using the `<filter-name>` value, we must ensure
we use `springSecurityFilterChain` as the value of `<filter-name>`. The pseudocode
for how `o.s.web.filter.DelegatingFilterProxy` works for our `web.xml` file can be
found in the following code snippet:

```
    public class DelegatingFilterProxy implements Filter {
        void doFilter(request, response, filterChain) {
            Filter delegate =
    applicationContet.getBean("springSecurityFilterChain")
            delegate.doFilter(request,response,filterChain);
        }
    }
```

The FilterChainProxy class

When working in conjunction with Spring Security,
`o.s.web.filter.DelegatingFilterProxy` will delegate to
the `o.s.s.web.FilterChainProxy` interface of Spring Security, which was created in our
minimal `security.xml` file. The `FilterChainProxy` class allows Spring Security to
conditionally apply any number of Servlet Filters to the servlet request. We will learn more
about each of the Spring Security filters, and their roles in ensuring that our application is
properly secured, throughout the rest of the book. The pseudocode for how
`FilterChainProxy` works are as follows:

```
    public class FilterChainProxy implements Filter {
        void doFilter(request, response, filterChain) {
        // lookup all the Filters for this request
        List<Filter> delegates =        lookupDelegates(request,response)
        // invoke each filter unless the delegate decided to stop
```

```
for delegate in delegates {
  if continue processing
    delegate.doFilter(request,response,filterChain)
}
// if all the filters decide it is ok allow the
// rest of the application to run
if continue processing
  filterChain.doFilter(request,response)   }
}
```

 Due to the fact that both `DelegatingFilterProxy` and `FilterChainProxy` are the front door to Spring Security, when used in a web application, you would add a debug point when trying to figure out what is happening.

Running a secured application

If you have not already done so, restart the application and visit `http://localhost:8080/`. You will be presented with the following screen:

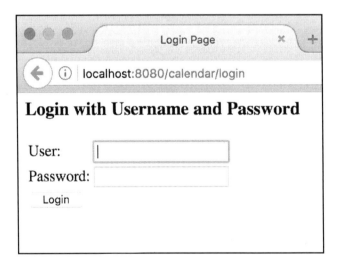

Great job! We've implemented a basic layer of security in our application using Spring Security. At this point, you should be able to log in using `user1@example.com` as **User** and `user1` as **Password**. You'll see the calendar welcome page, which describes at a high level what to expect from the application in terms of security.

Your code should now look like `chapter02.01-calendar`.

Common problems

Many users have trouble with the initial implementation of Spring Security in their application. A few common issues and suggestions are listed next. We want to ensure that you can run the example application and follow along!

- Make sure you can build and deploy the application before putting Spring Security in place.
- Review some introductory samples and documentation on your servlet container if needed.
- It's usually easiest to use an IDE, such as Eclipse, to run your servlet container. Not only is deployment typically seamless, but the console log is also readily available to review for errors. You can also set breakpoints at strategic locations, to be triggered by exceptions to better diagnose errors.
- Make sure the versions of Spring and Spring Security that you're using match and that there aren't any unexpected Spring JARs remaining as part of your application. As previously mentioned, when using Gradle, it can be a good idea to declare the Spring dependencies in the dependency management section.

A little bit of polish

Stop at this point and think about what we've just built. You may have noticed some obvious issues that will require some additional work and knowledge of the Spring Security product before our application is production-ready. Try to make a list of the changes that you think are required before this security implementation is ready to roll out on the public-facing website.

Applying the Hello World Spring Security implementation was blindingly fast and has provided us with a login page, username, and password-based authentication, as well as the automatic interception of URLs in our calendar application. However, there are gaps between what the automatic configuration setup provides and what our end goal is, which are listed as follows:

- While the login page is helpful, it's completely generic and doesn't look like the rest of our JBCP calendar application. We should add a login form that's integrated with our application's look and feel.
- There is no obvious way for a user to log out. We've locked down all pages in the application, including the **Welcome** page, which a potential user may want to browse anonymously. We'll need to redefine the roles required to accommodate anonymous, authenticated, and administrative users.
- We do not display any contextual information to indicate to the user that they are authenticated. It would be nice to display a greeting similar to welcome user1@example.com.
- We've had to hardcode the username, password, and role information of the user in the `SecurityConfig` configuration file. Recall this section of the `configure(AuthenticationManagerBuilder)` method we added:

  ```
  auth.inMemoryAuthentication().withUser("user1@example.com")
  .password("user1").roles("USER");
  ```

- You can see that the username and password are right there in the file. It's unlikely that we'd want to add a new declaration to the file for every user of the system! To address this, we'll need to update the configuration with another type of authentication.

We'll explore different authentication options throughout the first half of the book.

Customizing login

We've seen how Spring Security makes it very easy to get started. Now let's see how we can customize the login experience. In the following code snippet, we demonstrate the usage of some of the more common ways to customize login, but we encourage you to refer to the reference documentation of Spring Security, which includes an `Appendix`, *Additional Reference Material* with all of the supported attributes.

Let's take a look at the following steps to customize login:

1. First, update your `SecurityConfig.java` file as follows:

```
//src/main/java/com/packtpub/springsecurity/configuration/
SecurityConfig.java

    http.authorizeRequests()
        ...
        .formLogin()
            .loginPage("/login/form")
            .loginProcessingUrl("/login")
            .failureUrl("/login/form?error")
            .usernameParameter("username")
            .passwordParameter("password")
        ....
```

Let's take a look at the following methods depicted in the preceding code snippet:

- The `loginPage()` method specifies where Spring Security will redirect the browser if a protected page is accessed and the user is not authenticated. If a login page is not specified, Spring Security will redirect the user to `/spring_security_login`. Then `o.s.s.web.filter.FilterChainProxy` will choose `o.s.s.web.authentication.ui.DefaultLoginPageGeneratingFilter`, which renders the default login page as one of the delegates, since `DefaultLoginPageGeneratingFilter` is configured to process `/spring_security_login` by default. Since we have chosen to override the default URL, we are in charge of rendering the login page when the `/login/form` URL is requested.

- The `loginProcessingUrl()` method defaults to `/j_spring_security_check` and specifies the URL that the login form (which should include the username and password) should be submitted to, using an HTTP post. When Spring Security processes this request, it will attempt to authenticate the user.

- The `failureUrl()` method specifies the page that Spring Security will redirect to if the username and password submitted to `loginProcessingUrl()` are invalid.

- The `usernameParameter()` and `passwordParameter()` methods default to `j_username` and `j_password` respectively, and specify the HTTP parameters that Spring Security will use to authenticate the user when processing the `loginProcessingUrl()` method.

It may be obvious, but if we only wanted to add a custom login page, we would only need to specify the `loginPage()` method. We would then create our login form using the default values for the remaining attributes. However, it is often good practice to override the values of anything visible to users, to prevent exposing that we are using Spring Security. Revealing what frameworks we are using is a type of information leakage, making it easier for attackers to determine potential holes in our security.

2. The next step is to create a login page. We can use any technology we want to render the login page, as long as the login form produces the HTTP request that we specified with our Spring Security configuration when submitted. By ensuring the HTTP request conforms to our configuration, Spring Security can authenticate the request for us. Create the `login.html` file, as shown in the following code snippet:

```
//src/main/webapp/WEB-INF/tempates/login.html

    <div class="container">
<!--/*/ <th:block th:include="fragments/header :: header">
</th:block> /*/-->
<form th:action="@{/login}" method="POST"
cssClass="form-horizontal">
    <div th:if="${param.error != null}" class="alert
    alert-danger">
        <strong>Failed to login.</strong>
        <span
th:if="${session[SPRING_SECURITY_LAST_EXCEPTION]
        != null}">
            <span th:text="${session
            [SPRING_SECURITY_LAST_EXCEPTION].message}">
            Invalid credentials</span>
        </span>
    </div>
    <div th:if="${param.logout != null}"
    class="alert alert-success">You have been logged out.
    </div>
    <label for="username">Username</label>
    <input type="text" id="username" name="username"
    autofocus="autofocus"/>
    <label for="password">Password</label>
    <input type="password" id="password" name="password"/>
    <div class="form-actions">
        <input id="submit" class="btn" name="submit"
        type="submit"
        value="Login"/>
```

```
        </div>
      </form>
    </div>
```

 Remember that if you are having problems typing anything in the book, you can refer to the solution at the next checkpoint (chapter02.02-calendar).

The following number of items are worth highlighting in the preceding login.html file:

- The form action should be /login, to match the value provided for the loginProcessingUrl() method we specified. For security reasons, Spring Security only attempts to authenticate when using POST by default.
- We can use param.error to see whether there was a problem logging in, since the value of our failureUrl() method, /login/form?error, contains the HTTP parameter error.
- The session attribute, SPRING_SECURITY_LAST_EXCEPTION, contains the last o.s.s.core.AuthenticationException exception, which can be used to display the reason for a failed login. The error messages can be customized by leveraging Spring's internationalization support.
- The input names for the username and password inputs are chosen to correspond to the values we specified for the usernameParameter() and passwordParameter() methods in our SecurityConfig.java configuration.

3. The last step is to make Spring MVC aware of our new URL. This can be done by adding the following method to WebMvcConfig:

```
//src/main/java/com/packtpub/springsecurity/web/configuration/
WebMvcConfig.java

import org.springframework.web.servlet.config.annotation.
ViewControllerRegistry;
...
    public class WebMvcConfig extends WebMvcConfigurationSupport {
      public void addViewControllers(ViewControllerRegistry
      registry){
        registry.addViewController("/login/form")
          .setViewName("login");
      }
...
    }
```

Configuring logout

The HttpSecurity configuration of Spring Security automatically adds support for logging the user out. All that is needed is to create a link that points to /j_spring_security_logout. However, we will demonstrate how to customize the URL used to log the user out by performing the following steps:

1. Update the Spring Security configuration as follows:

   ```
   //src/main/java/com/packtpub/springsecurity/configuration/
   SecurityConfig.java

   http.authorizeRequests()
   ...
   .logout()
   .logoutUrl("/logout")
   .logoutSuccessUrl("/login?logout");
   ```

2. You have to provide a link for the user to click on that will log them out. We will update the header.html   file so that the Logout link appears on every page:

   ```
   //src/main/webapp/WEB-INF/templates/fragments/header.html

   <div id="navbar" ...>
     ...
       <ul class="nav navbar-nav pull-right">
         <li><a id="navLogoutLink" th:href="@{/logout}">
           Logout</a></li>
       </ul>
       ...
   </div>
   ```

3. The last step is to update the login.html file to display a message indicating logout was successful when the logout parameter is present:

   ```
   //src/main/webapp/WEB-INF/templates/login.html

   <div th:if=""${param.logout != null}" class="alert
   alert-success"> You have been logged out.</div>
     <label for="username">Username</label>
     ...
   ```

 Your code should now look like chapter02.02-calendar.

The page isn't redirecting properly

If you have not already, restart the application and visit `http://localhost:8080` in Firefox; you will see an error, as shown in the following screenshot:

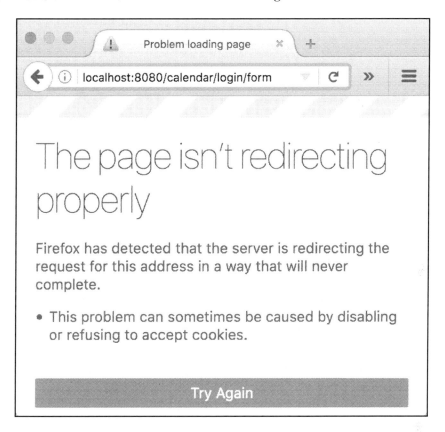

What went wrong? The problem is, since Spring Security is no longer rendering the login page, we must allow everyone (not just the USER role) to access the **Login** page. Without granting access to the **Login** page, the following happens:

1. We request the **Welcome** page in the browser.
2. Spring Security sees that the **Welcome** page requires the USER role and that we are not authenticated, so it redirects the browser to the **Login** page.

3. The browser requests the **Login** page.

4. Spring Security sees that the **Login** page requires the USER role and that we are still not authenticated, so it redirects the browser to the **Login** page again.

5. The browser requests the **Login** page again.

6. Spring Security sees that the **Login** page requires the USER role, as shown in the following diagram:

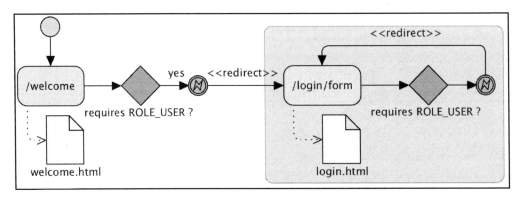

The process could just keep repeating indefinitely. Fortunately for us, Firefox realizes that there are too many redirects occurring, stops performing the redirect, and displays a very informative error message. In the next section, we will learn how to fix this error by configuring URLs differently, depending on the access that they require.

Basic role-based authorization

We can expand on the Spring Security configuration from Hello Spring Security to vary the access controls by URL. In this section, you will find a configuration that allows more granular control over how resources can be accessed. In the configuration, Spring Security does the following tasks:

- It completely ignores any request that starts with /resources/. This is beneficial since our images, CSS, and JavaScript do not need to use Spring Security.
- It allows anonymous users to access the **Welcome**, **Login**, and **Logout** pages.
- It only allows administrators access to the **All Events** page.
- It adds an administrator that can access the **All Events** page.

Take a look at the following code snippet:

```
//src/main/java/com/packtpub/springsecurity/configuration/
SecurityConfig.java

  http.authorizeRequests()
      .antMatchers("/resources/**").permitAll()
      .antMatchers("/").hasAnyRole("ANONYMOUS", "USER")
      .antMatchers("/login/*").hasAnyRole("ANONYMOUS", "USER")
      .antMatchers("/logout/*").hasAnyRole("ANONYMOUS", "USER")
      .antMatchers("/admin/*").hasRole("ADMIN")
      .antMatchers("/events/").hasRole("ADMIN")
      .antMatchers("/**").hasRole("USER")
      ...
  @Override
  public void configure(final AuthenticationManagerBuilder auth)
    throws Exception{
      auth.inMemoryAuthentication()
          .withUser("user1@example.com").password("user1").roles("USER")
    .and().withUser("admin1@example.com").password("admin1").
    roles("USER", "ADMIN");
  }
```

 Notice that we do not include `/calendar`, the application's context root, in the Spring Security configuration, because Spring Security takes care of the context root transparently for us. In this way, we do not need to update our configuration if we decide to deploy it to a different context root.

In Spring Security 4,2, you can specify multiple `RequestMatcher` entries using a builder pattern that allows you to have greater control over how security is applied to different portions of your application. The first `antMatchers()` method states that Spring Security should ignore any URL that starts with `/resources/`, and the second `antMatchers()` method states that any other request will be processed by it. There are a few important things to note about using multiple `antMatchers` methods, as follows:

- If no path attribute is specified, it is the equivalent of using a path of `/**`, which matches all requests.

- Each `antMatchers()` method is considered in order, and only the first match is applied. So, the order in which they appear in your configuration file is important. The implication is that only the last `antMatchers()` method can use a path that matches every request. If you do not follow this rule, Spring Security will produce an error. The following is invalid because the first matcher matches every request and will never get to the second mapping:

```
http.authorizeRequests()
    .antMatchers("/**").hasRole("USER")
    .antMatchers("/admin/**").hasRole("ADMIN")
```

- The default pattern is backed by `o.s.s.web.util.AntPathRequestMatcher`, which will compare the specified pattern to an ant pattern to determine whether it matches the `servletPath` and `pathInfo` methods of `HttpServletRequest`. Note that query strings are ignored when determining whether a request is a match. Internally, Spring Security uses `o.s.u.AntPathMatcher` to do all the work. A summary of the rules is listed as follows:

```
? matches a single character.
* matches zero or more characters, excluding /.
** matches zero or more directories in a path.

The pattern "/events/**" matches "/events", "/events/",
"/events/1", and "/events/1/form?test=1"; it does not
match "/events123".
The pattern "/events*" matches "/events", and "/events123";
it does not match "/events/" or "/events/1".
The pattern "/events*/**" matches "/events", "/events/",
"/events/1","/events123", "/events123/456", and
"/events/1/form?test=1".
```

- The path attribute on the `antMatchers()` method further refines the filtering of the request and allows access control to be applied. You can see that the updated configuration allows different types of access, depending on the URL pattern. The role `ANONYMOUS` is of particular interest since we have not defined it anywhere in `SecurityConfig.java`. This is the default authority assigned to a user that is not logged in. The following line, from the updates to our `SecurityConfig.java` file, is what allows anonymous (unauthenticated) users and users with the role `USER` authority to access the **Login** page. We will cover access control options in more detail in the second half of the book:

```
.antMatchers("/login/*").hasAnyRole("ANONYMOUS", "USER")
```

When defining the `antMatchers()` methods, there are a number of things to keep in mind, including the following:

- Just as each `http` method is considered from top to bottom, so are the `antMatchers()` methods. This means it is important to specify the most specific elements first. The following example illustrates a configuration that does not specify the more specific pattern first, which will result in warnings from Spring Security at startup:

```
http.authorizeRequests()
    ...
    // matches every request, so it will not continue
    .antMatchers("/**").hasRole("USER")
    // below will never match
    .antMatchers("/login/form").hasAnyRole("ANONYMOUS", "USER")
```

- It is important to note that if `http.authorizeRequests()` is marked `anyRequest()`, there can be no child `antMatchers()` method defined. This is because `anyRequest()` will match all requests that match this `http.authorizeRequests()` tag. Defining an `antMatchers()` child method with `anyRequest()` contradicts the `antMatchers()` declaration. An example is as follows:

```
http.authorizeRequests().anyRequest().permitAll()
    // This matcher will never be executed
    // and not produce an error.
    .antMatchers("/admin/*").hasRole("ADMIN")
```

- The path attribute of the `antMatchers()` element is independent and is not aware of the `anyRequest()` attribute of the `http` method.

If you have not done so already, restart the application and visit `http://localhost:8080`. Experiment with the application to see all the updates you have made, as follows:

1. Select a link that requires authentication and observes the new login page.
2. Try typing an invalid `username/password` and view the error message.
3. Try logging in as an admin (`admin1@example.com/admin1`), and view all of the events. Note that we are able to view all the events.

4. Try logging out and view the logout success message.

5. Try logging in as a regular user (`user1@example.com`/`user1`), and view all of the events. Note that we get an **Access Denied** page.

Your code should now look like `chapter02.03-calendar`.

Expression-based authorization

You may have noticed that granting access to everyone was not nearly as concise as we may have liked. Fortunately, Spring Security can leverage **Spring Expression Language (SpEL)** to determine whether a user has authorization. In the following code snippet, you can see the updates when using SpEL with Spring Security:

```
//src/main/java/com/packtpub/springsecurity/configuration/
SecurityConfig.java

http.authorizeRequests()
    .antMatchers("/").access("hasAnyRole('ANONYMOUS', 'USER')")
    .antMatchers("/login/*").access("hasAnyRole('ANONYMOUS', 'USER')")
    .antMatchers("/logout/*").access("hasAnyRole('ANONYMOUS', 'USER')")
    .antMatchers("/admin/*").access("hasRole('ADMIN')")
    .antMatchers("/events/").access("hasRole('ADMIN')")
    .antMatchers("/**").access("hasRole('USER')")
```

You may notice that the `/events/` security constraint is brittle. For example, the `/events` URL is not protected by Spring Security to restrict the `ADMIN` role. This demonstrates the need to ensure that we provide multiple layers of security. We will exploit this sort of weakness in `Chapter 11`, *Fine-Grained Access Control*.

Changing the `access` attribute from `hasAnyRole('ANONYMOUS', 'USER')` to `permitAll()` might not seem like much, but this only scratches the surface of the power of Spring Security's expressions. We will go into much greater detail about access control and Spring expressions in the second half of the book. Go ahead and verify that the updates work by running the application.

Your code should now look like `chapter02.04-calendar`.

Conditionally displaying authentication information

Currently, our application has no indication as to whether we are logged in or not. In fact, it appears as though we are always logged in since the `Logout` link is always displayed. In this section, we will demonstrate how to display the authenticated user's username and conditionally display portions of the page using Thymeleaf's Spring Security tag library. We do so by performing the following steps:

1. Update your dependencies to include the `thymeleaf-extras-springsecurity4` JAR file. Since we are using Gradle, we will add a new dependency declaration in our `build.gradle` file, as follows:

    ```
    //build.gradle

    dependency{
        ...
        compile 'org.thymeleaf.extras:thymeleaf-
        extras-springsecurity4'
    }
    ```

2. Next, we need to add `SpringSecurityDialect` to the Thymeleaf engine as follows:

    ```
    //src/com/packtpub/springsecurity/web/configuration/
    ThymeleafConfig.java

    @Bean
    public SpringTemplateEngine templateEngine(
      final ServletContextTemplateResolver resolver)
    {
        SpringTemplateEngine engine = new SpringTemplateEngine();
        engine.setTemplateResolver(resolver);
        engine.setAdditionalDialects(new HashSet<IDialect>() {{
            add(new LayoutDialect());
            add(new SpringSecurityDialect());
        }});
        return engine;
    }
    ```

3. Update the `header.html` file to leverage the Spring Security tag library. You can find the updates as follows:

```
//src/main/webapp/WEB-INF/templates/fragments/header.html
```

```html
<html xmlns:th="http://www.thymeleaf.org"
xmlns:sec="http://www.thymeleaf.org/thymeleaf-
extras-springsecurity4">
...
<div id="navbar" class="collapse navbar-collapse">
...
<ul class="nav navbar-nav pull-right"
sec:authorize="isAuthenticated()">
    <li>
        <p class="navbar-text">Welcome <div class="navbar-text"
        th:text="${#authentication.name}">User</div></p>
    </li>
    <li>
        <a id="navLogoutLink" class="btn btn-default"
        role="button" th:href="@{/logout}">Logout</a>
    </li>
    <li> | </li>
</ul>
<ul class="nav navbar-nav pull-right"
sec:authorize=" ! isAuthenticated()">
    <li><a id="navLoginLink" class="btn btn-default"
    role="button"
    th:href="@{/login/form}">Login</a></li>
    <li> | </li>
</ul>
...
```

The `sec:authorize` attribute determines whether the user is authenticated with the `isAuthenticated()` value, and displays the HTML node if the user is authenticated, and hides the node in the event that the user is not authenticated. The `access` attribute should be rather familiar from the `antMatcher().access()` element. In fact, both components leverage the same SpEL support. There are attributes in the Thymeleaf tag libraries that do not use expressions. However, using SpEL is typically the preferred method since it is more powerful.

The `sec:authentication` attribute will look up the current `o.s.s.core.Authentication` object. The `property` attribute will find the principal attribute of the `o.s.s.core.Authentication`,object, which in this case is `o.s.s.core.userdetails.UserDetails`. It then obtains the `UserDetails` username property and renders it to the page. Don't worry if the details of this are confusing. We are going to go over this in more detail in `Chapter 3`, *Custom Authentication*.

If you haven't done so already, restart the application to see the updates we have made. At this point, you may realize that we are still displaying links we do not have access to. For example, `user1@example.com` should not see a link to the **All Events** page. Rest assured, we'll fix this when we cover the tags in greater detail in `Chapter 11`, *Fine-Grained Access Control*.

 Your code should now look like this: `chapter02.05-calendar`.

Customizing behavior after login

We have already discussed how to customize a user's experience during login, but sometimes it is necessary to customize the behavior after login. In this section, we will discuss how Spring Security behaves after login and will provide a simple mechanism to customize this behavior.

In the default configuration, Spring Security has two different flows after successful authentication. The first scenario occurs if a user never visits a resource that requires authentication. In this instance, after a successful login attempt, the user will be sent to the `defaultSuccessUrl()` method chained to the `formLogin()` method. If left undefined, `defaultSuccessUrl()` will be the context root of the application.

If a user requests a protected page before being authenticated, Spring Security will remember the last protected page that was accessed prior to authenticating, using `o.s.s.web.savedrequest.RequestCache`. Upon successful authentication, Spring Security will send the user to the last protected page that was accessed prior to authentication. For example, if an unauthenticated user requests the **My Events** page, they will be sent to the **Login** page.

After successful authentication, they will be sent to the previously requested **My Events** page.

A common requirement is to customize Spring Security to send the user to a different `defaultSuccessUrl()` method, depending on the user's role. Let's take a look at how this can be accomplished by performing the following steps:

1. The first step is to configure the `defaultSuccessUrl()` method chained after the `formLogin()` method. Go ahead and update the `security.xml` file to use `/default` instead of the context root:

   ```
   //src/main/java/com/packtpub/springsecurity/configuration/
   SecurityConfig.java
   ```

   ```
   .formLogin()
                   .loginPage("/login/form")
                   .loginProcessingUrl("/login")
                   .failureUrl("/login/form?error")
                   .usernameParameter("username")
                   .passwordParameter("password")
                   .defaultSuccessUrl("/default")
                   .permitAll()
   ```

2. The next step is to create a controller that processes `/default`. In the following code, you will find a sample Spring MVC controller, `DefaultController`, which demonstrates how to redirect administrators to the **All Events** page and other users to the **Welcome** page. Create a new file in the following location:

   ```
   //src/main/java/com/packtpub/springsecurity/web/controllers/
   DefaultController.java
   ```

   ```java
   // imports omitted
   @Controller
   public class DefaultController {
   @RequestMapping("/default")
     public String defaultAfterLogin(HttpServletRequest request) {
         if (request.isUserInRole("ADMIN")) {
             return "redirect:/events/";
         }
         return "redirect:/";
     }
   }
   ```

In Spring Tool Suite, you can use *Shift + Ctrl + O* to automatically add the missing imports.

There are a few things to point out about `DefaultController` and how it works. The first is that Spring Security makes the `HttpServletRequest` parameter aware of the currently logged-in user. In this instance, we are able to inspect which role the user belongs to without relying on any of Spring Security's APIs. This is good because if Spring Security's APIs change or we decide we want to switch our security implementation, we have less code that needs to be updated. It should also be noted that while we implement this controller with a Spring MVC controller, our `defaultSuccessUrl()` method can be handled by any controller implementation (for example, Struts, a standard servlet, and so on) if we desire.

3. If you wish to always go to the `defaultSuccessUrl()` method, you can leverage the second parameter to the `defaultSuccessUrl()` method, which is a `Boolean` for always use. We will not do this in our configuration, but you can see an example of it as follows:

```
.defaultSuccessUrl("/default", true)
```

4. You are now ready to give it a try. Restart the application and go directly to the **My Events** page, then log in; you will see that you are on the **My Events** page.
5. Next, log out and try logging in as `user1@example.com`.
6. You should be on the **Welcome** page. Log out and log in as `admin1@example.com`, and you will be sent to the **All Events** page.

Your code should now look like `chapter02.06-calendar`.

Summary

In this chapter, we have applied a very basic Spring Security configuration, explained how to customize the user's login and logout experience, and demonstrated how to display basic information, such as a username, in our web application.

In the next chapter, we will discuss how authentication in Spring Security works and how we can customize it to our needs.

3
Custom Authentication

In Chapter 2, *Getting Started with Spring Security*, we demonstrated how to use an in-memory datastore to authenticate the user. In this chapter, we'll explore how to solve some common, real-world problems by extending Spring Security's authentication support to use our existing set of APIs. Through this exploration, we'll get an understanding of each of the building blocks that Spring Security uses in order to authenticate users.

During the course of this chapter, we will cover the following topics:

- Leverage Spring Security's annotations and Java-based configuration
- Discovering how to obtain the details of the currently logged-in user
- Adding the ability to log in after creating a new account
- Learning the simplest method for indicating to Spring Security, that a user is authenticated
- Creating custom `UserDetailsService` and `AuthenticationProvider` implementations that properly decouple the rest of the application from Spring Security
- Adding domain-based authentication to demonstrate how to authenticate with more than just a username and password

JBCP calendar architecture

In Chapter 1, *Anatomy of an Unsafe Application*, and Chapter 2, *Getting Started with Spring Security*, we used the Spring IO BOM to assist in dependency management, but the rest of the code in the projects was using the core Spring Framework and required manual configuration. Starting with this chapter, we will be using Spring Boot for the rest of the applications, to simplify the application configuration process. The Spring Security configuration we will be creating will be the same for both a Spring Boot and non-Boot application. We will cover more details on Spring IO and Spring Boot in the Appendix, *Additional Reference Material*.

Since this chapter is about integrating Spring Security with custom users and APIs, we will start with a quick introduction to the domain model within the JBCP calendar application.

The CalendarUser object

Our calendar application uses a domain object named CalendarUser, which contains information about our users, as follows:

```
//src/main/java/com/packtpub/springsecurity/domain/CalendarUser.java

public class CalendarUser implements Serializable {
    private Integer id;
    private String firstName;
    private String lastName;
    private String email;
    private String password;
    ... accessor methods omitted ..
}
```

The Event object

Our application has an Event object that contains information about each event, as follows:

```
//src/main/java/com/packtpub/springsecurity/domain/Event.java

public class Event {
    private Integer id;
    private String summary;
    private String description;
    private Calendar when;
    private CalendarUser owner;
    private CalendarUser attendee;
```

```
... accessor methods omitted ..
}
```

The CalendarService interface

Our application contains a `CalendarService` interface that can be used to access and store our domain objects. The code for `CalendarService` is as follows:

```
//src/main/java/com/packtpub/springsecurity/service/CalendarService.java

public interface CalendarService {
    CalendarUser getUser(int id);
    CalendarUser findUserByEmail(String email);
    List<CalendarUser> findUsersByEmail(String partialEmail);
    int createUser(CalendarUser user);
    Event getEvent(int eventId);
    int createEvent(Event event);
    List<Event> findForUser(int userId);
    List<Event> getEvents();
}
```

We won't go over the methods used in `CalendarService`, but they should be fairly straightforward. If you would like details about what each method does, please consult the Javadoc in the sample code.

The UserContext interface

Like most applications, our application requires us to interact with the currently logged-in user. We have created a very simple interface called `UserContext` to manage the currently logged-in user as follows:

```
//src/main/java/com/packtpub/springsecurity/service/UserContext.java

public interface UserContext {
    CalendarUser getCurrentUser();
    void setCurrentUser(CalendarUser user);
}
```

This means that our application can call `UserContext.getCurrentUser()` to obtain the details of the currently logged-in user. It can also call `UserContext.setCurrentUser(CalendarUser)` to specify which user is logged in. Later in this chapter, we will explore how we can write an implementation of this interface that uses Spring Security to access our current user and obtain their details using `SecurityContextHolder`.

Spring Security provides quite a few different methods for authenticating a user. However, the net result is that Spring Security will populate `o.s.s.core.context.SecurityContext` with `o.s.s.core.Authentication`. The `Authentication` object represents all the information we gathered at the time of authentication (username, password, roles, and so on). The `SecurityContext` interface is then set on the `o.s.s.core.context.SecurityContextHolder` interface. This means that Spring Security and developers can use `SecurityContextHolder` to obtain information about the currently logged-in user. An example of obtaining the current username is illustrated as follows:

```
String username = SecurityContextHolder.getContext()
    .getAuthentication()
    .getName();
```

It should be noted that `null` checks should always be done on the `Authentication` object, as this could be `null` if the user is not logged in.

The SpringSecurityUserContext interface

The current `UserContext` implementation, `UserContextStub`, is a stub that always returns the same user. This means that the **My Events** page will always display the same user no matter who is logged in. Let's update our application to utilize the current Spring Security user's username, to determine which events to display on the **My Events** page.

You should be starting with the sample code in `chapter03.00-calendar`.

Take a look at the following steps:

1. The first step is to comment out the `@Component` attribute on `UserContextStub`, so that our application no longer uses our scanned results.

 The `@Component` annotation is used in conjunction with the `@ComponentScan` annotation found in `com/packtpub/springsecurity/web/configuration/WebMvcConfig.java`, to automatically create a Spring bean rather than creating an explicit XML or Java configuration for each bean. You can learn more about the classpath of Spring scanning in the Spring Reference link at `http://static.springsource.org/spring/docs/current/spring-framework-reference/html/`.

Take a look at the following code snippet:

`//src/main/java/com/packtpub/springsecurity/service/UserContextStub.java`

```
...
//@Component
public class UserContextStub implements UserContext {
...
```

2. The next step is to utilize `SecurityContext` to obtain the currently logged-in user. We have included `SpringSecurityUserContext` within this chapter's code, which is wired up with the necessary dependencies but contains no actual functionality.

3. Open the `SpringSecurityUserContext.java` file and add the `@Component` annotation. Next, replace the `getCurrentUser` implementation, as illustrated in the following code snippet:

```
//src/main/java/com/packtpub/springsecurity/service/
SpringSecurityUserContext.java

@Component
public class SpringSecurityUserContext implements UserContext {
  private final CalendarService calendarService;
  private final UserDetailsService userDetailsService;
@Autowired
public SpringSecurityUserContext(CalendarService calendarService,
UserDetailsService userDetailsService) {
    this.calendarService = calendarService;
    this.userDetailsService = userDetailsService;
}
public CalendarUser getCurrentUser() {
```

```
      SecurityContext context = SecurityContextHolder.getContext();
      Authentication authentication = context.getAuthentication();
      if (authentication == null) {
        return null;
      }
      String email = authentication.getName();
      return calendarService.findUserByEmail(email);
  }
  public void setCurrentUser(CalendarUser user) {
      throw new UnsupportedOperationException();
  }
}
```

Our code obtains the username from the current Spring Security `Authentication` object and utilizes that to look up the current `CalendarUser` object by email address. Since our Spring Security username is an email address, we are able to use the email address to link `CalendarUser` with the Spring Security user. Note that if we were to link accounts, we would normally want to do this with a key that we generated rather than something that may change (that is, an email address). We follow the good practice of returning only our domain object to the application. This ensures that our application is only aware of our `CalendarUser` object and thus is not coupled to Spring Security.

This code may seem eerily similar to when we used the `sec:authorize="isAuthenticated()"` tag attribute in Chapter 2, *Getting Started with Spring Security,* to display the current user's username. In fact, the Spring Security tag library uses `SecurityContextHolder` in the same manner as we have done here. We could use our `UserContext` interface to place the current user on `HttpServletRequest` and thus remove our dependency on the Spring Security tag library.

4. Start up the application, visit `http://localhost:8080/`, and log in with `admin1@example.com` as the username and `admin1` as the password.

5. Visit the **My Events** page, and you will see that only the events for that current user, who is the owner or the attendee, are displayed.

6. Try creating a new event; you will observe that the owner of the event is now associated with the logged-in user.

7. Log out of the application and repeat these steps with `user1@example.com` as the username and `user1` as the password.

Your code should now look like `chapter03.01-calendar`.

Logging in new users using SecurityContextHolder

A common requirement is to allow users to create a new account and then automatically log them in to the application. In this section, we'll describe the simplest method for indicating that a user is authenticated, by utilizing `SecurityContextHolder`.

Managing users in Spring Security

The application provided in `Chapter 1`, *Anatomy of an Unsafe Application*, provides a mechanism for creating a new `CalendarUser` object, so it should be fairly trivial to create our `CalendarUser` object after a user signs up. However, Spring Security has no knowledge of `CalendarUser`. This means that we will need to add a new user in Spring Security too. Don't worry, we will remove the need for the dual maintenance of users later in this chapter.

Spring Security provides an `o.s.s.provisioning.UserDetailsManager` interface for managing users. Remember our in-memory Spring Security configuration?

```
auth.inMemoryAuthentication().
    withUser("user").password("user").roles("USER");
```

The `.inMemoryAuthentication()` method creates an in-memory implementation of `UserDetailsManager`, named `o.s.s.provisioning.InMemoryUserDetailsManager`, which can be used to create a new Spring Security user.

 While converting from an XML configuration to a Java-based configuration in Spring Security, there is currently a limitation with the Spring Security DSL where exposing multiple beans is not currently supported. There is a JIRA opened for this issue at `https://jira.spring. io/browse/SPR-13779`.

Let's see how we can manage users in Spring Security by performing the following steps:

1. In order to expose `UserDetailsManager` using a Java-based configuration, we need to create `InMemoryUserDetailsManager` outside of the `WebSecurityConfigurerAdapter` DSL:

    ```
    //src/main/java/com/packtpub/springsecurity/configuration/
    SecurityConfig.java

    @Bean
    @Override
    public UserDetailsManager userDetailsService() {
        InMemoryUserDetailsManager manager = new
        InMemoryUserDetailsManager();
        manager.createUser(
            User.withUsername("user1@example.com")
                .password("user1").roles("USER").build());
        manager.createUser(
            User.withUsername("admin1@example.com")
                .password("admin1").roles("USER", "ADMIN").build());
        return manager;
    }
    ```

2. Once we have an exposed `UserDetailsManager` interface in our Spring configuration, all we need to do is update our existing `CalendarService` implementation, `DefaultCalendarService`, to add a user in Spring Security. Make the following updates to the `DefaultCalendarService.java` file:

    ```
    //src/main/java/com/packtpub/springsecurity/service/
    DefaultCalendarService.java

    public int createUser(CalendarUser user) {
        List<GrantedAuthority> authorities = AuthorityUtils.
        createAuthorityList("ROLE_USER");
        UserDetails userDetails = new User(user.getEmail(),
        user.getPassword(), authorities);
        // create a Spring Security user
        userDetailsManager.createUser(userDetails);
        // create a CalendarUser
        return userDao.createUser(user);
    }
    ```

3. In order to leverage `UserDetailsManager`, we first convert `CalendarUser` into the `UserDetails` object of Spring Security.

4. Later, we use `UserDetailsManager` to save the `UserDetails` object. The conversion is necessary because Spring Security has no understanding of how to save our custom `CalendarUser` object, so we must map `CalendarUser` to an object Spring Security understands. You will notice that the `GrantedAuthority` object corresponds to the `authorities` attribute of our `SecurityConfig` file. We hardcode this for simplicity and due to the fact that there is no concept of roles in our existing system.

Logging in a new user to an application

Now that we are able to add new users to the system, we need to indicate that the user is authenticated. Update `SpringSecurityUserContext` to set the current user on the `SecurityContextHolder` object of Spring Security, as follows:

```
//src/main/java/com/packtpub/springsecurity/service/
SpringSecurityUserContext.java

public void setCurrentUser(CalendarUser user) {
  UserDetails userDetails = userDetailsService.
  loadUserByUsername(user.getEmail());
  Authentication authentication = new
  UsernamePasswordAuthenticationToken(userDetails, user.getPassword(),
  userDetails.getAuthorities());
  SecurityContextHolder.getContext().
  setAuthentication(authentication);
}
```

The first step we perform is to convert our `CalendarUser` object into the `UserDetails` object of Spring Security. This is necessary because, just as Spring Security didn't know how to save our custom `CalendarUser` object, Spring Security also does not understand how to make security decisions with our custom `CalendarUser` object. We use Spring Security's `o.s.s.core.userdetails.UserDetailsService` interface to obtain the same `UserDetails` object we saved with `UserDetailsManager`. The `UserDetailsService` interface provides a subset, lookup by username, of the functionality provided by Spring Security's `UserDetailsManager` object that we have already seen.

Next, we create a `UsernamePasswordAuthenticationToken` object and place `UserDetails`, the password, and `GrantedAuthority` in it. Lastly, we set the authentication on `SecurityContextHolder`. In a web application, Spring Security will automatically associate the `SecurityContext` object in `SecurityContextHolder` to our HTTP session for us.

It is important that Spring Security must not be instructed to ignore a URL (that is, using the `permitAll()` method), as discussed in Chapter 2, *Getting Started with Spring Security*, in which `SecurityContextHolder` is accessed or set. This is because Spring Security will ignore the request and thus not persist `SecurityContext` for subsequent requests. The proper method to allow access to the URL in which `SecurityContextHolder` is used is to specify the `access` attribute of the `antMatchers()` method (that is, `antMatchers(...).permitAll()`).

It is worth mentioning that we could have converted `CalendarUser` by creating a new `o.s.s.core.userdetails.User` object directly, instead of looking it up in `UserDetailsService`. For example, the following code would also authenticate the user:

```
List<GrantedAuthority> authorities =
AuthorityUtils.createAuthorityList("ROLE_USER");
UserDetails userDetails = new
User("username","password",authorities);
Authentication authentication = new
UsernamePasswordAuthenticationToken (
userDetails,userDetails.getPassword(),userDetails.getAuthorities())
;
SecurityContextHolder.getContext()
.setAuthentication(authentication);
```

The advantage of this approach is that there is no need to hit the datastore again. In our case, the datastore is an in-memory datastore, but this could be backed by a database, which could have some security implications. The disadvantage of this approach is that we do not get to reuse the code much. Since this method is invoked infrequently, we opt for reusing the code. In general, it is best to evaluate each situation separately to determine which approach makes the most sense.

Updating SignupController

The application has a `SignupController` object, which is what processes the HTTP request to create a new `CalendarUser` object. The last step is to update `SignupController` to create our user and then indicate that they are logged in. Make the following updates to `SignupController`:

```
//src/main/java/com/packtpub/springsecurity/web/controllers/
SignupController.java

@RequestMapping(value="/signup/new", method=RequestMethod.POST)
public String signup(@Valid SignupForm signupForm,
BindingResult result, RedirectAttributes redirectAttributes) {
... existing validation ...
user.setPassword(signupForm.getPassword());
int id = calendarService.createUser(user);
user.setId(id);
userContext.setCurrentUser(user);
redirectAttributes.addFlashAttribute("message", "Success");
return "redirect:/";
}
```

If you have not done so already, restart the application, visit `http://localhost:8080/`, create a new user, and see that the new user is automatically logged in.

Your code should now look like `chapter03.02-calendar`.

Creating a custom UserDetailsService object

While we are able to link our domain model (`CalendarUser`) with Spring Security's domain model (`UserDetails`), we have to maintain multiple representations of the user. To resolve this dual maintenance, we can implement a custom `UserDetailsService` object to translate our existing `CalendarUser` domain model into an implementation of Spring Security's `UserDetails` interface. By translating our `CalendarUser` object into `UserDetails`, Spring Security can make security decisions using our custom domain model. This means that we will no longer need to manage two different representations of a user.

The CalendarUserDetailsService class

Up to this point, we have needed two different representations of users: one for Spring Security to make security decisions, and one for our application to associate our domain objects to. Create a new class named `CalendarUserDetailsService` that will make Spring Security aware of our `CalendarUser` object. This will ensure that Spring Security can make decisions based upon our domain model. Create a new file named `CalendarUserDetailsService.java`, as follows:

```
//src/main/java/com/packtpub/springsecurity/core/userdetails/
CalendarUserDetailsService.java

// imports and package declaration omitted

@Component
public class CalendarUserDetailsService implements
UserDetailsService {
private final CalendarUserDao calendarUserDao;
@Autowired
public CalendarUserDetailsService(CalendarUserDao
    calendarUserDao) {
    this.calendarUserDao = calendarUserDao;
}
public UserDetails loadUserByUsername(String username) throws
    UsernameNotFoundException {
    CalendarUser user = calendarUserDao.findUserByEmail(username);
  if (user == null) {
     throw new UsernameNotFoundException("Invalid
       username/password.");
   }
   Collection<? extends GrantedAuthority> authorities =
     CalendarUserAuthorityUtils.createAuthorities(user);
   return new User(user.getEmail(), user.getPassword(),
     authorities);
 }
 }
```

 Within Spring Tool Suite, you can use *Shift+Ctrl+O* to easily add the missing imports. Alternatively, you can copy the code from the next checkpoint (`chapter03.03-calendar`).

Here, we utilize `CalendarUserDao` to obtain `CalendarUser` by using the email address. We take care not to return a `null` value; instead, a `UsernameNotFoundException` exception should be thrown, as returning `null` breaks the `UserDetailsService` interface.

We then convert `CalendarUser` into `UserDetails`, implemented by the user, as we did in the previous sections.

We now utilize a utility class named `CalendarUserAuthorityUtils` that we provided in the sample code. This will create `GrantedAuthority` based on the email address so that we can support users and administrators. If the email starts with `admin`, the user is treated as `ROLE_ADMIN`, `ROLE_USER`. Otherwise, the user is treated as `ROLE_USER`. Of course, we would not do this in a real application, but it's this simplicity that allows us to focus on this lesson.

Configuring UserDetailsService

Now that we have a new `UserDetailsService` object, let's update the Spring Security configuration to utilize it. Our `CalendarUserDetailsService` class is added to our Spring configuration automatically, since we leverage classpath scanning and the `@Component` annotation. This means we only need to update Spring Security to refer to the `CalendarUserDetailsService` class we just created. We are also able to remove the `configure()` and `userDetailsService()` methods, Spring Security's in-memory implementation of `UserDetailsService`, since we are now providing our own `UserDetailsService` implementation. Update the `SecurityConfig.java` file, as follows:

```
//src/main/java/com/packtpub/springsecurity/configuration/SecurityC
onfig.java

@Override
public void configure(AuthenticationManagerBuilder auth) throws
Exception {
    ...
}
@Bean
@Override
public UserDetailsManager userDetailsService() {
    ...
}
```

Removing references to UserDetailsManager

We need to remove the code we added in `DefaultCalendarService` that used `UserDetailsManager` to synchronize the Spring Security `o.s.s.core.userdetails.User` interface and `CalendarUser`. First, the code is not necessary, since Spring Security now refers to `CalendarUserDetailsService`. Second, since we removed the `inMemoryAuthentication()` method, there is no `UserDetailsManager` object defined in our Spring configuration. Go ahead and remove all references to `UserDetailsManager` found in `DefaultCalendarService`. The updates will look similar to the following sample snippets:

```
//src/main/java/com/packtpub/springsecurity/service/
DefaultCalendarService.java

public class DefaultCalendarService implements CalendarService {
    private final EventDao eventDao;
    private final CalendarUserDao userDao;
    @Autowired
    public DefaultCalendarService(EventDao eventDao, CalendarUserDao
userDao) {
        this.eventDao = eventDao;
        this.userDao = userDao;
    }
    ...
    public int createUser(CalendarUser user) {
        return userDao.createUser(user);
    }
}
```

Start up the application and see that Spring Security's in-memory `UserDetailsManager` object is no longer necessary (we removed it from our `SecurityConfig.java` file).

Your code should now look like `chapter03.03-calendar`.

The CalendarUserDetails object

We have successfully eliminated the need to manage both Spring Security users and our
CalendarUser objects. However, it is still cumbersome for us to continually need to
translate between the two objects. Instead, we will create a CalendarUserDetails object,
which can be referred to as both UserDetails and CalendarUser. Update
CalendarUserDetailsService to use CalendarUserDetails, as follows:

```
//src/main/java/com/packtpub/springsecurity/core/userdetails/
CalendarUserDetailsService.java

public UserDetails loadUserByUsername(String username) throws
UsernameNotFoundException {
...
return new CalendarUserDetails(user);
}
private final class CalendarUserDetails extends CalendarUser
implements UserDetails {
CalendarUserDetails(CalendarUser user) {
    setId(user.getId());
    setEmail(user.getEmail());
    setFirstName(user.getFirstName());
    setLastName(user.getLastName());
    setPassword(user.getPassword());
}
public Collection<? extends GrantedAuthority>
    getAuthorities() {
    return CalendarUserAuthorityUtils.createAuthorities(this);
}
public String getUsername() {
    return getEmail();
}
public boolean isAccountNonExpired() { return true; }
public boolean isAccountNonLocked() { return true; }
public boolean isCredentialsNonExpired() { return true; }
public boolean isEnabled() { return true; }
}
```

In the next section, we will see that our application can now refer to the principal
authentication on the current CalendarUser object. However, Spring Security can continue
to treat CalendarUserDetails as a UserDetails object.

The SpringSecurityUserContext simplifications

We have updated `CalendarUserDetailsService` to return a `UserDetails` object that extends `CalendarUser` and implements `UserDetails`. This means that, rather than having to translate between the two objects, we can simply refer to a `CalendarUser` object. Update `SpringSecurityUserContext` as follows:

```
public class SpringSecurityUserContext implements UserContext {
public CalendarUser getCurrentUser() {
   SecurityContext context =
SecurityContextHolder.getContext();
   Authentication authentication = context.getAuthentication();
   if(authentication == null) {
      return null;
   }
   return (CalendarUser) authentication.getPrincipal();
}

public void setCurrentUser(CalendarUser user) {
   Collection authorities =
     CalendarUserAuthorityUtils.createAuthorities(user);
   Authentication authentication = new
UsernamePasswordAuthenticationToken(user,user.getPassword(),
authorities);
   SecurityContextHolder.getContext()
     .setAuthentication(authentication);
}
}
```

The updates no longer require the use of `CalendarUserDao` or Spring Security's `UserDetailsService` interface. Remember our `loadUserByUsername` method from the previous section? The result of this method call becomes the principal of the authentication. Since our updated `loadUserByUsername` method returns an object that extends `CalendarUser`, we can safely cast the principal of the `Authentication` object to `CalendarUser`. We can pass a `CalendarUser` object as the principal into the constructor for `UsernamePasswordAuthenticationToken` when invoking the `setCurrentUser` method. This allows us to still cast the principal to a `CalendarUser` object when invoking the `getCurrentUser` method.

Displaying custom user attributes

Now that `CalendarUser` is populated into Spring Security's authentication, we can update our UI to display the name of the current user rather than the email address. Update the `header.html` file with the following code:

```
//src/main/resources/templates/fragments/header.html

<ul class="nav navbar-nav pull-right"
sec:authorize="isAuthenticated()">
    <li id="greeting">
        <p class="navbar-text">Welcome <div class="navbar-text"
        th:text="${#authentication.getPrincipal().getName()}">
        User</div></p>
    </li>
```

Internally, the `"${#authentication.getPrincipal().getName()}"` tag attribute executes the following code. Observe that the highlighted values correlate to the `property` attribute of the authentication tag we specified in the `header.html` file:

```
SecurityContext context = SecurityContextHolder.getContext();
Authentication authentication = context.getAuthentication();
CalendarUser user = (CalendarUser) authentication.getPrincipal();
String firstAndLastName = user.getName();
```

Restart the application, visit `http://localhost:8080/`, and log in to view the updates. Instead of seeing the current user's email, you should now see their first and last names.

 Your code should now look like `chapter03.04-calendar`.

Creating a custom AuthenticationProvider object

Spring Security delegates to an `AuthenticationProvider` object to determine whether a user is authenticated or not. This means we can write custom `AuthenticationProvider` implementations to inform Spring Security how to authenticate in different ways. The good news is that Spring Security provides quite a few `AuthenticationProvider` objects, so more often than not you will not need to create one. In fact, up until this point, we have been utilizing Spring Security's `o.s.s.authentication.dao.DaoAuthenticationProvider` object, which compares the username and password returned by `UserDetailsService`.

CalendarUserAuthenticationProvider

Throughout the rest of this section, we are going to create a custom `AuthenticationProvider` object named `CalendarUserAuthenticationProvider` that will replace `CalendarUserDetailsService`. Then, we will use `CalendarUserAuthenticationProvider` to consider an additional parameter to support authenticating users from multiple domains.

> We must use an `AuthenticationProvider` object rather than `UserDetailsService`, because the `UserDetails` interface has no concept of a domain parameter.

Create a new class named `CalendarUserAuthenticationProvider`, as follows:

```
//src/main/java/com/packtpub/springsecurity/authentication/
CalendarUserAuthenticationProvider.java

// ... imports omitted ...

@Component
public class CalendarUserAuthenticationProvider implements
AuthenticationProvider {
private final CalendarService calendarService;
@Autowired
public CalendarUserAuthenticationProvider
(CalendarService    calendarService) {
   this.calendarService = calendarService;
}
public Authentication authenticate(Authentication
```

```
authentication) throws AuthenticationException {
    UsernamePasswordAuthenticationToken token =
    (UsernamePasswordAuthenticationToken)
authentication;
String email = token.getName();
CalendarUser user = null;
if(email != null) {
  user = calendarService.findUserByEmail(email);
}
if(user == null) {
  throw new UsernameNotFoundException("Invalid
  username/password");
}
String password = user.getPassword();
if(!password.equals(token.getCredentials())) {
  throw new BadCredentialsException("Invalid
  username/password");
}
Collection<? extends GrantedAuthority> authorities =
  CalendarUserAuthorityUtils.createAuthorities(user);
return new UsernamePasswordAuthenticationToken(user, password,
  authorities);
}
public boolean supports(Class<?> authentication) {
    return UsernamePasswordAuthenticationToken
      .class.equals(authentication);
  }
}
```

 Remember that you can use *Shift+Ctrl+O* within Eclipse to easily add the missing imports. Alternatively, you can copy the implementation from `chapter03.05-calendar`.

Before Spring Security can invoke the `authenticate` method, the `supports` method must return `true` for the `Authentication` class that will be passed in. In this case, `AuthenticationProvider` can authenticate a username and password. We do not accept subclasses of `UsernamePasswordAuthenticationToken`, since there may be additional fields that we do not know how to validate.

The authenticate method accepts an Authentication object as an argument that represents an authentication request. In practical terms, it is the input from the user that we need to attempt to validate. If authentication fails, the method should throw an o.s.s.core.AuthenticationException exception. If authentication succeeds, it should return an Authentication object that contains the proper GrantedAuthority objects for the user. The returned Authentication object will be set on SecurityContextHolder. If authentication cannot be determined, the method should return null.

The first step in authenticating the request is to extract the information from the Authentication object that we need to authenticate the user. In our case, we extract the username and look up CalendarUser by email address, just as CalendarUserDetailsService did. If the provided username and password match CalendarUser, we will return a UsernamePasswordAuthenticationToken object with proper GrantedAuthority. Otherwise, we will throw an AuthenticationException exception.

Remember how the login page leveraged SPRING_SECURITY_LAST_EXCEPTION to explain why login failed? The message for the AuthenticationException exception thrown in AuthenticationProvider is the last AuthenticationException exception and will be displayed on our login page in the event of a failed login.

Configuring the CalendarUserAuthenticationProvider object

Let's perform the following steps to configure CalendarUserAuthenticationProvider:

1. Update the SecurityConfig.java file to refer to our newly created CalendarUserAuthenticationProvider object, and remove the reference to CalendarUserDetailsService, as shown in the following code snippet:

```
//src/main/java/com/packtpub/springsecurity/configuration/
SecurityConfig.java

@Autowired CalendarUserAuthenticationProvider cuap;
@Override
public void configure(AuthenticationManagerBuilder auth)
throws Exception {
    auth.authenticationProvider(cuap);
}
```

2. Restart the application and ensure everything is still working. As a user, we do not notice anything different. However, as a developer, we know that `CalendarUserDetails` is no longer required; we are still able to display the current user's first and last names, and Spring Security is still able to leverage `CalendarUser` for authentication.

 Your code should now look like `chapter03.05-calendar`.

Authenticating with different parameters

One of the strengths of `AuthenticationProvider` is that it can authenticate with any parameters you wish. For example, maybe your application uses a random identifier for authentication, or perhaps it is a multitenant application and requires a username, password, and domain. In the following section, we will update `CalendarUserAuthenticationProvider` to support multiple domains.

 A domain is a way to scope our users. For example, if we deploy our application once but have multiple clients using the same deployment, each client may want a user with the username `admin`. By adding a domain to our user object, we can ensure that each user is distinct and still supports this requirement.

The DomainUsernamePasswordAuthenticationToken class

When a user authenticates, Spring Security submits an `Authentication` object to `AuthenticationProvider` with the information provided by the user. The current `UsernamePasswordAuthentication` object only contains a username and password field. Create a `DomainUsernamePasswordAuthenticationToken` object that contains a `domain` field, as shown in the following code snippet:

```
//src/main/java/com/packtpub/springsecurity/authentication/
DomainUsernamePasswordAuthenticationToken.java

public final class DomainUsernamePasswordAuthenticationToken extends
UsernamePasswordAuthenticationToken {
        private final String domain;
```

```
            // used for attempting authentication
        public DomainUsernamePasswordAuthenticationToken(String
        principal, String credentials, String domain) {
           super(principal, credentials);
           this.domain = domain;
        }
    // used for returning to Spring Security after being
    //authenticated
    public DomainUsernamePasswordAuthenticationToken(CalendarUser
       principal, String credentials, String domain,
       Collection<? extends GrantedAuthority> authorities) {
         super(principal, credentials, authorities);
         this.domain = domain;
       }
    public String getDomain() {
       return domain;
    }
}
```

Updating CalendarUserAuthenticationProvider

Let's take a look at the following steps for updating the
CalendarUserAuthenticationProvider.java file:

1. Now, we need to update CalendarUserAuthenticationProvider to utilize
   the domain field as follows:

   ```
   //src/main/java/com/packtpub/springsecurity/authentication/
   CalendarUserAuthenticationProvider.java

   public Authentication authenticate(Authentication authentication)
   throws AuthenticationException {
       DomainUsernamePasswordAuthenticationToken token =
       (DomainUsernamePasswordAuthenticationToken) authentication;
   String userName = token.getName();
   String domain = token.getDomain();
   String email = userName + "@" + domain;
   ... previous validation of the user and password ...
   return new DomainUsernamePasswordAuthenticationToken(user,
   password, domain, authorities);
   }
   public boolean supports(Class<?> authentication) {
     return DomainUsernamePasswordAuthenticationToken
     .class.equals(authentication);
   }
   ```

2. We first update the `supports` method so that Spring Security will pass `DomainUsernamePasswordAuthenticationToken` into our `authenticate` method.

3. We then use the domain information to create our email address and authenticate, as we had previously done. Admittedly, this example is contrived. However, the example is able to illustrate how to authenticate with an additional parameter.

4. The `CalendarUserAuthenticationProvider` interface can now use the new domain field. However, there is no way for a user to specify the domain. For this, we must update our `login.html` file.

Adding domain to the login page

Open up the `login.html` file and add a new input named `domain`, as follows:

```
//src/main/resources/templates/login.html

...
<label for="username">Username</label>
<input type="text" id="username" name="username"/>
<label for="password">Password</label>
<input type="password" id="password" name="password"/>
<label for="domain">Domain</label>
<input type="text" id="domain" name="domain"/>
...
```

Now, a domain will be submitted when users attempt to log in. However, Spring Security is unaware of how to use that domain to create a `DomainUsernamePasswordAuthenticationToken` object and pass it into `AuthenticationProvider`. To fix this, we will need to create `DomainUsernamePasswordAuthenticationFilter`.

The DomainUsernamePasswordAuthenticationFilter class

Spring Security provides a number of servlet filters that act as controllers for authenticating users. The filters are invoked as one of the delegates of the `FilterChainProxy` object that we discussed in Chapter 2, *Getting Started with Spring Security*. Previously, the `formLogin()` method instructed Spring Security to use `o.s.s.web.authentication.UsernamePasswordAuthenticationFilter` to act as a login controller. The filter's job is to perform the following tasks:

- Obtain a username and password from the HTTP request.
- Create a `UsernamePasswordAuthenticationToken` object with the information obtained from the HTTP request.
- Request that Spring Security validates `UsernamePasswordAuthenticationToken`.
- If the token is validated, it will set the authentication returned to it on `SecurityContextHolder`, just as we did when a new user signed up for an account. We will need to extend `UsernamePasswordAuthenticationFilter` to leverage our newly created `DoainUsernamePasswordAuthenticationToken` object.
- Create a `DomainUsernamePasswordAuthenticationFilter` object, as follows:

```
//src/main/java/com/packtpub/springsecurity/web/authentication/
DomainUsernamePasswordAuthenticationFilter.java

public final class
DomainUsernamePasswordAuthenticationFilter extends
 UsernamePasswordAuthenticationFilter {
public Authentication attemptAuthentication
(HttpServletRequest request,HttpServletResponse response) throws
AuthenticationException {
        if (!request.getMethod().equals("POST")) {
          throw new AuthenticationServiceException
          ("Authentication method not supported: "
           + request.getMethod());
        }
    String username = obtainUsername(request);
    String password = obtainPassword(request);
    String domain = request.getParameter("domain");
    // authRequest.isAuthenticated() = false since no
    //authorities are specified
    DomainUsernamePasswordAuthenticationToken authRequest
    = new DomainUsernamePasswordAuthenticationToken(username,
```

```
   password, domain);
setDetails(request, authRequest);
return this.getAuthenticationManager()
.authenticate(authRequest);
}
}
```

The new `DomainUsernamePasswordAuthenticationFilter` object will perform the following tasks:

- Obtain a username, password, and domain from the `HttpServletRequest` method.
- Create our `DomainUsernamePasswordAuthenticationToken` object with information obtained from the HTTP request.
- Request that Spring Security validates `DomainUsernamePasswordAuthenticationToken`. The work is delegated to `CalendarUserAuthenticationProvider`.
- If the token is validated, its superclass will set the authentication returned by `CalendarUserAuthenticationProvider` on `SecurityContextHolder`, just as we did to authenticate a user after they created a new account.

Updating our configuration

Now that we have created all the code required for an additional parameter, we need to configure Spring Security to be aware of it. The following code snippet includes the required updates to our `SecurityConfig.java` file to support our additional parameter:

```
//src/main/java/com/packtpub/springsecurity/configuration/
SecurityConfig.java

@Override
protected void configure(final HttpSecurity http) throws
Exception {
   http.authorizeRequests()
      ...
      .and().exceptionHandling()
         .accessDeniedPage("/errors/403")
         .authenticationEntryPoint(
            loginUrlAuthenticationEntryPoint())
      .and().formLogin()
         .loginPage("/login/form")
         .loginProcessingUrl("/login")
         .failureUrl("/login/form?error")
         .usernameParameter("username")
```

```
            .passwordParameter("password")
            .defaultSuccessUrl("/default", true)
            .permitAll()
        ...
        // Add custom UsernamePasswordAuthenticationFilter
        .addFilterAt(
            domainUsernamePasswordAuthenticationFilter(),
            UsernamePasswordAuthenticationFilter.class)
    ;
}
@Bean
public DomainUsernamePasswordAuthenticationFilter
domainUsernamePasswordAuthenticationFilter()
        throws Exception {
    DomainUsernamePasswordAuthenticationFilter dupaf = new
DomainUsernamePasswordAuthenticationFilter(
                            super.authenticationManagerBean());
    dupaf.setFilterProcessesUrl("/login");
    dupaf.setUsernameParameter("username");
    dupaf.setPasswordParameter("password");
    dupaf.setAuthenticationSuccessHandler(
            new
SavedRequestAwareAuthenticationSuccessHandler(){{
                setDefaultTargetUrl("/default");
            }}
    );
    dupaf.setAuthenticationFailureHandler(
            new SimpleUrlAuthenticationFailureHandler(){{
                setDefaultFailureUrl("/login/form?error");
            }}
    );
    dupaf.afterPropertiesSet();
    return dupaf;
}
@Bean
public LoginUrlAuthenticationEntryPoint
loginUrlAuthenticationEntryPoint(){
    return new LoginUrlAuthenticationEntryPoint("/login/form");
}
```

 The preceding code snippet configures standard beans in our Spring Security configuration. We have shown this to demonstrate that it can be done. However, throughout much of the rest of the book, we include standard bean configuration in its own file, as this makes the configuration less verbose. If you are having trouble, or prefer not to type all of this, you may copy it from `chapter03.06-calendar`.

The following are a few highlights from the configuration updates:

- We overrode `defaultAuthenticationEntryPoint` and added a reference to `o.s.s.web.authentication.LoginUrlAuthenticationEntryPoint`, which determines what happens when a request for a protected resource occurs and the user is not authenticated. In our case, we are redirected to a login page.
- We removed the `formLogin()` method and used a `.addFilterAt()` method to insert our custom filter into `FilterChainProxy`. The position indicates the order in which the delegates of `FilterChain` are considered and cannot overlap with another filter, but can replace the filter at the current position. We replaced `UsernamePasswordAuthenticationFilter` with our custom filter.
- We added the configuration for our custom filter, which refers to the authentication manager created by the `configure(AuthenticationManagerBuilder)` method.

Take a look at the following diagram for your reference:

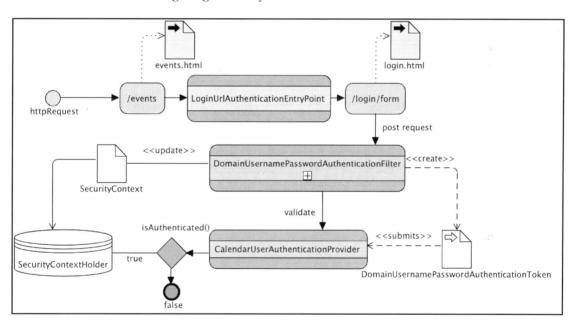

You can now restart the application and try the following steps, depicted in the preceding diagram, to understand how all the pieces fit together:

1. Visit `http://localhost:8080/events`.

2. Spring Security will intercept the secured URL and use the `LoginUrlAuthenticationEntryPoint` object to process it.

3. The `LoginUrlAuthenticationEntryPoint` object will send the user to the login page. Enter `admin1` as the username, `example.com` as the domain, and `admin1` as the password.

4. The `DomainUsernamePasswordAuthenticationFilter` object will intercept the process of the login request. It will then obtain the username, domain, and password from the HTTP request and create a `DomainUsernamePasswordAuthenticationToken` object.

5. The `DomainUsernamePasswordAuthenticationFilter` object submits `DomainUsernamePasswordAuthenticationToken` to `CalendarUserAuthenticationProvider`.

6. The `CalendarUserAuthenticationProvider` interface validates `DomainUsernamePasswordAuthenticationToken` and then returns an authenticated `DomainUsernamePasswordAuthenticationToken` object (that is, `isAuthenticated()` returns `true`).

7. The `DomainUserPasswordAuthenticationFilter` object updates `SecurityContext` with `DomainUsernamePasswordAuthenticationToken` and places it on `SecurityContextHolder`.

 Your code should look like `chapter03.06-calendar`.

Which authentication method to use?

We have covered the three main methods of authenticating, so which one is the best? Like all solutions, each comes with its pros and cons. You can find a summary of when to use a specific type of authentication by referring to the following list:

- SecurityContextHolder: Interacting directly with SecurityContextHolder is certainly the easiest way of authenticating a user. It works well when you are authenticating a newly created user or authenticating in an unconventional way. By using SecurityContextHolder directly, we do not have to interact with so many Spring Security layers. The downside is that we do not get some of the more advanced features that Spring Security provides automatically. For example, if we want to send the user to the previously requested page after logging in, we would have to manually integrate that into our controller.

- UserDetailsService: Creating a custom UserDetailsService object is an easy mechanism that allows for Spring Security to make security decisions based on our custom domain model. It also provides a mechanism to hook into other Spring Security features. For example, Spring Security requires UserDetailsService in order to use the built-in remember-me support covered in Chapter 7, *Remember-Me Services*. The UserDetailsService object does not work when authentication is not based on a username and password.

- AuthenticationProvider: This is the most flexible method for extending Spring Security. It allows a user to authenticate with any parameters that we wish. However, if we wish to leverage features such as Spring Security's remember-me, we will still need UserDetailsService.

Summary

This chapter has used real-world problems to introduce the basic building blocks used in Spring Security. It also demonstrates to us how we can make Spring Security authenticate against our custom domain objects by extending those basic building blocks. In short, we have learned that the SecurityContextHolder interface is the central location for determining the current user. Not only can it be used by developers to access the current user, but also to set the currently logged-in user.

We also explored how to create custom UserDetailsService and AuthenticationProvider objects and how to perform authentication with more than just a username and password.

In the next chapter, we will explore some of the built-in support for JDBC-based authentication.

4
JDBC-Based Authentication

In the previous chapter, we saw how we can extend Spring Security to utilize our `CalendarDao` interface and our existing domain model to authenticate users. In this chapter, we will see how we can use Spring Security's built-in JDBC support. To keep things simple, this chapter's sample code is based on our Spring Security setup from Chapter 2, *Getting Started with Spring Security*. In this chapter, we will cover the following topics:

- Using Spring Security's built-in JDBC-based authentication support
- Utilizing Spring Security's group-based authorization to make administering users easier
- Learning how to use Spring Security's `UserDetailsManager` interface
- Configuring Spring Security to utilize the existing `CalendarUser` schema to authenticate users
- Learning how we can secure passwords using Spring Security's new cryptography module
- Using Spring Security's default JDBC authentication

If your application has not yet implemented security, or if your security infrastructure is using a database, Spring Security provides out-of-the-box support that can simplify the solving of your security needs. Spring Security provides a default schema for users, authorities, and groups. If that does not meet your needs, it allows for the querying and managing of users to be customized. In the next section, we are going to go through the basic steps for setting up JDBC authentication with Spring Security.

Required dependencies

Our application has already defined all the necessary dependencies required for this chapter. However, if you are using Spring Security's JDBC support, you are likely going to want the following dependencies listed in your `build.gradle` file. It is important to highlight that the JDBC driver that you will use will depend on which database you are using. Consult your database vendor's documentation for details on which driver is needed for your database.

 Remember that all the Spring versions need to match, and all Spring Security versions need to match (this includes transitive dependency versions). If you are having difficulty getting this to work in your own application, you may want to define the dependency management section in `build.gradle` to enforce this, as shown in Chapter 2, *Getting Started with Spring Security*. As previously mentioned, you will not need to worry about this when using the sample code, since we have already set up the necessary dependencies for you.

The following snippet defines the required dependencies needed for this chapter, including Spring Security and JDBC dependencies:

```
//build.gradle

dependencies {
...
// Database:
 compile('org.springframework.boot:spring-boot-starter-jdbc')
 compile('com.h2database:h2')
// Security:
 compile('org.springframework.boot:spring-boot-starter-security')
 testCompile('org.springframework.security:spring-security-test')
    ....
}
```

Using the H2 database

The first portion of this exercise involves setting up an instance of the Java-based H2 relational database, populated with the Spring Security default schema. We'll configure H2 to run in memory using Spring's `EmbeddedDatabase` configuration feature—a significantly simpler method of configuration than
setting up the database by hand. You can find additional information on the H2 website at `http://www.h2database.com/`.

Keep in mind that in our sample application, we'll primarily use H2 due to its ease of setup. Spring Security will work with any database that supports ANSI SQL out of the box. We encourage you to tweak the configuration and use the database of your preference if you're following along with the examples. As we didn't want this portion of the book to focus on the complexities of database setup, we chose convenience over realism for the purpose of the exercises.

Provided JDBC scripts

We've supplied all the SQL files that are used for creating the schema and data in an H2 database for this chapter in the `src/main/resources/database/h2/` folder. Any files prefixed with `security` are to support Spring Security's default JDBC implementation. Any SQL files prefixed with `calendar` are custom SQL files for the JBCP calendar application. Hopefully, this will make running the samples a little easier. If you're following along with your own database instance, you may have to adjust the schema definition syntax to fit your particular database. Additional database schemas can be found in the Spring Security reference. You can find a link to the Spring Security Reference in the book's `Appendix`, *Additional Reference Material*.

Configuring the H2 embedded database

To configure the H2 embedded database, we need to create a `DataSource` and run SQL to create the Spring Security table structure. We will need to update the SQL that is loaded at startup to include Spring Security's basic schema definition, Spring Security user definitions, and the authority mappings for users. You can find the `DataSource` definition and the relevant updates in the following code snippet:

```
//src/main/java/com/packtpub/springsecurity/configuration/DataSourceConfig.
java

    @Bean
    public DataSource dataSource() {
    return new EmbeddedDatabaseBuilder()
        .setName("dataSource")
        .setType(EmbeddedDatabaseType.H2)
        .addScript("/database/h2/calendar-schema.sql")
        .addScript("/database/h2/calendar-data.sql")
        .addScript("/database/h2/security-schema.sql")
        .addScript("/database/h2/security-users.sql")
        .addScript("/database/h2/security-user-authorities.sql")
        .build();
```

```
        }
```

Remember that the `EmbeddedDatabaseBuilder()` method creates this database only in memory, so you won't see anything on the disk, and you won't be able to use standard tools to query it. However, you can use the H2 console that is embedded in the application to interact with the database. See the instructions on the **Welcome** page of our application to learn how to use it.

Configuring a JDBC UserDetailsManager implementation

We'll modify the `SecurityConfig.java` file to declare that we're using a JDBC `UserDetailsManager` implementation, instead of the Spring Security in-memory `UserDetailsService` implementation that we configured in Chapter 2, *Getting Started with Spring Security*. This is done with a simple change to the `UserDetailsManager` declaration, as follows:

```
//src/main/java/com/packtpub/springsecurity/configuration/SecurityConfig.ja
va

    ...
    @Bean
    @Override
    public UserDetailsManager userDetailsService() {
        JdbcUserDetailsManager manager = new JdbcUserDetailsManager();
        manager.setDataSource(dataSource);
        return manager;
    }
    ...
```

We replace the previous `configure(AuthenticationManagerBuilder)` method, along with all of the child elements, with the `userDetailsService()` method, as shown in the preceding code snippet.

The default user schema of Spring Security

Let's take a look at each of the SQL files used to initialize the database. The first script we added contains the default Spring Security schema definition for users and their authorities. The following script has been adapted from Spring Security's Reference, which is listed in the Appendix, *Additional Reference Material* to have explicitly named constraints, to make troubleshooting easier:

```
//src/main/resources/database/h2/security-schema.sql

create table users(
    username varchar(256) not null primary key,
    password varchar(256) not null,
    enabled boolean not null
);
create table authorities (
    username varchar(256) not null,
    authority varchar(256) not null,
    constraint fk_authorities_users
        foreign key(username) references users(username)
);
create unique index ix_auth_username on authorities
(username,authority);
```

Defining users

The next script is in charge of defining the users in our application. The included SQL statement creates the same users that we have used throughout the entire book so far. The file also adds an additional user, disabled1@example.com, who will not be able to log in since we indicate the user as disabled:

```
//src/main/resources/database/h2/security-users.sql

insert into users (username,password,enabled)
    values ('user1@example.com','user1',1);
insert into users (username,password,enabled)
    values ('admin1@example.com','admin1',1);
insert into users (username,password,enabled)
    values ('user2@example.com','admin1',1);
insert into users (username,password,enabled)
    values ('disabled1@example.com','disabled1',0);
```

Defining user authorities

You may have noticed that there is no indication if a user is an administrator or a regular user. The next file specifies a direct mapping of the user to the corresponding authorities. If a user did not have an authority mapped to it, Spring Security would not allow that user to be logged in:

```
//src/main/resources/database/h2/security-user-authorities.sql

insert into authorities(username,authority)
```

```
          values ('user1@example.com','ROLE_USER');
      insert into authorities(username,authority)
        values ('admin1@example.com','ROLE_ADMIN');
      insert into authorities(username,authority)
        values ('admin1@example.com','ROLE_USER');
      insert into authorities(username,authority)
        values ('user2@example.com','ROLE_USER');
      insert into authorities(username,authority)
        values ('disabled1@example.com','ROLE_USER');
```

After the SQL is added to the embedded database configuration, we should be able to start the application and log in. Try logging in with the new user using `disabled1@example.com` as the `username` and `disabled1` as the `password`. Notice that Spring Security does not allow the user to log in and provides the error message `Reason: User is disabled`.

 Your code should now look like this: `calendar04.01-calendar`.

The UserDetailsManager interface

We have already leveraged the `InMemoryUserDetailsManager` class in Spring Security in `Chapter 3`, *Custom Authentication*, to look up the current `CalendarUser` application in our `SpringSecurityUserContext` implementation of `UserContext`. This allowed us to determine which `CalendarUser` should be used when looking up the events for the **My Events** page. `Chapter 3`, *Custom Authentication*, also demonstrated how to update the `DefaultCalendarService.java` file to utilize `InMemoryUserDetailsManager`, to ensure that we created a new Spring Security user when we created `CalendarUser`. This chapter reuses exactly the same code. The only difference is that the `UserDetailsManager` implementation is backed by the `JdbcUserDetailsManager` class of Spring Security, which uses a database instead of an in-memory datastore.

What other features does `UserDetailsManager` provide out of the box?

Although these types of functions are relatively easy to write with additional JDBC statements, Spring Security actually provides out-of-the-box functionality to support many common **create, read, update, and delete (CRUD)** operations on users in JDBC databases. This can be convenient for simple systems, and a good base to build on for any custom requirements that a user may have:

Method	Description
`void createUser(UserDetails user)`	It creates a new user with the given `UserDetails` information, including any declared `GrantedAuthority` authorities.
`void updateUser(final UserDetails user)`	It updates a user with the given `UserDetails` information. It updates `GrantedAuthority` and removes the user from the user cache.
`void deleteUser(String username)`	It deletes the user with the given username and removes the user from the user cache.
`boolean userExists(String username)`	It indicates whether or not a user (active or inactive) exists with the given username.
`void changePassword(String oldPassword, String newPassword)`	It changes the password of the currently logged-in user. The user must then supply the correct password in order for the operation to succeed.

If `UserDetailsManager` does not provide all the methods that are necessary for your application, you can extend the interface to provide these custom requirements. For example, if you needed the ability to list all of the possible users in an administrative view, you could write your own interface with this method and provide an implementation that points to the same datastore as the `UserDetailsManager` implementation you are currently using.

Group-based access control

The `JdbcUserDetailsManager` class supports the ability to add a level of indirection between the users and the `GrantedAuthority` declarations by grouping `GrantedAuthority` into logical sets called groups.

Users are then assigned one or more groups, and their membership confers a set of the `GrantedAuthority` declarations:

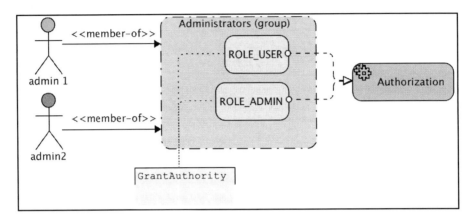

As you can see in the preceding diagram, this indirection allows the assignment of the same set of roles to multiple users, by simply assigning any new users to existing groups. This is different behavior that we've seen so far, where previously we assigned `GrantedAuthority` directly to individual users.

This bundling of common sets of authorities can be helpful in the following scenarios:

- You need to segregate users into communities, with some overlapping roles between groups.
- You want to globally change the authorization for a class of user. For example, if you have a supplier group, you might want to enable or disable their access to particular portions of the application.
- You have a large number of users, and you don't need user-level authority configuration.

Unless your application has a very small user base, there is a very high likelihood that you'll be using group-based access control. While group-based access control is slightly more complex than other strategies, the flexibility and simplicity of managing a user's access makes this complexity worthwhile. This indirect technique of aggregating user privileges by group is commonly referred to as **group-based access control (GBAC)**.

GBAC is an approach common to almost every secured operating system or software package on the market. **Microsoft Active Directory** (**AD**) is one of the most visible implementations of large-scale GBAC, due to its design of slotting AD users into groups and assigning privileges to those groups. Management of privileges in large AD-based organizations is made exponentially simpler through the use of GBAC.

Try to think of the security models of the software you use—how are the users, groups, and privileges managed? What are the pros and cons of the way the security model is written?

Let's add a level of abstraction to the JBCP calendar application and apply the concept of group-based authorization to the site.

Configuring group-based access control

We'll add two groups to the application: regular users, which we'll call Users, and administrative users, which we'll call Administrators. Our existing accounts will be associated with the appropriate groups through an additional SQL script.

Configuring JdbcUserDetailsManager to use groups

By default, Spring Security does not use GBAC. Therefore, we must instruct Spring Security to enable the use of groups. Modify the SecurityConfig.java file to use GROUP_AUTHORITIES_BY_USERNAME_QUERY, as follows:

```
//src/main/java/com/packtpub/springsecurity/configuration/SecurityConfig.java

    private static String GROUP_AUTHORITIES_BY_USERNAME_QUERY = " "+
                "select g.id, g.group_name, ga.authority " +
                "from groups g, group_members gm, " +
                "group_authorities ga where gm.username = ? " +
                "and g.id = ga.group_id and g.id = gm.group_id";
    @Override
    public void configure(AuthenticationManagerBuilder auth) throws
Exception {
      auth
        .jdbcAuthentication()
        .dataSource(dataSource)
        .groupAuthoritiesByUsername(
          GROUP_AUTHORITIES_BY_USERNAME_QUERY
      );
    }
```

Utilizing GBAC JDBC scripts

Next, we need to update the scripts that are being loaded at startup. We need to remove the `security-user-authorities.sql` mapping so that our users no longer obtain their authorities with direct mapping. We then need to add two additional SQL scripts. Update the `DataSource` bean configuration to load the SQL required for GBAC, as follows:

```
//src/main/java/com/packtpub/springsecurity/configuration/DataSourceConfig.
java
```

```java
@Bean
public DataSource dataSource() {
    return new EmbeddedDatabaseBuilder()
        .setName("dataSource")
        .setType(EmbeddedDatabaseType.H2)
        .addScript("/database/h2/calendar-schema.sql")
        .addScript("/database/h2/calendar-data.sql")
        .addScript("/database/h2/security-schema.sql")
        .addScript("/database/h2/security-users.sql")
        .addScript("/database/h2/security-groups-schema.sql")
        .addScript("/database/h2/security-groups-mappings.sql")
        .build();
}
```

The group-based schema

It may be obvious, but the first SQL file we added contains updates to the schema to support group-based authorization. You can find the contents of the file in the following code snippet:

```
//src/main/resources/database/h2/security-groups-schema.sql
```

```sql
create table groups (
id bigint generated by default as identity(start with 0) primary key,
group_name varchar(256) not null
);
create table group_authorities (
  group_id bigint not null,
  authority varchar(256) not null,
  constraint fk_group_authorities_group
  foreign key(group_id) references groups(id)
);
create table group_members (
  id bigint generated by default as identity(start with 0) primary key,
  username varchar(256) not null,
  group_id bigint not null,\
```

```
   constraint fk_group_members_group
   foreign key(group_id) references groups(id)\
);
```

Group authority mappings

Now we need to map our existing users to groups, and the groups to authorities. This is done in the `security-groups-mappings.sql` file. Mapping based on groups can be convenient because often, organizations already have a logical group of users for various reasons. By utilizing the existing groupings of users, we can drastically simplify our configuration. This is how a layer of indirection helps us. We have included the group definitions, group to authority mappings, and a few users in the following group mapping:

```
//src/main/resources/database/h2/security-groups-mappings.sql

-- Create the Groups

insert into groups(group_name) values ('Users');
insert into groups(group_name) values ('Administrators');

-- Map the Groups to Roles

insert into group_authorities(group_id, authority)
select id,'ROLE_USER' from groups where group_name='Users';
insert into group_authorities(group_id, authority)
select id,'ROLE_USER' from groups where
group_name='Administrators';
insert into group_authorities(group_id, authority)
select id,'ROLE_ADMIN' from groups where
group_name='Administrators';

-- Map the users to Groups

insert into group_members(group_id, username)
select id,'user1@example.com' from groups where
group_name='Users';
insert into group_members(group_id, username)
select id,'admin1@example.com' from groups where
group_name='Administrators';
...
```

Go ahead and start the application, and it will behave just as before; however, the additional layer of abstraction between the users and roles simplifies the managing of large groups of users.

Your code should now look like `calendar04.02-calendar`.

Support for a custom schema

It's common for new users of Spring Security to begin their experience by adapting the JDBC user, group, or role mapping to an existing schema. Even though a legacy database doesn't conform to the expected Spring Security schema, we can still configure `JdbcDaoImpl` to map to it.

We will now update Spring Security's JDBC support to use our existing `CalendarUser` database along with a new `calendar_authorities` table.

We can easily change the configuration of `JdbcUserDetailsManager` to utilize this schema and override Spring Security's expected table definitions and columns, which we're using for the JBCP calendar application.

Determining the correct JDBC SQL queries

The `JdbcUserDetailsManager` class has three SQL queries that have a well-defined parameter and a set of returned columns. We must determine the SQL that we'll assign to each of these queries, based on the intended functionality. Each SQL query used by `JdbcUserDetailsManager` takes the username presented at login as its one and only parameter:

Namespace query attribute name	Description	Expected SQL columns
users-by-username-query	Returns one or more users matching the username; only the first user is used.	Username (string) Password (string) Enabled (Boolean)

authorities-by-username-query	Returns one or more granted authorities directly provided to the user. Typically used when GBAC is disabled.	Username (string) GrantedAuthority (string)
group-authorities-by-username-query	Returns granted authorities and group details provided to the user through group membership. Used when GBAC is enabled.	Group Primary Key (any) Group Name (any) GrantedAuthority (string)

Be aware that in some cases, the return columns are not used by the default `JdbcUserDetailsManager` implementation, but they must be returned anyway.

Updating the SQL scripts that are loaded

We need to initialize the `DataSource` with our custom schema, rather than with Spring Security's default schema. Update the `DataSourceConfig.java` file, as follows:

```
//src/main/java/com/packtpub/springsecurity/configuration/DataSourceConfig.
java

@Bean
public DataSource dataSource() {
return new EmbeddedDatabaseBuilder()
   .setName("dataSource")
 .setType(EmbeddedDatabaseType.H2)
   .addScript("/database/h2/calendar-schema.sql")
   .addScript("/database/h2/calendar-data.sql")
  .addScript("/database/h2/calendar-authorities.sql")
   .build();
}
```

Notice that we have removed all of the scripts that start with security, and replaced them with `calendar-authorities.sql`.

The CalendarUser authority SQL

You can view the `CalendarUser` authority mappings in the following code snippet:

```
//src/main/resources/database/h2/calendar-authorities.sql

create table calendar_user_authorities (
    id bigint identity,
    calendar_user bigint not null,
    authority varchar(256) not null,
);
-- user1@example.com
insert into calendar_user_authorities(calendar_user, authority)
    select id,'ROLE_USER' from calendar_users where
    email='user1@example.com';
-- admin1@example.com
insert into calendar_user_authorities(calendar_user, authority)
    select id,'ROLE_ADMIN' from calendar_users where
    email='admin1@example.com';
insert into calendar_user_authorities(calendar_user, authority)
    select id,'ROLE_USER' from calendar_users where
    email='admin1@example.com';
-- user2@example.com
insert into calendar_user_authorities(calendar_user, authority)
    select id,'ROLE_USER' from calendar_users where
 email='user2@example.com';
```

 Notice that we use the `id` as the foreign key, which is better than utilizing the username as a foreign key (as Spring Security does). By using the `id` as the foreign key, we can allow users to easily change their username.

Inserting custom authorities

We need to update `DefaultCalendarService` to insert the authorities for the user using our custom schema when we add a new `CalendarUser` class. This is because while we reused the schema for the user definition, we did not define custom authorities in our existing application. Update `DefaultCalendarService`, as follows:

```
//src/main/java/com/packtpub/springsecurity/service/DefaultCalendarService.
java

import org.springframework.jdbc.core.JdbcOperations;
...
public class DefaultCalendarService implements CalendarService {
```

```
...
private final JdbcOperations jdbcOperations;
@Autowired
   public DefaultCalendarService(EventDao eventDao,
   CalendarUserDao userDao, JdbcOperations jdbcOperations) {
      ...
      this.jdbcOperations = jdbcOperations;
   }
...
public int createUser(CalendarUser user) {
    int userId = userDao.createUser(user);
    jdbcOperations.update(
      "insert into
calendar_user_authorities(calendar_user,authority)
      values(?,?)", userId, "ROLE_USER");
    return userId;
   }
}
```

 You may have noticed the JdbcOperations interface that is used for inserting our user. This is a convenient template provided by Spring that helps manage boilerplate code, such as connection and transaction handling. For more details, refer to the Appendix, *Additional Reference Material* of this book to find the Spring Reference.

Configuring JdbcUserDetailsManager to use custom SQL queries

In order to use custom SQL queries for our non-standard schema, we'll simply update our userDetailsService() method to include new queries. This is quite similar to how we enabled support for GBAC, except instead of using the default SQL, we will use our modified SQL. Notice that we remove our old setGroupAuthoritiesByUsernameQuery() method call, since we will not be using it in this example, in order to keep things simple:

```
//src/main/java/com/packtpub/springsecurity/configuration/SecurityConfig.java

private static String CUSTOM_USERS_BY_USERNAME_QUERY = ""+
                        "select email, password, true " +
                        "from calendar_users where email = ?";
private static String CUSTOM_AUTHORITIES_BY_USERNAME_QUERY = ""+
            "select cua.id, cua.authority " +
            "from calendar_users cu, calendar_user_authorities "+
```

```
                       "cua where cu.email = ? "+
                       "and cu.id = cua.calendar_user";
        @Override
        public void configure(AuthenticationManagerBuilder auth) throws
    Exception {
        auth
            .jdbcAuthentication()
            .dataSource(dataSource)
            .usersByUsernameQuery(USERS_BY_USERNAME_QUERY)
            .authoritiesByUsernameQuery(
              AUTHORITIES_BY_USERNAME_QUERY
            );
        }
```

This is the only configuration required to use Spring Security to read settings from an existing, non-default schema! Start up the application and ensure that everything is working properly.

Your code should now look like this: `calendar04.03-calendar`.

Keep in mind that the utilization of an existing schema commonly requires an extension of `JdbcUserDetailsManager` to support the changing of passwords, the renaming of user accounts, and other user-management functions.

If you are using `JdbcUserDetailsManager` to perform user-management tasks, then there are over 20 SQL queries utilized by the class that are accessible through the configuration. However, only the three covered are available through the namespace configuration. Please refer to the Javadoc or source code to review the defaults for the queries used by `JdbcUserDetailsManager`.

Configuring secure passwords

You might recall from the security audit in Chapter 1, *Anatomy of an Unsafe Application*, that the security of passwords stored in cleartext was a top priority of the auditors. In fact, in any secured system, password security is a critical aspect of trust and authoritativeness of an authenticated principal. Designers of a fully secured system must ensure that passwords are stored in a way in which malicious users would have an impractically difficult time compromising them.

The following general rules should be applied to passwords stored in a database:

- Passwords must not be stored in cleartext (plaintext)
- Passwords supplied by the user must be compared to the recorded passwords in the database
- A user's password should not be supplied to the user upon demand (even if the user forgets it)

For the purposes of most applications, the best fit for these requirements involves one-way encoding, known as the **hashing** of the passwords. Using a cryptographic hash provides properties such as security and uniqueness that are important to properly authenticate users, with the added bonus that once it is hashed, the password cannot be extracted from the value that is stored.

In most secure application designs, it is neither required nor desirable to ever retrieve the user's actual password upon request, as providing the user's password to them without the proper additional credentials could present a major security risk. Instead, most applications provide the user the ability to reset their password, either by presenting additional credentials (such as their social security number, date of birth, tax ID, or other personal information), or through an email-based system.

Storing other types of sensitive information

Many of the guidelines listed that apply to passwords apply equally to other types of sensitive information, including social security numbers and credit card information (although, depending on the application, some of these may require the ability to decrypt). Storing this type of information to represent it in multiple ways, for example, a customer's full 16-digit credit card number, would be stored in a highly encrypted form, but the last four digits might be stored in cleartext. For reference, think of any internet commerce site that displays XXXX XXXX XXXX 1234 to help you identify your stored credit cards.

You may already be thinking ahead and wondering, given our admittedly unrealistic approach of using SQL to populate our H2 database with users, how do we encode the passwords? H2, or most other databases for that matter, don't offer encryption methods as built-in database functions.

Typically, the bootstrap process (populating a system with initial users and data) is handled through a combination of SQL loads and Java code. Depending on the complexity of your application, this process can get very complicated.

For the JBCP calendar application, we'll retain the `dataSource()` bean declaration and `DataSource` is a name in code in the corresponding SQL, and then add some SQL that will modify the passwords to their hashed values.

The PasswordEncoder method

Password hashing in Spring Security is encapsulated and defined by implementations of the `o.s.s.authentication.encoding.PasswordEncoder` interface. The simple configuration of a password encoder is possible through the `passwordEncoder()` method within the `AuthenticationManagerBuilder` element, as follows:

```
auth
    .jdbcAuthentication()
    .dataSource(dataSource)
    .usersByUsernameQuery(CUSTOM_USERS_BY_USERNAME_QUERY)
    .authoritiesByUsernameQuery(CUSTOM_AUTHORITIES_BY_USERNAME_QUERY)
    .passwordEncoder(passwordEncoder());
```

You'll be happy to learn that Spring Security ships with a number of implementations of `passwordEncoder`, which are applicable for different needs and security requirements.

The following table provides a list of the out-of-the-box implementation classes and their benefits. Note that all implementations reside in the `o.s.s.authentication.encoding` package:

Implementation class	Description	Hash value
`PlaintextPasswordEncoder`	It encodes the password as plaintext; this is the default.	`&lt;p>plaintext`
`Md4PasswordEncoderPasswordEncoder`	This encoder utilizes the MD4 hash algorithm. The MD4 hash algorithm is not a secure algorithm—use of this encoder is not recommended.	`md4`
`Md5PasswordEncoderPassword`	This encoder utilizes the MD5 one-way encoding algorithm.	

Implementation class	Description	Hash value
`ShaPasswordEncoderPasswordEncoder`	This encoder utilizes the `SHA` one-way encoding algorithm. This encoder can support configurable levels of encoding strength.	`sha` `sha-256`
`LdapShaPasswordEncoder`	An implementation of `LdapSha` and `LdapSsha` algorithms used in integration with LDAP authentication stores. We'll learn more about this algorithm in `Chapter 6`, *LDAP Directory Services*, where we will cover LDAP.	`{sha}` `{ssha}`

As with many other areas of Spring Security, it's also possible to reference a bean definition by implementing `PasswordEncoder` to provide more precise configuration and allowing `PasswordEncoder` to be wired into other beans through the dependency injection. For the JBCP calendar application, we'll need to use this bean reference method in order to hash the passwords of the newly created users.

Let's walk through the process of configuring basic password encoding for the JBCP calendar application.

Configuring password encoding

Configuring basic password encoding involves two steps: hashing the passwords we load into the database after the SQL script executes, and ensuring that Spring Security is configured to work with `PasswordEncoder`.

Configuring the PasswordEncoder method

First, we'll declare an instance of PasswordEncoder as a normal Spring bean, as follows:

```
//src/main/java/com/packtpub/springsecurity/configuration/SecurityConfig.ja
va

@Bean
public ShaPasswordEncoder passwordEncoder(){
    return new ShaPasswordEncoder(256);
}
```

You'll notice that we're using the SHA-256 PasswordEncoder implementation. This is an efficient one-way encryption algorithm, commonly used for password storage.

Making Spring Security aware of the PasswordEncoder method

We'll need to configure Spring Security to have a reference to PasswordEncoder, so that it can encode and compare the presented password during user login. Simply add a passwordEncoder method and refer to the bean ID we defined in the previous step:

```
//src/main/java/com/packtpub/springsecurity/configuration/SecurityConfig.ja
va

@Override
public void configure(AuthenticationManagerBuilder auth)
throws Exception {
auth
    .jdbcAuthentication()
    .dataSource(dataSource)
    .usersByUsernameQuery(CUSTOM_USERS_BY_USERNAME_QUERY)
    .authoritiesByUsernameQuery(
        CUSTOM_AUTHORITIES_BY_USERNAME_QUERY)
    .passwordEncoder(passwordEncoder())
  ;
}
```

If you were to try the application at this point, you'd notice that what were previously valid login credentials would now be rejected. This is because the passwords stored in the database (loaded with the calendar-users.sql script) are not stored as a hash that matches the password encoder. We'll need to update the stored passwords to be hashed values.

Hashing the stored passwords

As illustrated in the following diagram, when a user submits a password, Spring Security hashes the submitted password and then compares that against the unhashed password in the database:

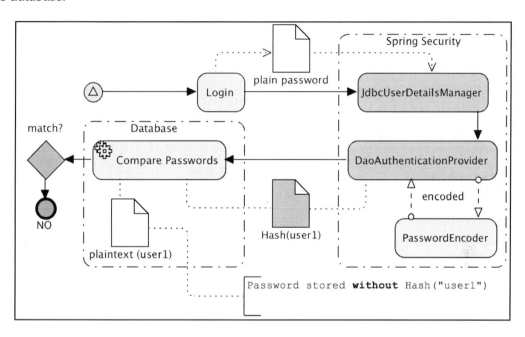

This means that users cannot log in to our application. To fix this, we will update the SQL that is loaded at startup time to update the passwords to be the hashed values. Update the DataSourceConfig.java file, as follows:

```
//src/main/java/com/packtpub/springsecurity/configuration/DataSourceConfig.
java

@Bean
public DataSource dataSource() {
return new EmbeddedDatabaseBuilder()
    .setName("dataSource")
    .setType(EmbeddedDatabaseType.H2)
    .addScript("/database/h2/calendar-schema.sql")
    .addScript("/database/h2/calendar-data.sql")
    .addScript("/database/h2/calendar-authorities.sql")
    .addScript("/database/h2/calendar-sha256.sql")
    .build();
}
```

The `calendar-sha256.sql` file simply updates the existing passwords to their expected hashed values, as follows:

```
update calendar_users set password =
'0a041b9462caa4a31bac3567e0b6e6fd9100787db2ab433d96f6d178cabfce90'
where email = 'user1@example.com';
```

How did we know what value to update the password to? We have provided `o.s.s.authentication.encoding.Sha256PasswordEncoderMain` to demonstrate how to use the configured `PasswordEncoder` interface to hash the existing passwords. The relevant code is as follows:

```
ShaPasswordEncoder encoder = new ShaPasswordEncoder(256);
String encodedPassword = encoder.encodePassword(password, null);
```

Hashing the passwords of new users

If we tried running the application and creating a new user, we would not be able to log in. This is because the newly-created user's password would not be hashed. We need to update `DefaultCalendarService` to hash the password. Make the following updates to ensure that the newly-created users' passwords are hashed:

```
//src/main/java/com/packtpub/springsecurity/service/DefaultCalendarService.
java

    import
org.springframework.security.authentication.encoding.PasswordEncoder;
    // other imports omitted
    public class DefaultCalendarService implements CalendarService {
        ...
        private final PasswordEncoder passwordEncoder;
        @Autowired
        public DefaultCalendarService(EventDao eventDao,
        CalendarUserDao userDao, JdbcOperations jdbcOperations,
        PasswordEncoder passwordEncoder) {
        ...
        this.passwordEncoder = passwordEncoder;
        }
        ...
        public int createUser(CalendarUser user) {
            String encodedPassword = passwordEncoder.
            encodePassword(user.getPassword(), null);
            user.setPassword(encodedPassword);
```

```
        ...
        return userId;
    }
}
```

Not quite secure

Go ahead and start the application. Try creating a new user with `user1` as the password. Log out of the application, then use the instructions on the **Welcome** page to open the H2 console and view all of the users' passwords. Did you notice that the hashed values for the newly created user and `user1@example.com` are the same value? The fact that we have now figured out another user's password is a little disturbing. We will solve this with a technique known as **salting**.

 Your code should now look like this: `calendar04.04-calendar`.

Would you like some salt with that password? If the security auditor were to examine the encoded passwords in the database, he'd find something that would still make him concerned about the website's security. Let's examine the following stored username and password values for a few of our users:

Username	Plaintext password	Hashed password
admin1@example.com	admin1	25f43b1486ad95a1398e3eeb3d83bc4010015fcc9bed b35b432e00298d5021f7
user1@example.com	user1	0a041b9462caa4a31bac3567e0b6e6fd9100787db2ab 433d96f6d178cabfce90

This looks very secure—the encrypted passwords obviously bear no resemblance to the original passwords. What could the auditor be concerned about? What if we add a new user who happens to have the same password as our `user1@example.com` user?

Username	Plaintext password	Hashed password
`hacker@example.com`	`user1`	`0a041b9462caa4a31bac3567e0b6e6fd9100787d` `b2ab433d96f6d178cabfce90`

Now, note that the encrypted password of the `hacker@example.com` user is exactly the same as the real user! Thus, a hacker who had somehow gained the ability to read the encrypted passwords in the database could compare their known password's encrypted representation with the unknown one for the user account, and see they are the same! If the hacker had access to an automated tool to perform this analysis, they could likely compromise the user's account within a matter of hours.

While it is difficult to guess a single password, hackers can calculate all the hashes ahead of time and store a mapping of the hash to the original password. Then, figuring out the original password is a matter of looking up the password by its hashed value in constant time. This is a hacking technique known as **rainbow tables**.

One common and effective method of adding another layer of security to encrypted passwords is to incorporate a **salt**. A salt is a second plaintext component, which is concatenated with the plaintext password prior to performing the hash, in order to ensure that two factors must be used to generate (and thus compare) the hashed password values. Properly selected salts can guarantee that no two passwords will ever have the same hashed value, thus preventing the scenario that concerned our auditor, and avoiding many common types of brute force password cracking techniques.

Best practice salts generally fall into one of the following three categories:

- They are algorithmically generated from some pieces of data associated with the user, for example, the timestamp that the user created
- They are randomly generated and stored in some form
- They are plaintext or two-way encrypted along with the user's password record

Remember that because the `salt` is added to the plaintext password, it can't be one-way encrypted—the application needs to be able to look up or derive the appropriate `salt` value for a given user's record in order to calculate the `hash` of the password, and to compare it with the stored `hash` of the user when performing authentication.

Using salt in Spring Security

Spring Security 3.1 provides a new cryptography module that is included in the `spring-security-core` module and is available separately in `spring-security-crypto`. The `crypto` module contains its own `o.s.s.crypto.password.PasswordEncoder` interface. In fact, using this interface is the preferred method for encoding passwords, because it will salt passwords using a random `salt`. At the time of this writing, there are the following three implementations of `o.s.s.crypto.password.PasswordEncoder`:

Class	Description
`o.s.s.crypto.bcrypt.BCryptPasswordEncoder`	This class uses the `bcrypt` hashing function. It supports `salt` and the ability to slow down to perform over time as technology improves. This helps protect against brute-force search attacks.
`o.s.s.crypto.password.NoOpPasswordEncoder`	This class does no encoding (it returns the password in its plaintext form).
`o.s.s.crypto.password.StandardPasswordEncoder`	This class uses SHA-256 with multiple iterations and a random `salt` value.

 For those who are familiar with Spring Security 3.0, `salt` used to be provided using `o.s.s.authentication.dao.SaltSource`. While still supported, this mechanism is not demonstrated in this book, since it is not the preferred mechanism for providing `salt`.

Updating the Spring Security configuration

This can be done by updating the Spring Security configuration. Remove the old
`ShaPasswordEncoder` encoder and add the new `StandardPasswordEncoder` encoder, as
follows:

```
//src/main/java/com/packtpub/springsecurity/configuration/SecurityConfig.ja
va

@Bean
public PasswordEncoder passwordEncoder(){
    return new StandardPasswordEncoder();
}
```

Migrating existing passwords

Let's take a look at the following steps and learn about migrating existing passwords:

1. We need to update our existing passwords to use the values produced by the
   new `PasswordEncoder` class. If you would like to generate your own passwords,
   you can use the following code snippet:

   ```
   StandardPasswordEncoder encoder = new StandardPasswordEncoder();
   String encodedPassword = encoder.encode("password");
   ```

2. Remove the previously used `calendar-sha256.sql` file, and add the provided
   `saltedsha256.sql` file as follows:

   ```
   //src/main/java/com/packtpub/springsecurity/configuration/
   DataSourceConfig.java

   @Bean
   public DataSource dataSource() {
   return new EmbeddedDatabaseBuilder()
       .setName("dataSource")
       .setType(EmbeddedDatabaseType.H2)
       .addScript("/database/h2/calendar-schema.sql")
       .addScript("/database/h2/calendar-data.sql"
       .addScript("/database/h2/calendar-authorities.sql")
       .addScript("/database/h2/calendar-saltedsha256.sql")
       .build();
   }
   ```

Updating DefaultCalendarUserService

The `passwordEncoder()` method we defined previously is smart enough to handle the new password encoder interface. However, `DefaultCalendarUserService` needs to update to the new interface. Make the following updates to the `DefaultCalendarUserService` class:

```
//src/main/java/com/packtpub/springsecurity/service/DefaultCalendarService.
java

    import
org.springframework.security.authentication.encoding.PasswordEncoder;
    import org.springframework.security.crypto.password.PasswordEncoder;

    // other imports omitted

    public class DefaultCalendarService implements CalendarService {
    ...
    public int createUser(CalendarUser user) {
        String encodedPassword = passwordEncoder.encode(user.getPassword());
        user.setPassword(encodedPassword);
        ...
        return userId;
    }
    }
```

Trying out the salted passwords

Start up the application and try creating another user with the password `user1`. Use the H2 console to compare the new user's password, and observe that they are different.

> Your code should now look like this: `calendar04.05-calendar`.

Spring Security now generates a random `salt` and combines this with the password before hashing our password. It then adds the random `salt` to the beginning of the password in plaintext, so that passwords can be checked. The stored password can be summarized as follows:

```
salt = randomsalt()
hash = hash(salt+originalPassword)
storedPassword = salt + hash
```

This is the pseudocode for hashing a newly created password.

To authenticate a user, `salt` and `hash` can be extracted from the stored password, since both `salt` and `hash` are fixed lengths. Then, the extracted `hash` can be compared against a new `hash`, computed with extracted `salt` and the inputted password:

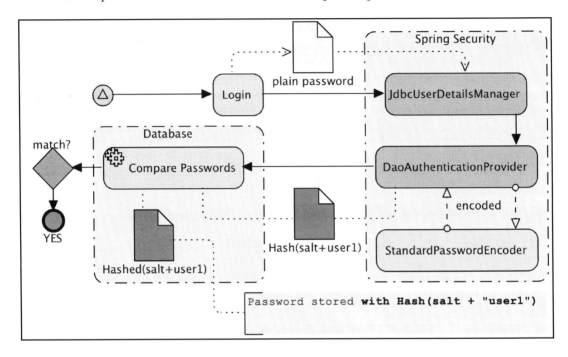

The following is the pseudocode for validating a salted password:

```
storedPassword = datasource.lookupPassword(username)
salt, expectedHash = extractSaltAndHash(storedPassword)
actualHash = hash(salt+inputedPassword)
authenticated = (expectedHash == actualHash)
```

Summary

In this chapter, we learned how to use Spring Security's built-in JDBC support. Specifically, we have learned that Spring Security provides a default schema for new applications. We also explored how to implement GBAC and how it can make managing users easier.
We also learned how to integrate Spring Security's JDBC support with an existing database and also how to secure our passwords by hashing them and using a randomly-generated salt.

In the next chapter, we will explore the **Spring Data** project and how to configure Spring Security to use **object-relational mapping (ORM)** to connect to an RDBMS, as well as a document database.

5
Authentication with Spring Data

In the previous chapter, we covered how to leverage Spring Security's built-in JDBC support. In this chapter, we will look at the Spring Data project, and how to leverage JPA to perform authentication against a relational database. We will also explore how to perform authentication against a document database using MongoDB. This chapter's sample code is based on the Spring Security setup from `Chapter 4`, *JDBC-Based Authentication*, and has been updated to refactor out the need for SQL and to use ORM for all database interactions.

During the course of this chapter, we will cover the following topics:

- Some of the basic concepts related to the Spring Data project
- Utilizing Spring Data JPA to authenticate against a relational database
- Utilizing Spring Data MongoDB to authenticate against a document database
- How to customize Spring Security for more flexibility when dealing with Spring Data integration
- Understanding the Spring Data project

The Spring Data project's mission is to provide a familiar and consistent Spring-based programming model for data access, while still retaining the special traits of the underlying data provider.

The following are just a few of the powerful features in this Spring Data project:

- Powerful repository and custom object-mapping abstractions
- Dynamic query derivation from repository method names
- Implementation of domain base classes, providing basic properties
- Support for transparent auditing (created and last changed)
- The ability to integrate custom repository code

- Easy Spring integration via Java-based configuration and custom XML namespaces
- Advanced integration with Spring MVC controllers
- Experimental support for cross-store persistence

This project simplifies the use of data access technologies, relational and non-relational databases, map-reduce frameworks, and cloud-based data services. This umbrella project contains many subprojects that are specific to a given database. These projects were developed by working together with many of the companies and developers that are behind these exciting technologies. There are also many community maintained modules and other related modules including **JDBC Support** and **Apache Hadoop**.

The following table describes the main modules that make up the Spring Data project:

Module	Description
Spring Data Commons	Applies core Spring concepts all Spring Data projects
Spring Data Gemfire	Provides easy configuration and access to Gemfire from Spring applications
Spring Data JPA	Makes it easy to implement JPA-based repositories
Spring Data Key Value	Map-based repositories and SPIs, which can easily build a Spring Data module for key-value stores
Spring Data LDAP	Provides Spring Data repository support for Spring LDAP
Spring Data MongoDB	Spring-based, object-document support, and repositories for MongoDB
Spring Data REST	Exports Spring Data repositories as hypermedia-driven RESTful resources
Spring Data Redis	Provides easy configuration and access to Redis from Spring applications
Spring Data for Apache Cassandra	Spring Data module for Apache Cassandra
Spring Data for Apache Solr	Spring Data module for Apache Solr

Spring Data JPA

The Spring Data JPA project aims to significantly improve the ORM implementation of data access layers by reducing the effort to the amount that's actually needed. A developer only needs to write repository interfaces, including custom finder methods, and Spring will provide the implementation automatically.

The following are just a few of the powerful features specific to the Spring Data JPA project:

- Sophisticated support for building repositories based on Spring and JPA
- Support for **Querydsl** predicates, and thus, type-safe JPA queries
- Transparent auditing of domain classes
- Pagination support, dynamic query execution, and the ability to integrate custom data access code
- Validation of `@Query` annotated queries at bootstrap time
- Support for XML based entity mapping
- The `JavaConfig` based repository configuration by introducing `@EnableJpaRepositories`

Updating our dependencies

We have already included all the dependencies you need for this chapter, so you will not need to make any updates to your `build.gradle` file. However, if you are just adding Spring Data JPA support to your own application, you need to add `spring-boot-starter-data-jpa` as a dependency in the `build.gradle` file, as follows:

```
//build.gradle

dependencies {
    . . .
// REMOVE: compile('org.springframework.boot:spring-boot-starter-jdbc')
    compile('org.springframework.boot:spring-boot-starter-data-jpa')
    . . .
}
```

Notice we removed the `spring-boot-starter-jdbc` dependency. The `spring-boot-starter-data-jpa` dependency will contain all the dependencies needed to wire our domain objects to our embedded database with JPA.

Updating the JBCP calendar to use Spring Data JPA

To get familiar with Spring Data, we will first convert the JBCP calendar SQL to leverage ORM, using the Spring Data JPA starter.

Creating and maintaining SQL can be quite tedious. In the previous chapters, when we wanted to create a new `CalendarUser` table in the database, we had to create a fair amount of boilerplate code, as follows:

```
//src/main/java/com/packtpub/springsecurity/
dataaccess/JdbcCalendarUserDao.java

public int createUser(final CalendarUser userToAdd) {
if (userToAdd == null) {
    throw new IllegalArgumentException("userToAdd cannot be null");
}
if (userToAdd.getId() != null) {
    throw new IllegalArgumentException("userToAdd.getId() must be
    null when creating a
    "+CalendarUser.class.getName());
}
 KeyHoldener keyHolder = new GeratedKeyHolder();
 this.jdbcOperations.update(new PreparedStatementCreator() {
   public PreparedStatement createPreparedStatement
   (Connection connection)
   throws SQLException {
     PreparedStatement ps = connection.prepareStatement("insert into
     calendar_users (email, password, first_name, last_name)
     values (?, ?, ?, ?)", new String[] {
      "id" });
     ps.setString(1, userToAdd.getEmail());
     ps.setString(2, userToAdd.getPassword());
     ps.setString(3, userToAdd.getFirstName());
     ps.setString(4, userToAdd.getLastName());
     return ps;
   }
 }, keyHolder);
return keyHolder.getKey().intValue();
 }
```

To create this object, we technically need 12 lines of code to perform the operation.

Now, with Spring Data JPA, the same implementation can be reduced to the following code snippet:

```
//src/main/java/com/packtpub/springsecurity/dataaccess/JpaCalendarUserDao.java

    public int createUser(final CalendarUser userToAdd) {
    if (userToAdd == null) {
        throw new IllegalArgumentException("userToAdd cannot be null");
    }
    if (userToAdd.getId() != null) {
        throw new IllegalArgumentException("userToAdd.getId()
        must be null when creating a "+CalendarUser.class.getName());
    }
    Set<Role> roles = new HashSet<>();
    roles.add(roleRepository.findOne(0));
    userToAdd.setRoles(roles);
    CalendarUser result = repository.save(userToAdd);
    repository.flush();
    return result.getId();
    }
```

Now, to create this object using JPA, we technically need five lines of code to perform the operation. We now need less than half the amount of code to perform the same operation.

Reconfiguring the database configuration

Firstly, we will convert the current JBCP calendar project. Let's begin by reconfiguring the database.

We can begin by removing the DataSourceConfig.java file, as we will be leveraging Spring Boot's built-in support for an embedded H2 database. We will also need to remove the reference to DataSourceConfig.java in the JavaConfig.java file, as there is currently a reference to JavaConfig.java inside the @Import annotation.

Initializing the database

We can now remove the src/main/resources/database directory and all contents in that directory. This directory contains several .sql files, and we will consolidate and move them to the next step:

Now, we need to create a `data.sql` file that will contain our seed data, as follows:

```
//src/main/resources/data.sql:
```

- Take a look at the following SQL statement, depicting the password for `user1`:

```
insert into calendar_users(id,username,email,password,
first_name,last_name)
values(0,'user1@example.com','user1@example.com',
'$2a$04$qr7RWyqOnWWC1nwotUW1nOe1RD5.
mKJVHK16WZy6v49pymu1WDHmi','User','1');
```

- Take a look at the following SQL statement, depicting the password for `admin1` :

```
insert into calendar_users(id,username,email,password,
first_name,last_name)
values (1,'admin1@example.com','admin1@example.com',
'$2a$04$0CF/Gsquxlel3fWq5Ic/ZOGDCaXbMfXYiXsviTNMQofWRXhvJH3IK',
'Admin','1');
```

- Take a look at the following SQL statement, depicting the password for `user2`:

```
insert into calendar_users(id,username,email,password,first_name,
last_name)
values (2,'user2@example.com','user2@example.com',
'$2a$04$PiVhNPAxunf0Q4IMbVeNIuH4M4ecySWHihyrclxW..PLArjLbg8CC',
'User2','2');
```

- Take a look at the following SQL statement, depicting the user roles:

```
insert into role(id, name) values (0, 'ROLE_USER');
insert into role(id, name) values (1, 'ROLE_ADMIN');
```

- Here, `user1` has one role:

```
insert into user_role(user_id,role_id) values (0, 0);
```

- Here, `admin1` has two roles:

```
insert into user_role(user_id,role_id) values (1, 0);
insert into user_role(user_id,role_id) values (1, 1);
```

- Take a look at the following SQL statement, depicting events:

```
insert into events (id,when,summary,description,owner,attendee)
values (100,'2017-07-03 20:30:00','Birthday Party',
'This is going to be a great birthday',0,1);
insert into events (id,when,summary,description,owner,attendee)
values (101,'2017-12-23 13:00:00','Conference Call','Call with
the client',2,0);
insert into events (id,when,summary,description,owner,attendee)
values (102,'2017-09-14 11:30:00','Vacation',
'Paragliding in Greece',1,2);
```

Now, we can update the application properties to define our embedded database properties in the `src/main/resources/application.yml` file as follows:

```
# Embedded Database
datasource:
url: jdbc:h2:mem:dataSource;DB_CLOSE_DELAY=-1;DB_CLOSE_ON_EXIT=FALSE
driverClassName: org.h2.Driver
username: sa
password:
continue-on-error: true
jpa:
  database-platform: org.hibernate.dialect.H2Dialect
  show-sql: true
  hibernate:
    ddl-auto: create-drop
```

At this point, we have removed the old database configuration and added the new configuration. The application will not work at this point, but this can still be considered a marker point before we continue on to the next steps of conversion.

 Your code should now look like `calendar05.01-calendar`.

Refactoring from SQL to ORM

Refactoring from an SQL to an ORM implementation is simpler than you might think. Most of the refactoring involves the removal of excess code in the form of an SQL. In this next section, we will refactor our SQL implementation to a JPA implementation.

In order for JPA to map our domain objects to our database, we need to perform some mapping on our domain objects.

Mapping domain objects using JPA

Take a look at the following steps to learn about mapping the domain objects:

1. Let's begin by mapping our `Event.java` file so all the domain objects will use JPA, as follows:

```
//src/main/java/com/packtpub/springsecurity/domain/Event.java

import javax.persistence.*;
@Entity
@Table(name = "events")
public class Event implements Serializable{
 @Id
 @GeneratedValue(strategy = GenerationType.AUTO)
private Integer id;
@NotEmpty(message = "Summary is required")
private String summary;
@NotEmpty(message = "Description is required")
private String description;
@NotNull(message = "When is required")
private Calendar when;
@NotNull(message = "Owner is required")
 @ManyToOne(fetch = FetchType.LAZY)
 @JoinColumn(name="owner", referencedColumnName="id")
private CalendarUser owner;
 @ManyToOne(fetch = FetchType.LAZY)
 @JoinColumn(name="attendee", referencedColumnName="id")
private CalendarUser attendee;
```

2. We need to create a `Role.java` file with the following contents:

```
//src/main/java/com/packtpub/springsecurity/domain/Role.java

import javax.persistence.*;
@Entity
@Table(name = "role")
public class Role implements Serializable {
 @Id
 @GeneratedValue(strategy = GenerationType.AUTO)
private Integer id;
private String name;
 @ManyToMany(fetch = FetchType.EAGER, mappedBy = "roles")
private Set<CalendarUser> users;
```

3. The `Role` object will be used to map authorities to our `CalendarUser` table. Let's map our `CalendarUser.java` file, now that we have a `Role.java` file:

```
//src/main/java/com/packtpub/springsecurity/domain/CalendarUser
.java

import javax.persistence.*;
import java.io.Serializable;
import java.util.Set;
@Entity
@Table(name = "calendar_users")
public class CalendarUser implements Serializable {
    @Id
    @GeneratedValue(strategy = GenerationType.AUTO)
    private Integer id;
    private String firstName;
    private String lastName;
    private String email;
    private String password;
    @ManyToMany(fetch = FetchType.EAGER)
    @JoinTable(name = "user_role",
            joinColumns = @JoinColumn(name = "user_id"),
            inverseJoinColumns = @JoinColumn(name = "role_id"))
    private Set<Role> roles;
```

At this point, we have mapped our domain objects with the required JPA annotation, including `@Entity` and `@Table` to define the RDBMS location, as well as structural, reference, and association mapping annotations.

The application will not work at this point, but this can still be considered a marker point before we continue on to the next steps of conversion.

You should be starting with the source from `chapter05.02-calendar`.

Spring Data repositories

We will now add the required interfaces for Spring Data to map our required CRUD operations to our embedded database, by performing the following steps:

1. We begin by adding a new interface in a new package, which will be `com.packtpub.springsecurity.repository`. The new file will be called `CalendarUserRepository.java`, as follows:

```
//com/packtpub/springsecurity/repository/CalendarUserRepository.java

    package com.packtpub.springsecurity.repository;
    import com.packtpub.springsecurity.domain.CalendarUser;
    import org.springframework.data.jpa.repository.JpaRepository;

    public interface CalendarUserRepository
            extends JpaRepository<CalendarUser, Integer> {
        CalendarUser findByEmail(String email);
    }
```

This will allow for standard CRUD operations such as `find()`, `save()`, and `delete()` on our `CalendarUser` objects.

2. We can now continue by adding a new interface in the same repository package, which will be `com.packtpub.springsecurity.repository`, and the new file will be called `EventRepository.java`:

```
    //com/packtpub/springsecurity/repository/EventRepository.java

    package com.packtpub.springsecurity.repository;
    import com.packtpub.springsecurity.domain.Event;
    import org.springframework.data.jpa.repository.JpaRepository;

    public interface EventRepository extends JpaRepository<Event,
    Integer> {}
```

This will allow for standard CRUD operations such as `find()`, `save()`, and `delete()` on our `Event` objects.

3. Finally, we will be adding a new interface in the same repository package, which will be `com.packtpub.springsecurity.repository`, and the new file will be called `RoleRepository.java`. This `CrudRepository` interface will be used to manage the `Role` object for our security roles associated with a given `CalendarUser`:

```
//com/packtpub/springsecurity/repository/

package com.packtpub.springsecurity.repository;
import com.packtpub.springsecurity.domain.Event;
import org.springframework.data.jpa.repository.JpaRepository;

public interface RoleRepository extends JpaRepository<Role,
Integer> {}
```

This will allow for standard CRUD operations such as `find()`, `save()`, and `delete()` on our `Role` objects.

Data access objects

We need to refactor the `JdbcEventDao.java` file with a new name, `JpaEventDao.java`, so we can replace the JDBC SQL code with our new Spring Data code. Let's take a look at the following steps:

1. Specifically, we need to add the new `EventRepository` interface, and replace the SQL code with the new ORM repository, as shown in the following code:

```
//com/packtpub/springsecurity/dataaccess/JpaEventDao.java

package com.packtpub.springsecurity.dataaccess;
import com.packtpub.springsecurity.domain.CalendarUser;
import com.packtpub.springsecurity.domain.Event;
import com.packtpub.springsecurity.repository.EventRepository;
import org.springframework.beans.factory.annotation.Autowired;
import org.springframework.data.domain.Example;
import org.springframework.stereotype.Repository;
import org.springframework.transaction.annotation.Transactional;
...
@Repository
 public class JpaEventDao implements EventDao {
    private EventRepository repository;
   @Autowired
   public JpaEventDao(EventRepository repository) {
       if (repository == null) {
```

```java
            throw new IllegalArgumentException("repository
            cannot be null");
        }
        this.repository = repository;
    }
    @Override
    @Transactional(readOnly = true)
    public Event getEvent(int eventId) {
        return repository.findOne(eventId);
    }
    @Override
    public int createEvent(final Event event) {
        ...
        final Calendar when = event.getWhen();
        if(when == null) {
            throw new IllegalArgumentException("event.getWhen()
            cannot be null");
        }
        Event newEvent = repository.save(event);
        ...
    }
    @Override
    @Transactional(readOnly = true)
    public List<Event> findForUser(final int userId) {
        Event example = new Event();
        CalendarUser cu = new CalendarUser();
        cu.setId(userId);
        example.setOwner(cu);
        return repository.findAll(Example.of(example));
    }
    @Override
    @Transactional(readOnly = true)
    public List<Event> getEvents() {
        return repository.findAll();
    }
}
```

2. At this point, we need to refactor the DAO classes to support the new
   `CrudRepository` interfaces we have created. Let's begin with refactoring the
   `JdbcCalendarUserDao.java` file. First, we can rename the file to
   `JpaCalendarUserDao.java` to indicate that this is using JPA, and not standard
   JDBC:

   ```java
   //com/packtpub/springsecurity/dataaccess/JpaCalendarUserDao.java

   package com.packtpub.springsecurity.dataaccess;
   ... omitted for brevity ...
   ```

```java
@Repository
public class JpaCalendarUserDao
        implements CalendarUserDao {
    private CalendarUserRepository userRepository;
    private RoleRepository roleRepository;
    @Autowired
    public JpaCalendarUserDao(CalendarUserRepository repository,
    RoleRepository roleRepository) {
        if (repository == null) {
            throw new IllegalArgumentException("repository
            cannot be null");
        }
        if (roleRepository == null) {
            throw new IllegalArgumentException("roleRepository
            cannot be null");
        }
        this. userRepository = repository;
        this.roleRepository = roleRepository;
    }
    @Override
    @Transactional(readOnly = true)
    public CalendarUser getUser(final int id) {
        return userRepository.findOne(id);
    }
    @Override
    @Transactional(readOnly = true)
    public CalendarUser findUserByEmail(final String email) {
        if (email == null) {
            throw new IllegalArgumentException
            ("email cannot be null");
        }
        try {
            return userRepository.findByEmail(email);
        } catch (EmptyResultDataAccessException notFound) {
            return null;
        }
    }
    @Override
    @Transactional(readOnly = true)
    public List<CalendarUser> findUsersByEmail(final String email) {
        if (email == null) {
            throw new IllegalArgumentException("email
            cannot be null");
        }
        if ("".equals(email)) {
            throw new IllegalArgumentException("email
            cannot be empty string");
        }
```

```
        return userRepository.findAll();
    }
    @Override
    public int createUser(final CalendarUser userToAdd) {
        if (userToAdd == null) {
            throw new IllegalArgumentException("userToAdd
            cannot be null");
        }
        if (userToAdd.getId() != null) {
            throw new IllegalArgumentException("userToAdd.getId()
            must be null when creating a "+
            CalendarUser.class.getName());
        }
        Set<Role> roles = new HashSet<>();
        roles.add(roleRepository.findOne(0));
        userToAdd.setRoles(roles);
        CalendarUser result = userRepository.save(userToAdd);
        userRepository.flush();
        return result.getId();
    }
}
```

As you can see in the preceding code, the update fragments to leverage the amount needed for JPA are quite a bit less than the required code for JDBC. This means we can focus on business logic and not worry about the plumbing.

3. We continue by refactoring the `JdbcEventDao.java` file. First, we can rename the file to `JpaEventDao.java`, to indicate that this is using JPA and not standard JDBC, as follows:

```
//com/packtpub/springsecurity/dataaccess/JpaEventDao.java

package com.packtpub.springsecurity.dataaccess;
... omitted for brevity ...
@Repository
public class JpaEventDao implements EventDao {
    private EventRepository repository;
    @Autowired
    public JpaEventDao(EventRepository repository) {
        if (repository == null) {
            throw new IllegalArgumentException("repository
            cannot be null");
        }
        this.repository = repository;
    }
    @Override
    @Transactional(readOnly = true)
```

```java
public Event getEvent(int eventId) {
    return repository.findOne(eventId);
}
@Override
public int createEvent(final Event event) {
    if (event == null) {
        throw new IllegalArgumentException("event cannot be
null");
    }
    if (event.getId() != null) {
        throw new IllegalArgumentException
        ("event.getId() must be null when creating a new
Message");
    }
    final CalendarUser owner = event.getOwner();
     if (owner == null) {
        throw new IllegalArgumentException("event.getOwner()
        cannot be null");
    }
    final CalendarUser attendee = event.getAttendee();
    if (attendee == null) {
        throw new
IllegalArgumentException("attendee.getOwner()
        cannot be null");
    }
    final Calendar when = event.getWhen();
    if(when == null) {
        throw new IllegalArgumentException
        ("event.getWhen()cannot be null");
    }
    Event newEvent = repository.save(event);
    return newEvent.getId();
}
    @Override
@Transactional(readOnly = true)
public List<Event> findForUser(final int userId) {
    Event example = new Event();
    CalendarUser cu = new CalendarUser();
    cu.setId(userId);
    example.setOwner(cu);
    return repository.findAll(Example.of(example));
}
    @Override
@Transactional(readOnly = true)
public List<Event> getEvents() {
    return repository.findAll();
}
}
```

In the preceding code, the update fragments to leverage the JPA repositories have been placed in bold, so now the `Event` and `CalendarUser` objects are mapped to our underlying RDBMS.

The application will not work at this point, but this can still be considered a marker point before we continue on to the next steps of conversion.

 At this point, your source code should look the same as `chapter05.03-calendar`.

Application services

The only thing left to do is configure Spring Security to use the new artifacts.

We need to edit the `DefaultCalendarService.java` file and only remove the remaining code that was used to add `USER_ROLE` to any new `User` object that was created as follows:

```
//com/packtpub/springsecurity/service/DefaultCalendarService.java

package com.packtpub.springsecurity.service;
... omitted for brevity ...
@Repository
public class DefaultCalendarService implements CalendarService {
    @Override
    public int createUser(CalendarUser user) {
        String encodedPassword =
passwordEncoder.encode(user.getPassword());
        user.setPassword(encodedPassword);
        int userId = userDao.createUser(user);
        //jdbcOperations.update("insert into
        calendar_user_authorities(calendar_user,authority)
        values (?,?)", userId,
        //"ROLE_USER");
        return userId;
    }
}
```

The UserDetailsService object

Let's take a look at the following steps to add the UserDetailsService object:

1. Now, we need to add a new implementation of the UserDetailsService object, we will use our CalendarUserRepository interface to authenticate and authorize users again, with the same underlying RDBMS, but using our new JPA implementation as follows:

```
//com/packtpub/springsecurity/service/UserDetailsServiceImpl.java

package com.packtpub.springsecurity.service;
... omitted for brevity ...
@Service
public class UserDetailsServiceImpl
    implements UserDetailsService {
  @Autowired
  private CalendarUserRepository userRepository;
  @Override
  @Transactional(readOnly = true)
 public UserDetails loadUserByUsername(final String username)
  throws UsernameNotFoundException {
   CalendarUser user = userRepository.findByEmail(username);
   Set<GrantedAuthority> grantedAuthorities = new HashSet<>();
  for (Role role : user.getRoles()){
      grantedAuthorities.add(new SimpleGrantedAuthority
      (role.getName()));
  }
   return new org.springframework.security.core.userdetails.User(
    user.getEmail(), user.getPassword(), grantedAuthorities);
  }
}
```

2. Now, we have to configure Spring Security to use our custom UserDetailsService object, as follows:

```
//com/packtpub/springsecurity/configuration/SecurityConfig.java

package com.packtpub.springsecurity.configuration;
... omitted for brevity ...
@Configuration
@EnableWebSecurity
public class SecurityConfig extends WebSecurityConfigurerAdapter {\
    @Autowired
    private UserDetailsService userDetailsService;
    @Override
```

```
public void configure(AuthenticationManagerBuilder auth)
throws Exception {
auth
 .userDetailsService(userDetailsService)
 .passwordEncoder(passwordEncoder());
 }
@Bean
@Override
public UserDetailsService userDetailsService() {
    return new UserDetailsServiceImpl();
}
...
}
```

3. Start the application and try logging in to the application. Any of the configured users can now log in and create new events. You can also create a new user and will be able to log in as the new user immediately.

 Your code should now look like `calendar05.04-calendar`.

Refactoring from an RDBMS to a document database

Luckily, with the Spring Data project, once we have a Spring Data implementation, we have most of the difficult work completed. Now, there are only a few implementation-specific changes that need to be refactored.

Document database implementation with MongoDB

We are now going to work on refactoring our RDBMS implementation—with JPA as our ORM provider—into a document database implementation, using MongoDB as our underlying database provider. MongoDB (from humongous) is a free and open source cross-platform document-oriented database program. Classified as a NoSQL database program, MongoDB uses JSON-like documents with schemas. MongoDB is developed by MongoDB Inc. and is located at `https://github.com/mongodb/mongo`.

Updating our dependencies

We have already included all of the dependencies you need for this chapter, so you will not need to make any updates to your `build.gradle` file. However, if you are just adding Spring Data JPA support to your own application, you will need to add `spring-boot-starter-data-jpa` as a dependency in the `build.gradle` file, as follows:

```
//build.gradle
// JPA / ORM / Hibernate:
//compile('org.springframework.boot:spring-boot-starter-data-jpa')
// H2 RDBMS
//runtime('com.h2database:h2')
// MongoDB:

compile('org.springframework.boot:spring-boot-starter-data-mongodb')
compile('de.flapdoodle.embed:de.flapdoodle.embed.mongo')
```

Notice we removed the `spring-boot-starter-jpa` dependency. The `spring-boot-starter-data-mongodb` dependency will contain all the dependencies needed to wire our domain objects to our embedded MongoDB database, with a mix of Spring and MongoDB annotations.

We also added the **Flapdoodle** embedded MongoDB database, but this is only meant for testing and demonstration purposes. Embedded MongoDB will provide a platform neutral way for running MongoDB in unit tests. This embedded database is located at `https://github.com/flapdoodle-oss/de.flapdoodle.embed.mongo`.

Reconfiguring the database configuration in MongoDB

First, we will begin to convert the current JBCP calendar project. Let's begin by reconfiguring the database to use the Flapdoodle embedded MongoDB database. Previously, when we updated the dependencies for this project, we added a Flapdoodle dependency that gave the project an embedded MongoDB database which we could automatically use instead of installing a full version of MongoDB installation. To stay consistent with the JBCP application, we need to change the name of our database. With Spring Data, we can change the MongoDB configuration using the YAML configuration, as follows:

```
//src/main/resources/application.yml

spring
```

```
# MongoDB
data:
    mongodb:
        host: localhost
        database: dataSource
```

The most important configuration for our current requirements is changing the database name to dataSource, which is the same name we have been using throughout this book.

Initializing the MongoDB database

With the JPA implementation, we used the data.sql file to initialize the data in our database. For MongoDB implementation, we can remove the data.sql file and replace it with a Java configuration file, which we will call MongoDataInitializer.java:

```
//src/main/java/com/packtpub/springsecurity/configuration/
MongoDataInitializer.java

...
@Configuration
public class MongoDataInitializer {
    @Autowired
    private RoleRepository roleRepository;
    @Autowired
    private CalendarUserRepository calendarUserRepository;
    @Autowired
    private EventRepository eventRepository;
    @PostConstruct
    public void setUp() {
        calendarUserRepository.deleteAll();
        roleRepository.deleteAll();
        eventRepository.deleteAll();
        seedRoles();
        seedCalendarUsers();
        seedEvents();
    }
    CalendarUser user1, admin, user2;
    {
        user1 = new CalendarUser(0, "user1@example.com",
        "$2a$04$qr7RWyqOnWWC1nwotUW1nOe1RD5.mKJVHK16WZy6v49pymu1WDHmi",
        "User","1");
        admin = new    CalendarUser(1,"admin1@example.com",
        "$2a$04$0CF/Gsquxle13fWq5Ic/ZOGDCaXbMfXYiXsviTNMQofWRXhvJH3IK",
        "Admin","1");
        user2 = new CalendarUser(2,"user2@example.com",
        "$2a$04$PiVhNPAxunf0Q4IMbVeNIuH4M4ecySWHihyrclxW..PLArjLbg8CC",
```

```
                "User2","2");
        }
        Role user_role, admin_role;
        private void seedRoles(){
            user_role = new Role(0, "ROLE_USER");
            admin_role = new Role(1, "ROLE_ADMIN");
            user_role = roleRepository.save(user_role);
            admin_role = roleRepository.save(admin_role);
        }
        private void seedEvents(){
            // Event 1
            Event event1 = new Event(100, "Birthday Party", "This is
            going to be a great birthday", new
            GregorianCalendar(2017,6,3,6,36,00), user, admin);
            // Event 2
            Event event2 = new Event(101, "Conference Call",
            "Call with the client",new
            GregorianCalendar(2017,11,23,13,00,00),user2, user);
            // Event 3
            Event event3 = new Event(102, "Vacation",
            "Paragliding in Greece",new
GregorianCalendar(2017,8,14,11,30,00),
            admin, user2);
            // Save Events
            eventRepository.save(event1);
            eventRepository.save(event2);
            eventRepository.save(event3);
        }
        private void seedCalendarUsers(){
            // user1
            user1.addRole(user_role);
           // admin2
            admin.addRole(user_role);
            admin.addRole(admin_role);
            // user2
            user2.addRole(user_role);
            calendarUserRepository.save(user1);
            calendarUserRepository.save(admin);
            calendarUserRepository.save(user2);
        }
    }
```

This will be executed at load time and will seed the same data into our MongoDB as we did with our H2 database.

Mapping domain objects with MongoDB

Let's begin by mapping our `Event.java` file so that each of the domain objects are saved as a document in our MongoDB database. This can be done by performing the following steps:

1. With a document database, domain object mapping is a little different, but the same ORM concepts hold true. Let's begin with the Event JPA implementation, then take a look how we can transform our `Entity` to document mapping:

   ```
   //src/main/java/com/packtpub/springsecurity/domain/Event.java

   ...
   import javax.persistence.*;
   @Entity
   @Table(name = "events")
   public class Event implements Serializable{
       @Id
       @GeneratedValue(strategy = GenerationType.AUTO)
       private Integer id;
       private String summary;
       private String description;
       private Calendar when;
       @ManyToOne(fetch = FetchType.LAZY)
       @JoinColumn(name="owner", referencedColumnName="id")
       private CalendarUser owner;
       @ManyToOne(fetch = FetchType.LAZY)
       @JoinColumn(name="attendee", referencedColumnName="id")
       private CalendarUser attendee;
       ...
   ```

2. In Entity-based JPA mapping, we needed to use six different annotations to create the required mapping. Now, with document-based MongoDB mapping, we need to change all the previous mapping annotations. Here is a fully refactored example of our `Event.java` file:

   ```
   //src/main/java/com/packtpub/springsecurity/domain/Event.java

   import org.springframework.data.annotation.Id;
   import org.springframework.data.annotation.PersistenceConstructor;
   import org.springframework.data.domain.Persistable;
   import org.springframework.data.mongodb.core.mapping.DBRef;
   import org.springframework.data.mongodb.core.mapping.Document;
   ...
   @Document(collection="events")
   public class Event implements Persistable<Integer>, Serializable{
   ```

```
@Id
private Integer id;
private String summary;
private String description;
private Calendar when;
@DBRef
private CalendarUser owner;
@DBRef
private CalendarUser attendee;
@PersistenceConstructor
public Event(Integer id,
        String summary,
        String description,
        Calendar when,
        CalendarUser owner,
        CalendarUser attendee) {
    ...
}
```

In the preceding code, we can see a following few notable changes:

1. First, we declare the class to be of type
   `@o.s.d.mongodb.core.mapping.Document`, and provide a collection name for these documents.

2. Next, the `Event` class must implement the `o.s.d.domain.Persistable` interface, providing the primary key type (`Integer`) for our document.

3. Now, we change the annotation for our domain ID to `@o.s.d.annotation.Id`, to define the domain primary key.

4. Previously, we had to map our owner and attendee `CalendarUser` object to two different mapping annotations.

5. Now, we only have to define the two types to be of type
   `@o.s.d.mongodb.core.mapping.DBRef`, and allow Spring Data to take care of the underlying references.

6. The final annotation we have to add defines a specific constructor to be used for new documents to be added to our document, by using the
   `@o.s.d.annotation.PersistenceConstructor` annotation.

7. Now that we have reviewed the changes needed to refactor from JPA to MongoDB, let's refactor the other domain object starting with the `Role.java` file, as follows:

```
//src/main/java/com/packtpub/springsecurity/domain/Role.java

    ...
```

```
import org.springframework.data.annotation.Id;
import org.springframework.data.annotation.PersistenceConstructor;
import org.springframework.data.domain.Persistable;
import org.springframework.data.mongodb.core.mapping.Document;
@Document(collection="role")
public class Role implements Persistable<Integer>, Serializable {
    @Id
    private Integer id;
    private String name;
    public Role(){}
    @PersistenceConstructor
public Role(Integer id, String name) {
    this.id = id;
    this.name = name;
  }
```

8. The final domain object that we need to refactor is our `CalendarUser.java` file. After all, this is the most complex domain object we have in this application:

`//src/main/java/com/packtpub/springsecurity/domain/CalendarUser.java`

```
...
import org.springframework.data.annotation.Id;
import org.springframework.data.annotation.PersistenceConstructor;
import org.springframework.data.domain.Persistable;
import org.springframework.data.mongodb.core.mapping.DBRef;
import org.springframework.data.mongodb.core.mapping.Document;
@Document(collection="calendar_users")
public class CalendarUser implements Persistable<Integer>,
Serializable {
    @Id
    private Integer id;
    private String firstName;
    private String lastName;
    private String email;
    private String password;
    @DBRef(lazy = false)
    private Set<Role> roles = new HashSet<>(5);
    public CalendarUser() {}
    @PersistenceConstructor
    public CalendarUser(Integer id,String email, String password,
    String firstName,String lastName) {
        this.id = id;
        this.firstName = firstName;
        this.lastName = lastName;
        this.email = email;
        this.password = password;
    }
```

As you can see, the effort to refactor our domain objects from JPA to MongoDB is fairly simple, and requires less annotation configuration than the JPA configuration.

Spring Data repositories of MongoDB

We now have only a few changes to make to refactor from a JPA implementation to a MongoDB implementation. We will begin by refactoring our `CalendarUserRepository.java` file by changing the interface that our repository extends, as follows:

```
//com/packtpub/springsecurity/repository/CalendarUserRepository.java

...
import org.springframework.data.mongodb.repository.MongoRepository;
public interface CalendarUserRepository extends MongoRepository
<CalendarUser, Integer> {
    ...
```

This same change needs to be applied to the `EventRepository.java` file and the `RoleRepository.java` files accordingly.

> If you need help with any of these changes, remember the source for `chapter05.05` will have the completed code available for your reference.

Data access objects in MongoDB

In our `EventDao` interface, we are required to create a new `Event` object. With JPA, we can have our object ID automatically generated. With MongoDB, there are several ways to assign primary key identifiers, but for the sake of this demonstration, we are just going to use an atomic counter, as follows:

```
//src/main/java/com/packtpub/springsecurity/dataaccess/MongoEventDao.java

...
import java.util.concurrent.atomic.AtomicInteger;
@Repository
public class MongoEventDao implements EventDao {
    // Simple Primary Key Generator
    private AtomicInteger eventPK = new AtomicInteger(102);
    ...
    @Override
```

```
public int createEvent(Event event) {
    ...
    // Get the next PK instance
    event.setId(eventPK.incrementAndGet());
    Event newEvent = repository.save(event);
    return newEvent.getId();
}
...
```

There was technically no change to our `CalendarUserDao` object, but for consistency in this book, we renamed the implementation file to denote the use of `Mongo`:

```
@Repository
public class MongoCalendarUserDao implements CalendarUserDao {
```

There are no other **Data Access Objects** (**DAO**) changes required for this refactoring example.

Go ahead and start the application, and it will behave just as before. Try to log in as `user1` and `admin1`, and test it to ensure that both users can add new events to the system, to ensure the mapping is correct for the entire application.

 You should be starting with the source from `chapter05.05-calendar`.

Summary

We have looked at the power and flexibility of the Spring Data project and explored several aspects related to application development, as well as its integration with Spring Security. In this chapter, we covered the Spring Data project and a few of its capabilities. We also saw the refactoring process to convert from legacy JDBC code using SQL, to ORM with JPA, and from a JPA implementation with Spring Data to a MongoDB implementation using Spring Data. We also covered configuring Spring Security to leverage an ORM `Entity` in a relational database and in a document database.

In the next chapter, we will explore Spring Security's built-in support for LDAP-based authentication.

6
LDAP Directory Services

In this chapter, we will review the **Lightweight Directory Access Protocol (LDAP)** and learn how it can be integrated into a Spring Security-enabled application to provide authentication, authorization, and user information services to interested constituents.

During the course of this chapter, we will cover the following topics:

- Learning some of the basic concepts related to the LDAP protocol and server implementations
- Configuring a self-contained LDAP server within Spring Security
- Enabling LDAP authentication and authorization
- Understanding the model behind LDAP search and user matching
- Retrieving additional user details from standard LDAP structures
- Differentiating between LDAP authentication methods and evaluating the pros and cons of each type
- Explicitly configuring Spring Security LDAP using **Spring bean** declarations
- Connecting to external LDAP directories
- Exploring the built-in support for Microsoft AD
- We will also explore how to customize Spring Security for more flexibility when dealing with custom AD deployments

Understanding LDAP

LDAP has its roots in logical directory models dating back over 30 years—conceptually akin to a combination of an organizational chart and an address book. Today, LDAP is used more and more as a way to centralize corporate user information, partition thousands of users into logical groups, and allow unified sharing of user information between many disparate systems.

For security purposes, LDAP is quite commonly used to facilitate centralized username and password authentication—users' credentials are stored in the LDAP directory, and authentication requests can be made against the directory on the user's behalf. This eases management for administrators, as user credentials—login ID, password, and other details—are stored in a single location in the LDAP directory. Additionally, organizational information, such as group or team assignments, geographic location, and corporate hierarchy membership, are defined based on the user's location in the directory.

LDAP

At this point, if you have never used LDAP before, you may be wondering what it is. We'll illustrate a sample LDAP schema with a screen from the Apache Directory Server 2.0.0-M231.5 example directory, as shown in the following screenshot:

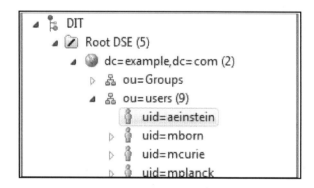

Starting at a particular user entry for `uid=admin1@example.com` (highlighted in the preceding screenshot), we can infer the organizational membership of `admin1` by starting at this node in the tree and moving upward. We can see that the user `aeinstein` is a member of the organizational unit (`ou=users`), which itself is a part of the domain `example.com` (the abbreviation `dc` shown in the preceding screenshot stands for domain component). Preceding this are the organizational elements (`DIT` and `Root DSE`) of the LDAP tree itself, which don't concern us in the context of Spring Security. The position of the user `aeinstein` in the LDAP hierarchy is semantically and definitively meaningful—you can imagine a much more complex hierarchy easily illustrating the organizational and departmental boundaries of a huge organization.

The complete top-to-bottom path formed by walking down the tree to an individual leaf node forms a string composed of all intervening nodes along the way, as with the node path of `admin1`, as follows:

```
uid=admin1,ou=users,dc=example,dc=com
```

The preceding node path is unique and is known as a node's **distinguished name** (**DN**). The distinguished name is akin to a database primary key, allowing a node to be uniquely identified and located in a complex tree structure. We'll see a node's DN used extensively throughout the authentication and searching process with Spring Security LDAP integration.

Note that there are several other users listed at the same level of organization as `admin1`. All of these users are assumed to be within the same organizational position as `admin1`. Although this example organization is relatively simple and flat, the structure of LDAP is arbitrarily flexible, with many levels of nesting and logical organization possible.

Spring Security LDAP support is assisted by the Spring LDAP module (`http://www.springsource.org/ldap`), which is actually a separate project from the core Spring Framework and Spring Security projects. It's considered to be stable and provides a helpful set of wrappers around the standard Java LDAP functionality.

Common LDAP attribute names

Each actual entry in the tree is defined by one or more object classes. An object class is a logical unit of organization, grouping a set of semantically-related attributes. By declaring an entry in the tree as an instance of a particular object class, such as a person, the organizer of the LDAP directory is able to provide users of the directory with a clear indication of what each element of the directory represents.

LDAP has a rich set of standard schemas covering the available LDAP object classes and their applicable attributes (along with gobs of other information). If you are planning on doing extensive work with LDAP, it's highly advised that you review a good reference guide, such as the appendix of the book *Zytrax OpenLDAP* (http://www.zytrax.com/books/ldap/ape/), or *Internet2 Consortium's Guide to Person-related Schemas* (http://middleware.internet2.edu/eduperson/).

In the previous section, we were introduced to the fact that each entry in an LDAP tree has a DN, which uniquely identifies it in the tree. The DN is composed of a series of attributes, one (or more) of which is used to uniquely identify the path down the tree of the entry represented by the DN. As each segment of the path described by the DN represents an LDAP attribute, you could refer to the available, well-defined LDAP schemas and object classes to determine what each of the attributes in any given DN means.

We've included some of the common attributes and their meanings in the following table. These attributes tend to be organizing attributes—meaning that they are typically used to define the organizational structure of the LDAP tree—and are ordered from top to bottom in the structure that you're likely to see in a typical LDAP installation:

Attribute name	Description	Example
dc	**Domain component**: Generally, the highest level of organization in an LDAP hierarchy.	dc=jbcpcalendar,dc=com
c	**Country**: Some LDAP hierarchies are structured at a high level by country.	c=US
o	**Organization name**: It is a parent business organization used for classifying LDAP resources.	o=Oracle Corporation
ou	**Organizational unit**: It is a divisional business organization which is generally within an organization.	ou=Product Development
cn	**Common name**: This is a common name, or a unique or human-readable name for the object. For humans, this is usually the person's full name, while for other resources in LDAP (computers, and so on), it's typically the hostname.	cn=Super Visor cn=Jim Bob

Attribute name	Description	Example
uid	**User ID**: Although not organizational in nature, the uid attribute is generally what Spring looks for during user authentication and search.	uid=svisor
userPassword	**User password**: This attribute stores the password for the person object to which this attribute is associated. It is typically one-way hashed using SHA or something similar.	userPassword=plaintext userPassword={SHA}cryptval

The attributes in the preceding table do, however, tend to be organizing attributes on the directory tree and, as such, will probably form various search expressions or mappings that you will use to configure Spring Security to interact with the LDAP server.

 Remember that there are hundreds of standard LDAP attributes—these represent a very small fraction of those you are likely to see when integrating with a fully-populated LDAP server.

Updating our dependencies

We have already included all of the dependencies you need for this chapter, so you will not need to make any updates to your build.gradle file. However, if you were just adding LDAP support to your own application, you would need to add spring-security-ldap as a dependency in build.gradle, as follows:

```
//build.gradle

dependencies {
// LDAP:
compile('org.springframework.boot:spring-boot-starter-data-ldap')
compile("org.springframework.ldap:spring-ldap-core")
compile("org.springframework.security:spring-security-ldap")
compile("org.springframework:spring-tx")
compile("com.unboundid:unboundid-ldapsdk")
    ...
}
```

Due to an artifact resolution issue with Gradle, `spring-tx` must be pulled in or Gradle will fetch an older one that doesn't work.

As mentioned previously, Spring Security's LDAP support is built on top of Spring LDAP. Gradle will automatically bring this dependency in as a transitive dependency, so there is no need to explicitly list it.

If you were using **ApacheDS** to run an LDAP server within your web application, as we are doing in our calendar application, you would need to add dependencies on the relevant ApacheDS JARs. There is no need to make these updates to our sample application, since we have already included them. Note that these dependencies are not necessary if you are connecting to an external LDAP server:

```
//build.gradle

    compile 'org.apache.directory.server:apacheds-core:2.0.0-M23'
    compile 'org.apache.directory.server:apacheds-protocol-ldap:2.0.0-M23'
    compile 'org.apache.directory.server:apacheds-protocol-shared:2.0.0
    -M23'
```

Configuring embedded LDAP integration

Let's now enable the JBCP calendar application to support LDAP-based authentication. Fortunately, this is a relatively simple exercise, using the embedded LDAP server and a sample LDIF file. For this exercise, we will be using an LDIF file created for this book, intended to capture many of the common configuration scenarios with LDAP and Spring Security. We have included several more sample LDIF files, some from Apache DS 2.0.0-M23 and one from the Spring Security unit tests, which you may choose to experiment with as well.

Configuring an LDAP server reference

The first step is to configure the embedded LDAP server. Spring Boot will automatically configure an embedded LDAP server, but we will need to tweak the configuration a bit. Make the following updates to your `application.yml` file:

```
//src/main/resources/application.yml

spring:
## LDAP
 ldap:
    embedded:
```

```
ldif: classpath:/ldif/calendar.ldif
base-dn: dc=jbcpcalendar,dc=com
port: 33389
```

You should be starting with the source from `chapter06.00-calendar`.

We are loading the `calendar.ldif` file from `classpath`, and using it to populate the LDAP server. The `root` attribute declares the root of the LDAP directory using the specified DN. This should correspond to the logical root DN in the LDIF file we're using.

Be aware that for embedded LDAP servers, the `base-dn` attribute is required. If it is not specified or is specified incorrectly, you may receive several odd errors upon initialization of the Apache DS server. Also, be aware that the `ldif` resource should only load a single `ldif`, otherwise the server will fail to start up. Spring Security requires a single resource, since using something such as `classpath*:calendar.ldif` does not provide the deterministic ordering that is required.

We'll reuse the bean ID defined here later, in the Spring Security configuration files, when we declare the LDAP user service and other configuration elements. All other attributes on the `<ldap-server>` declaration are optional when using the embedded LDAP mode.

Enabling the LDAP AuthenticationProviderNext interface

Next, we'll need to configure another `AuthenticationProvider` interface that checks user credentials against the LDAP provider. Simply update the Spring Security configuration to use an `o.s.s.ldap.authentication.LdapAuthenticationProvider` reference, as follows:

```
//src/main/java/com/packtpub/springsecurity/configuration/SecurityConfig.ja
va

@Override
public void configure(AuthenticationManagerBuilder auth)
throws Exception {
    auth
        .ldapAuthentication()
        .userSearchBase("")
        .userSearchFilter("(uid={0})")
```

```
        .groupSearchBase("ou=Groups")
        .groupSearchFilter("(uniqueMember={0})")
        .contextSource(contextSource())
        .passwordCompare()
        .passwordAttribute("userPassword");
}
@Bean
public DefaultSpringSecurityContextSource contextSource() {
    return new DefaultSpringSecurityContextSource(
            Arrays.asList("ldap://localhost:33389/"),
            "dc=jbcpcalendar,dc=com");
}
```

We'll discuss these attributes a bit more later. For now, get the application back up and running, and try logging in with `admin1@example.com` as the username and `admin1` as the password. You should be logged in!

 Your source code should look like `chapter05.01-calendar`.

Troubleshooting embedded LDAP

It is quite possible that you will run into hard-to-debug problems with embedded LDAP. Apache DS is not usually very friendly with its error messages, doubly so in Spring Security embedded mode. If you are getting a `404` error when trying to access the application in your browser, there is a good chance that things did not start up properly. Some things to double-check if you can't get this simple example running are as follows:

- Ensure the `baseDn` attribute is set on the `DefaultSpringSecurityContextSource` declaration in your `configuration` file, and make sure it matches the root defined in the LDIF file that's loaded at startup. If you get errors referencing missing partitions, it's likely that either the `root` attribute was missed or doesn't match your LDIF file.

- Be aware that a failure starting up the embedded LDAP server is not a fatal failure. In order to diagnose errors loading LDIF files, you will need to ensure that the appropriate log settings, including logging for the Apache DS server, are enabled, at least at error level. The LDIF loader is under the `org.apache.directory.server.protocol.shared.store` package, and this should be used to enable the logging of LDIF load errors.
- If the application server shuts down non-gracefully, you may be required to delete some files in your temporary directory (`%TEMP%` on Windows systems or `/tmp` on Linux-based systems) in order to start the server again. The error messages regarding this are (fortunately) fairly clear. Unfortunately, embedded LDAP isn't as seamless and easy to use as the embedded H2 database, but it is still quite a bit easier than trying to download and configure many of the freely-available external LDAP servers.

An excellent tool for troubleshooting or accessing LDAP servers in general is the Apache Directory Studio project, which offers standalone and Eclipse plugin versions. The free download is available at `http://directory.apache.org/studio/`. If you want to follow along with the book, you may want to download Apache Directory Studio 2.0.0-M23 now.

Understanding how Spring LDAP authentication works

We saw that we were able to log in using a user defined in the LDAP directory. But what exactly happens when a user issues a login request for a user in LDAP? There are the following three basic steps to the LDAP authentication process:

1. Authenticate the credentials supplied by the user against the LDAP directory.
2. Determine the `GrantedAuthority` object that the user has, based on their information in LDAP.
3. Pre-load information from the LDAP entry for the user into a custom `UserDetails` object, for further use by the application.

Authenticating user credentials

For the first step, authentication against the LDAP directory, a custom authentication provider is wired into `AuthenticationManager`. The `o.s.s.ldap.authentication.LdapAuthenticationProvider` interface takes the user's provided credentials and verifies them against the LDAP directory, as illustrated in the following diagram:

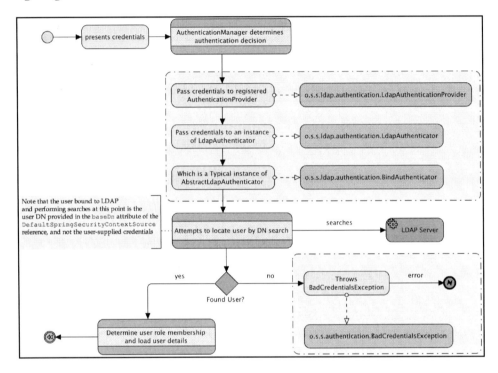

We can see that the `o.s.s.ldap.authentication.LdapAuthenticator` interface defines a delegate to allow the provider to make the authentication request in a customizable way. The implementation that we've implicitly configured to this point, `o.s.s.ldap.authentication.BindAuthenticator`, attempts to use the user's credentials to bind (log in) to the LDAP server as if it were the user themselves making a connection. For an embedded server, this is sufficient for our authentication needs; however, external LDAP servers may be stricter, and in these, users may not be allowed to bind to the LDAP directory. Fortunately, an alternative method of authentication exists, which we will explore later in this chapter.

As noted in the preceding diagram, keep in mind that the search is performed under an LDAP context created by the credentials specified in the `DefaultSpringSecurityContextSource` reference's `baseDn` attribute. With an embedded server, we don't use this information, but with an external server reference, unless `baseDn` is supplied, anonymous binding is used. Retaining some control over the public availability of information in the directory is very common for organizations which require valid credentials to search an LDAP directory, and as such, `baseDn` will be almost always required in real-world scenarios. The `baseDn` attribute represents the full DN of a user with valid access to bind the directory and perform searches.

Demonstrating authentication with Apache Directory Studio

We are going to demonstrate how the authentication process works by using Apache Directory Studio 1.5 to connect to our embedded LDAP instance and performing the same steps that Spring Security is performing. We will use `user1@example.com` throughout the simulation. These steps will help to ensure a firm grasp of what is happening behind the scenes and will help in the event that you are having difficulty figuring out the correct configuration.

Ensure that the calendar application is started up and working. Next, start Apache Directory Studio 1.5 and close the **Welcome** screen.

Binding anonymously to LDAP

The first step is to bind anonymously to LDAP. The bind is done anonymously because we did not specify the `baseDn` and `password` attributes on our `DefaultSpringSecurityContextSource` object. Within Apache Directory Studio, create a connection using the following steps:

1. Click on **File | New | LDAP Browser | LDAP Connection**.
2. Click on **Next**.

3. Enter the following information, and then click on **Next**:
   - **Connection name**: `calendar-anonymous`
   - **Hostname**: `localhost`
   - **Port**: `33389`

4. We did not specify `baseDn`, so select **No Authentication** as the **Authentication Method**.

5. Click on **Finish**.

You can safely ignore the message indicating no default schema information is present. You should now see that you are connected to the embedded LDAP instance.

Searching for the user

Now that we have a connection, we can use it to look up the user's DN that we wish to bind to, by performing the following steps:

1. Right-click on `DIT` and select **New** | **New Search**.

2. Enter a search base of `dc=jbcpcalendar,dc=com`. This corresponds to the `baseDn` attribute of our `DefaultSpringSecurityContextSource` object that we specified.

3. Enter a filter of `uid=user1@example.com`. This corresponds to the value we specified for the `userSearchFilter` method of `AuthenticationManagerBuilder`. Note that we have included the parentheses and have substituted the username we are attempting to log in with with the `{0}` value.

4. Click on **Search**.

5. Click on the DN of the single result returned by our search. You can now see that our LDAP user is displayed. Note that this DN matches the value we searched for. Remember this DN, as it will be used in our next step.

Binding as a user to LDAP

Now that we have found the full DN of our user, we need to try to bind to LDAP as that user to validate the submitted password. These steps are the same as in the anonymous bind we already did, except that we will specify the credentials of the user that we are authenticating.

Within ApacheDS, create a connection using the following steps:

1. Select **File** | **New** | **LDAP Browser** | **LDAP Connection**.
2. Click on **Next**.
3. Enter the following information and click on **Next**:
   - **Connection name**: `calendar-user1`
   - **Hostname**: `localhost`
   - **Port**: `33389`
4. Leave **Authentication Method** as **Simple Authentication**.
5. Enter the DN from our search result as `Bind DN`. The value should be `uid=admin1@example.com,ou=Users,dc=jbcpcalendar,dc=com`.
6. The `Bind` password should be the password that was submitted at the time of login. In our case, we want to use `admin1` to successfully authenticate. If the wrong password was entered, we would fail to connect and Spring Security would report an error.
7. Click on **Finish**.

Spring Security will determine that the username and password were correct for this user when it is able to successfully bind with the provided username and password (similar to how we were able to create a connection). Spring Security will then proceed with determining the user's role membership.

Determining user role membership

After the user has been successfully authenticated against the LDAP server, authorization information must be determined next. Authorization is defined by a principal's list of roles, and an LDAP-authenticated user's role membership is determined, as illustrated in the following diagram:

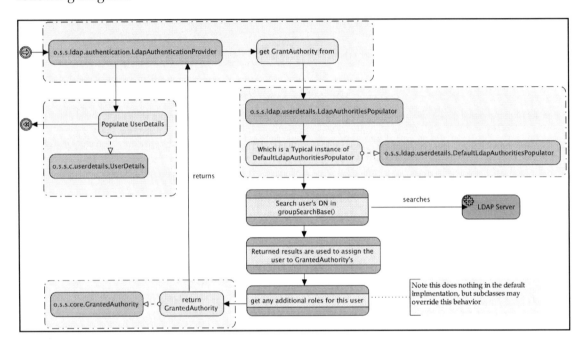

We can see that after authenticating the user against LDAP, LdapAuthenticationProvider delegates to LdapAuthoritiesPopulator. The DefaultLdapAuthoritiesPopulator interface will attempt to locate the authenticated user's DN in an attribute located at or below another entry in the LDAP hierarchy. The DN of the location searched for user role assignments is defined in the groupSearchBase method; in our sample, we set this to groupSearchBase("ou=Groups"). When the user's DN is located within an LDAP entry below the DN of groupSearchBase, an attribute on the entry in which their DN is found is used to confer a role to them.

How Spring Security roles are associated with LDAP users can be a little confusing, so let's look at the JBCP calendar LDAP repository and see how the association of a user with a role works. The DefaultLdapAuthoritiesPopulator interface uses several methods of the AuthenticationManagerBuilder declaration to govern the searching of roles for the user. These attributes are used approximately in the following order:

1. groupSearchBase: It defines the base DN under which the LDAP integration should look for one or more matches for the user's DN. The default value performs a search from the LDAP root, which may be expensive.

2. groupSearchFilter: It defines the LDAP search filter used to match the user's DN to an attribute of an entry located under groupSearchBase. This search filter is parameterized with two parameters—the first ({0}) being the user's DN, and the second ({1}) being the user's username. The default value is uniqueMember={0}.

3. groupRoleAttribute: It defines the attribute of the matching entries, which will be used to compose the user's GrantedAuthority object. The default value is cn.

4. rolePrefix: It is the prefix that will be prepended to the value found in groupRoleAttribute, to make a Spring Security GrantedAuthority object. The default value is ROLE_.

This can be a little abstract and hard for new developers to follow because it's very different from anything we've seen so far with our JDBC and JPA-based UserDetailsService implementations. Let's continue walking through the login process with our user1@example.com user in the JBCP calendar LDAP directory.

Determining roles with Apache Directory Studio

We will now try to determine the roles for our user with Apache Directory Studio. Using the calendar-user1 connection we created previously, perform the following steps:

1. Right-click on DIT and select **New | New Search**.

2. Enter a search base of ou=Groups,dc=jbcpcalendar,dc=com. This corresponds to the baseDn attribute of the DefaultSpringSecurityContextSource object we specified, plus the groupSearchBase attribute we specified for the AuthenticationManagerBuilder object.

3. Enter a filter of uniqueMember=uid=user1@example.com,ou=Users,dc=jbcpcalendar,dc=com. This corresponds to the default groupSearchFilter attribute of (uniqueMember={0}). Notice that we have substituted the full DN of the user we found in our previous exercise for the {0} value.

4. Click on **Search**.

5. You will observe that the User group is the only group returned in our search results. Click on the DN of the single result returned by our search. You can now see the User group displayed in Apache DS. Note that the group has a uniqueMember attribute with the full DN of our user and other users.

Spring Security now creates the GrantedAuthority object for each result by forcing the name of the group that was found into uppercase and prepending ROLE_ to the group name. The pseudocode would look similar to the following code snippet:

```
foreach group in groups:

authority = ("ROLE_"+group).upperCase()

grantedAuthority = new GrantedAuthority(authority)
```

Spring LDAP is as flexible as your gray matter. Keep in mind that, although this is one way to organize an LDAP directory to be compatible with Spring Security, typical usage scenarios are exactly the opposite—an LDAP directory already exists that Spring Security needs to be wired into. In many cases, you will be able to reconfigure Spring Security to deal with the hierarchy of the LDAP server; however, it's key that you plan effectively and understand how Spring works with LDAP when it's querying. Use your brain, map out the user search and group search, and come up with the most optimal plan you can think of—keep the scope of searches as minimal and as precise as possible.

Can you describe how the results of the login process would differ for our admin1@example.com user? If you are confused at this point, we'd suggest that you take a breather and try using Apache Directory Studio to work through browsing the embedded LDAP server, configured by the running of an application. It can be easier to grasp the flow of Spring Security's LDAP configuration if you attempt to search the directory yourself by following the algorithm described previously.

Mapping additional attributes of UserDetails

Finally, once the LDAP lookup has assigned the user a set of the GrantedAuthority objects, o.s.s.ldap.userdetails.LdapUserDetailsMapper will consult o.s.s.ldap.userdetails.UserDetailsContextMapper to retrieve any additional details to populate the UserDetails object for application use.

Using `AuthenticationManagerBuilder`, we've configured up until this point that `LdapUserDetailsMapper` will be used to populate a `UserDetails` object with information gleaned from the user's entry in the LDAP directory:

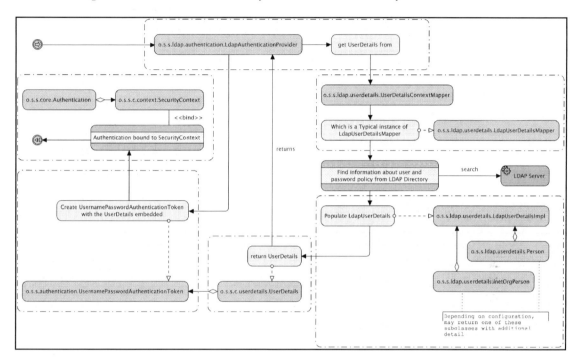

We'll see in a moment how `UserDetailsContextMapper` can be configured to pull a wealth of information from the standard LDAP `person` and `inetOrgPerson` objects. With the baseline `LdapUserDetailsMapper`, little more than `username`, `password`, and `GrantedAuthority` is stored.

Although there is more machinery involved behind the scenes in LDAP user authentication and detail retrieval, you'll notice that the overall process seems somewhat similar to the JDBC authentication that we studied in `Chapter 4`, *JDBC-Based Authentication* (authenticating the user and populating `GrantedAuthority`). As with JDBC authentication, there is the ability to perform advanced configuration of LDAP integration. Let's dive deeper and see what's possible!

Advanced LDAP configuration

Once we get beyond the basics of LDAP integration, there's a plethora of additional configuration capabilities in the Spring Security LDAP module that are still within the security `WebSecurityConfigurerAdapter` style of configuration. These include retrieval of user personal information, additional options for user authentication, and the use of LDAP as the `UserDetailsService` interface in conjunction with a standard `DaoAuthenticationProvider` class.

Sample JBCP LDAP users

We've supplied a number of different users in the JBCP calendar `LDIF` file. The following quick reference chart may help you with the advanced configuration exercises, or with self-exploration:

Username/password	Role(s)	Password encoding
admin1@example.com/admin1	ROLE_ADMIN, ROLE_USER	Plaintext
user1@example.com/user1	ROLE_USER	Plaintext
shauser@example.com/shauser	ROLE_USER	{sha}
sshauser@example.com/sshauser	ROLE_USER	{ssha}
hasphone@example.com/hasphone	ROLE_USER	Plaintext (in the `telephoneNumber` attribute)

We'll explain why password encoding matters in the next section.

Password comparison versus bind authentication

Some LDAP servers will be configured so that certain individual users are not allowed to bind directly to the server, or so that anonymous binding (what we have been using for user search up until this point) is disabled. This tends to occur in very large organizations which want a restricted set of users to be able to read information from the directory.

In these cases, the standard Spring Security LDAP authentication strategy will not work, and an alternative strategy must be used, implemented by
`o.s.s.ldap.authentication.PasswordComparisonAuthenticator` (a sibling class of `BindAuthenticator`):

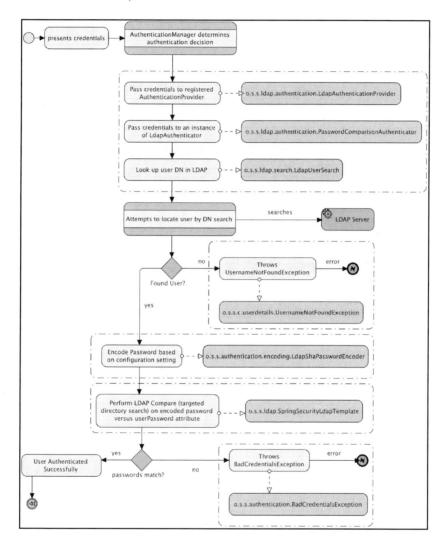

The `PasswordComparisonAuthenticator` interface binds to LDAP and searches for the DN matching the username provided by the user. It then compares the user-supplied password with the `userPassword` attribute stored on the matching LDAP entry. If the encoded password matches, the user is authenticated and the flow proceeds, as with `BindAuthenticator`.

Configuring basic password comparison

Configuring password comparison authentication instead of bind authentication is as simple as adding a method to the `AuthenticationManagerBuilder` declaration. Update the `SecurityConfig.java` file, as follows:

```
//src/main/java/com/packtpub/springsecurity/configuration/SecurityConfig.ja
va

    @Override
    public void configure(AuthenticationManagerBuilder auth)
        throws Exception {
        auth
          .ldapAuthentication()
          .userSearchBase("")
          .userSearchFilter("(uid={0})")
          .groupSearchBase("ou=Groups")
          .groupSearchFilter("(uniqueMember={0})")
          .contextSource(contextSource())
          .passwordCompare()
            .passwordEncoder(new LdapShaPasswordEncoder())
            .passwordAttribute("userPassword");
    }
```

The `PasswordCompareConfigurer` class, that is used by declaring the `passwordCompare` method, uses `PlaintextPasswordEncoder` for password encoding. To use the SHA-1 password algorithm, we need to set a password encoder, and we can use `o.s.s.a.encoding.LdapShaPasswordEncoder` for SHA support (recall that we discussed the SHA-1 password algorithm extensively in Chapter 4, *JDBC-Based Authentication*).

In our `calendar.ldif` file, we have the `password` field set to `userPassword`. The default `password` attribute for the `PasswordCompareConfigurer` class is `password`. So, we also need to override the `password` attribute with the `passwordAttribute` method.

After restarting the server, you can attempt to log in using `shauser@example.com` as the `username` and `shauser` as `password`.

 Your code should look like `chapter06.02-calendar`.

LDAP password encoding and storage

LDAP has general support for a variety of password encoding algorithms, ranging from plaintext to one-way hash algorithms—similar to those we explored in the previous chapter—with database-backed authentication. The most common storage formats for LDAP passwords are `SHA` (SHA-1 one-way hashed), and `SSHA` (SHA-1 one-way hashed with a salt value). Other password formats often supported by many LDAP implementations are thoroughly documented in *RFC 2307, An Approach to Using LDAP as a Network Information Service* (`http://tools.ietf.org/html/rfc2307`). The designers of *RFC 2307* did a very clever thing with regards to password storage. Passwords retained in the directory are, of course, encoded with whatever algorithm is appropriate (`SHA` and so on), but then, they are prefixed with the algorithm used to encode the password. This makes it very easy for the LDAP server to support multiple algorithms for password encoding. For example, an `SHA` encoded password is stored in the directory as `{SHA}5baa61e4c9b93f3f0682250b6cf8331b7ee68fd8`.

We can see that the password storage algorithm is very clearly indicated with the `{SHA}` notation and stored along with the password.

The `SSHA` notation is an attempt to combine the strong `SHA-1` hash algorithm with password salting to prevent dictionary attacks. As with password salting, which we reviewed in the previous chapter, the salt is added to the password prior to calculating the hash. When the hashed password is stored in the directory, the salt value is appended to the hashed password. The password is prepended with `{SSHA}` so that the LDAP directory knows that the user-supplied password needs to be compared differently. The majority of modern LDAP servers utilize `SSHA` as their default password storage algorithm.

The drawbacks of a password comparison authenticator

Now that you know a bit about how LDAP uses passwords, and we have `PasswordComparisonAuthenticator` set up, what do you think will happen if you log in using our `sshauser@example.com` user with their password, stored in the `SSHA` format?

Go ahead, put the book aside and try it, and then come back.

Your login was denied, right? And yet you were still able to log in as the user with the SHA-encoded password. Why? The password encoding and storage didn't matter when we were using bind authentication. Why do you think that is?

The reason it didn't matter with bind authentication was that the LDAP server was taking care of the authentication and validation of the user's password. With password compare authentication, Spring Security LDAP is responsible for encoding the password in the format expected by the directory and then matching it against the directory to validate the authentication.

For security purposes, password comparison authentication can't actually read the password from the directory (reading directory passwords is often denied by the security policy). Instead, `PasswordComparisonAuthenticator` performs an LDAP search, rooted at the user's directory entry, attempting to match with a `password` attribute and value as determined by the password that's been encoded by Spring Security.

So, when we try to log in with `sshauser@example.com`, `PasswordComparisonAuthenticator` is encoding the password using the configured `SHA` algorithm and attempting to do a simple match, which fails, as the directory password for this user is stored in the `SSHA` format.

Our current configuration, using `LdapShaPasswordEncoder`, already supports `SHA` and `SSHA`, so currently, it still doesn't work. Let's think why that might be. Remember that `SSHA` uses a salted password, with the salt value stored in the LDAP directory along with the password. However, `PasswordComparisonAuthenticator` is coded so that it cannot read anything from the LDAP server (this typically violates the security policy with companies that don't allow binding). Thus, when `PasswordComparisonAuthenticator` computes the hashed password, it has no way to determine what salt value to use.

In conclusion, `PasswordComparisonAuthenticator` is valuable in certain limited circumstances where the security of the directory itself is a concern, but it will never be as flexible as straight bind authentication.

Configuring the UserDetailsContextMapper object

As we noted earlier, an instance of the `o.s.s.ldap.userdetails.UserDetailsContextMapper` interface is used to map a user's entry into the LDAP server to a `UserDetails` object in memory. The default `UserDetailsContextMapper` object behaves similarly to `JpaDaoImpl`, given the level of detail that is populated on the returned `UserDetails` object—that is to say, not a lot of information is returned besides the username and password.

However, an LDAP directory potentially contains many more details about individual users than usernames, passwords, and roles. Spring Security ships with two additional methods of pulling more user data from two of the standard LDAP object schemas—`person` and `inetOrgPerson`.

Implicit configuration of UserDetailsContextMapper

In order to configure a different `UserDetailsContextMapper` implementation than the default, we simply need to declare which `LdapUserDetails` class we want `LdapAuthenticationProvider` to return. The security namespace parser will be smart enough to instantiate the correct `UserDetailsContextMapper` implementation based on the type of the `LdapUserDetails` interface requested.

Let's reconfigure our `SecurityConfig.java` file to use the `inetOrgPerson` version of the mapper. Update the `SecurityConfig.java` file, as illustrated in the following code:

```
//src/main/java/com/packtpub/springsecurity/configuration/SecurityConfig.ja
va

    @Override
    public void configure(AuthenticationManagerBuilder auth)
    throws Exception {
        auth
            .ldapAuthentication()
```

```
        .userSearchBase("")
        .userSearchFilter("(uid={0})")
        .groupSearchBase("ou=Groups")
        .groupSearchFilter("(uniqueMember={0})")
        .userDetailsContextMapper(
            new InetOrgPersonContextMapper())
        .contextSource(contextSource())
        .passwordCompare()
            // Supports {SHA} and {SSHA}
            .passwordEncoder(new LdapShaPasswordEncoder())
            .passwordAttribute("userPassword");
}
```

 If we remove the `passwordEncoder` method, then the LDAP users that are using `SHA` passwords will fail to authenticate.

If you were to restart the application and attempt to log in as an LDAP user, you would see that nothing changed. In fact, `UserDetailsContextMapper` has changed behind the scenes to read the additional details in the case where attributes from the `inetOrgPerson` schema are available in the user's directory entry.

Try authenticating with `admin1@example.com` as the `username` and `admin1` as the `password`. It should fail to authenticate.

Viewing additional user details

To assist you in this area, we'll add the ability to view the current account to the JBCP calendar application. We'll use this page to illustrate how the richer person and the `inetOrgPerson` LDAP schemas can provide additional (optional) information to your LDAP-enabled application.

You may have noticed that this chapter came with an additional controller named `AccountController`. You can see the relevant code, as follows:

```
//src/main/java/com/packtpub/springsecurity/web/controllers/AccountControll
er.java

    ...
    @RequestMapping("/accounts/my")
    public String view(Model model) {
    Authentication authentication = SecurityContextHolder.
    getContext().getAuthentication();
```

```
// null check on authentication omitted
Object principal = authentication.getPrincipal();
model.addAttribute("user", principal);
model.addAttribute("isLdapUserDetails", principal instanceof
LdapUserDetails);
model.addAttribute("isLdapPerson", principal instanceof Person);
model.addAttribute("isLdapInetOrgPerson", principal instanceof
InetOrgPerson);
return "accounts/show";
}
...
```

The preceding code will retrieve the `UserDetails` object (principal) stored in the `Authentication` object by `LdapAuthenticationProvider` and determine what type of `LdapUserDetailsImplinterface` it is. The page code itself will then display various details depending on the type of `UserDetails` object that has been bound to the user's authentication information, as we see in the following JSP code. We have already included JSP as well:

```
//src/main/resources/templates/accounts/show.html

<dl>
    <dt>Username</dt>
    <dd id="username" th:text="${user.username}">ChuckNorris</dd>
    <dt>DN</dt>
    <dd id="dn" th:text="${user.dn}"></dd>
    <span th:if="${isLdapPerson}">
        <dt>Description</dt>
        <dd id="description" th:text="${user.description}"></dd>
        <dt>Telephone</dt>
        <dd id="telephoneNumber" th:text="${user.telephoneNumber}"></dd>
        <dt>Full Name(s)</dt>
        <span th:each="cn : ${user.cn}">
        <dd th:text="${cn}"></dd>
        </span>
    </span>
    <span th:if="${isLdapInetOrgPerson}">
        <dt>Email</dt>
        <dd id="email" th:text="${user.mail}"></dd>
        <dt>Street</dt>
        <dd id="street" th:text="${user.street}"></dd>
    </span>
</dl>
```

The only work that actually needs to be done is to add a link in our `header.html` file, as shown in the following code snippet:

```
//src/main/resources/templates/fragments/header.html

<li>
<p class="navbar-text">Welcome  
    <a id="navMyAccount" th:href="@{/accounts/my}">
      <div class="navbar-text" th:text="${#authentication.name}">
      User</div>
    </a>
</p>
</li>
```

We've added the following two more users that you can use to examine the differences in the available data elements:

Username	Password	Type
shainet@example.com	shainet	inetOrgPerson
shaperson@example.com	shaperson	person

Your code should look like `chapter05.03-calendar`.

Restart the server and examine the **Account Details** page for each of the types of users by clicking on **username** in the upper-right corner. You'll note that when `UserDetails` class is configured to use `inetOrgPerson`, although `o.s.s.ldap.userdetails.InetOrgPerson` is what is returned, the fields may or may not be populated depending on the available attributes in the directory entry.

In fact, `inetOrgPerson` has many more attributes that we've illustrated on this simple page. You can review the full list in *RFC 2798, Definition of the inetOrgPerson LDAP Object Class* (`http://tools.ietf.org/html/rfc2798`).

One thing you may notice is that there is no facility to support additional attributes that may be specified on an Object entry, but don't fall into a standard schema. The standard `UserDetailsContextMapper` interfaces don't support arbitrary lists of attributes, but it is possible nonetheless to customize it with a reference to your own `UserDetailsContextMapper` interface through the use of the `userDetailsContextMapper` method.

Using an alternate password attribute

In some cases, it may be necessary to use an alternate LDAP attribute instead of `userPassword`, for authentication purposes. This can happen during occasions when companies have deployed custom LDAP schemas or don't have the requirement for strong password management (arguably, this is never a good idea, but it definitely does occur in the real world).

The `PasswordComparisonAuthenticator` interface also supports the ability to verify the user's password against an alternate LDAP entry attribute instead of the standard `userPassword` attribute. This is very easy to configure, and we can demonstrate a simple example using the plaintext `telephoneNumber` attribute. Update the `SecurityConfig.java`, as follows:

```
//src/main/java/com/packtpub/springsecurity/configuration/SecurityConfig.ja
va

@Override
public void configure(AuthenticationManagerBuilder auth)
throws Exception {
    auth
        .ldapAuthentication()
        .userSearchBase("")
        .userSearchFilter("(uid={0})")
      .groupSearchBase("ou=Groups")
        .groupSearchFilter("(uniqueMember={0})")
        .userDetailsContextMapper(new InetOrgPersonContextMapper())
        .contextSource(contextSource())
        .passwordCompare()
            .passwordAttribute("telephoneNumber");
}
```

We can restart the server and attempt to log in with `hasphone@example.com` as the `username` and `0123456789` as the `password` (telephone number) attributes.

 Your code should look like `chapter05.04-calendar`.

Of course, this type of authentication has all of the perils we discussed earlier regarding authentication based on `PasswordComparisonAuthenticator`; however, it's good to be aware of it on the off-chance that it comes up with an LDAP implementation.

Using LDAP as UserDetailsService

One thing to note is that LDAP may also be used as UserDetailsService. As we will discuss later in the book, UserDetailsService is required to enable various other bits of functionality in the Spring Security infrastructure, including the remember-me and OpenID authentication features.

We will modify our AccountController object to use the LdapUserDetailsService interface to obtain the user. Before doing this, make sure to remove the passwordCompare method, as shown in the following code snippet:

```
//src/main/java/com/packtpub/springsecurity/configuration/SecurityConfig.ja
va

    @Override
    public void configure(AuthenticationManagerBuilder auth)
    throws Exception {
        auth
            .ldapAuthentication()
            .userSearchFilter("(uid={0})")
            .groupSearchBase("ou=Groups")
            .userDetailsContextMapper(new InetOrgPersonContextMapper())
            .contextSource(contextSource());
    }
```

Configuring LdapUserDetailsService

The configuration of LDAP as a UserDetailsService function is very similar to the configuration of an LDAP AuthenticationProvider. Like the JDBC UserDetailsService, an LDAP UserDetailsService interface is configured as a sibling to the <http> declaration. Make the following updates to the SecurityConfig.java file:

```
//src/main/java/com/packtpub/springsecurity/configuration/SecurityConfig.ja
va

    @Bean
    @Override
    public UserDetailsService userDetailsService() {
        return super.userDetailsService();
    }
```

Functionally, o.s.s.ldap.userdetails.LdapUserDetailsService is configured in almost exactly the same way as LdapAuthenticationProvider, with the exception that there is no attempt to use the principal's username to bind to LDAP. Instead, the credentials supplied by the `DefaultSpringSecurityContextSource` reference itself, and are used to perform the user lookup.

> Do not make the very common mistake of configuring `AuthenticationManagerBuilder` with the `UserDetailsService` referring to `LdapUserDetailsService` if you intend to authenticate the user against LDAP itself! As discussed previously, the `password` attribute often cannot be retrieved from LDAP due to security reasons, which makes `UserDetailsService` useless for authenticating. As noted previously, `LdapUserDetailsService` uses the `baseDn` attribute supplied with the `DefaultSpringSecurityContextSource` declaration to get its information—this means that it does not attempt to bind the user to LDAP and, as such, may not behave as you expect.

Updating AccountController to use LdapUserDetailsService

We will now update the `AccountController` object to use the `LdapDetailsUserDetailsService` interface to look up the user that it displays:

```
//src/main/java/com/packtpub/springsecurity/web/controllers/AccountControll
er.java

@Controller
public class AccountController {
private final UserDetailsService userDetailsService;
@Autowired
public AccountController(UserDetailsService userDetailsService) {
    this.userDetailsService = userDetailsService;
}
@RequestMapping("/accounts/my")
public String view(Model model) {
    Authentication authentication = SecurityContextHolder.
    getContext().getAuthentication();
    // null check omitted
    String principalName = authentication.getName();
    Object principal = userDetailsService.
    loadUserByUsername(principalName);
    ...
}
}
```

Obviously, this example is a bit silly, but it demonstrates the use of `LdapUserDetailsService`. Go ahead and restart the application and give this a try with the `username` as `admin1@example.com` and the `password` as `admin1`. Can you figure out how to modify the controller to display an arbitrary user's information?

Can you figure out how you should modify the security settings to restrict access to an administrator?

 Your code should look like `chapter05.05-calendar`.

Integrating Spring Security with an external LDAP server

It is likely that once you test basic integration with the embedded LDAP server, you will want to interact with an external LDAP server. Fortunately, this is very straightforward and can be done using a slightly different syntax along with the same `DefaultSpringSecurityContextSource` instructions we provided to set up the embedded LDAP server.

Update the Spring Security configuration to connect to an external LDAP server on port `33389`, as follows:

```
//src/main/java/com/packtpub/springsecurity/configuration/SecurityConfig.java

    @Override
    public void configure(AuthenticationManagerBuilder auth)
    throws Exception {
        auth
          .ldapAuthentication()
           .userSearchFilter("(uid={0})")
           .groupSearchBase("ou=Groups")
           .userDetailsContextMapper(new InetOrgPersonContextMapper())
           //.contextSource(contextSource())
           .contextSource()
              .managerDn("uid=admin,ou=system")
              .managerPassword("secret")
              .url("ldap://localhost:33389/dc=jbcpcalendar,dc=com");
    }
```

The notable differences here (aside from the LDAP URL) are that the DN and password for an account are provided. The account (which is actually optional) should be allowed to bind to the directory and perform searches across all relevant DNs for user and group information. The binding resulting from the application of these credentials against the LDAP server URL is used for the remaining LDAP operations across the LDAP-secured system.

Be aware that many LDAP servers also support SSL-encrypted LDAP (LDAPS)—this is, of course, preferred for security purposes and is supported by the Spring LDAP stack. Simply use `ldaps://` at the beginning of the LDAP server URL. LDAPS typically runs on TCP port 636. Note that there are many commercial and non-commercial implementations of LDAP. The exact configuration parameters that you will use for connectivity, user binding, and the population of `GrantedAuthoritys` will wholly depend on both the vendor and the structure of the directory. We will cover one very common LDAP implementation, Microsoft AD, in the next section.

If you do not have an LDAP server handy and would like to give this a try, go ahead and add the following code to your `SecurityConfig.java` file, which starts up the embedded LDAP server we have been using:

```
//src/main/java/com/packtpub/springsecurity/configuration/SecurityConfig.java

@Override
public void configure(AuthenticationManagerBuilder auth)
throws Exception {
    auth
        .ldapAuthentication()
        .userSearchBase("")
        .userSearchFilter("(uid={0})")
        .groupSearchBase("ou=Groups")
        .groupSearchFilter("(uniqueMember={0})")
        .userDetailsContextMapper(new InetOrgPersonContextMapper())
        .contextSource()
          .managerDn("uid=admin,ou=system")
          .managerPassword("secret")
          .url("ldap://localhost:10389/dc=jbcpcalendar,dc=com")
          .root("dc=jbcpcalendar,dc=com")
          .ldif("classpath:/ldif/calendar.ldif")
          .and()
              .passwordCompare()
               .passwordEncoder(new LdapShaPasswordEncoder())
               .passwordAttribute("userPassword")
    ;
}
```

If this isn't convincing, start up an LDAP server using Apache Directory Studio and import `calendar.ldif` into it. You can then connect to the external LDAP server. Go ahead and restart the application and give this a try with the `username` as `shauser@example.com` and the `password` as `shauser`.

 Your code should look like `chapter05.06-calendar`.

Explicit LDAP bean configuration

In this section, we'll lead you through the set of bean configurations required to explicitly configure both a connection to an external LDAP server and the `LdapAuthenticationProvider` interface required to support authentication against an external server. As with other explicit bean-based configurations, you really want to avoid doing this unless you find yourself in a situation where the capabilities of the security namespace style of configuration will not support your business or your technical requirements. In which case, read on!

Configuring an external LDAP server reference

To implement this configuration, we'll assume that we have a local LDAP server running on port `10389`, with the same configuration corresponding to the `DefaultSpringSecurityContextSource` interface example provided in the previous section. The required bean definition is already provided in the `SecurityConfig.java` file. In fact, to keep things simple, we have provided the entire `SecurityConfig.java` file. Review the LDAP server reference in the following code snippet:

```
//src/main/java/com/packtpub/springsecurity/configuration/SecurityConfig.java

@Bean
public DefaultSpringSecurityContextSource contextSource() {return new
DefaultSpringSecurityContextSource(
    Arrays.asList("ldap://localhost:10389/"),
    "dc=jbcpcalendar,dc=com") {{
        setUserDn("uid=admin,ou=system");
        setPassword("secret");
}};
}
```

Next, we'll need to configure `LdapAuthenticationProvider`, which is a bit more complex.

Configuring the LdapAuthenticationProvider interface

If you've read and understood the explanations throughout this chapter, describing how Spring Security LDAP authentication works behind the scenes, this bean configuration will be perfectly understandable, albeit a bit complex. We'll configure `LdapAuthenticationProvider` with the following characteristics:

- User credential binding authentication (not password comparison)
- Use of `InetOrgPerson` in `UserDetailsContextMapper`

Take a look at the following steps:

1. Let's get to it—we'll explore the already configured `LdapAuthenticationProvider` interface first, as follows:

   ```
   //src/main/java/com/packtpub/springsecurity/configuration/
   SecurityConfig.java

   @Bean
   public LdapAuthenticationProvider authenticationProvider
   (BindAuthenticator ba,LdapAuthoritiesPopulator lap,
   \UserDetailsContextMapper cm){
       return new LdapAuthenticationProvider(ba, lap){{
         setUserDetailsContextMapper(cm);
      }};
   }
   ```

2. The next bean provided for us is `BindAuthenticator`, and the supporting `FilterBasedLdapUserSearch` bean is used to locate the user's DN in the LDAP directory prior to binding, as follows:

   ```
   //src/main/java/com/packtpub/springsecurity/configuration/
   SecurityConfig.java

   @Bean
   public BindAuthenticator bindAuthenticator
   (FilterBasedLdapUserSearch userSearch)
   {
       return new BindAuthenticator(contextSource()){{
   ```

```
                setUserSearch(userSearch);
        }};
    }
    @Bean
    public FilterBasedLdapUserSearch filterBasedLdapUserSearch(){
        return new FilterBasedLdapUserSearch("",
        //user-search-base "(uid={0})", //user-search-filter
        contextSource()); //ldapServer
    }
```

Finally, `LdapAuthoritiesPopulator` and `UserDetailsContextMapper` perform the roles we examined earlier in the chapter:

```
//src/main/java/com/packtpub/springsecurity/configuration/
SecurityConfig.java

@Bean
public LdapAuthoritiesPopulator authoritiesPopulator(){
    return new DefaultLdapAuthoritiesPopulator(contextSource(),
    "ou=Groups"){{
        setGroupSearchFilter("(uniqueMember={0})");
    }};
}
@Bean
public userDetailsContextMapper userDetailsContextMapper(){
    return new InetOrgPersonContextMapper();
}
```

3. In the next step, we must update Spring Security to utilize our explicitly configured `LdapAuthenticationProvider` interface. Update the `SecurityConfig.java` file to use our new configuration, ensuring you remove the old `ldapAuthentication` method, as follows:

```
//src/main/java/com/packtpub/springsecurity/configuration/
SecurityConfig.java

@Autowired
private LdapAuthenticationProvider authenticationProvider;
@Override
public void configure(AuthenticationManagerBuilder auth)
throws Exception {
    auth.authenticationProvider(authenticationProvider);
}
```

At this point, we have fully configured LDAP authentication with explicit Spring bean notation. Employing this technique in the LDAP integration is useful in a few cases, such as when the security namespace does not expose certain configuration attributes, or when custom implementation classes are required to provide functionality tailored to a particular business scenario. We'll explore one such scenario later in this chapter when we examine how to connect to Microsoft AD via LDAP.

4. Go ahead and start the application and give the configuration a try with the `username` as `shauser@example.com` and the `password` as `shauser`. Assuming you have an external LDAP server running, or you have kept the configured in-memory `DefaultSpringSecurityContextSource` object, everything should still be working.

 Your code should look like `chapter05.07-calendar`.

Delegating role discovery to UserDetailsService

One technique for populating user roles that are available to use with explicit bean configuration is implementing the support for looking up a user by username in `UserDetailsService`, and getting the `GrantedAuthority` objects from this source. The configuration is as simple as replacing the bean with the `ldapAuthoritiesPopulator` ID bean with an updated `UserDetailsServiceLdapAuthoritiesPopulator` object, with a reference to `UserDetailsService`. Make the following updates to the `SecurityConfig.java` file, ensuring you remove the previous `ldapAuthoritiesPopulator` bean definition:

```
//src/main/java/com/packtpub/springsecurity/configuration/SecurityConfig.java

    //@Bean
    //public LdapAuthoritiesPopulator authoritiesPopulator(){
        //return new DefaultLdapAuthoritiesPopulator(contextSource(),
        //"ou=Groups"){{
                //setGroupSearchFilter("(uniqueMember={0})");
        //     }};
    //}
    @Bean
    public LdapAuthoritiesPopulator authoritiesPopulator(
```

```
         UserDetailsService userDetailsService) {
            return new UserDetailsServiceLdapAuthoritiesPopulator
            (userDetailsService);
    }
```

We will also need to ensure that we have defined `userDetailsService`. To keep things simple, add an in-memory `UserDetailsService` interface, as follows:

```
//src/main/java/com/packtpub/springsecurity/configuration/SecurityConfig.ja
va

@Bean
@Override
public UserDetailsManager userDetailsService() {
    InMemoryUserDetailsManager manager = new
     InMemoryUserDetailsManager();
    manager.createUser(User.withUsername("user1@example.com")
    .password("user1").roles("USER").build());
    manager.createUser(
        User.withUsername("admin1@example.com")
            .password("admin1").roles("USER", "ADMIN").build());
    return manager;
}
```

You should now be able to authenticate with `admin1@example.com` as the `username` and `admin1` as the `password`. Naturally, we could also substitute this in-memory `UserDetailsService` interface for the JDBC or JPA-based one we discussed in Chapter 4, *JDBC-Based Authentication*, and in Chapter 5, *Authentication with Spring Data*.

 Your code should look like `chapter05.08-calendar`.

The logistical and managerial problem you may notice with this is that the usernames and roles must be managed both in the LDAP server and the repository used by `UserDetailsService`—this is probably not a scalable model for a large user base.

The more common use of this scenario is when LDAP authentication is required to ensure that users of the secured application are valid corporate users, but the application itself wants to store authorization information. This keeps potentially application-specific data out of the LDAP directory, which can be a beneficial separation of concerns.

Integrating with Microsoft Active Directory via LDAP

One of the convenient features of Microsoft AD is not only its seamless integration with Microsoft Windows-based network architectures, but also that it can be configured to expose the contents of AD using the LDAP protocol. If you are working in a company that is heavily leveraging Microsoft Windows, it is probable that any LDAP integration you do will be against your AD instance.

Depending on your configuration of Microsoft AD (and the directory administrator's willingness to configure it to support Spring Security LDAP), you may have a difficult time, not with the authentication and binding process, but with the mapping of AD information to the user's `GrantedAuthority` objects within the Spring Security system.

The sample AD LDAP tree for JBCP calendar corporate within our LDAP browser looks similar to the following screenshot:

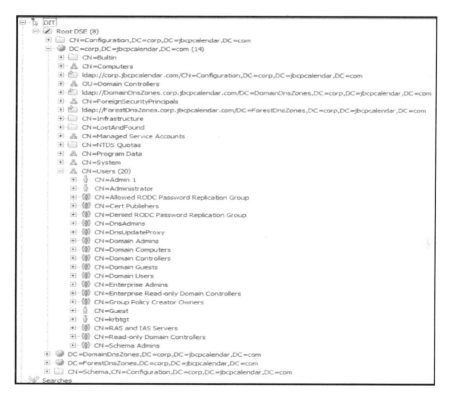

What you do not see here is `ou=Groups`, which we saw in our sample LDAP structure earlier; this is because AD stores group membership as attributes on the LDAP entries of the users themselves.

Let's use our recently acquired knowledge of explicit bean configuration to write an `LdapAuthoritiesPopulator` implementation that obtains `GrantedAuthority` from the user's `memberOf` attribute. In the following section, you will find the `ActiveDirectoryLdapAuthoritiesPopulator.java` file that is provided in this chapter's sample code:

```
//src/main/java/com/packtpub/springsecurity/ldap/userdetails/ad/
ActiveDirectoryLdapAuthoritiesPopulator.java

public final class ActiveDirectoryLdapAuthoritiesPopulator
implements LdapAuthoritiesPopulator {
   public Collection<? extends GrantedAuthority>
     getGrantedAuthorities(DirContextOperations userData, String
     username) {
       String[] groups = userData.getStringAttributes("memberOf");
       List<GrantedAuthority> authorities = new
        ArrayList<GrantedAuthority>();
     for (String group : groups) {
       LdapRdn authority = new DistinguishedName(group).removeLast();
       authorities.add(new SimpleGrantedAuthority
       (authority.getValue()));
   }
   return authorities;
 }
}
```

Now, we need to alter our configuration to support our AD structure. Assuming we are starting with the bean configuration detailed in the previous section, make the following updates:

```
//src/main/java/com/packtpub/springsecurity/configuration/SecurityConfig.ja
va

@Bean
public DefaultSpringSecurityContextSource contextSource() {
    return new DefaultSpringSecurityContextSource(Arrays.asList
    ("ldap://corp.jbcpcalendar.com/"), "dc=corp,dc=jbcpcalendar,
    dc=com"){{
         setUserDn("CN=Administrator,CN=Users," +
         "DC=corp,DC=jbcpcalendar,DC=com");
         setPassword("admin123!");
    }};
}
```

```
@Bean
public LdapAuthenticationProvider authenticationProvider(
BindAuthenticator ba, LdapAuthoritiesPopulator lap){
    // removed UserDetailsContextMapper
    return new LdapAuthenticationProvider(ba, lap);
}
@Bean
public FilterBasedLdapUserSearch filterBasedLdapUserSearch(){
    return new FilterBasedLdapUserSearch("CN=Users", //user-search-base
    "(sAMAccountName={0})", //user-search-filter
    contextSource()); //ldapServer
}
@Bean
public LdapAuthoritiesPopulator authoritiesPopulator(){
    return new ActiveDirectoryLdapAuthoritiesPopulator();
}
```

If you have it defined, you will want to remove the `UserDetailsService` declaration in the `SecurityConfig.java` file. Finally, you will want to remove the references to `UserDetailsService` from `AccountController`.

The `sAMAccountName` attribute is the AD equivalent of the `uid` attribute we use in a standard LDAP entry. Although most AD LDAP integrations are likely to be more complex than this example, this should give you a starting point to jump off and explore your conceptual understanding of the inner workings of Spring Security LDAP integration; supporting even a complex integration will be much easier.

> If you want to run this sample, you will need an instance of AD up and running that matches the schema displayed in the screenshot. The alternative is to adjust the configuration to match your AD schema. A simple way to play around with AD is to install **Active Directory Lightweight Directory Services**, which can be found at `http://www.microsoft.com/download/en/details.aspx?id=14683`. Your code should look like `chapter05.09-calendar`.

Built-in AD support in Spring Security 4.2

Spring Security added AD support in Spring Security 3.1. In fact, the `ActiveDirectoryLdapAuthoritiesPopulator` class from the previous section is based on the newly-added support. To utilize the built-in support in Spring Security 4.2, we can replace our entire `SecurityConfig.java` file with the following configuration:

```
//src/main/java/com/packtpub/springsecurity/configuration/SecurityConfig.ja
```

```
va

    @Bean
    public AuthenticationProvider authenticationProvider(){
        ActiveDirectoryLdapAuthenticationProvider ap = new
        ActiveDirectoryLdapAuthenticationProvider("corp.jbcpcalendar.com",
        "ldap://corp.jbcpcalendar.com/");
        ap.setConvertSubErrorCodesToExceptions(true);
        return ap;
    }
```

Of course, if you are going to use it, you need to ensure that you wire it to
AuthenticationManager. We have already done this, but a reminder of what the
configuration looks like can be found in the following code snippet:

```
//src/main/java/com/packtpub/springsecurity/configuration/SecurityConfig.ja
va

    @Autowired
    private AuthenticationProvider authenticationProvider;
    @Override
    public void configure(AuthenticationManagerBuilder auth)
    throws Exception {
        auth.authenticationProvider(authenticationProvider);
    }
```

There are a few things that should be noted about the provided
ActiveDirectoryLdapAuthenticationProvider class, as follows:

- The users that need to be authenticated must be able to bind to AD (there is no
  manager user.
- The default method for populating users' authorities is to search the users'
  memberOf attributes.
- Users must contain an attribute named userPrincipalName, which is in the
  username@<domain> format. Here, <domain> is the first constructor argument
  to ActiveDirectoryLdapAuthenticationProvider. This is due to the fact
  that, after the bind occurs, this is how the context for the memberOf lookup is
  found.

Due to the complex LDAP deployments that occur in the real world, the built-in support
will most likely provide a guide to as how you can integrate with your custom LDAP
schema.

Summary

We have seen that LDAP servers can be relied on to provide authentication and authorization information, as well as rich user profile information when requested. In this chapter, we covered the LDAP terminology and concepts, and how LDAP directories might be commonly organized to work with Spring Security. We also explored the configuration of both standalone (embedded) and external LDAP servers from a Spring Security configuration file.

We covered authentication and authorization of users against LDAP repositories, and subsequent mapping to Spring Security actors. We also saw the differences in authentication schemes, password storage, and security mechanisms in LDAP, and how they are treated in Spring Security. We also learned to map user detail attributes from the LDAP directory to the `UserDetails` object for rich information exchange between LDAP and the Spring-enabled application. We also explicited bean configuration for LDAP, and the pros and cons of this approach.

We also covered integration with AD.

In the next chapter, we will discuss Spring Security's **remember-me** feature, which allows a user's session to securely persist even after closing the browser.

7
Remember-Me Services

In this chapter, we'll add the ability for an application to remember a user even after their session has expired and the browser is closed. The following topics will be covered in this chapter:

- Discussing what remember-me is
- Learning how to use the **token-based remember-me** feature
- Discussing how secure remember-me is, and various ways of making it more secure
- Enabling the persistent-based remember-me feature, and how to handle additional considerations for using it
- Presenting the overall remember-me architecture
- Learning how to create a custom remember-me implementation that is restricted to the user's IP address

What is remember-me?

A convenient feature to offer frequent users of a website is the remember-me feature. This feature allows a user to elect to be remembered even after their browser is closed. In Spring Security, this is implemented through the use of a remember-me cookie that is stored in the user's browser. If Spring Security recognizes that the user is presenting a remember-me cookie, then the user will automatically be logged into the application, and will not need to enter a username or password.

What is a cookie?
A cookie is a way for a client (that is, a web browser) to persist the state. For more information about cookies, refer to additional online resources, such as Wikipedia (http://en.wikipedia.org/wiki/HTTP_cookie).

Spring Security provides the following two different strategies that we will discuss in this chapter:

- The first is the token-based remember-me feature, which relies on a cryptographic signature
- The second method, the **persistent-based remember-me** feature, requires a datastore (a database)

As we previously mentioned, we will discuss these strategies in much greater detail throughout this chapter. The remember-me feature must be explicitly configured in order to enable it. Let's start off by trying the token-based remember-me feature and see how it affects the flow of the login experience.

Dependencies

The token-based remember-me section does not need any additional dependencies other than the basic setup from Chapter 2, *Getting Started with Spring Security*. However, you will want to ensure you include the following additional dependencies in your pom.xml file if you are leveraging the persistent-based remember-me feature. We have already included these dependencies in the chapter's sample, so there is no need to update the sample application:

```
//build.gradle

dependencies {
// JPA / ORM / Hibernate:
  compile('org.springframework.boot:spring-boot-starter-data-jpa')
// H2 RDBMS
  runtime('com.h2database:h2')
    ...
}
```

The token-based remember-me feature

Spring Security provides two different implementations of the remember-me feature. We will start off by exploring how to set up token-based remember-me services.

Configuring the token-based remember-me feature

Completing this exercise will allow us to provide a simple and secure method to keep users logged in for extended periods of time. To start, perform the following steps:

1. Modify the `SecurityConfig.java` configuration file and add the `rememberMe` method.

   Take a look at the following code snippet:

   ```
   //src/main/java/com/packtpub/springsecurity/configuration/
   SecurityConfig.java

   @Override
   protected void configure(HttpSecurity http) throws Exception {
       ...
       http.rememberMe().key("jbcpCalendar")
       ...
   }
   ```

   You should start with `chapter07.00-calendar`.

2. If we try running the application now, we'll see nothing different in the flow. This is because we also need to add a field to the login form that allows the user to opt for this functionality. Edit the `login.html` file and add a checkbox, as shown in the following code snippet:

   ```
   //src/main/resources/templates/login.html

   <input type="password" id="password" name="password"/>
   <label for="remember-me">Remember Me?</label>
   <input type="checkbox" id="remember-me" name="remember_me"
   value="true"/>
   <div class="form-actions">
      <input id="submit" class="btn" name="submit" type="submit"
      value="Login"/>
   </div>
   ```

Your code should look like `chapter07.01-calendar`.

3. When we next log in, if the remember-me box is selected, a remember-me cookie is set in the user's browser.

   Spring Security understands that it should remember the user by inspecting the HTTP parameter `remember_me`.

 In Spring Security 3.1 and earlier versions, the default parameter for the remember-me form field was `spring_security_remember_me`. Now, in Spring Security 4.x, the default remember-me form field is `remember-me`. This can be overridden with the `rememberMeParameter` method.

4. If the user then closes his/her browser and reopens it to an authenticated page on the JBCP calendar website, he/she won't be presented with the login page a second time. Try it yourself now—log in with the remember-me option selected, bookmark the home page, then restart the browser and access the home page. You'll see that you're immediately logged in successfully without needing to supply your login credentials again. If this appears to be happening to you, it means that your browser or a browser plugin is restoring the session.

 Try closing the tab first and then close the browser.

One more effective solution is to use a browser plugin, such as **Firebug** (`https://addons.mozilla.org/en-US/firefox/addon/firebug/`), to remove the `JSESSIONID` cookie. This can often save time and annoyance during the development and verification of this type of feature on your site.

After logging in and selecting remember-me, you should see two cookies have been set, JSESSIONID and remember-me, as shown in the following screenshot:

How the token-based remember-me feature works

The remember-me feature sets a cookie in the user's browser containing a Base64-encoded string with the following pieces:

- The username
- An expiration date/time
- An MD5 hash value of the expiration date/time, username, password, and the key attribute of the rememberMe method

These are combined into a single cookie value that is stored in the browser for later use.

MD5

MD5 is one of the several well-known cryptographic hash algorithms. Cryptographic hash algorithms compute a compact and unique text representation of input data with arbitrary length, called a **digest**. This digest can be used to determine if an untrusted input should be trusted by comparing the digest of the untrusted input to a known valid digest of the expected input.

The following diagram illustrates how this works:

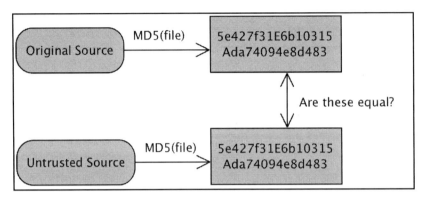

For example, many open source software sites allow mirrors to distribute their software to help increase download speeds. However, as a user of the software, we would want to be sure that the software is authentic and doesn't include any viruses. The software distributor will calculate and publish the expected MD5 checksum on their website with their known, good version of the software. Then, we can download the file from any location. Before we install the software, we calculate the untrusted MD5 checksum on the file we downloaded. We then compare the untrusted MD5 checksum to the expected MD5 checksum. If the two values match, we know that we can safely install the file we downloaded. If the two values do not match, we should not trust the downloaded file and delete it.

Although it is impossible to obtain the original data from the hash value, MD5 is vulnerable to several types of attack, including the exploitation of weaknesses in the algorithm itself and rainbow table attacks. Rainbow tables typically contain the pre-computed hash values of millions of input values. This allows attackers to look for the hash value in the rainbow table and determine the actual (unhashed) value. Spring Security combats this by including the expiration date, the user's password, and the remember-me key in the hashed value.

Remember-me signature

We can see how MD5 can ensure that we have downloaded the correct file, but how does this apply to Spring Security's remember-me service? Much like the file we downloaded, the cookie is untrusted, but we can trust it if we can validate the signature that originated from our application. When a request comes in with the remember-me cookie, its contents are extracted and the expected signature is compared to the signature found in the cookie. The steps in calculating the expected signature are illustrated in the following diagram:

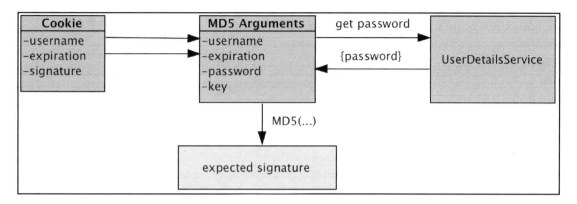

The remember-me cookie contains the **username, expiration**, and a **signature**. Spring Security will extract the **username** and **expiration** from the cookie. It will then utilize the username from the cookie to look up the **password** using `UserDetailsService`. The **key** is already known because it was provided using the `rememberMe` method. Now that all of the arguments are known, Spring Security can calculate the expected signature using the **username, expiration, password**, and **key**. It then compares the **expected signature** against the cookie's **signature**.

If the two signatures match, we can trust that the **username** and **expiration** date are valid. Forging a **signature** is next to impossible without knowing the remember-me key (which only the application knows) and the user's password (which only this user knows). This means if the signatures match and if the token is not expired, the user can be logged in.

You have anticipated that if the user changes their username or password, any remember-me token set will no longer be valid. Make sure that you provide appropriate messaging to users if you allow them to change these bits of their account. Later in this chapter, we will look at an alternative remember-me implementation that is reliant only on the username and not on the password.

Note that it is still possible to differentiate between users who have been authenticated with a remember-me cookie and users who have presented the username and password (or equivalent) credentials. We'll experiment with this shortly when we investigate the security of the remember-me feature.

Token-based remember-me configuration directives

The following two configuration changes are commonly made to alter the default behavior of the remember-me functionality:

Attribute	Description
`key`	Defines a unique key used when producing the remember-me cookie's signature.
`tokenValiditySeconds`	Defines the length of time (in seconds). The remember-me cookie will be considered valid for authentication. It is also used to set the cookie expiration timestamp.

As you may infer from the discussion of how the cookie contents are hashed, the `key` attribute is critical for the security of the remember-me feature. Make sure that the key you choose is likely to be unique to your application and long enough so that it can't be easily guessed.

Keeping in mind the purpose of this book, we've kept the key values relatively simple, but if you're using remember-me in your own application, it's suggested that your key contains the unique name of your application and is at least 36 random characters long. Password generator tools (search Google for "online password generator") are a great way to get a pseudo-random mix of alphanumeric and special characters to compose your remember-me key. For applications that exist in multiple environments (such as development, test, and production), the remember-me cookie value should include this fact as well. This will prevent remember-me cookies from inadvertently being used in the wrong environment during testing!

An example key value in a production application might be similar to the following:

```
prodJbcpCalendar-rmkey-paLLwApsifs24THosE62scabWow78PEaCh99Jus
```

The `tokenValiditySeconds` method is used to set the number of seconds after which the remember-me token will not be accepted for the automatic login function, even if it is otherwise a valid token. The same attribute is also used to set the maximum lifetime of the remember-me cookie on the user's browser.

Configuration of the remember-me session cookies

If `tokenValiditySeconds` is set to -1, the login cookie will be set to a session cookie, which does not persist after the browser is closed by the user. The token will be valid (assuming the user doesn't close the browser) for a non-configurable length of two weeks. Don't confuse this with the cookie that stores your user's session ID—they're two different things with similar names!

You may have noticed that we listed very few attributes. Don't worry, we will spend time covering some of the other configuration attributes throughout this chapter.

Is remember-me secure?

Any feature related to security that has been added for user convenience has the potential to expose our carefully-protected site to a security risk. The remember-me feature, in its default form, runs the risk of the user's cookie being intercepted and reused by a malicious user. The following diagram illustrates how this might happen:

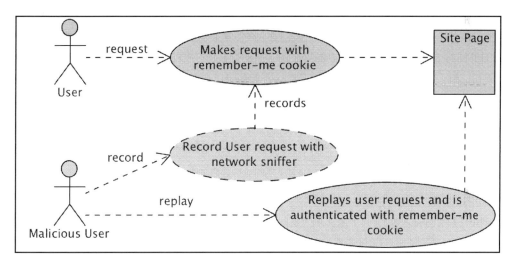

The use of SSL (covered in the `Appendix`, *Additional Reference Material*) and other network security techniques can mitigate this type of attack, but be aware that there are other techniques, such as **cross-site scripting** (**XSS**), that can steal or compromise a remembered user session. While convenient for the user, we don't want to risk financial or other personal information being inadvertently changed or possibly stolen if the remembered session is misused.

Although we don't cover malicious user behavior in detail in this book, when implementing any secured system, it is important to understand the techniques employed by users who may be trying to hack your customers or employees. XSS is one such technique, but many others exist. It's highly recommended that you review the *OWASP Top Ten article* (`http://www.owasp.org/index.php/Category:OWASP_Top_Ten_Project`) for a good list, and also pick up a web application security reference book in which many of the techniques demonstrated are illustrated to apply to any technology.

One common approach for maintaining the balance between convenience and security is identifying the functional locations on the site where personal or sensitive information could be present. You can then use the `fullyAuthenticated` expression to ensure these locations are protected using an authorization that checks not just the user's role, but that they have been authenticated with a full username and password. We will explore this feature in greater detail in the next section.

Authorization rules for remember-me

We'll fully explore the advanced authorization techniques later in Chapter 11, *Fine-Grained Access Control*, however, it's important to realize that it's possible to differentiate access rules based on whether or not an authenticated session was remembered.

Let's assume we want to limit users trying to access the H2 admin console to administrators who have been authenticated using a username and password. This is similar to the behavior found in other major consumer-focused commerce sites, which restrict access to the elevated portions of the site until a password is entered. Keep in mind that every site is different, so don't blindly apply such rules to your secure site. For our sample application, we'll concentrate on protecting the H2 database console. Update the `SecurityConfig.java` file to use the keyword `fullyAuthenticated`, which ensures that remembered users who try to access the H2 database are denied access. This is shown in the following code snippet:

```
//src/main/java/com/packtpub/springsecurity/configuration/SecurityConfig.java

@Override
protected void configure(HttpSecurity http) throws Exception {
    ...
    http.authorizeRequests()
        .antMatchers("/admin/*")
        .access("hasRole(ADMIN) and isFullyAuthenticated()")
    ...
```

```
http.rememberMe().key("jbcpCalendar")
}
```

The existing rules remain unchanged. We've added a rule that requires requests for account information to have the appropriate `GrantedAuthority` of ROLE_ADMIN, and that the user is fully authenticated; that is, during this authenticated session, they have actually presented a username and password or other suitable credentials. Note the syntax of the SpEL logical operators here—AND, OR, and NOT are used for logical operators in SpEL. This was thoughtful of the SpEL designers, as the `&&` operator would be awkward to represent in XML, even though the preceding example is using Java-based configuration!

 Your code should look like `chapter07.02-calendar`.

Go ahead and log in with the username `admin1@example.com` and the password `admin1`, ensuring you select the remember-me feature. Access the H2 database console and you will see that the access is granted. Now, delete the `JSESSIONID` cookie (or close the tab and then all of the browser instances), and ensure that access is still granted to the **All Events** page. Now, navigate to the H2 console and observe that the access is denied.

This approach combines the usability enhancements of the remember-me feature with an additional level of security by requiring a user to present a full set of credentials to access sensitive information. Throughout the rest of the chapter, we will explore other ways of making the remember-me feature more secure.

Persistent remember-me

Spring Security provides the capability to alter the method for validating the remember-me cookie by leveraging different implementations of the `RememberMeServices` interface. In this section, we will discuss how we can use persistent remember-me tokens using a database, and how this can increase the security of our application.

Using the persistent-based remember-me feature

Modifying our remember-me configuration at this point to persist to the database is surprisingly trivial. The Spring Security configuration parser will recognize a new `tokenRepository` method on the `rememberMe` method, and simply switch implementation classes for `RememberMeServices`. Let's now review the steps required to accomplish this.

Adding SQL to create the remember-me schema

We have placed the SQL file containing the expected schema in our `resources` folder in the same place we did in Chapter 3, *Custom Authentication*. You can view the schema definition in the following code snippet:

```
//src/main/resources/schema.sql

...
create table persistent_logins (
    username varchar_ignorecase(100) not null,
    series varchar(64) primary key,
    token varchar(64) not null,
    last_used timestamp not null
);
...
```

Initializing the data source with the remember-me schema

Spring Data will automatically initialize the embedded database with the `schema.sql`, as described in the preceding section. Note, however, that with JPA, in order for the schema to be created and the `data.sql` file used to seed the database, we must ensure we set `ddl-auto` to none, as shown in the following code:

```
//src/main/resources/application.yml

spring:
jpa:
    database-platform: org.hibernate.dialect.H2Dialect
    hibernate:
      ddl-auto: none
```

Configuring the persistent-based remember-me feature

Finally, we'll need to make some brief configuration changes to the `rememberMe` declaration to point it to the data source we're using, as shown in the following code snippet:

```java
//src/main/java/com/packtpub/springsecurity/configuration/SecurityConfig.java

@Autowired
@SuppressWarnings("SpringJavaAutowiringInspection")
    private DataSource dataSource;
@Autowired
private PersistentTokenRepository persistentTokenRepository;
@Override
protected void configure(HttpSecurity http) throws Exception {
    ...
    http.rememberMe()
        .key("jbcpCalendar")
        .tokenRepository(persistentTokenRepository)
    ...
}
@Bean
public PersistentTokenRepository persistentTokenRepository() {
    JdbcTokenRepositoryImpl db = new JdbcTokenRepositoryImpl();
    db.setDataSource(dataSource);
    return db;
}
```

This is all we need to do to switch over to using persistent-based remember-me authentication. Go ahead and start up the application and give it a try. From a user standpoint, we do not notice any differences, but we know that the implementation backing this feature has changed.

 Your code should look like `chapter07.03-calendar`.

How does the persistent-based remember-me feature work?

Instead of validating a signature present in the cookie, the persistent-based remember-me service validates if the token exists in a database. Each persistent remember-me cookie consists of the following:

- **Series identifier**: This identifies the initial login of a user and remains consistent each time the user is automatically logged in to the original session
- **Token value**: A unique value that changes each time a user is authenticated using the remember-me feature

Take a look at the following diagram:

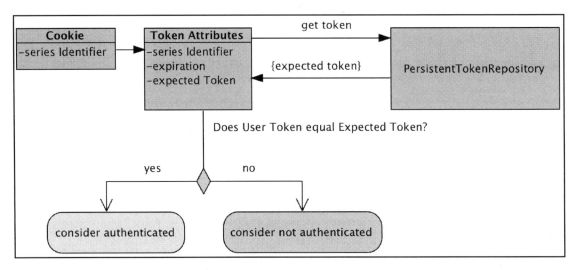

When the remember-me cookie is submitted, Spring Security will use an `o.s.s.web.authentication.rememberme.PersistentTokenRepository` implementation to look up the expected token value and an expiration using the submitted series identifier. It will then compare the token value in the cookie to the expected token value. If the token is not expired and the two tokens match, the user is considered authenticated. A new remember-me cookie with the same series identifier, a new token value, and an updated expiration date will be generated.

If the series token submitted is found in the database, but the tokens do not match, it can be assumed that someone stole the remember-me cookie. In this case, Spring Security will terminate these series of remember-me tokens and warn the user that their login has been compromised.

The persisted tokens can be found in the database and viewed with the H2 console, as shown in the following screenshot:

JPA-based PersistentTokenRepository

As we have seen in the earlier chapters, using a Spring Data project for our database mapping can greatly simplify our work. So, to keep things consistent, we are going to refactor our JDBC-based `PersistentTokenRepository` interface that uses `JdbcTokenRepositoryImpl` to one that is JPA-based. We will do so by performing the following steps:

1. First, let's create a domain object to hold the persistent logins, as shown in the following code snippet:

```
//src/main/java/com/packtpub/springsecurity/domain/
PersistentLogin.java

import org.springframework.security.web.authentication.rememberme.
PersistentRememberMeToken;
import javax.persistence.*;
import java.io.Serializable;
import java.util.Date;
@Entity
@Table(name = "persistent_logins")
public class PersistentLogin implements Serializable {
    @Id
    private String series;
    private String username;
    private String token;
```

```
        private Date lastUsed;
        public PersistentLogin(){}
        public PersistentLogin(PersistentRememberMeToken token){
            this.series = token.getSeries();
            this.username = token.getUsername();
            this.token = token.getTokenValue();
            this.lastUsed = token.getDate();
        }
    ...
```

2. Next, we need to create a `o.s.d.jpa.repository.JpaRepository` repository instance, as shown in the following code snippet:

```
//src/main/java/com/packtpub/springsecurity/repository/
RememberMeTokenRepository.java

import com.packtpub.springsecurity.domain.PersistentLogin;
import org.springframework.data.jpa.repository.JpaRepository;
import java.util.List;
public interface RememberMeTokenRepository extends
JpaRepository<PersistentLogin, String> {
    PersistentLogin findBySeries(String series);
    List<PersistentLogin> findByUsername(String username);
}
```

3. Now, we need to create a custom `PersistentTokenRepository` interface to replace the `Jdbc` implementation. We have four methods we must override, but the code should look fairly familiar as we will be using JPA for all of the operations:

```
//src/main/java/com/packtpub/springsecurity/web/authentication/
rememberme/JpaPersistentTokenRepository.java:

...
public class JpaPersistentTokenRepository implements
PersistentTokenRepository {
    private RememberMeTokenRepository rememberMeTokenRepository;
    public JpaPersistentTokenRepository
    (RememberMeTokenRepository rmtr) {
        this.rememberMeTokenRepository = rmtr;
    }
    @Override
    public void createNewToken(PersistentRememberMeToken token) {
        PersistentLogin newToken = new PersistentLogin(token);
        this.rememberMeTokenRepository.save(newToken);
    }
    @Override
```

```
      public void updateToken(String series, String tokenValue,
      Date lastUsed) {
            PersistentLogin token = this.rememberMeTokenRepository
            .findBySeries(series);
            if (token != null) {
                token.setToken(tokenValue);
                token.setLastUsed(lastUsed);
                this.rememberMeTokenRepository.save(token);
            }
      }
@Override
    public PersistentRememberMeToken
    getTokenForSeries(String seriesId) {
            PersistentLogin token = this.rememberMeTokenRepository
            .findBySeries(seriesId);
            return new PersistentRememberMeToken(token.getUsername(),
            token.getSeries(), token.getToken(), token.getLastUsed());
    }
    @Override
    public void removeUserTokens(String username) {
        List<PersistentLogin> tokens = this.rememberMeTokenRepository
        .findByUsername(username);
         this.rememberMeTokenRepository.delete(tokens);
    }
}
```

4. Now, we need to make a few changes in the `SecurityConfig.java` file to
   declare the new `PersistentTokenTokenRepository` interface, but the rest of
   the configuration from the last section does not change, as shown in the following
   code snippet:

```
//src/main/java/com/packtpub/springsecurity/configuration/
SecurityConfig.java

//@Autowired
//@SuppressWarnings("SpringJavaAutowiringInspection")
//private DataSource dataSource;
@Autowired
private PersistentTokenRepository persistentTokenRepository;
...
@Bean
public PersistentTokenRepository persistentTokenRepository(
    RememberMeTokenRepository rmtr) {
    return new JpaPersistentTokenRepository(rmtr);
}
```

5. This is all we need to do to switch JDBC to JPA persistent-based remember-me authentication. Go ahead and start up the application and give it a try. From a user standpoint, we do not notice any differences, but we know that the implementation backing this feature has changed.

Your code should look like `chapter07.04-calendar`.

Custom RememberMeServices

Up to this point, we have used a fairly simple implementation of `PersistentTokenRepository`. We have used a JDBC-backed and JPA-backed implementation. This provided limited control over the cookie persistence; if we want more control, we wrap our `PersistentTokenRepository` interface in `RememberMeServices`. Barry Jaspan has a great article on *Improved Persistent Login Cookie Best Practice* (`http://jaspan.com/improved_persistent_login_cookie_best_practice`). Spring Security has a slightly modified version, as previously described, called `PersistentTokenBasedRememberMeServices`, which we can wrap our custom `PersistentTokenRepository` interface in and use in our remember-me service.

In the following section, we are going to wrap our existing `PersistentTokenRepository` interface with `PersistentTokenBasedRememberMeServices` and the use of the `rememberMeServices` method to wire it into our remember-me declaration:

```
//src/main/java/com/packtpub/springsecurity/configuration/SecurityConfig.java

    //@Autowired
    //private PersistentTokenRepository persistentTokenRepository;
    @Autowired
    private RememberMeServices rememberMeServices;
    @Override
    protected void configure(HttpSecurity http) throws Exception {
        ...
        http.rememberMe()
            .key("jbcpCalendar")
            .rememberMeServices(rememberMeServices)
        ...
    }
    @Bean
    public RememberMeServices rememberMeServices
```

```
(PersistentTokenRepository ptr){
    PersistentTokenBasedRememberMeServices rememberMeServices = new
    PersistentTokenBasedRememberMeServices("jbcpCalendar",
    userDetailsService, ptr);
    rememberMeServices.setAlwaysRemember(true);
    return rememberMeServices;
}
```

 Your code should look like `chapter07.05-calendar`.

Are database-backed persistent tokens more secure?

Just like `TokenBasedRememberMeServices`, persistent tokens may be compromised by cookie theft or other man-in-the-middle techniques. The use of SSL, as covered in the `Appendix`, *Additional Reference Material* can circumvent man-in-the-middle techniques. If you are using a Servlet 3.0 environment (that is, Tomcat 7+), Spring Security will mark the cookie as `HttpOnly`, which will help to mitigate against the cookie being stolen in the event of an XSS vulnerability in the application. To learn more about the `HttpOnly` attribute, refer to the external resource on cookies provided earlier in the chapter.

One of the advantages of using the persistent-based remember-me feature is that we can detect if the cookie is compromised. If the correct series token and an incorrect token is presented, we know that any remember-me feature using that series token should be considered compromised, and we should terminate any sessions associated with it. Since the validation is stateful, we can also terminate the specific remember-me feature without needing to change the user's password.

Cleaning up the expired remember-me sessions

The downside of using the persistent-based remember-me feature is that there is no built-in support for cleaning up the expired sessions. In order to do this, we need to implement a background process that cleans up the expired sessions. We have included code in the chapter's sample code to perform the cleanup.

For conciseness, we display a version that does not do validation or error handling in the following code snippet. You can view the full version in the sample code of this chapter:

```
//src/main/java/com/packtpub/springsecurity/web/authentication/rememberme/
    JpaTokenRepositoryCleaner.java

    public class JpaTokenRepositoryImplCleaner
    implements Runnable {
        private final RememberMeTokenRepository repository;
        private final long tokenValidityInMs;
        public JpaTokenRepositoryImplCleaner(RememberMeTokenRepository
        repository, long tokenValidityInMs) {
            if (rememberMeTokenRepository == null) {
                throw new IllegalArgumentException("jdbcOperations cannot
                be null");
            }
            if (tokenValidityInMs < 1) {
                throw new IllegalArgumentException("tokenValidityInMs
                must be greater than 0. Got " + tokenValidityInMs);
            }
            this. repository = repository;
            this.tokenValidityInMs = tokenValidityInMs;
        }
        public void run() {
        long expiredInMs = System.currentTimeMillis()
        - tokenValidityInMs;
            try {
            Iterable<PersistentLogin> expired =
            rememberMeTokenRepository
            .findByLastUsedAfter(new Date(expiredInMs));
            for(PersistentLogin pl: expired){
                rememberMeTokenRepository.delete(pl);
            }
        } catch(Throwable t) {...}
    }
}
```

The sample code for this chapter also includes a simple Spring configuration that will execute the cleaner every ten minutes. If you are unfamiliar with Spring's task abstraction and want to learn it, then you may want to read more about it in the Spring Reference at https://docs.spring.io/spring/docs/current/spring-framework-reference/html/ scheduling.html. You can find the relevant configuration in the following code snippet. For clarity, we are putting this scheduler in the JavaConfig.java file:

```
//src/main/java/com/packtpub/springsecurity/configuration/
JavaConfig.java@Configuration
```

```
@Import({SecurityConfig.class})
@EnableScheduling
public class JavaConfig {
    @Autowired
    private RememberMeTokenRepository rememberMeTokenRepository;
    @Scheduled(fixedRate = 10_000)
    public void tokenRepositoryCleaner(){
        Thread trct = new Thread(new JpaTokenRepositoryCleaner(
        rememberMeTokenRepository, 60_000L));
        trct.start();
    }
}
```

Keep in mind that this configuration is not cluster-aware. Therefore, if this is deployed to a cluster, the cleaner will execute once for every JVM that the application is deployed to.

Start up the application and give the updates a try. The configuration that was provided will ensure that the cleaner is executed every ten minutes. You may want to change the cleaner task to run more frequently and to clean up the more recently used remember-me tokens by modifying the @Scheduled declaration. You can then create a few remember-me tokens and see that they get deleted by querying for them in the H2 database console.

Your code should look like chapter07.06-calendar.

The remember-me architecture

We have gone over the basic architecture of both TokenBasedRememberMeServices and PersistentTokenBasedRememberMeServices, but we have not described the overall architecture. Let's see how all of the remember-me pieces fit together.

The following diagram illustrates the different components involved in the process of validating a token-based remember-me token:

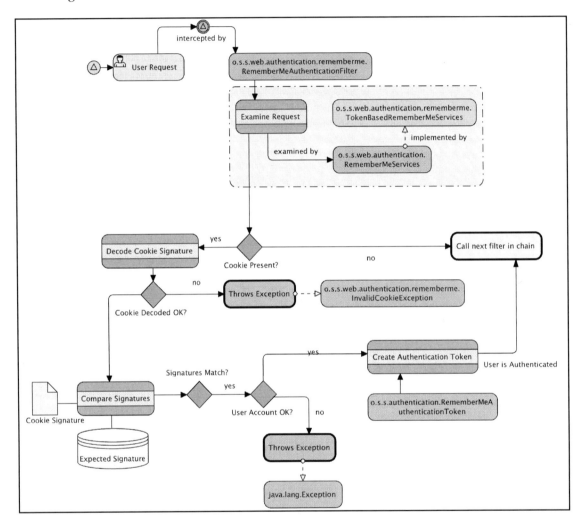

As with any of the Spring Security filters, `RememberMeAuthenticationFilter` is invoked from within `FilterChainProxy`. The job of `RememberMeAuthenticationFilter` is to inspect the request, and if it is of interest, an action is taken. The `RememberMeAuthenticationFilter` interface will use the `RememberMeServices` implementation to determine if the user is already logged in. The `RememberMeServices` interface does this by inspecting the HTTP request for a remember-me cookie that is then validated using either the token-based validation or the persistent-based validation we previously discussed. If the token checks out, the user will be logged in.

Remember-me and the user life cycle

The implementation of `RememberMeServices` is invoked at several points in the user life cycle (the life cycle of an authenticated user's session). To assist you in your understanding of the remember-me functionality, it can be helpful to be aware of the points in time when remember-me services are informed of life cycle functions:

Action	What should happen?	The RememberMeServices method invoked
Successful login	Implementation sets a remember-me cookie (if the `form` parameter has been sent)	`loginSuccess`
Failed login	Implementation should cancel the cookie, if it's present	`loginFailed`
User logout	Implementation should cancel the cookie, if it's present	`logout`

The `logout` method is not present on the `RememberMeServices` interface. Instead, each `RememberMeServices` implementation also implements the `LogoutHandler` interface, which contains the `logout` method. By implementing the `LogoutHandler` interface, each `RememberMeServices` implementation can perform the necessary cleanup when the user logs out.

Knowing where and how `RememberMeServices` ties into the user's life cycle will be important when we begin to create custom authentication handlers, because we need to ensure that any authentication processor treats `RememberMeServices` consistently to preserve the usefulness and security of this functionality.

Restricting the remember-me feature to an IP address

Let's put our understanding of the remember-me architecture to use. A common requirement is that any remember-me token should be tied to the IP address of the user that created it. This adds additional security to the remember-me feature. To do this, we only need to implement a custom `PersistentTokenRepository` interface. The configuration changes that we will make will illustrate how to configure a custom `RememberMeServices`. Throughout this section, we will take a look at `IpAwarePersistentTokenRepository`, which is included in the chapter's source code. The `IpAwarePersistenTokenRepository` interface ensures that the series identifier is internally combined with the current user's IP address, and the series identifier includes only the identifier externally. This means that whenever a token is looked up or saved, the current IP address is used to lookup or persist the token. In the following code snippets, you can see how `IpAwarePersistentTokenRepository` works. If you want to dig in even deeper, we encourage you to view the source code included with the chapter.

The trick to looking up the IP address is using `RequestContextHolder` of Spring Security. The relevant code is as follows:

 It should be noted that in order to use `RequestContextHolder`, you need to ensure you have set up your `web.xml` file to use `RequestContextListener`. We have already performed this setup for our sample code. However, this can be useful when utilizing the example code in an external application. Refer to the Javadoc of `IpAwarePersistentTokenRepository` for details on how to set this up.

Take a look at the following code snippet:

```
//src/main/java/com/packtpub/springsecurity/web/authentication/rememberme/
    IpAwarePersistentTokenRepository.java

    private String ipSeries(String series) {
    ServletRequestAttributes attributes = (ServletRequestAttributes)
    RequestContextHolder.getRequestAttributes();
    return series + attributes.getRequest().getRemoteAddr();
    }
```

We can build on this method to force tokens that are saved to include the IP address in the series identifier, as follows:

```
public void createNewToken(PersistentRememberMeToken token) {
    String ipSeries = ipSeries(token.getSeries());
    PersistentRememberMeToken ipToken = tokenWithSeries(token, ipSeries);
    this.delegateRepository.createNewToken(ipToken);
}
```

You can see that we first created a new series with the IP address concatenated to it. The `tokenWithSeries` method is just a helper that creates a new token with all of the same values, except a new series. We then submit the new token with a series identifier that includes the IP address to `delegateRepsository`, which is the original implementation of `PersistentTokenRepository`.

Whenever the tokens are looked up, we require that the current user's IP address is appended to the series identifier. This means that there is no way for a user to obtain a token for a user with a different IP address:

```
public PersistentRememberMeToken getTokenForSeries(String seriesId) {
    String ipSeries = ipSeries(seriesId);
    PersistentRememberMeToken ipToken = delegateRepository.
    getTokenForSeries(ipSeries);
    return tokenWithSeries(ipToken, seriesId);
}
```

The remainder of the code is quite similar. Internally, we construct the series identifier to be appended to the IP address, and externally, we present only the original series identifier. By doing this, we enforce the constraint that only the user who created the remember-me token can use it.

Let's review the Spring configuration included in this chapter's sample code for `IpAwarePersistentTokenRepository`. In the following code snippet, we first create the `IpAwarePersistentTokenRepository` declaration that wraps a new `JpaPersistentTokenRepository` declaration. We then initialize a `RequestContextFilter` class by instantiating an `OrderedRequestContextFilter` interface:

```
//src/main/java/com/packtpub/springsecurity/web/configuration/WebMvcConfig.
java

@Bean
public IpAwarePersistentTokenRepository
tokenRepository(RememberMeTokenRepository rmtr) {
    return new IpAwarePersistentTokenRepository(
```

```
                    new JpaPersistentTokenRepository(rmtr)
        );
    }
    @Bean
    public OrderedRequestContextFilter requestContextFilter() {
        return new OrderedRequestContextFilter();
    }
```

In order for Spring Security to utilize our custom `RememberMeServices`, we need to update our security configuration to point to it. Go ahead and make the following updates to `SecurityConfig.java`:

```
//src/main/java/com/packtpub/springsecurity/configuration/SecurityConfig.ja
va

    @Override
    protected void configure(HttpSecurity http) throws Exception {
        ...
      // remember me configuration
      http.rememberMe()
            .key("jbcpCalendar")
            .rememberMeServices(rememberMeServices);
    }
    @Bean
    public RememberMeServices rememberMeServices
    (PersistentTokenRepository ptr){
        PersistentTokenBasedRememberMeServices rememberMeServices = new
        PersistentTokenBasedRememberMeServices("jbcpCalendar",
        userDetailsService, ptr);
        return rememberMeServices;
    }
```

Now, go ahead and start up the application. You can use the second computer along with a plugin, such as Firebug, to manipulate your remember-me cookie. If you try to use the remember-me cookie from one computer on another computer, Spring Security will now ignore the remember-me request and delete the associated cookie.

 Your code should look like `chapter07.07-calendar`.

Note that the IP-based remember-me tokens may behave unexpectedly if the user is behind a shared or load balanced network infrastructure, such as a multi-WAN corporate environment. In most scenarios, however, the addition of an IP address to the remember-me function provides an additional, welcome layer of security to a helpful user feature.

Custom cookie and HTTP parameter names

Curious users may wonder if the expected value of the remember-me form field checkbox to be remember-me, or the cookie name to be remember-me, can be changed to obscure the use of Spring Security. This change can be made in one of two locations. Take a look at the following steps:

1. First, we can add additional methods to the `rememberMe` method, as follows:

```
//src/main/java/com/packtpub/springsecurity/configuration/
SecurityConfig.java

http.rememberMe()
        .key("jbcpCalendar")
        .rememberMeParameter("jbcpCalendar-remember-me")
        .rememberMeCookieName("jbcpCalendar-remember-me");
```

2. Additionally, now that we've declared our own `RememberMeServices` implementation as a Spring bean, we can simply define more properties to change the checkbox and cookie names, as follows:

```
//src/main/java/com/packtpub/springsecurity/configuration/
SecurityConfig.java

@Bean
public RememberMeServices rememberMeServices
(PersistentTokenRepository ptr){
    PersistentTokenBasedRememberMeServices rememberMeServices = new
    PersistentTokenBasedRememberMeServices("jbcpCalendar",
    userDetailsService, ptr);
    rememberMeServices.setParameter("obscure-remember-me");
    rememberMeServices.setCookieName("obscure-remember-me");
    return rememberMeServices;
}
```

3. Don't forget to change the `login.html` page to set the name of the checkbox `form` field and to match the parameter value we declared. Go ahead and make the updates to `login.html`, as follows:

```
//src/main/resources/templates/login.html

<input type="checkbox" id="remember" name=" obscure-remember-me"
value="true"/>
```

4. We'd encourage you to experiment here to ensure you understand how these settings are related. Go ahead and start up the application and give it a try.

Your code should look like `chapter07.08-calendar`.

Summary

This chapter explained and demonstrated the use of the remember-me feature in Spring Security. We started with the most basic setup and learned how to gradually make the feature more secure. Specifically, we learned about a token-based remember-me service and how to configure it. We also explore how persistent-based remember-me services can provide additional security, how it works, and the additional considerations necessary when using them.

We also covered the creation of a custom remember-me implementation that restricts the remember-me token to a specific IP address. We saw various other ways to make the remember-me feature more secure.

Up next is certificate-based authentication, and we will discuss how to use trusted client-side certificates to perform authentication.

8
Client Certificate Authentication with TLS

Although username and password authentication is extremely common, as we discussed in Chapter 1, *Anatomy of an Unsafe Application*, and in Chapter 2, *Getting Started with Spring Security*, forms of authentication exist that allow users to present different types of credentials. Spring Security caters to these requirements as well. In this chapter, we'll move beyond form-based authentication to explore authentication using trusted client-side certificates.

During the course of this chapter, we will cover the following topics:

- Learning how client certificate authentication is negotiated between the user's browser and a compliant server
- Configuring Spring Security to authenticate users with client certificates
- Understanding the architecture of client certificate authentication in Spring Security
- Exploring advanced configuration options related to client certificate authentication
- Reviewing pros, cons, and common troubleshooting steps when dealing with client certificate authentication

How does client certificate authentication work?

Client certificate authentication requires a request for information from the server and a response from the browser to negotiate a trusted authentication relationship between the client (that is, a user's browser) and the server application. This trusted relationship is built through the use of the exchange of trusted and verifiable credentials, known as **certificates**.

Unlike much of what we have seen up to this point, with client certificate authentication, the servlet container or application server itself is typically responsible for negotiating the trust relationship between the browser and server by requesting a certificate, evaluating it, and accepting it as valid.

Client certificate authentication is also known as **mutual authentication** and is part of the **Secure Sockets Layer (SSL)** protocol and its successor, **Transport Layer Security (TLS)**. As mutual authentication is part of the SSL and TLS protocols, it follows that an HTTPS connection (secured with SSL or TLS) is required in order to make use of client certificate authentication. For more details on SSL/TLS support in Spring Security, please refer to our discussion and the implementation of SSL/TLS in the Appendix, *Additional Reference Material*. Setting up SSL/TLS in Tomcat (or the application server you have been using to follow along with the examples) is required to implement client certificate authentication. As in the Appendix, *Additional Reference Material* we will refer to SSL/TLS as SSL for the remainder of this chapter.

The following sequence diagram illustrates the interaction between the client browser and the web server when negotiating an SSL connection and validating the trust of a client certificate used for mutual authentication:

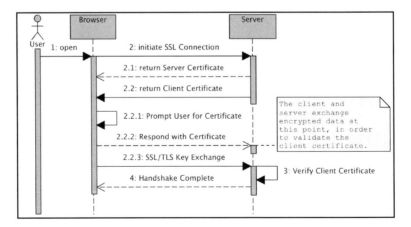

We can see that the exchange of two certificates, the server and client certificates, provides the authentication that both parties are known and can be trusted to continue their conversation securely. In the interest of clarity, we omit some details of the SSL handshake and trust the checking of the certificates themselves; however, you are encouraged to do further reading in the area of the SSL and TLS protocols, and certificates in general, as many good reference guides on these subjects exist. *RFC 5246, The Transport Layer Security (TLS) Protocol Version 1.2* (`http://tools.ietf.org/html/rfc5246`), is a good place to begin reading about client certificate presentation, and if you'd like to get into more detail, *SL and TLS: Designing and Building Secure Systems, Eric Rescorla, Addison-Wesley* (`https://www.amazon.com/SSL-TLS-Designing-Building-Systems/dp/0201615983`) has an incredibly detailed review of the protocol and its implementation.

An alternative name for client certificate-based authentication is X.509 authentication. The term X.509 is derived from the X.509 standard, originally published by the ITU-T organization for use in directories based on the X.500 standard (the origins of LDAP, as you may recall from `Chapter 6`, *LDAP Directory Services*). Later, this standard was adapted for use in securing internet communications.

We mention this here because many of the classes in Spring Security related to this subject refer to X.509. Remember that X.509 doesn't define the mutual authentication protocol itself, but defines the format and structure of the certificates and the encompassing trusted certificate authorities instead.

Setting up the client certificate authentication infrastructure

Unfortunately for you as an individual developer, being able to experiment with client certificate authentication requires some non-trivial configuration and setup prior to the relatively easy integration with Spring Security. As these setup steps tend to cause a lot of problems for first-time developers, we felt it was important to walk you through them.

We assume that you are using a local, self-signed server certificate, self-signed client certificates, and Apache Tomcat. This is typical of most development environments; however, it's possible that you may have access to a valid server certificate, a **certificate authority** (**CA**), or another application server. If this is the case, you may use these setup instructions as guidelines and configure your environment in an analogous manner. Please refer to the SSL setup instructions in the `Appendix`, *Additional Reference Material* for assistance on configuring Tomcat and Spring Security to work with SSL in a standalone environment.

Understanding the purpose of a public key infrastructure

This chapter focuses on setting up a self-contained development environment for the purposes of learning and education. However, in most cases where you are integrating Spring Security into an existing client certificate-secured environment, there will be a significant amount of infrastructure (usually a combination of hardware and software) in place to provide functionality, such as certificate granting and management, user self-service, and revocation. Environments of this type define a public key infrastructure—a combination of hardware, software, and security policies that result in a highly secure authentication-driven network ecosystem.

In addition to being used for web application authentication, certificates or hardware devices in these environments can be used for secure, non-repudiated email (using S/MIME), network authentication, and even physical building access (using PKCS 11-based hardware devices).

While the management overhead of such an environment can be high (and requires both IT and process excellence to implement well), it is arguably one of the most secure operating environments possible for technology professionals.

Creating a client certificate key pair

The self-signed client certificate is created in the same way as the self-signed server certificate is created—by generating a key pair using the `keytool` command. A client certificate key pair differs in that it requires the key store to be available to the web browser and requires the client's public key to be loaded into the server's trust store (we'll explain what this is in a moment).

If you do not wish to generate your own key right now, you may skip to the next section and use the sample certificates in the `./src/main/resources/keys` folder in the sample chapter. Otherwise, create the client key pair, as follows:

```
keytool -genkeypair -alias jbcpclient -keyalg RSA -validity 365 -keystore
jbcp_clientauth.p12 -storetype PKCS12
```

 You can find additional information about `keytool`, along with all of the configuration options, at Oracle's site, here `http://docs.oracle.com/javase/8/docs/technotes/tools/unix/keytool.html/keytool.html`.

Most of the arguments to `keytool` are fairly arbitrary for this use case. However, when prompted to set up the first and last name (the common name, or CN, the portion of the owner's DN) for the client certificate, ensure that the answer to the first prompt matches a user that we have set up in our Spring Security JDBC store. For example, `admin1@example.com` is an appropriate value since we have the `admin1@example.com` user setup in Spring Security. An example of the command-line interaction is as follows:

```
What is your first and last name?
[Unknown]: admin1@example.com
... etc
Is CN=admin1@example.com, OU=JBCP Calendar, O=JBCP, L=Park City, ST=UT,
C=US correct?
[no]: yes
```

We'll see why this is important when we configure Spring Security to access the information from the certificate-authenticated user. We have one final step before we can set up certificate authentication within Tomcat, which is explained in the next section.

Configuring the Tomcat trust store

Recall that the definition of a key pair includes both a private and public key. Similar to SSL certificates verifying and securing server communication, the validity of the client certificate needs to be verified by the certifying authority that created it.

As we have created our own self-signed client certificate using the `keytool` command, the Java VM will not implicitly trust it as having been assigned by a trusted certificate authority.

Let's take a look at the following steps:

1. We will need to force Tomcat to recognize the certificate as a trusted certificate. We do this by exporting the public key from the key pair and adding it to the Tomcat trust store.
2. Again, if you do not wish to perform this step now, you can use the existing trust store in `.src/main/resources/keys` and skip to where we configure `server.xml` later in this section.

3. We'll export the public key to a standard certificate file named
   `jbcp_clientauth.cer`, as follows:

```
keytool -exportcert -alias jbcpclient -keystore jbcp_clientauth.p12
-storetype PKCS12 -storepass changeit -file jbcp_clientauth.cer
```

4. Next, we'll import the certificate into the trust store (this will create the trust
   store, but in a typical deployment scenario you'd probably already have some
   other certificates in the trust store):

```
keytool -importcert -alias jbcpclient -keystore tomcat.truststore
-file jbcp_clientauth.cer
```

The preceding command will create the trust store called `tomcat.truststore`
and prompt you for a password (we chose the password `changeit`). You'll also
see some information about the certificate and will finally be asked to confirm that
you do trust the certificate, as follows:

```
Owner: CN=admin1@example.com, OU=JBCP Calendar, O=JBCP, L=Park City,
ST=UT, C=US
Issuer: CN=admin1@example.com, OU=JBCP Calendar, O=JBCP, L=Park City,
ST=UT, C=US
Serial number: 464fc10c
Valid from: Fri Jun 23 11:10:19 MDT 2017 until: Thu Feb 12 10:10:19
MST 2043

//Certificate fingerprints:

MD5:  8D:27:CE:F7:8B:C3:BD:BD:64:D6:F5:24:D8:A1:8B:50
SHA1:  C1:51:4A:47:EC:9D:01:5A:28:BB:59:F5:FC:10:87:EA:68:24:E3:1F
SHA256:  2C:F6:2F:29:ED:09:48:FD:FE:A5:83:67:E0:A0:B9:DA:C5:3B:
FD:CF:4F:95:50:3A:
2C:B8:2B:BD:81:48:BB:EF
Signature algorithm name: SHA256withRSA
Version: 3

//Extensions

#1: ObjectId: 2.5.29.14 Criticality=false
SubjectKeyIdentifier [
KeyIdentifier [
0000: 29 F3 A7 A1 8F D2 87 4B   EA 74 AC 8A 4B BC 4B 5D
)......K.t..K.K]
0010: 7C 9B 44 4A                                        ..DJ
]
]
Trust this certificate? [no]: yes
```

Remember the location of the new `tomcat.truststore` file, as we will need to reference it in our Tomcat configuration.

What's the difference between a key store and a trust store?

The **Java Secure Socket Extension** (**JSSE**) documentation defines a key store as a storage mechanism for private keys and their corresponding public keys. The key store (containing key pairs) is used to encrypt or decrypt secure messages, and so on. The trust store is intended to store only public keys for trusted communication partners when verifying an identity (similar to how the trust store is used in certificate authentication). In many common administration scenarios, however, the key store and trust store are combined into a single file (in Tomcat, this would be done through the use of the `keystoreFile` and `truststoreFile` attributes of the connector). The format of the files themselves can be exactly the same. Really, each file can be any JSSE-supported keystore format, including **Java KeyStore** (**JKS**), PKCS 12, and so on.

5. As previously mentioned, we assume you have already configured the SSL Connector, as outlined in the `Appendix`, *Additional Reference Material*. If you do not see the `keystoreFile` or `keystorePass` attributes in `server.xml`, it means you should visit the `Appendix`, *Additional Reference Material* to get SSL set up.

6. Finally, we'll need to point Tomcat at the trust store and enable client certificate authentication. This is done by adding three additional attributes to the SSL connector in the Tomcat `server.xml` file, as follows:

```
//sever.xml

<Connector port="8443" protocol="HTTP/1.1" SSLEnabled="true"
maxThreads="150" scheme="https" secure="true"
sslProtocol="TLS"
keystoreFile="<KEYSTORE_PATH>/tomcat.keystore"
keystorePass="changeit"
truststoreFile="<CERT_PATH>/tomcat.truststore"
truststorePass="changeit"
clientAuth="true"
/>
```

The `server.xml` file can be found at `TOMCAT_HOME/conf/server.xml`. If you are interacting with Tomcat using Eclipse or Spring Tool Suite, you will find a project named `Servers` that contains `server.xml`. For example, if you are using Tomcat 8, the path in your Eclipse workspace might look something similar to `/Servers/Tomcat v7.0 Server` at `localhost-config/server.xml`.

7. This should be the remaining configuration required to trigger Tomcat to request a client certificate when an SSL connection is made. Of course, you will want to ensure you replace both `<CERT_PATH>` and `<KEYSTORE_PATH>` with the full paths. For example, on a Unix-based operating system, the path might look like this: `/home/mickknutson/packt/chapter8/keys/tomcat.keystore`.

8. Go ahead and try to start up Tomcat to ensure that the server starts up without any errors in the logs.

There's also a way to configure Tomcat to optionally use client certificate authentication—we'll enable this later in the chapter. For now, we require the use of client certificates to even connect to the Tomcat server in the first place. This makes it easier to diagnose whether or not you have set this up correctly!

Configuring Tomcat in Spring Boot

We can also configure the embedded Tomcat instance within Spring Boot, which is how we will be working with Tomcat for the rest of this chapter.

Configuring Spring Boot to use our newly created certificates is as straightforward as properties of the YAML entry, as shown in the following code snippet:

```
server:
port: 8443
ssl:
    key-store: "classpath:keys/jbcp_clientauth.p12"
    key-store-password: changeit
    keyStoreType: PKCS12
    keyAlias: jbcpclient
    protocol: TLS
```

The final step is to import the certificate into the client browser.

Importing the certificate key pair into a browser

Depending on what browser you are using, the process of importing a certificate may differ. We will provide instructions for installations of Firefox, Chrome, and Internet Explorer here, but if you are using another browser, please consult its help section or your favorite search engine for assistance.

Using Firefox

Perform the following steps to import the key store containing the client certificate key pair in Firefox:

1. Click on **Edit | Preferences**.
2. Click on the **Advanced** button.
3. Click on the **Encryption** tab.
4. Click on the **View Certificates** button. The **Certificate Manager** window should open up.
5. Click on the **Your Certificates** tab.
6. Click on the **Import...** button.
7. Browse to the location where you saved the `jbcp_clientauth.p12` file and select it. You will need to enter the password (that is, `changeit`) that you used when you created the file.

The client certificate should be imported, and you should see it on the list.

Using Chrome

Perform the following steps to import the key store containing the client certificate key pair in Chrome:

1. Click on the wrench icon on the browser toolbar.
2. Select **Settings**.
3. Click on **Show advanced settings...**.
4. In the **HTTPS/SSL** section, click on the **Manage certificates...** button.
5. In the **Your Certificates** tab, click on the **Import...** button.

6. Browse to the location where you saved the `jbcp_clientauth.p12` file and select it.

7. You will need to enter the password (that is, `changeit`) that you used when you created the file.

8. Click on **OK**.

Using Internet Explorer

As Internet Explorer is tightly integrated into the Windows OS, it's a bit easier to import the key store. Let's take a look at the following steps:

1. Double-click on the `jbcp_clientauth.p12` file in Windows Explorer. The **Certificate Import Wizard** window should open.

2. Click on **Next** and accept the default values until you are prompted for the certificate password.

3. Enter the certificate password (that is, `changeit`) and click **Next**.

4. Accept the default **Automatically select the certificate store** option and click **Next**.

5. Click on **Finish**.

To verify that the certificate was installed correctly, you will need to perform another series of steps:

1. Open the **Tools** menu (*Alt* + *X*) in Internet Explorer.

2. Click on the **Internet Options** menu item.

3. Click on the **Content** tab.

4. Click on the **Certificates** button.

5. Click on the **Personal** tab, if it is not already selected. You should see the certificate listed here.

Wrapping up testing

You should now be able to connect to the JBCP calendar site using the client certificate. Navigate to `https://localhost:8443/`, taking care to use HTTPS and `8443`. If all is set up correctly, you should be prompted for a certificate when you attempt to access the site—in Firefox, the certificate is displayed as follows:

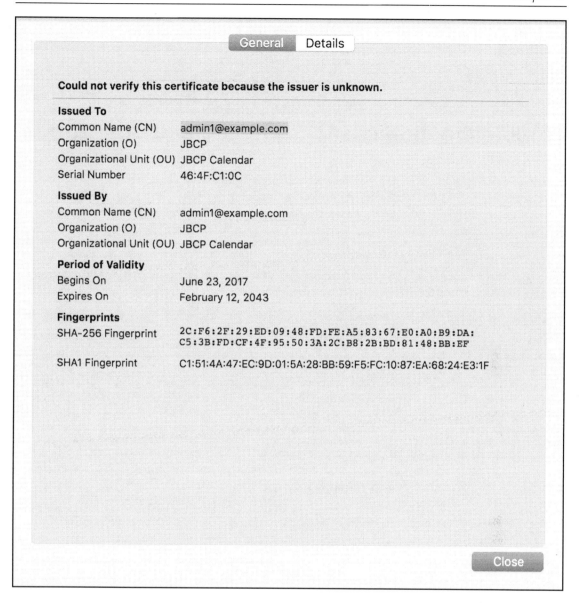

You'll notice, however, that if you attempt to access a protected section of the site, such as the **My Events** section, you'll be redirected to the login page. This is because we haven't yet configured Spring Security to recognize the information in the certificate—at this point, the negotiation between the client and server has stopped at the Tomcat server itself.

You should start with the code from `chapter08.00-calendar`.

Troubleshooting client certificate authentication

Unfortunately, if we said that getting client certificate authentication configured correctly for the first time—without anything going wrong—was easy, we'd be lying to you. The fact is, although this is a great and very powerful security apparatus, it is poorly documented by both the browser and web server manufacturers, and the error messages, when present, can be confusing at best and misleading at worst.

Remember that, at this point, we have not involved Spring Security in the equation at all, so a debugger will most likely not help you (unless you have the Tomcat source code handy). There are some common errors and things to check.

You aren't prompted for a certificate when you access the site. There are many possible causes for this, and this can be the most puzzling problem to try to solve. Here are some things to check:

1. Ensure that the certificate has been installed in the browser client you are using. Sometimes, you need to restart the whole browser (close all windows) if you attempted to access the site previously and were rejected.

2. Ensure you are accessing the SSL port for the server (typically `8443` in a development setup), and have selected the HTTPS protocol in your URL. The client certificates are not presented in insecure browser connections. Make sure the browser also trusts the server SSL certificate, even if you have to force it to trust a self-signed certificate.

3. Ensure you have added the `clientAuth` directive to your Tomcat configuration (or the equivalent for whatever application server you are using).

4. If all else fails, use a network analyzer or packet sniffer, such as Wireshark (`http://www.wireshark.org/`) or Fiddler2 (`http://www.fiddler2.com/`), to review the traffic and SSL key exchange over the wire (check with your IT department first—many companies do not allow tools of this kind on their networks).

5. If you are using a self-signed client certificate, make sure the public key has been imported into the server's trust store. If you are using a CA-assigned certificate, make sure the CA is trusted by the JVM or that the CA certificate is imported into the server's trust store.

6. Internet Explorer, in particular, does not report details of client certificate failures at all (it simply reports a generic `Page Cannot be Displayed` error). Use Firefox for diagnosing if an issue you are seeing is related to client certificates or not.

Configuring client certificate authentication in Spring Security

Unlike the authentication mechanisms that we have utilized thus far, the use of client certificate authentication results in the user's request being preauthenticated by the server. As the server (Tomcat) has already established that the user has provided a valid and trustworthy certificate, Spring Security can simply trust this assertion of validity.

An important component of the secure login process is still missing, that is, the authorization of the authenticated user. This is where our configuration of Spring Security comes in—we must add a component to Spring Security that will recognize the certificate authentication information from the user's HTTP session (populated by Tomcat), and then validate the presented credentials against the Spring Security `UserDetailsService` invocation. The invocation of `UserDetailsService` will result in the determination of whether the user declared in the certificate is known to Spring Security at all, and then it will assign `GrantedAuthority` as per the usual login rules.

Configuring client certificate authentication using the security namespace

With all of the complexity of LDAP configuration, configuring client certificate authentication is a welcome reprieve. If we are using the security namespace style of configuration, the addition of client certificate authentication is a simple one-line configuration change, added within the `HttpSecurity` declaration. Go ahead and make the following changes to the provided `SecurityConfig.java` configuration:

```
//src/main/java/com/packtpub/springsecurity/configuration/SecurityConfig.ja
va
    http.x509().userDetailsService(userDetailsService);
```

Observe that the `.x509()` method references our existing
`userDetailsService()` configuration. For simplicity, we use the
`UserDetailsServiceImpl` implementation covered in Chapter 5,
Authentication with Spring Data. However, we could easily swap this out
with any other implementation (that is, the LDAP or JDBC-based
implementation covered in Chapter 4, *JDBC-Based Authentication*).

After restarting the application, you'll again be prompted for a client certificate, but this
time, you should be able to access areas of the site requiring authorization. You can see
from the logs (if you have them enabled) that you have been logged in as the
`admin1@example.com` user.

 Your code should look like `chapter08.01-calendar`.

How does Spring Security use certificate information?

As previously discussed, Spring Security's involvement in certificate exchange is to pick up
information from the presented certificate and map the user's credentials to a user service.
What we did not see in the use of the `.x509()` method was the magic that makes this
happen. Recall that when we set the client certificate up, a DN similar to an LDAP DN was
associated with the certificate:

```
Owner: CN=admin@example.com, OU=JBCP Calendar, O=JBCP, L=Park City,
ST=UT, C=US
```

Spring Security uses the information in this DN to determine the actual username of the
principal and it will look for this information in `UserDetailsService`. In particular, it
allows for the specification of a regular expression, which is used to match a portion of the
DN established with the certificate, and the utilization of this portion of the DN as the
principal name. The implicit, default configuration for the `.x509()` method would be as
follows:

```
http.x509()
  .userDetailsService(userDetailsService)
  .subjectPrincipalRegex("CN=(.*?),");
```

We can see that this regular expression would match the `admin1@example.com` value as the principal's name. This regular expression must contain a single matching group, but it can be configured to support the username and DN issuance requirements of your application. For example, if the DNs for your organization's certificates include the `email` or `userid` fields, the regular expression can be modified to use these values as the authenticated principal's name.

How Spring Security certificate authentication works

Let's review the various actors involved in the review and evaluation of the client certificates and translation into a Spring Security-authenticated session, with the help of the following diagram:

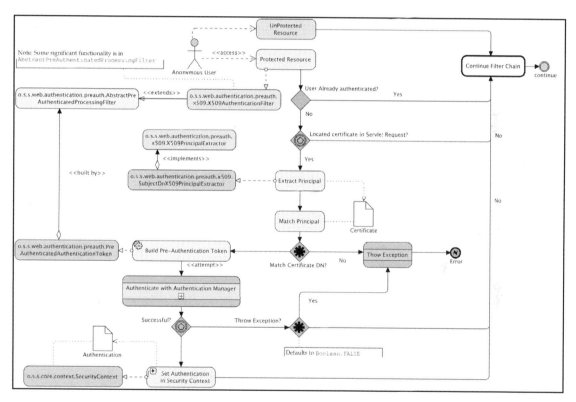

We can see that
`o.s.s.web.authentication.preauth.x509.X509AuthenticationFilter` is
responsible for examining the request of an unauthenticated user for the presentation of
client certificates. If it sees that the request includes a valid client certificate, it will extract
the principal using
`o.s.s.web.authentication.preauth.x509.SubjectDnX509PrincipalExtractor`,
using a regular expression matching the certificate owner's DN, as previously described.

Be aware that although the preceding diagram indicates that examination
of the certificate occurs for unauthenticated users, a check can also be
performed when the presented certificate identifies a different user than
the one that was previously authenticated. This would result in a new
authentication request using the newly provided credentials. The reason
for this should be clear—any time a user presents a new set of credentials,
the application must be aware of this and react in a responsible fashion by
ensuring that the user is still able to access it.

Once the certificate has been accepted (or rejected/ignored), as with other authentication
mechanisms, an `Authentication` token is built and passed along
to `AuthenticationManager` for authentication. We can now review the very brief
illustration of the
`o.s.s.web.authentication.preauth.PreAuthenticatedAuthenticationProvider`
handling of the authentication token:

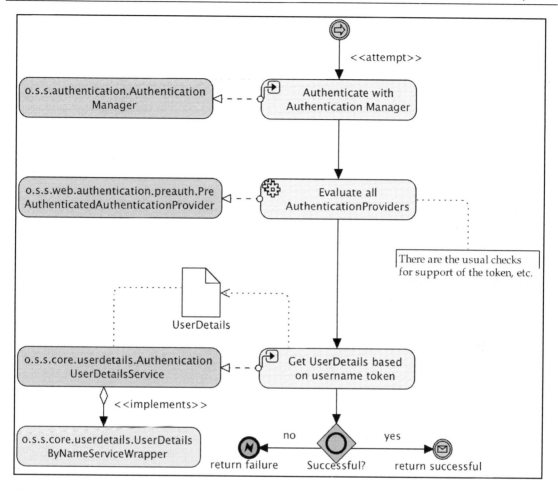

Though we will not go over them in detail, there are a number of other preauthenticated mechanisms supported by Spring Security. Some examples include Java EE role mapping (`J2eePreAuthenticatedProcessingFilter`), WebSphere integration (`WebSpherePreAuthenticatedProcessingFilter`), and Site Minder-style authentication (`RequestHeaderAuthenticationFilter`). If you understand the process flow of client certificate authentication, understanding these other authentication types is significantly easier.

Handling unauthenticated requests with AuthenticationEntryPoint

Since `X509AuthenticationFilter` will continue processing the request if authentication fails, we'll need to handle situations where the user does not authenticate successfully and has requested a protected resource. The way that Spring Security allows developers to customize this is by plugging in a custom `o.s.s.web.AuthenticationEntryPoint` implementation. In a default form login scenario, `LoginUrlAuthenticationEntryPoint` is used to redirect the user to a login page if they have been denied access to a protected resource and are not authenticated.

In contrast, in typical client certificate authentication environments, alternative methods of authentication are simply not supported (remember that Tomcat expects the certificate well before the Spring Security form login takes place anyway). As such, it doesn't make sense to retain the default behavior of redirection to a form login page. Instead, we'll modify the entry point to simply return an `HTTP 403 Forbidden` message, using the `o.s.s.web.authentication.Http403ForbiddenEntryPoint`. Go ahead and make the following updates in your `SecurityConfig.java` file, as follows:

```
//src/main/java/com/packtpub/springsecurity/configuration/SecurityConfig.java

    @Autowired
    private Http403ForbiddenEntryPoint forbiddenEntryPoint;
    http.exceptionHandling()
        .authenticationEntryPoint(forbiddenEntryPoint)
        .accessDeniedPage("/errors/403");
    ...
    @Bean
    public Http403ForbiddenEntryPoint forbiddenEntryPoint(){
        return new Http403ForbiddenEntryPoint();
    }
```

Now, if a user tries to access a protected resource and is unable to provide a valid certificate, they will be presented with the following page, instead of being redirected to the login page:

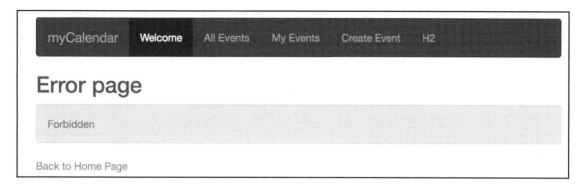

 Your code should now look like `chapter08.02-calendar`.

Other configuration or application flow adjustments that are commonly performed with client certificate authentication are as follows:

- Removal of the form-based login page altogether
- Removal of the logout link (as there's no reason to log out because the browser will always present the user's certificate)
- Removal of the functionality to rename the user account and change the password
- Removal of the user registration functionality (unless you are able to tie it into the issuance of a new certificate)

Supporting dual-mode authentication

It is also possible that some environments may support both certificate-based and form-based authentication. If this is the case in your environment, it is also possible (and trivial) to support it with Spring Security. We can simply leave the default `AuthenticationEntryPoint` interface (redirecting to the form-based login page) intact and allow the user to log in using the standard login form if they do not supply a client certificate.

If you choose to configure your application this way, you'll need to adjust the Tomcat SSL settings (change as appropriate for your application server). Simply change the `clientAuth` directive to `want`, instead of `true`:

```
<Connector port="8443" protocol="HTTP/1.1" SSLEnabled="true"
    maxThreads="150" scheme="https" secure="true"
    sslProtocol="TLS"
    keystoreFile="conf/tomcat.keystore"
    keystorePass="password"
    truststoreFile="conf/tomcat.truststore"
    truststorePass="password"
    clientAuth="want"
    />
```

We'll also need to remove the `authenticationEntryPoint()` method that we configured in the previous exercise, so that the standard form-based authentication workflow takes over if the user isn't able to supply a valid certificate upon the browser first being queried.

Although this is convenient, there are a few things to keep in mind about dual-mode (form-based and certificate-based) authentication, as follows:

- Most browsers will not reprompt the user for a certificate if they have failed certificate authentication once, so make sure that your users are aware that they may need to reenter the browser to present their certificate again.
- Recall that a password is not required to authenticate users with certificates; however, if you are still using `UserDetailsService` to support your form-based authenticated users, this may be the same `UserDetailsService` object that you use to give the `PreAuthenticatedAuthenticationProvider` information about your users. This presents a potential security risk, as users who you intend to sign in only with certificates could potentially authenticate using form login credentials.

There are several ways to solve this problem, and they are described in the following list:

- Ensure that the users authenticating with certificates have an appropriately strong password in your user store.
- Consider customizing your user store to clearly identify users who are enabled for form-based login. This can be tracked with an additional field in the table holding user account information, and with minor adjustments to the SQL queries used by the `JpaDaoImpl` object.

- Configure a separate user details store altogether for users who are logging in as certificate-authenticated users, to completely segregate them from users that are allowed to use form-based login.
- Dual-mode authentication can be a powerful addition to your site and can be deployed effectively and securely, provided that you keep in mind the situations under which users will be granted access to it.

Configuring client certificate authentication using Spring beans

Earlier in this chapter, we reviewed the flow of the classes involved in client certificate authentication. As such, it should be straightforward for us to configure the JBCP calendar using explicit beans. By using the explicit configuration, we will have additional configuration options at our disposal. Let's take a look and see how to use explicit configuration:

```
//src/main/java/com/packtpub/springsecurity/configuration/SecurityConfig.java

    @Bean
    public X509AuthenticationFilter x509Filter(AuthenticationManager
    authenticationManager){
        return new X509AuthenticationFilter(){{
            setAuthenticationManager(authenticationManager);
        }};
    }
    @Bean
    public PreAuthenticatedAuthenticationProvider
    preauthAuthenticationProvider(AuthenticationUserDetailsService
    authenticationUserDetailsService){
        return new PreAuthenticatedAuthenticationProvider(){{
    setPreAuthenticatedUserDetailsService(authenticationUserDetailsService);
        }};
    }
    @Bean
    public UserDetailsByNameServiceWrapper
    authenticationUserDetailsService(UserDetailsService
    userDetailsService){
        return new UserDetailsByNameServiceWrapper(){{
            setUserDetailsService(userDetailsService);
        }};
    }
```

We'll also need to remove the x509() method and add x509Filter to our filter chain, and add our AuthenticationProvider implementation to AuthenticationManger:

```
//src/main/java/com/packtpub/springsecurity/configuration/SecurityConfig.ja
va

    @Override
    protected void configure(HttpSecurity http) throws Exception {
        http.x509()
            //.userDetailsService(userDetailsService)
            .x509AuthenticationFilter(x509Filter());
        ...
    }
    @Override
    public void configure(AuthenticationManagerBuilder auth)
    throws Exception {
        auth
            .authenticationProvider(preAuthAuthenticationProvider)
            .userDetailsService(userDetailsService)
            .passwordEncoder(passwordEncoder());
    }
```

Now, give the application a try. Nothing much has changed from a user perspective, but as developers, we have opened the door to a number of additional configuration options.

 Your code should now look like chapter08.03-calendar.

Additional capabilities of bean-based configuration

The use of Spring bean-based configuration provides us with additional capabilities through the exposure of bean properties that aren't exposed via the security namespace style of configuration.

Additional properties available on X509AuthenticationFilter are as follows:

Property	Description	Default
continueFilterChainOn UnsuccessfulAuthentication	If false, a failed authentication will throw an exception rather than allow the request to continue. This would typically be set in cases where a valid certificate is expected and required to access the secured site. If true, the filter chain will proceed, even if there is a failed authentication.	true
checkForPrincipalChanges	If true, the filter will check to see if the currently authenticated username differs from the username presented in the client certificate. If so, authentication against the new certificate will be performed and the HTTP session will be invalidated (optionally, see the next attribute). If false, once the user is authenticated, they will remain authenticated even if they present different credentials.	false
invalidateSessionOn PrincipalChange	If true, and the principal in the request changes, the user's HTTP session will be invalidated prior to being reauthenticated. If false, the session will remain—note that this may introduce security risks.	true

The `PreAuthenticatedAuthenticationProvider` implementation has a couple of interesting properties available to us, which are listed in the following table:

Property	Description	Default
`preAuthenticatedUser DetailsService`	This property is used to build a full `UserDetails` object from the username extracted from the certificate.	None
`throwExceptionWhen TokenRejected`	If true, a `BadCredentialsException` exception will be thrown when the token is not constructed properly (does not contain a username or certificate). It is typically set to `true` in environments where certificates are used exclusively.	None

In addition to these properties, there are a number of other opportunities for implementing interfaces or extending classes involved in certificate authentication to further customize your implementation.

Considerations when implementing client certificate authentication

Client certificate authentication, while highly secure, isn't for everyone and isn't appropriate for every situation.

The pros of client certificate authentication are listed, as follows:

- Certificates establish a framework of mutual trust and verifiability that both parties (client and server) are who they say they are
- Certificate-based authentication, if implemented properly, is much more difficult to spoof or tamper with than other forms of authentication
- If a well-supported browser is used and configured correctly, client certificate authentication can effectively act as a single sign-on solution, enabling transparent login to all certificate-secured applications

The cons of client certificate authentication are listed, as follows:

- The use of certificates typically requires the entire user population to have them. This can lead to both a user training burden and an administrative burden. Most organizations deploying certificate-based authentication on a large scale must have sufficient self-service and helpdesk support for certificate maintenance, expiration tracking, and user assistance.
- The use of certificates is generally an all-or-nothing affair, meaning that mixed-mode authentication and offering support for non-certificated users is not provided due to the complexity of web server configuration, or poor application support.
- The use of certificates may not be well supported by all users in your user population, including the ones who use mobile devices.
- The correct configuration of the infrastructure required to support certificate-based authentication may require advanced IT knowledge.

As you can see, there are both benefits and drawbacks to client certificate authentication. When implemented correctly, it can be a very convenient mode of access for your users and has extremely attractive security and non-repudiation properties. You will need to determine your particular situation to see whether or not this type of authentication is appropriate.

Summary

In this chapter, we examined the architecture, flow, and Spring Security support for client certificate-based authentication. We have covered the concepts and overall flow of client certificate (mutual) authentication. We explored the important steps required to configure Apache Tomcat for a self-signed SSL and client certificate scenario.

We also learned about configuring Spring Security to understand certificate-based credentials presented by clients. We covered the architecture of Spring Security classes related to certificate authentication. We also know how to configure a Spring bean-style client certificate environment. We also covered the pros and cons of this type of authentication.

It's quite common for developers unfamiliar with client certificates to be confused by many of the complexities of this type of environment. We hope that this chapter has made this complicated subject a bit easier to understand and implement! In the next chapter, we will discuss how you can accomplish single sign-on with OpenID.

9
Opening up to OAuth 2

OAuth 2 is a very popular form of trusted identity management that allows users to manage their identity through a single trusted provider. This convenient feature provides users with the security of storing their password and personal information with the trusted OAuth 2 provider, optionally disclosing personal information upon request. Additionally, the OAuth 2-enabled website offers the confidence that the users providing OAuth 2 credentials are who they say they are.

In this chapter, we will cover the following topics:

- Learning to set up your own OAuth 2 application in less than 5 minutes
- Configuring the JBCP calendar application with a very rapid implementation of OAuth 2
- Learning the conceptual architecture of OAuth 2 and how it provides your site with trustworthy user access
- Implementing OAuth 2-based user registration
- Experimenting with OAuth 2 attribute exchange for user profile functionality
- Demonstrating how we can trigger automatic authentication to the previous OAuth 2 provider
- Examining the security offered by OAuth 2-based login

The promising world of OAuth 2

As an application developer, you may have heard the term OAuth 2 thrown around a lot. OAuth 2 has been widely adopted by web service and software companies around the world and is integral to the way these companies interact and share information. But what exactly is it? In a nutshell, OAuth 2 is a protocol that allows distinct parties to share information and resources in a secure and reliable manner.

What about OAuth 1.0?

Built with the same motivation, OAuth 1.0 was designed and ratified in 2007. However, it was criticized for being overly complex and also had issues with imprecise specifications, which led to insecure implementation. All of these issues contributed to poor adoption for OAuth 1.0, and eventually led to the design and creation of OAuth 2. OAuth 2 is the successor to OAuth 1.0.

It is also important to note that OAuth 2 is not backward compatible with OAuth 1.0, and so OAuth 2 applications cannot integrate with OAuth 1.0 service providers.

This type of login—through a trusted third-party—has been in existence for a long time, in many different forms (for example, **Microsoft Passport** became one of the more notable central login services on the web for some time). The distinct advantage of OAuth 2 is that the OAuth 2 provider needs to implement only the public OAuth 2 protocol to be compatible with any site seeking to integrate login with OAuth 2.

You can refer to the OAuth 2.0 specification at `https://tools.ietf.org/html/rfc6749`.

The following diagram illustrates the high-level relationship between a site integrating OAuth 2 during the login process and the Facebook OAuth 2 provider, for example:

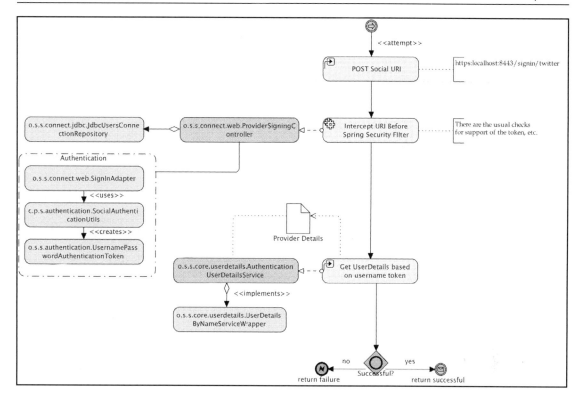

We can see that submitting a form post will initiate a request to the OAuth provider, resulting in the provider displaying an authorization dialog asking the user to allow `jbcpcalendar` to gain permission to specific information from your OAuth provider account. This request contains a `uri` parameter called `code`. Once granted, the user is redirected back to `jbcpcalendar`, and the `code` parameter is included in the `uri` parameter. Then, the request is redirected to the OAuth provider again, to authorize `jbcpcalendar`. The OAuth provider then responds with an `access_token` that can be used to access the user's OAuth information that `jbcpcalendar` was granted access to.

Don't trust OAuth 2 unequivocally!

Here, you can see a fundamental assumption that can fool users of the system. It is possible for us to sign up for an OAuth 2 provider account, which would make it appear as though we were James Gosling, even though we obviously are not. Do not make the false assumption that just because a user has a convincing-sounding OAuth 2 (or OAuth 2 delegate provider), that he/she is the authentic person without requiring additional forms of identification. Thinking about it another way, if someone came to your door just claiming he was James Gosling, would you let him in without verifying his ID?

The OAuth 2-enabled application then redirects the user to the OAuth 2 provider, and the user presents his credentials to the provider, which is then responsible for making an access decision. Once the access decision has been made by the provider, the provider redirects the user to the originating site, which is now assured of the user's authenticity. OAuth 2 is much easier to understand once you have tried it. Let's add OAuth 2 to the JBCP calendar login screen now!

Signing up for an OAuth 2 application

In order to get the full value out of the exercise in this section (and be able to test login), you will need to create an application with a service provider. Currently, Spring Social supports Twitter, Facebook, Google, LinkedIn, and GitHub, and the list is growing.

To get the full value out of the exercises in this chapter, we recommend you have accounts with at least Twitter and GitHub. We have set up accounts for the jbcpcalendar application, which we will be using for the remainder of this chapter.

Enabling OAuth authentication with Spring Security

We can see a common theme among the external authentication providers examined over the next several chapters. Spring Security provides convenient wrappers around the provider integrations that are actually developed outside the Spring ecosystem.

In this vein, the Spring Social project (`http://projects.spring.io/spring-social/`) provides the underlying OAuth 2 provider discovery and request/response negotiation for the Spring Security OAuth 2 functionality.

Additional required dependencies

Let's take a look at the following steps:

1. In order to utilize OAuth, we will need to include provider-specific dependencies and their transitive dependencies. This can be done in Gradle by updating the `build.gradle` file, as shown in the following code snippet:

   ```
   //build.gradle

   compile("org.springframework.boot:spring-boot-starter-
   social-facebook")
   compile("org.springframework.boot:spring-boot-starter-
   social-linkedin")
   compile("org.springframework.boot:spring-boot-starter-
   social-twitter")
   ```

2. Using Spring Boot includes references to Facebook, Twitter, and LinkedIn starter dependencies, as shown in the preceding code snippet. To add other providers, we must include the provider dependency and include the version. This can be done in Gradle by updating the `build.gradle` file, as shown in the following code snippet:

   ```
   //build.gradle

   compile("org.springframework.social:spring-social-google:
   latest.release ")
   compile("org.springframework.social:spring-social-github:
   latest.release ")
   compile("org.springframework.social:spring-social-linkedin:
   latest.release ")
   ```

    You should start with the source in `chapter09.00-calendar`.

3. When writing the OAuth login form, we will need to replace the `username` and `password` fields with OAuth fields. Go ahead and make the following updates to your `login.html` file:

```
//src/main/resources/templates/login.html

  <div class="form-actions">
     <input id="submit" class="btn" name="submit" type="submit"
     value="Login"/>
     </div>
  </form>
<br/>
  <h3>Social Login</h3>
<br />
<form th:action="@{/signin/twitter}" method="POST"
class="form-horizontal">
 <input type="hidden" name="scope" value="public_profile" />
<div class="form-actions">
<input id="twitter-submit" class="btn" type="submit"
value="Login using
Twitter"/>
  </div>
  </form>
</div>
```

4. We can make similar edits to the signup form, as shown in the following code snippet:

```
//src/main/resources/templates/signup/form.html

</fieldset>
</form>
 <br/>
   <h3>Social Login</h3>
 <br/>
   <form th:action="@{/signin/twitter}" method="POST"
   class="form-horizontal">
   <input type="hidden" name="scope" value="public_profile" />
<div class="form-actions">
 <input id="twitter-submit" class="btn" type="submit"
 value="Login using Twitter"/>
 </div>
 </form>
 </div>
```

You will notice that we have added a scope field to define the OAuth 2 details we are interested in retrieving during authentication.

 OAuth 2.0 API Scopes: Scopes allow a provider to define the API data accessible to client applications. When an API is created by a provider, they define one scope for each API represented and action. Once an API is created and define the scopes, the client applications can request these defined permissions when they initiate an authorization flow and include them in the access token as part of the scope request parameter.

Each provider might have slightly different API scopes, such as `r_basicprofile` and `r_emailaddress`, but the API scope is also limited to the application configuration. As such, an application might only request access to email or contacts, not the entire user profile or provider actions such as posting to a user's wall.

You'll notice that we don't offer the **remember me** option with OAuth 2 login. This is due to the fact that the redirection to and from the vendor causes the **remember me** checkbox value to be lost so that when the user is successfully authenticated, they no longer have the **remember me** option indicated. This is unfortunate, but ultimately increases the security of OAuth 2 as a login mechanism for our site, as OAuth 2 forces the user to establish a trusted relationship with the provider with each and every login.

Configuring OAuth 2 support in Spring Security

Using **Spring Social**, we can enable OAuth 2-specific provider endpoints for intercepting provider form submissions.

Local UserConnectionRepository

The `UsersConnectionRepository` interface is a data access interface for managing a global store of users' connections to service providers. It provides data access operations that apply to multiple user records, as shown in the following code snippet:

```
//src/main/java/com/packtpub/springsecurity/configuration/SocialConfig.java

@Autowired
private UsersConnectionRepository usersConnectionRepository;
@Autowired
 private ProviderConnectionSignup providerConnectionSignup;
```

```
@Bean
public ProviderSignInController providerSignInController() {
    ((JdbcUsersConnectionRepository) usersConnectionRepository)
    .setConnectionSignUp(providerConnectionSignup);
    ...
}
```

Creating local database entries for provider details

Spring Security provides support to save provider details in a separate set of database tables, in case we want to save the user in a local data store, but don't want to include that data in an existing User table:

```
//src/main/java/com/packtpub/springsecurity/configuration/
SocialDatabasePopulator.java

@Component
public class SocialDatabasePopulator
implements InitializingBean {
    private final DataSource dataSource;
    @Autowired
public SocialDatabasePopulator(final DataSource dataSource) {
this.dataSource = dataSource;
    }
@Override
public void afterPropertiesSet() throws Exception {
    ClassPathResource resource = new ClassPathResource(
    "org/springframework/social/connect/jdbc/
    JdbcUsersConnectionRepository.sql");
    executeSql(resource);
    }
  private void executeSql(final Resource resource) {
  ResourceDatabasePopulator populator = new ResourceDatabasePopulator();
  populator.setContinueOnError(true);
  populator.addScript(resource);
  DatabasePopulatorUtils.execute(populator, dataSource);
    }
}
```

This InitializingBean interface is executed at load time and will execute JdbcUsersConnectionRepository.sql which is located in the spring-social-core-[VERSION].jar file on the classpath, seeding the following schema into our local database:

```
spring-social-core-
```

```
[VERSION].jar#org/springframework/social/connect/jdbc/
    JdbcUsersConnectionRepository.sql

    create table UserConnection(
      userId varchar(255) not null,
      providerId varchar(255) not null,
      providerUserId varchar(255),
      rank int not null,
      displayName varchar(255),
      profileUrl varchar(512),
      imageUrl varchar(512),
      accessToken varchar(512) not null,
      secret varchar(512),
      refreshToken varchar(512),
      expireTime bigint,
      primary key (userId, providerId, providerUserId));

      create unique index UserConnectionRank on UserConnection(userId,
  providerId,
      rank);
```

Now that we have a table to store provider details, we can configure
ConnectionRepository to save provider details at runtime.

The custom UserConnectionRepository interface

We need to create a UserConnectionRepository interface, and we can leverage
JdbcUsersConnectionRepository as the implementation, which is based on the
JdbcUsersConnectionRepository.sql schema we generated at load time, as follows:

```
//src/main/java/com/packtpub/springsecurity/configuration/
DatabaseSocialConfigurer.java

public class DatabaseSocialConfigurer extends SocialConfigurerAdapter
{

  private final DataSource dataSource;
  public DatabaseSocialConfigurer(DataSource dataSource) {
    this.dataSource = dataSource;
  }
@Override
public UsersConnectionRepository getUsersConnectionRepository(
ConnectionFactoryLocator connectionFactoryLocator) {
    TextEncryptor textEncryptor = Encryptors.noOpText();
    return new JdbcUsersConnectionRepository(
    dataSource, connectionFactoryLocator, textEncryptor);
  }
```

```
        @Override
    public void addConnectionFactories(ConnectionFactoryConfigurer config,
    Environment env) {
        super.addConnectionFactories(config, env);
    }
    }
```

Now, every time a user connects to a registered provider, the connection details will be saved into our local database.

The ConnectionSignup flow

In order to save the provider details into a local repository, we have created a ConnectionSignup object, which is a command that signs up a new user in the event that no userid can be mapped from Connection which allows for implicitly creating a local user profile from connection data during a provider sign-in attempt:

```
//src/main/java/com/packtpub/springsecurity/authentication/
ProviderConnectionSignup.java

@Service
 public class ProviderConnectionSignup implements ConnectionSignUp {
      ...;
@Override
public String execute(Connection<?> connection) {
    ...
  }
 }
```

Executing the OAuth 2 provider connection workflow

In order to save the provider details, we need to fetch the available details from the provider, available via the OAuth 2 connection. Next, we create a CalendarUser table from the available details. Note that we need to create at least one GrantedAuthority role. Here, we have used CalendarUserAuthorityUtils#createAuthorities to create ROLE_USER GrantedAuthority:

```
//src/main/java/com/packtpub/springsecurity/authentication/
ProviderConnectionSignup.java

@Service
```

```
public class ProviderConnectionSignup implements ConnectionSignUp {
    ...
@Override
public String execute(Connection<?> connection) {
    UserProfile profile = connection.fetchUserProfile();
    CalendarUser user = new CalendarUser();
    if(profile.getEmail() != null){
        user.setEmail(profile.getEmail());
    }
    else if(profile.getUsername() != null){
        user.setEmail(profile.getUsername());
    }
    else {
        user.setEmail(connection.getDisplayName());
    }

        user.setFirstName(profile.getFirstName());
        user.setLastName(profile.getLastName());
        user.setPassword(randomAlphabetic(32));
        CalendarUserAuthorityUtils.createAuthorities(user);
        ...

    }
}
```

Adding OAuth 2 users

Now that we have created `CalendarUser` from our provider details, we need to save that
`User` account into our database using `CalendarUserDao`. We then return the
`CalendarUser` email, as that is what we have been using in the JBCP calendar for the
username, as follows:

```
//src/main/java/com/packtpub/springsecurity/authentication/
ProviderConnectionSignup.java

@Service
public class ProviderConnectionSignup
implements ConnectionSignUp {
 @Autowired
   private CalendarUserDao calendarUserDao;
  @Override
 public String execute(Connection<?> connection) {...
calendarUserDao.createUser(user);
return user.getEmail();
    }
}
```

Now, we have a local `User` account in our database based on the provider details.

 This is an additional database entry, as we have already saved the provider details into the `UserConnection` table earlier.

OAuth 2 controller sign-in flow

Now, to complete the `SocialConfig.java` configuration, we need to construct `ProviderSignInController`, which is initialized with `ConnectionFactoryLocator`, `usersConnectionRepository`, and `SignInAdapter`. The `ProviderSignInController` interface is a Spring MVC controller for handling the provider user sign-in flow. An HTTP `POST` request to `/signin/{providerId}` initiates a user sign-in with `{providerId}`. Submitting an HTTP `GET` request to `/signin/{providerId}?oauth_token&amp;oauth_verifier||code` will receive the `{providerId}` authentication callback and establish the connection.

A `ServiceLocator` interface is used for creating the `ConnectionFactory` instances. This factory supports lookup by `providerId` and by `apiType`, based on the included service providers found within Spring Boot's `AutoConfiguration`:

```
//src/main/java/com/packtpub/springsecurity/configuration/SocialConfig.java

    @Autowired
    private ConnectionFactoryLocator connectionFactoryLocator;
    @Bean
    public ProviderSignInController providerSignInController() {
        ...
        return new ProviderSignInController(connectionFactoryLocator,
        usersConnectionRepository, authSignInAdapter());
    }
```

This will allow submissions to a specific provider `uri` to be intercepted, and will begin the OAuth 2 connection flow.

Automatic user authentication

Let's take a look at the following steps:

1. The `ProviderSignInController` controller is initialized with an authentication `SignInAdapter`, which is used to complete a provider sign-in attempt by signing in the local user account with the specified ID:

    ```
    //src/main/java/com/packtpub/springsecurity/configuration/
    SocialConfig.java

    @Bean
    public SignInAdapter authSignInAdapter() {
        return (userId, connection, request) -> {
          SocialAuthenticationUtils.authenticate(connection);
          return null;
        };
    }
    ```

2. In the `SingInAdapter` bean, from the preceding code snippet, we used a custom authentication utility method to create an `Authentication` object in the form of `UsernamePasswordAuthenticationToken`, and added it to `SecurityContext` based on the details returned from the OAuth 2 provider:

    ```
    //src/main/java/com/packtpub/springsecurity/authentication/
    SocialAuthenticationUtils.java

    public class SocialAuthenticationUtils {
     public static void authenticate(Connection<?> connection) {
      UserProfile profile = connection.fetchUserProfile();
      CalendarUser user = new CalendarUser();
      if(profile.getEmail() != null){
         user.setEmail(profile.getEmail());
       }
      else if(profile.getUsername() != null){
         user.setEmail(profile.getUsername());
       }
      else {
         user.setEmail(connection.getDisplayName());
       }
         user.setFirstName(profile.getFirstName());
         user.setLastName(profile.getLastName());
         UsernamePasswordAuthenticationToken authentication = new
         UsernamePasswordAuthenticationToken(user, null,
         CalendarUserAuthorityUtils.createAuthorities(user));
         SecurityContextHolder.getContext()
         .setAuthentication(authentication);
    ```

```
    }
  }
```

The final details required to connect to a provider is the application ID and secret key obtained when creating the provider application are as follows:

```
//src/main/resources/application.yml:

spring
## Social Configuration:
social:
twitter:
  appId: cgceheRX6a8EAE74JUeiRi8jZ
  appSecret: XROJ2N0Inzy2y2poxzot9oSAaE6MIOs4QHSWzT8dyeZaaeawep
```

3. Now we have the required details to connect to the Twitter JBCP calendar, and we can start the JBCP calendar and log in with a Twitter provider.

> Your code should now look like `chapter09.01-calendar`.

4. At this point, you should be able to complete a full login using Twitter's OAuth 2 provider. The redirects that occur are as follows, first, we initiate the OAuth 2 provider login as shown in the following screenshot:

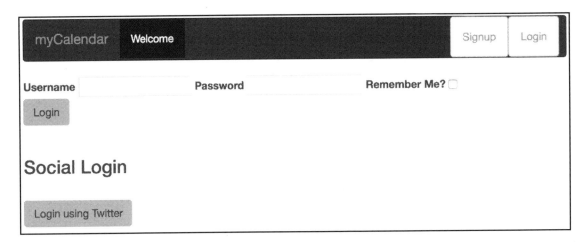

We are then redirected to the provider authorization page, requesting the user to grant permission to the `jbcpcalendar` application as shown in the following screenshot:

Authorize jbcpcalendar to use your account?

jbcpcalendar

By BASE Logic, Inc.

127.0.0.1:8443

jbcpcalendar Spring Security 3rd Edition Demo

Privacy Policy

Terms and Conditions

| Authorize app | Cancel |

This application will be able to:

- Read Tweets from your timeline.
- See who you follow, and follow new people.
- Update your profile.
- Post Tweets for you.
- Access your direct messages.
- See your email address.

Will not be able to:

- See your Twitter password.

5. After authorizing the `jbcpcalendar` application, the user is redirected to the `jbcpcalendar` application and automatically logged in using the provider display name:

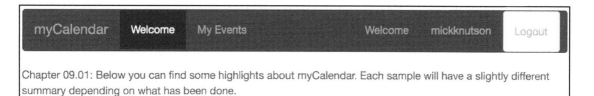

Chapter 09.01: Below you can find some highlights about myCalendar. Each sample will have a slightly different summary depending on what has been done.

6. At this point, the user exists in the application and is authenticated and authorized with a single `GrantedAuthority` of `ROLE_USER`, but if we navigate to **My Events**, the user will be allowed to view this page. However, no events exist for `CalendarUser`:

7. Try to create an event for this user to verify that the user credentials that were created correctly in the `CalendarUser` table.

8. To verify that the provider details were created correctly, we can open the H2 admin console and query the `USERCONNECTION` table to verify that standard connection details were saved, as shown in the following screenshot:

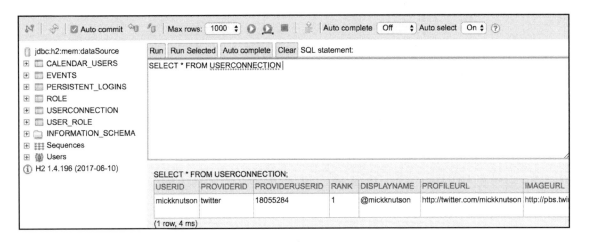

9. Additionally, we can verify the `CALENDAR_USERS` table, which has also been populated with the provider details:

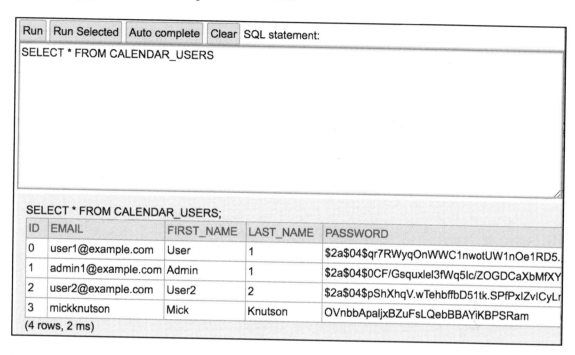

ID	EMAIL	FIRST_NAME	LAST_NAME	PASSWORD
0	user1@example.com	User	1	$2a$04$qr7RWyqOnWWC1nwotUW1nOe1RD5.
1	admin1@example.com	Admin	1	$2a$04$0CF/Gsquxlel3fWq5lc/ZOGDCaXbMfXY
2	user2@example.com	User2	2	$2a$04$pShXhqV.wTehbffbD51tk.SPfPxlZvlCyLr
3	mickknutson	Mick	Knutson	OVnbbApaljxBZuFsLQebBBAYiKBPSRam

(4 rows, 2 ms)

Now we have the user registered in our local database, and we also have the ability to interact with the registered provider based on authorized access to specific provider details.

Additional OAuth 2 providers

We have successfully integrated a single OAuth 2 provider using one of the three current support providers for Spring Social. There are several other providers available; we are going to add a few more providers so our users have more than one option. Spring Social currently supports Twitter, Facebook, and LinkedIn providers natively. Including additional providers will require additional libraries to gain this support, which will be covered later in this chapter.

Let's take a look at the following steps:

1. In order to add Facebook or LinkedIn providers into the JBCP calendar application, additional application properties need to be set, and each configured provider will automatically be registered with the `appId` and `appSecret` keys from the provider application, as follows:

```
//src/main/resources/application.yml

spring:
social:
 # Twitter
 twitter:
     appId: cgceheRX6a8EAE74JUeiRi8jZ
     appSecret: XR0J2N0Inzy2y2poxzot9oSAaE6MIOs4QHSWzT8dyeZaaeawep
 # facebook
 facebook:
     appId: 299089913898983
     appSecret: 01639f125103752ec408affc92515d0e
 # Linked
     linkedin:
     appId: 866qpyhnq6f6o5
     appSecret: KsFKoOmcGCiLfGfO
```

2. We can now add the new login options to our `login.html` file, and the `form.html` signup page, to include one new `<form>` tag for each new provider:

```
//src/main/resources/templates/login.html

<h3>Social Login</h3>
<form th:action="@{/signin/twitter}" method="POST"
class="form-horizontal">
 <input type="hidden" name="scope" value="public_profile" />
 <div class="form-actions">
   <input id="twitter-submit" class="btn" type="submit"
   value="Login using Twitter"/>
 </div>
</form>
<br />
 <form th:action="@{/signin/facebook}" method="POST"
 class="form-horizontal"
 <input type="hidden" name="scope" value="public_profile" />
 <div class="form-actions">
    <input id="facebook-submit" class="btn" type="submit"
    value="Login using Facebook"/> </div>
</form>
```

```
<br/>
  <form th:action="@{/signin/linkedin}" method="POST"
  class="form-horizontal">
  <input type="hidden" name="scope" value="r_basicprofile,
  r_emailaddress" />
  <div class="form-actions">
    <input id="linkedin-submit" class="btn" type="submit"
    value="Login using Linkedin"/>
  </div>
</form>
```

3. Now we have the required details to connect to the additional providers for the JBCP calendar, and we can restart the JBCP calendar application and test logging in with the other OAuth 2 providers.

> Your code should now look like `chapter09.02-calendar`.

When logging in now, we should be presented with additional provider options, as shown in the following screenshot:

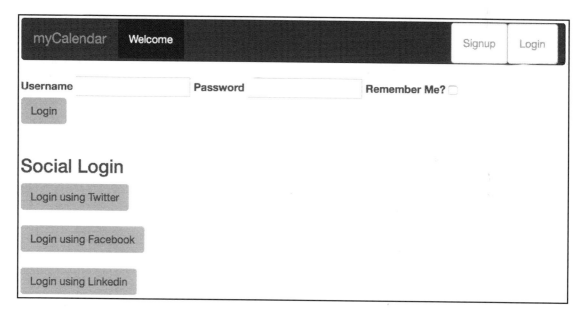

The OAuth 2 user registration problem

One issue that would need to be resolved if supporting multiple providers is username conflicts between the various provider details returned.

If you log in to the JBCP calendar application with each of the listed providers—which then query the data that was stored in H2—you will find the data could be similar, if not exactly the same, based on the user's account details.

In the following USERCONNECTION table, we can see that the USERID column data from each provider, is similar:

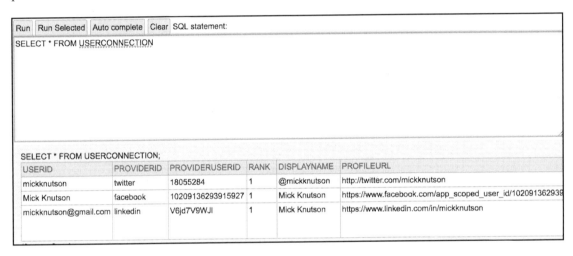

In the CALENDARUSER table, we have two possible issues. First, the user details used for EMAIL, which is the JBCP calendar user ID , is not an email for some of the providers. Second, it is still possible that the user identifier for two different providers will be the same:

```
SELECT * FROM CALENDAR_USERS;
```

ID	EMAIL	FIRST_NAME	LAST_NAME	PASSWORD
0	user1@example.com	User	1	$2a$04$qr7RWyqOnWWC1nwotUW1nOe1RD5.mKJVHK16WZy6v49pymu1WDHmi
1	admin1@example.com	Admin	1	$2a$04$0CF/Gsquxlel3fWq5Ic/ZOGDCaXbMfXYiXsviTNMQofWRXhvJH3IK
2	user2@example.com	User2	2	$2a$04$pShXhqV.wTehbffbD51tk.SPfPxIZvICyLn9WvQ8YhIXcYqWtW2Mm
3	mickknutson	Mick	Knutson	wDKwNPcTfPJcxuOmQTIdAtveUibHKtIQ
4	Mick Knutson	Mick	Knutson	pUlufjsVBpJrdxFWiXsLUYjZPxltvSTY
5	mickknutson@gmail.com	Mick	Knutson	eYpAXBszkkQFQkqXKMxKgPUGsJOmRXOg

We are not going to dive into the various ways to detect and correct this possible issue, but it is worth noting for future reference.

Registering non-standard OAuth 2 providers

In order to include additional providers, we need to perform a few extra steps to include custom providers into the login flow, as follows:

1. For each provider, we need to include the provider dependencies in our `build.gradle` file, as follows:

```
//build.gradle

dependencies {
   ...
   compile("org.springframework.social:spring-social-google:
   ${springSocialGoogleVersion}")
   compile("org.springframework.social:spring-social-github:
   ${springSocialGithubVersion}")
}
```

2. Next, we will register the providers into the JBCP calendar application with the following additional application properties for the `appId` and `appSecret` key for each provider:

```
//src/main/resources/application.yml

spring:
  social:
    # Google
      google:
        appId: 947438796602-uiob88a5kg1j9mcljfmk00quok7rphib.apps.
        googleusercontent.com
        appSecret: lpYZpF2IUgNXyXdZn-zY3gpR
    # Github
      github:
        appId: 71649b756d29b5a2fc84
        appSecret: 4335dcc0131ed62d757cc63e2fdc1be09c38abbf
```

3. Each new provider must be registered by adding the respective `ConnectionFactory` interface. We can add a new `ConnectionFactory` entry for each new Provider we intend to support, to the custom `DatabaseSocialConfigurer.java` file as seen in the following:

```
//src/main/java/com/packtpub/springsecurity/configuration/
DatabaseSocialConfigurer.java

public class DatabaseSocialConfigurer
extends SocialConfigurerAdapter {

    ...
@Override
public void addConnectionFactories(
ConnectionFactoryConfigurer config, Environment env) {
        super.addConnectionFactories(config, env);

    // Adding GitHub Connection with properties
    // from application.yml
        config.addConnectionFactory(
            new GitHubConnectionFactory(
              env.getProperty("spring.social.github.appId"),
                env.getProperty("spring.social.github.appSecret")));
    // Adding Google Connection with properties
```

```
// from application.yml
    config.addConnectionFactory(
    new GoogleConnectionFactory(
    env.getProperty("spring.social.google.appId"),
    env.getProperty("spring.social.google.appSecret")));
    }
  }
```

4. We can now add the new login options to our `login.html` file and `form.html` sign up page to include one new `<form>` tag for each new provider:

```
//src/main/resources/templates/login.html

<h3>Social Login</h3>
...
<form th:action="@{/signin/google}" method="POST"
class="form-horizontal">
<input type="hidden" name="scope" value="profile" />
<div class="form-actions">
   <input id="google-submit" class="btn" type="submit"
   value="Login using
   Google"/>
</div>
</form>
<br />

<form th:action="@{/signin/github}" method="POST"
class="form-horizontal">
<input type="hidden" name="scope" value="public_profile" />
<div class="form-actions">
   <input id="github-submit" class="btn" type="submit"
   value="Login using
   Github"/>
</div>
</form&gt;
```

5. Now, we have the required details to connect to the additional providers for the JBCP calendar. We can restart the JBCP calendar application and test logging in with the additional OAuth 2 providers. When logging in now, we should be presented with additional provider options, as shown in the following screenshot:

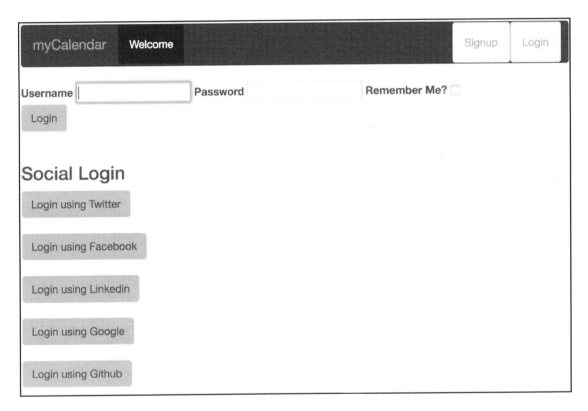

Is OAuth 2 secure?

As support for OAuth 2 relies on the trustworthiness of the OAuth 2 provider and the verifiability of the provider's response, security and authenticity are critical in order for the application to have confidence in the user's OAuth 2-based login.

Fortunately, the designers of the OAuth 2 specification were very aware of this concern, and implemented a series of verification steps to prevent response forgery, replay attacks, and other types of tampering, which are explained as follows:

- **Response forgery** is prevented due to a combination of a shared secret key (created by the OAuth 2-enabled site prior to the initial request), and a one-way hashed message signature on the response itself. A malicious user tampering with the data in any of the response fields without having access to the shared secret key—and signature algorithm—would generate an invalid response.

- **Replay attacks** are prevented due to the inclusion of a nonce, or a one-time use, random key, which should be recorded by the OAuth 2-enabled site so that it cannot ever be reused. In this way, even a user attempting to reissue the response URL would be foiled because the receiving site would determine that the nonce had been previously used, and would invalidate the request.

- The most likely form of attack that could result in a compromised user interaction would be a man-in-the-middle attack, where a malicious user could intercept the user's interaction between their computer and the OAuth 2 provider. A hypothetical attacker in this situation could be in a position to record the conversation between the user's browser and the OAuth 2 provider, and record the secret key used when the request was initiated. The attacker, in this case, would need a very high level of sophistication and reasonably a complete implementation of the OAuth 2 signature specification—in short, this is not likely to occur with any regularity.

Summary

In this chapter, we reviewed OAuth 2, a relatively recent technology for user authentication and credentials management. OAuth 2 has a very wide reach on the web and has made great strides in usability and acceptance within the past year or two. Most public-facing sites on the modern web should plan on having some form of OAuth 2 support, and the JBCP calendar application is no exception!

In this chapter, we learned about the following topics the OAuth 2 authentication mechanism and its high-level architecture and key terminology. We also learned about the OAuth 2 login and automatic user registration with the JBCP calendar application.

We also covered automatic login with OAuth 2 and the security of OAuth 2's login responses.

We covered one of the simplest single sign-on mechanisms to implement with Spring Security. One of the downsides is that it does not support a standard mechanism for a single logout. In the next chapter, we will explore CAS, another standard, single sign-on protocol that also supports single logout.

10
Single Sign-On with the Central Authentication Service

In this chapter, we'll examine the use of the **Central Authentication Service (CAS)** as a single sign-on portal for Spring Security-based applications.

During the course of this chapter, we'll cover the following topics:

- Learning about CAS, its architecture, and how it benefits system administrators and organizations of any size
- Understanding how Spring Security can be reconfigured to handle the interception of authentication requests and redirecting it to CAS
- Configuring the JBCP calendar application to utilize CAS single sign-on
- Gaining an understanding of how a single logout can be performed, and configuring our application to support it
- Discussing how to use CAS proxy ticket authentication for services, and configuring our application to utilize proxy ticket authentication
- Discussing how to customize the out-of-the-box **JA-SIG CAS** server using the recommended war overlay approach
- Integrating the CAS server with LDAP, and passing data from LDAP to Spring Security via CAS

Introducing the Central Authentication Service

CAS is an open source, single sign-on server, providing centralized access control, and authentication to web-based resources within an organization. The benefits of CAS are numerous to administrators, and it supports many applications and diverse user communities. The benefits are as follows:

- Individual or group access to resources (applications) can be configured in one location
- Broad support for a wide variety of authentication stores (to centralize user management) provides a single point of authentication and control to a widespread, cross-machine environment
- Wide authentication support is provided for web-based and non-web-based Java applications through CAS client libraries
- A single point of reference for user credentials (via CAS) is provided so that CAS client applications are not required to have any knowledge of the user's credentials, or knowledge of how to verify them

In this chapter, we'll not focus much on the management of CAS, but on authentication and how CAS can act as an authentication point for the users of our site. Although CAS is commonly seen in intranet environments for enterprises or educational institutions, it can also be found in use at high profile locations such as Sony Online Entertainment's public-facing site.

High-level CAS authentication flow

At a high level, CAS is composed of a CAS server, which is the central web application for determining authentication, and one or more CAS services, which are distinct web applications that use the CAS server to get authenticated. The basic authentication flow of CAS proceeds via the following actions:

1. The user attempts to access a protected resource on the website.
2. The user is redirected through the browser from the CAS service to the CAS server to request a login.
3. The CAS server is responsible for user authentication. If the user is not already authenticated to the CAS server, it requests credentials from the user. In the following diagram, the user is presented with a login page.
4. The user submits the credentials (that is, the username and password).
5. If the user's credentials are valid, the CAS server responds with a redirect through the browser with a service ticket. A service ticket is a one-time use token used to identify a user.
6. The CAS service calls the CAS server back to verify that the ticket is valid, has not expired, and so on. Note that this step does not occur through the browser.
7. The CAS server responds with an assertion indicating that trust has been established. If the ticket is acceptable, trust has been established and the user may proceed via normal authorization checking.

Visually, this behaves as illustrated in the following diagram:

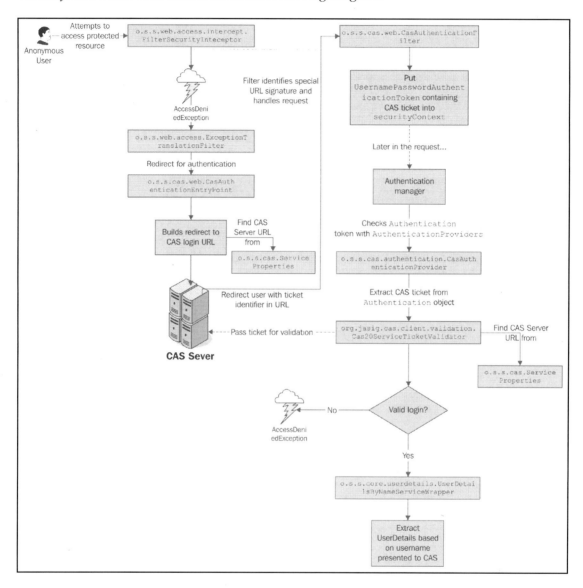

We can see that there is a high level of interaction between the CAS server and the secured application, with several data exchange handshakes required before the trust of the user can be established. The result of this complexity is a single sign-on protocol that is quite hard to spoof through common techniques (assuming other network security precautions, such as the use of SSL and network monitoring, are in place).

Now that we understand how CAS authentication works in general, let's see how it applies to Spring Security.

Spring Security and CAS

Spring Security has a strong integration capability with CAS, although it's not as tightly integrated into the security namespace style of configuration like the OAuth2 and LDAP integrations that we've explored thus far in the latter part of this book. Instead, much of the configuration relies on bean wiring and configuration by reference, from the security namespace elements to bean declarations.

The two basic pieces of CAS authentication when using Spring Security involve the following:

- Replacement of the standard `AuthenticationEntryPoint` implementation, which typically handles redirection of unauthenticated users to the login page with an implementation that redirects the user to the CAS server instead
- Processing the service ticket when the user is redirected back from the CAS server to the protected resource, through the use of a custom servlet filter

An important thing to understand about CAS is that in typical deployments, CAS is intended to replace all of the alternative login mechanisms of your application. As such, once we configure CAS for Spring Security, our users must use CAS exclusively as an authentication mechanism to our application. In most cases, this is not a problem; as we discussed in the previous section, CAS is designed to proxy authentication requests to one or more authentication stores (similar to what Spring Security does when delegating to a database or LDAP for authentication). From the previous diagram, we can see that our application is no longer checking its own authentication store to validate users. Instead, it determines the user through the use of the service ticket. However, as we will discuss later, initially, Spring Security still needs a data store to determine the user's authorization. We will discuss how to remove this restriction later on in the chapter.

After completing the basic CAS integration with Spring Security, we can remove the login link from the home page and enjoy automatic redirection to CAS's login screen, where we attempt to access a protected resource. Of course, depending on the application, it can also be beneficial to still allow the user to explicitly log in (so that they can see customized content, and so on).

Required dependencies

Before we got too far, we should ensure that our dependencies are updated. A list of the dependencies that we have added with comments about when they are needed can be seen, as follows:

```
//build.gradle

dependencies {
// CAS:
compile('org.springframework.security:spring-security-cas')
...
}
```

Installing and configuring CAS

CAS has the benefit of having an extremely dedicated team behind it that has done an excellent job of developing both quality software and accurate, straightforward documentation on how to use it. Should you choose to follow along with the examples in this chapter, you are encouraged to read the appropriate getting started manual for your CAS platform. You can find this manual at `https://apereo.github.io/cas/5.1.x/index.html`.

In order to make integration as simple as possible, we have included a CAS server application for this chapter, which can be deployed in the Spring Tool Suite or in IntelliJ, along with the calendar application. For the examples in this chapter, we will assume that CAS is deployed at `https://localhost:9443/cas/` and the calendar application is deployed at `https://localhost:8443/`. In order to work, CAS requires the use of HTTPS. For detailed instructions on setting up HTTPS, refer to the Appendix, *Additional Reference Material*.

> The examples in this chapter were written using the most recent, available version of the CAS server, 5.1.2 at the time of writing. Be aware that some significant changes to some of the backend classes were made to CAS in the 5.x time frame. So, if you are on an earlier version of the server, these instructions may be slightly or significantly different for your environment.

Let's go ahead and configure the components required for CAS authentication.

> You should start the chapter off with the source from `chapter10.00-calendar` and `chapter10.00-cas-server`.

Configuring basic CAS integration

Since the Spring Security namespace does not support CAS configuration, there are quite a few more steps that we need to implement in order to get a basic setup working. In order to get a high-level understanding of what is happening, you can refer to the following diagram.

Don't worry about understanding the entire diagram right now, as we will break it into small chunks in order to make it easy to digest:

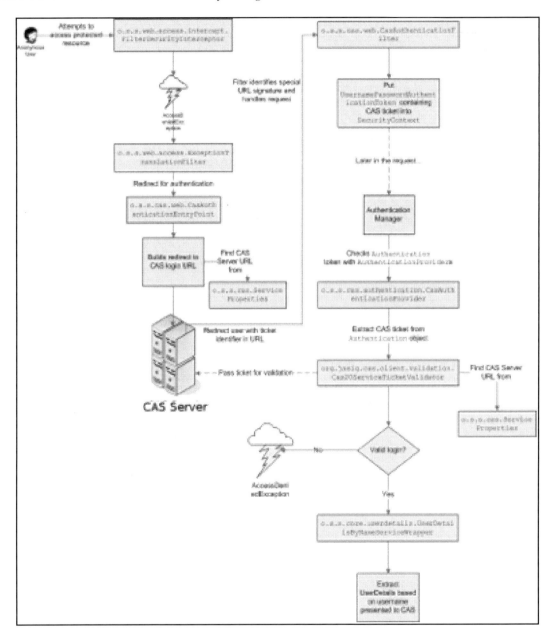

Creating the CAS ServiceProperties object

The Spring Security setup relies on an `o.s.s.cas.ServiceProperties` bean in order to store common information about the CAS service. The `ServiceProperties` object plays a role in coordinating the data exchange between the various CAS components—it is used as a data object to store CAS configuration settings that are shared (and are expected to match) by the varying participants in the Spring CAS stack. You can view the configuration included in the following code snippet:

```
//src/main/java/com/packtpub/springsecurity/configuration/CasConfig.java

static{
System.setProperty("cas.server", "https://localhost:9443/cas");
 System.setProperty("cas.server.login",
 "https://localhost:9443/cas/login");
System.setProperty("cas.service",
 "https://localhost:8443");
System.setProperty("cas.service.login",
"https://localhost:8443/login");
 }
@Value("#{systemProperties['cas.service.login']}")
private String calendarServiceLogin;
@Bean
public ServiceProperties serviceProperties(){
 return new ServiceProperties(){{
setService(calendarServiceLogin);
 }};
 }
```

You probably noticed that we leveraged system properties to use variables named `${cas.service}` and `${cas.server}`. Both of these values can be included in your application, and Spring will automatically replace them with the values provided in the `PropertySources` configuration. This is a common strategy when deploying a CAS service, since the CAS server will likely change as we progress from development to production. In this instance, we use `localhost:9443` by default for the CAS server and `localhost:8443` for the calendar application. This configuration can be overridden using a system argument when the application is taken to production. Alternatively, the configuration can be externalized into a Java properties files. Either mechanism allows us to externalize our configuration properly.

Adding the CasAuthenticationEntryPoint object

As we briefly mentioned earlier in this chapter, Spring Security uses an `o.s.s.web.AuthenticationEntryPoint` interface to request credentials from the user. Typically, this involves redirecting the user to the login page. With CAS, we will need to redirect the CAS server to request a login. When we redirect to the CAS server, Spring Security must include a `service` parameter that indicates where the CAS server should send the service ticket. Fortunately, Spring Security provides the `o.s.s.cas.web.CasAuthenticationEntryPoint` object, which is specifically designed for this purpose. The configuration that is included in the sample application is as follows:

```
//src/main/java/com/packtpub/springsecurity/configuration/CasConfig.java

@Value("#{systemProperties['cas.server.login']}")
private String casServerLogin;
@Bean
public CasAuthenticationEntryPoint casAuthenticationEntryPoint(){
  return new CasAuthenticationEntryPoint(){{
  setServiceProperties(serviceProperties());
  setLoginUrl(casServerLogin);
  }};
}
```

The `CasAuthenticationEntryPoint` object uses the `ServiceProperties` class to specify where to send the service ticket once the user is authenticated. CAS allows for the selective granting of access per user, per application, based on configuration. We'll examine the particulars of this URL in a moment when we configure the servlet filter that is expected to process it. Next, we will need to update Spring Security to utilize the bean with the `casAuthenticationEntryPoint` ID. Make the following update to our `SecurityConfig.java` file:

```
//src/main/java/com/packtpub/springsecurity/configuration/
SecurityConfig.java

@Autowired
private CasAuthenticationEntryPoint casAuthenticationEntryPoint;
@Override
protected void configure(HttpSecurity http) throws Exception {
  ...
// Exception Handling
 http.exceptionHandling()
 .authenticationEntryPoint(casAuthenticationEntryPoint)
 .accessDeniedPage("/errors/403");
 ...
```

Lastly, we need to ensure that the `CasConfig.java` file is loaded by Spring. Update the `SecurityConfig.java` file, as follows:

```
//src/main/java/com/packtpub/springsecurity/configuration/
SecurityConfig.java

@Configuration
@EnableWebSecurity(debug = true)
@EnableGlobalAuthentication
@Import(CasConfig.class)
public class SecurityConfig extends WebSecurityConfigurerAdapter {
```

The last thing you need to do is to remove the existing `UserDetailsService` object as the `userDetailsService` implementation of the `AuthenticationManager`, as it is no longer required as the `CasAuthenticationEntryPoint` replaces it in the SecurityConfig.java file:

```
src/main/java/com/packtpub/springsecurity/configuration/
SecurityConfig.java
@Override
public void configure(AuthenticationManagerBuilder auth)
throws Exception {
super.configure(auth);
//auth.userDetailsService(userDetailsService)
 // .passwordEncoder(passwordEncoder());
 }
```

If you start the application at this point and attempt to access the **My Events** page, you will immediately be redirected to the CAS server for authentication. The default configuration of CAS allows authentication for any user whose username is equal to the password. So, you should be able to log in with the username `admin1@example.com` and the password `admin1@example.com` (or `user1@example.com`/`user1@example.com`).

You'll notice, however, that even after the login, you will immediately be redirected back to the CAS server. This is because although the destination application was able to receive the ticket, it wasn't able to be validated, and as such the `AccessDeniedException` object is handled by CAS as a rejection of the ticket.

Enabling CAS ticket verification

Referring to the diagram that we saw earlier in the *Configuring basic CAS integration* section, we can see that Spring Security is responsible for identifying an unauthenticated request and redirecting the user to CAS via the `FilterSecurityInterceptor` class. Adding the `CasAuthenticationEntryPoint` object has overridden the standard redirect to the login page functionality and provided the expected redirection from the application to the CAS server. Now, we need to configure things so that, once authenticated to CAS, the user is properly authenticated to the application.

If you remember from `Chapter 9`, *Opening up to OAuth2*, OAuth2 uses a similar redirection approach by redirecting unauthenticated users to the OAuth2 provider for authentication, and then back to the application with verifiable credentials. CAS differs from OAuth2. In the CAS protocol, upon the user's return to the application, the application is expected to call back the CAS server to explicitly validate that the credentials provided are valid and accurate. Compare this with OAuth2, which uses the presence of a date-based nonce and key-based signature so that the credentials passed by the OAuth2 provider can be independently verified.

The benefit of the CAS approach is that the information passed on from the CAS server to authenticate the user is much simpler—only a single URL parameter is returned to the application by the CAS server. Additionally, the application itself need not track the active or valid tickets, and instead can wholly rely on CAS to verify this information. Much as we saw with OAuth2, a servlet filter is responsible for recognizing a redirect from CAS and processing it as an authentication request. We can see how this is configured in our `CasConfig.java` file, as follows:

```
//src/main/java/com/packtpub/springsecurity/configuration/CasConfig.java

@Autowired
private AuthenticationManager authenticationManager;
@Bean
public CasAuthenticationFilter casAuthenticationFilter() {
CasAuthenticationFilter casAuthenticationFilter =
new CasAuthenticationFilter();
casAuthenticationFilter.setAuthenticationManager
(authenticationManager);
 casAuthenticationFilter.setFilterProcessesUrl("/login");
return casAuthenticationFilter;
}
```

We'll then replace the `formLogin()` method with the custom servlet filter declaration in our `SecurityConfig.java` file:

```
//src/main/java/com/packtpub/springsecurity/configuration/SecurityC
onfig.java

@Autowired
private CasAuthenticationFilter casFilter;
@Override
protected void configure(HttpSecurity http) throws Exception {
    ...
/*http.formLogin()
    .loginPage("/login/form")
    .loginProcessingUrl("/login")
.failureUrl("/login/form?error")
.usernameParameter("username")
.passwordParameter("password")
.defaultSuccessUrl("/default", true
    .permitAll();*/
    http.addFilterAt(casFilter, CasAuthenticationFilter.class);
    // Exception Handling
    http.exceptionHandling()
        .authenticationEntryPoint(casAuthenticationEntryPoint)
        .accessDeniedPage("/errors/403");
    ...
```

Finally, a reference to the `AuthenticationManager` implementation is required by the `CasAuthenticationFilter` object—this is added (if not already present) by exposing the `AuthenticationManager` implementation as a bean declaration in `SecurityConfig.java`:

```
//src/main/java/com/packtpub/springsecurity/configuration/
SecurityConfig.java

@Bean
@Override
public AuthenticationManager authenticationManager()
throws Exception {
  return super.authenticationManager();
}
```

You may have noticed that the CAS service name from the
`ServiceProperties` configuration evaluates to
`https://localhost:8443/login`. As we've seen with other
authentication filters, it is best to override the default URL
`/j_spring_cas_security_check` to ensure that we do not
unnecessarily disclose to malicious users that we are using Spring
Security.

The `CasAuthenticationFilter` object populates an `Authentication` implementation (a
`UsernamePasswordAuthenticationToken` object) with special credentials that are
recognizable by the next and final elements of a minimal CAS configuration.

Proving authenticity with the CasAuthenticationProvider object

If you have been following the logical flow of Spring Security throughout the rest of this
book, hopefully, you already know what comes next—the `Authentication` token must be
inspected by an appropriate `AuthenticationProvider` object. CAS is no different, and as
such, the final piece of the puzzle is the configuration of an
`o.s.s.cas.authentication.CasAuthenticationProvider` object within
`AuthenticationManager`.

Let's take a look at the following steps:

1. First, we'll declare the Spring bean in the `CasConfig.java` file, as follows:

```
//src/main/java/com/packtpub/springsecurity/configuration/
CasConfig.java

@Bean
public CasAuthenticationProvider casAuthenticationProvider() {
    CasAuthenticationProvider casAuthenticationProvider = new
    CasAuthenticationProvider();
    casAuthenticationProvider.setTicketValidator(ticketValidator());
    casAuthenticationProvider.setServiceProperties
    (serviceProperties());
    casAuthenticationProvider.setKey("casJbcpCalendar");
    casAuthenticationProvider.setAuthenticationUserDetailsService(
        userDetailsByNameServiceWrapper);
        return casAuthenticationProvider;
}
```

2. Next, we'll configure a reference to this new `AuthenticationProvider` object in `SecurityConfig.java`, where our `AuthenticationManager` declaration resides:

```
//src/main/java/com/packtpub/springsecurity/configuration/
SecurityConfig.java

@Autowired
private CasAuthenticationProvider casAuthenticationProvider;
@Override
public void configure(final AuthenticationManagerBuilder auth)
throws Exception
{
  auth.authenticationProvider(casAuthenticationProvider);
}
```

3. If you have any other `AuthenticationProvider` references remaining from prior exercises, please remember to remove them from work with CAS. All of these changes are illustrated in the preceding code. Now, we'll need to take care of the other attributes and bean references within the `CasAuthenticationProvider` class. The `ticketValidator` attribute refers to an implementation of the `org.jasig.cas.client.validation.TicketValidator` interface; as we are using the CAS 3.0 authentication, we'll declare an `org.jasig.cas.client.validation.Cas30ServiceTicketValidator` instance, as follows:

```
//src/main/java/com/packtpub/springsecurity/configuration/
CasConfig.java

@Bean
public Cas30ProxyTicketValidator ticketValidator(){
  return new Cas30ProxyTicketValidator(casServer);
}
```

The constructor argument supplied to this class should refer (once again) to the URL used to access the CAS server. You'll note that at this point, we have moved out of the `org.springframework.security` package into `org.jasig`, which is part of the CAS client's JAR files. Later in this chapter, we'll see that the `TicketValidator` interface also has implementations (still within the CAS client's JAR files) that support other methods of authentication with CAS, such as the proxy ticket and SAML authentications.

Next, we can see the `key` attribute; this is simply used to validate the integrity of `UsernamePasswordAuthenticationToken` and can be arbitrarily defined.

Just as we saw in Chapter 8, *Client Certificate Authentication with TLS*, the `authenticationUserDetailsService` attribute refers to an `o.s.s.core.userdetails.AuthenticationUserDetailsService` object that is used to translate the username information from the `Authentication` token to a fully-populated `UserDetails` object. The current implementation does this translation by looking up the username returned by the CAS server and looking up `UserDetails` using the `UserDetailsService` object. Obviously, this technique would only ever be used when we have confirmed that the integrity of the `Authentication` token has not been compromised. We configure this object with a reference to our `CalendarUserDetailsService` implementation of the `UserDetailsService` interface:

```
//src/main/java/com/packtpub/springsecurity/configuration/CasConfig.java

@Bean
public UserDetailsByNameServiceWrapper
authenticationUserDetailsService(
   final UserDetailsService userDetailsService) {
   return new UserDetailsByNameServiceWrapper() {{
   setUserDetailsService(userDetailsService);
   }};
}
```

You may wonder why a `UserDetailsService` interface isn't directly referenced; it's because, just as with OAuth2, there will be additional advanced configuration options later, which will allow details from the CAS server to be used to populate the `UserDetails` object.

 Your code should look like `chapter10.01-calendar` and `chapter10.01-cas-server`.

At this point, we should be able to start both the CAS server and JBCP calendar application. You can then visit `https://localhost:8443/` and select **All Events**, which will redirect you to the CAS server. You can then log in using the username `admin1@example.com` and the password `admin1@example.com`. Upon successful authentication, you will be redirected back to the JBCP calendar application. Excellent job!

If you are experiencing issues, it is most likely due to an improper SSL configuration. Ensure that you have set up the trust store file as `tomcat.keystore`, as described in the `Appendix`, *Additional reference Material*.

Single logout

You may notice that if you log out of the application, you get the logout confirmation page. However, if you click on a protected page, such as the **My Events** page, you are still authenticated. The problem is that the logout is only occurring locally. So, when you request another protected resource in the JBCP calendar application, a login is requested from the CAS server. Since the user is still logged in to the CAS server, it immediately returns a service ticket and logs the user back into the JBCP calendar application.

This also means that if the user had signed in to other applications using the CAS server, they would still be authenticated to those applications, since our calendar application does not know anything about the other applications. Fortunately, CAS and Spring Security offer a solution to this problem. Just as we can request a login from the CAS server, we can also request a logout. You can see a high-level diagram of how a logout works within CAS, as follows:

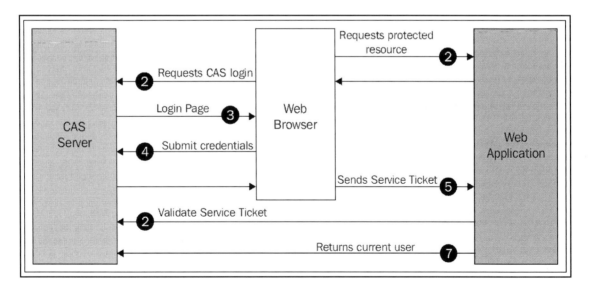

The following steps explain how a single logout takes place:

1. The user requests to log out of the web application.
2. The web application then requests to log out of CAS by sending a redirect through the browser to the CAS server.
3. The CAS server recognizes the user and then sends a logout request to each CAS service that was authenticated. Note that these logout requests do not occur through the browser.
4. The CAS server indicates which user should log out by providing the original service ticket that was used to log the user in. The application is then responsible for ensuring that the user is logged out.
5. The CAS server displays the logout success page to the user.

Configuring single logout

The configuration for a single logout is relatively simple:

1. The first step is to specify a `logout-success-url` attribute to be the logout URL of the CAS server in our `SecurityConfig.java` file. This means that after we log out locally, we will automatically redirect the user to the CAS server's logout page:

```
//src/main/java/com/packtpub/springsecurity/configuration/
SecurityConfig.java

@Value("#{systemProperties['cas.server']}/logout")
private static String casServerLogout;
@Override
protected void configure(final HttpSecurity http)
throws Exception {
  ...
 http.logout()
.logoutUrl("/logout")
.logoutSuccessUrl(casServerLogout)
.permitAll();
}
```

Since we only have one application, this is all we need to make it appear as though a single logout is occurring. This is because we log out of our calendar application before redirecting to the CAS server logout page. This means that by the time the CAS server sends the logout request to the calendar application, the user has already been logged out.

2. If there were multiple applications and the user logged out of another application, the CAS server would send a logout request to our calendar application and not process the logout event. This is because our application is not listening to these logout events. The solution is simple; we must create the SingleSignoutFilter object, as follows:

```
//src/main/java/com/packtpub/springsecurity/configuration/
CasConfig.java

@Bean
public SingleSignOutFilter singleSignOutFilter() {
    return new SingleSignOutFilter();
}
```

3. Next, we need to make Spring Security aware of the singleLogoutFilter object in our SecurityCOnfig.java file by including it as a <custom-filter> element. Place the single logout filter before the regular logout to ensure that it receives the logout events, as follows:

```
//src/main/java/com/packtpub/springsecurity/configuration/
SecurityConfig.java

@Autowired
private SingleSignOutFilter singleSignOutFilter;
@Override
protected void configure(HttpSecurity http) throws Exception {
  ...
  http.addFilterAt(casFilter, CasAuthenticationFilter.class);
  http.addFilterBefore(singleSignOutFilter, LogoutFilter.class);
// Logout
http.logout()
 .logoutUrl("/logout")
 .logoutSuccessUrl(casServerLogout)
 .permitAll();
}
```

4. Under normal circumstances, we would need to make a few updates to the `web.xml` or `ApplicationInitializer` file. However, for our calendar application, we have already made the updates to our `CasConfig.java` file, as follows:

```java
//src/main/java/com/packtpub/springsecurity/configuration/
CasConfig.java

@Bean
public ServletListenerRegistrationBean
<SingleSignOutHttpSessionListener>
singleSignOutHttpSessionListener() {
    ServletListenerRegistrationBean<SingleSignOutHttpSessionListener>
    listener = new
    ServletListenerRegistrationBean<>();
    listener.setEnabled(true);
    listener.setListener(new SingleSignOutHttpSessionListener());
    listener.setOrder(1);
    return listener;
}
@Bean
public FilterRegistrationBean
characterEncodingFilterRegistration() {
    FilterRegistrationBean registrationBean =
    new FilterRegistrationBean
    (characterEncodingFilter());
    registrationBean.setName("CharacterEncodingFilter");
    registrationBean.addUrlPatterns("/*");
    registrationBean.setOrder(1);
    return registrationBean;
}
private CharacterEncodingFilter characterEncodingFilter() {
    CharacterEncodingFilter filter = new CharacterEncodingFilter(
        filter.setEncoding("UTF-8");
        filter.setForceEncoding(true);
        return filter;
}
```

First, we added the `SingleSignoutHttpSessionListener` object to ensure that the mapping of the service ticket to `HttpSession` was removed. We have also added `CharacterEncodingFilter`, as recommended by the JA-SIG documentation, to ensure that character encoding is correct when using `SingleSignOutFilter`.

5. Go ahead and start up the application and try logging out now. You will observe that you are actually logged out.

6. Now, try logging back in and visiting the CAS server's logout URL directly. For our setup, the URL is `https://localhost:9443/cas/logout`.

7. Now, try to visit the JBCP calendar application. You will observe that you are unable to access the application without authenticating again. This demonstrates that a single logout works.

> Your code should look like `chapter10.02-calendar` and `chapter10.02-cas-server`.

Clustered environments

One of the things that we failed to mention in our initial diagram of a single logout was how the logout is performed. Unfortunately, it is implemented by storing a mapping of the service ticket to `HttpSession` as an in-memory map. This means that a single logout will not work properly within a clustered environment:

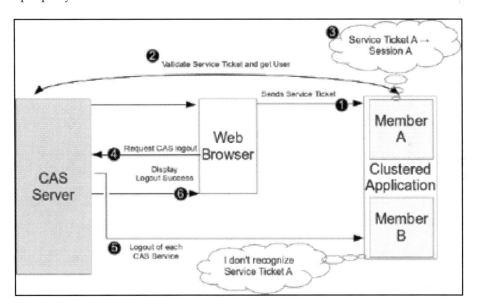

Consider the following situation:

- The user logs in to **Cluster Member A**
- **Cluster Member A** validates the service ticket
- It then remembers, in memory, the mapping of the service ticket to the user's session
- The user requests to log out from the **CAS Server**

The **CAS Server** sends a logout request to the CAS service, but the **Cluster Member B** receives the logout request. It looks in its memory but does not find a session for **Service Ticket A**, because it only exists in **Cluster Member A**. This means, the user has not been logged out successfully.

Users looking for this functionality might consider looking in the JA-SIG JIRA queue and forums for solutions to this problem. In fact, a working patch has been submitted on `https://issues.jasig.org/browse/CASC-114`. Keep in mind that there are a number of ongoing discussions and proposals on the forums and in the JA-SIG JIRA queue, so you may want to look around before deciding which solution to use. For more information about clustering with CAS, refer to JA-SIG's clustering documentation at `https://wiki.jasig.org/display/CASUM/Clustering+CAS`.

Proxy ticket authentication for stateless services

Centralizing our authentication using CAS seems to work rather well for web applications, but what if we want to call a web service using CAS? In order to support this, CAS has a notion of **proxy tickets** (**PT**). The following is a diagram of how it works:

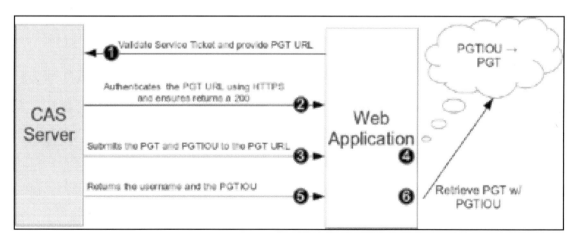

The flow is the same as standard CAS authentication until the following things take place:

1. The **Service Ticket** is validated when an additional parameter is included called the proxy ticket callback URL (**PGT URL**).
2. The **CAS Server** calls the **PGT URL** over **HTTPS** to validate that the **PGT URL** is what it claims to be. Like most of CAS, this is done by performing an SSL handshake to the appropriate URL.
3. The **CAS Server** submits the **Proxy Granting Ticket** (**PGT**) and the **Proxy Granting Ticket I Owe You** (**PGTIOU**) to the **PGT URL** over **HTTPS** to ensure that the tickets are submitted to the source they claim to be.
4. The **PGT URL** receives the two tickets and must store an association of the **PGTIOU** to the **PGT**.
5. The **CAS Server** finally returns a response to the request in *step 1* that includes the username and the **PGTIOU**.
6. The CAS service can look up the **PGT** using the **PGTIOU**.

Configuring proxy ticket authentication

Now that we know how PT authentication works, we will update our current configuration to obtain a PGT by performing the following steps:

1. The first step is to add a reference to a `ProxyGrantingTicketStorage` implementation. Go ahead and add the following code to our `CasConfig.java` file:

   ```
   //src/main/java/com/packtpub/springsecurity/configuration/
   CasConfig.java

   @Bean
   public ProxyGrantingTicketStorage pgtStorage() {
    return new ProxyGrantingTicketStorageImpl();
   }
   @Scheduled(fixedRate = 300_000)
   public void proxyGrantingTicketStorageCleaner(){
     pgtStorage().cleanUp();
   }
   ```

2. The `ProxyGrantingTicketStorageImpl` implementation is an in-memory mapping of the PGTIOU to a PGT. Just as with logging out, this means we would have problems in a clustered environment using this implementation. Refer to the JA-SIG documentation to determine how to set this up in a clustered environment: `https://wiki.jasig.org/display/CASUM/Clustering+CAS`.

3. We also need to periodically clean `ProxyGrantingTicketStorage` by invoking its `cleanUp()` method. As you can see, Spring's task abstraction makes this very simple. You may consider tweaking the configuration to clear the `Ticket`'s, in a separate a thread pool that makes sense for your environment. For more information, refer to the *Task Execution* and *Scheduling* section of the Spring Framework Reference documentation at `http://static.springsource.org/spring/docs/current/spring-framework-reference/html/scheduling.html`.

4. Now we need to use `ProxyGrantingTicketStorage`, which we have just created. We just need to update the `ticketValidator` method to refer to our storage and to know the PGT URL. Make the following updates to `CasConfig.java`:

```
//src/main/java/com/packtpub/springsecurity/configuration/
CasConfig.java

@Value("#{systemProperties['cas.calendar.service']}/pgtUrl")
private String calendarServiceProxyCallbackUrl;
@Bean
public Cas30ProxyTicketValidator ticketValidator(){
  Cas30ProxyTicketValidator tv = new
  Cas30ProxyTicketValidator(casServer);
  tv.setProxyCallbackUrl(calendarServiceProxyCallbackUrl);
  tv.setProxyGrantingTicketStorage(pgtStorage());
  return tv;
    }
```

5. The last update we need to make is to our `CasAuthenticationFilter` object, to store the PGTIOU to the PGT mapping in our `ProxyGrantingTicketStorage` implementation when the PGT URL is called. It is critical to ensure that the `proxyReceptorUrl` attribute matches the `proxyCallbackUrl` attribute of the `Cas20ProxyTicketValidator` object, to ensure that the CAS server sends the ticket to the URL that our application is listing to. Make the following changes to `security-cas.xml`:

```
//src/main/java/com/packtpub/springsecurity/configuration/
CasConfig.java
```

```
@Bean
public CasAuthenticationFilter casFilter() {
    CasAuthenticationFilter caf = new CasAuthenticationFilter();
caf.setAuthenticationManager(authenticationManager);
caf.setFilterProcessesUrl("/login");
caf.setProxyGrantingTicketStorage(pgtStorage());
caf.setProxyReceptorUrl("/pgtUrl");
 return caf;
}
```

Now that we have a PGT, what do we do with it? A service ticket is a one-time use token. However, a PGT can be used to produce PT. Let's see how we can create a PT using a PGT.

 You will observe that the `proxyCallBackUrl` attribute matches the absolute path of our context-relative `proxyReceptorUrl` attribute path. Since we are deploying our base application to `https://${cas.service }/`, the full path of our `proxyReceptor` URL will be `https://${cas.service }/pgtUrl`.

Using proxy tickets

We can now use our PGT to create a PT to authenticate it to a service. The code to do this is quite trivially demonstrated in the `EchoController` class that we have included with this chapter. You can see the relevant portions of it in the following code snippet. For additional details, refer to the sample's source code:

```
//src/main/java/com/packtpub/springsecurity/web/controllers/
EchoController.java

@ResponseBody
@RequestMapping("/echo")
 public String echo() throws UnsupportedEncodingException {
    final CasAuthenticationToken token = (CasAuthenticationToken)
 SecurityContextHolder.getContext().getAuthentication();
 final String proxyTicket = token.getAssertion().getPrincipal()
.getProxyTicketFor(targetUrl);
return restClient.getForObject(targetUrl+"?ticket={pt}",
String.class, proxyTicket);
}
```

This controller is a contrived example that will obtain a PT that will be used to authenticate a RESTful call to obtain all of the events for the currently logged-in user. It then writes the JSON response to the page. The thing that may confuse some users is that the EchoController object is actually making a RESTful call to the MessagesController object that is in the same application. This means that the calendar application makes a RESTful call to itself.

Go ahead and visit https://localhost:8443/echo to see it in action. The page looks a lot like the CAS login page (minus the CSS). This is because the controller attempts to echo our **My Events** page, and our application does not yet know how to authenticate a PT. This means it is redirected to the CAS login page. Let's see how we can authenticate proxy tickets.

 Your code should look like chapter10.03-calendar and chapter10.03-cas-server.

Authenticating proxy tickets

Let's take a look at the following steps to learn about authenticating proxy tickets:

1. We first need to tell the ServiceProperties object that we want to authenticate all of the tickets and not just those submitted to the filterProcessesUrl attribute. Make the following updates to CasConfig.java:

```
//src/main/java/com/packtpub/springsecurity/configuration/
CasConfig.java

@Bean
public ServiceProperties serviceProperties(){
  return new ServiceProperties(){{
     setService(calendarServiceLogin);
     setAuthenticateAllArtifacts(true);
  }};
}
```

2. We then need to update our `CasAuthenticationFilter` object for it to know that we want to authenticate all artifacts (that is, tickets) instead of only listening to a specific URL. We also need to use an `AuthenticationDetailsSource` interface that can dynamically provide the CAS service URL when validating proxy tickets on arbitrary URLs. This is important because when a CAS service asks whether a ticket is valid or not, it must also provide the CAS service URL that was used to create the ticket. Since proxy tickets can occur at any URL, we must be able to dynamically discover this URL. This is done by leveraging the `ServiceAuthenticationDetailsSource` object, which will provide the current URL from the HTTP request:

```
//src/main/java/com/packtpub/springsecurity/configuration/
CasConfig.java

@Bean
public CasAuthenticationFilter casFilter() {
  CasAuthenticationFilter caf = new CasAuthenticationFilter();
  caf.setAuthenticationManager(authenticationManager);
  caf.setFilterProcessesUrl("/login");
  caf.setProxyGrantingTicketStorage(pgtStorage());
  caf.setProxyReceptorUrl("/pgtUrl");
  caf.setServiceProperties(serviceProperties());
  caf.setAuthenticationDetailsSource(new
  ServiceAuthenticationDetailsSource(serviceProperties())
);
  return caf;
}
```

3. We will also need to ensure that we are using the `Cas30ProxyTicketValidator` object and not the `Cas30ServiceTicketValidator` implementation, and indicate which proxy tickets we will want to accept. We will configure ours to accept a proxy ticket from any CAS service. In a production environment, you will want to consider restricting yourself to only those CAS services that are trusted:

```
//src/main/java/com/packtpub/springsecurity/configuration/
CasConfig.java

@Bean
public Cas30ProxyTicketValidator ticketValidator(){
  Cas30ProxyTicketValidator tv = new
  Cas30ProxyTicketValidator(casServer);
  tv.setProxyCallbackUrl(calendarServiceProxyCallbackUrl);
```

```
        tv.setProxyGrantingTicketStorage(pgtStorage());
        tv.setAcceptAnyProxy(true);
        return tv;
    }
```

4. Lastly, we will want to provide a cache for our `CasAuthenticationProvider` object so that we do not need to hit the CAS service for every call to our service:

```
//src/main/java/com/packtpub/springsecurity/configuration/
CasConfig.java

@Bean
public CasAuthenticationProvider casAuthenticationProvider() {
  CasAuthenticationProvider cap = new CasAuthenticationProvider();
  cap.setTicketValidator(ticketValidator());
  cap.setServiceProperties(serviceProperties());
  cap.setKey("casJbcpCalendar");
  cap.setAuthenticationUserDetailsService
  (userDetailsByNameServiceWrapper);
  cap.setStatelessTicketCache(ehCacheBasedTicketCache());
  return cap;
 }
@Bean
public EhCacheBasedTicketCache ehCacheBasedTicketCache() {
  EhCacheBasedTicketCache cache = new EhCacheBasedTicketCache();
  cache.setCache(ehcache());
  return cache;
 }
@Bean(initMethod = "initialise", destroyMethod = "dispose")
public Cache ehcache() {
  Cache cache = new Cache("casTickets", 50, true, false, 3_600, 900);
  return cache;
 }
```

5. As you might have suspected, the cache requires the `ehcache` dependency that we mentioned at the beginning of the chapter. Go ahead and start the application back up and visit `https://localhost:8443/echo` again. This time, you should see a JSON response to calling our **My Events** page.

Your code should look like `chapter10.04-calendar` and `chapter10.04-cas-server`.

Customizing the CAS server

All of the changes in this section will be to the CAS server and not the calendar application. This section is only meant to be an introduction to configuring the CAS server, as a detailed setup is certainly beyond the scope of this book. Just as with the changes for the calendar application, we encourage you to follow along with the changes in this chapter. For more information, you can refer to the JA-SIG CAS Wikipedia page at `https://wiki.jasig.org/display/CAS/Home`.

CAS WAR overlay

The preferred way to customize CAS is to use a Maven or Gradle War overlay. With this mechanism, you can change everything from the UI to the method in which you authenticate to the CAS server. The concept of a WAR overlay is simple. You add a WAR overlay, `cas-server-webapp`, as a dependency, and then provide additional files that will be merged with the existing WAR overlay. For more information about the CAS WAR overlay, refer to the JA-SIG documentation at `https://wiki.jasig.org/display/CASUM/Best+Practice+-+Setting+Up+CAS+Locally+using+the+Maven2+WAR+Overlay+Method`.

How does the CAS internal authentication work?

Before we jump into CAS configuration, we'll briefly illustrate the standard behavior of CAS authentication processing. The following diagram should help you follow the configuration steps required to allow CAS to talk to our embedded LDAP server:

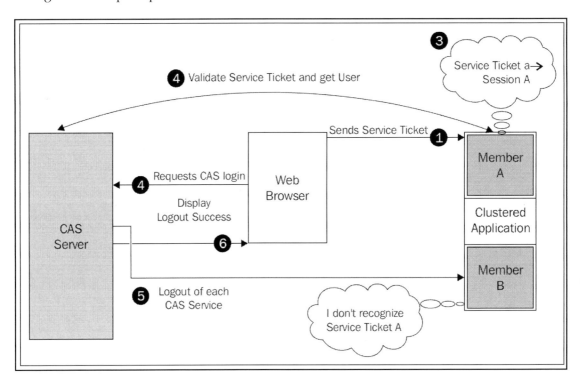

While the previous diagram describes the internal flow of authentication within the CAS server itself, it is likely that if you are implementing integration between Spring Security and CAS, you will need to adjust the configuration of the CAS server as well. It's important, therefore, that you understand how CAS authentication works at a high level.

The CAS server's `org.jasig.cas.authentication.AuthenticationManager` interface (not to be confused with the Spring Security interface of the same name) is responsible for authenticating the user based on the provided credentials. Much as with Spring Security, the actual processing of the credentials is delegated to one (or more) processing class implementing the `org.jasig.cas.authentication.handler.AuthenticationHandler` interface (we recognize that the analogous interface in Spring Security would be `AuthenticationProvider`).

Finally, a `org.jasig.cas.authentication.principal.CredentialsToPrincipalResolver` interface is used to translate the credentials passed into a full `org.jasig.cas.authentication.principal.Principal` object (similar behavior in Spring Security occurs during the implementation of `UserDetailsService`).

While not a full review of the behind-the-scenes functionality of the CAS server, this should help you understand the configuration steps in the next several exercises. We encourage you to read the source code for CAS and consult the web-based documentation available at the JA-SIG CAS Wikipedia page at `http://www.ja-sig.org/wiki/display/CAS`.

Configuring CAS to connect to our embedded LDAP server

The `org.jasig.cas.authentication.principal.UsernamePasswordCredentialsToPrincipalResolver` object that comes configured, by default, with CAS doesn't allow us to pass back attribute information and demonstrate this feature of Spring Security CAS integration, so we'd suggest using an implementation that does allow this.

An easy authentication handler to configure and use (especially if you have gone through the previous chapter's LDAP exercises) is `org.jasig.cas.adaptors.ldap.BindLdapAuthenticationHandler`, which communicates with the embedded LDAP server that we used in the previous chapter. We'll lead you through the configuration of CAS that returns user LDAP attributes in the following guide.

All of the CAS configuration will take place in the `WEB-INF/deployerConfigContext.xml` file of the CAS installation, and will typically involve inserting class declarations into configuration file segments that already exist. We have already extracted the default `WEB-INF/deployerConfigContext.xml` file from `cas-server-webapp` and placed it in `cas-server/src/main/webapp/WEB-INF`.

If the contents of this file look familiar to you, it's because CAS uses the Spring Framework for its configuration just like the JBCP calendar! We'd recommend using a good IDE with a handy reference to the CAS source code if you want to dig into what these configuration settings do. Remember that in this section, and all sections where we refer to `WEB-INF/deployerConfigContext.xml`, we are referring to the CAS installation and not JBCP calendar.

Let's take a look at the following steps:

1. First, we'll add a new `BindLdapAuthenticationHandler` object in place of the `SimpleTestUsernamePasswordAuthenticationHandler` object, which will attempt to bind the user to LDAP (just as we did in Chapter 6, *LDAP Directory Services*).

2. The `AuthenticationHandler` interface will be placed in the `authenticationHandlers` property of the `authenticationManager` bean:

   ```
   //cas-server/src/main/webapp/WEB-INF/deployerConfigContext.xml

   <property name="authenticationHandlers">
   <list>
    ... remove ONLY
   SimpleTestUsernamePasswordAuthenticationHandler ...
   <bean class="org.jasig.cas.adaptors
   .ldap.BindLdapAuthenticationHandler">
   <property name="filter" value="uid=%u"/>
   <property name="searchBase" value="ou=Users"/>
   <property name="contextSource" ref="contextSource"/>
    </bean>
   </list>
   </property>
   ```

   Don't forget to remove the reference to the `SimpleTestUsernamePasswordAuthenticationHandler` object, or at least move its definition to after that of the `BindLdapAuthenticationHandler` object, otherwise, your CAS authentication will not use LDAP and use the stub handler instead!

3. You'll notice the bean reference to a `contextSource` bean; this defines the `org.springframework.ldap.core.ContextSource` implementation, which CAS will use to interact with LDAP (yes, CAS uses Spring LDAP as well). We'll define this at the end of the file using the Spring Security namespace to simplify its definition, as follows:

```
//cas-server/src/main/webapp/WEB-INF/deployerConfigContext.xml

<sec:ldap-server id="contextSource"
 ldif="classpath:ldif/calendar.ldif" root="dc=jbcpcalendar,dc=com" />
</beans>
```

This creates an embedded LDAP instance that uses the `calendar.ldif` file included with this chapter. Of course, in a production environment, you would want to point to a real LDAP server.

4. Finally, we'll need to configure a new `org.jasig.cas.authentication.principal.CredentialsToPrincipalResolver` object. This is responsible for translating the credentials that the user has provided (that CAS has already authenticated using the `BindLdapAuthenticationHandler` object) into a full `org.jasig.cas.authentication.principal.Principal` authenticated principal. You'll notice many configuration options in this class, which we'll skim over. You are welcome to dive into them as you explore CAS further.

5. Remove `UsernamePasswordCredentialsToPrincipalResolver` and add the following bean definition inline to the `credentialsToPrincipalResolvers` property of the CAS `authenticationManager` bean:

```
//cas-server/src/main/webapp/WEB-INF/deployerConfigContext.xml

<property name="credentialsToPrincipalResolvers">
<list>
<!-- REMOVE UsernamePasswordCredentialsToPrincipalResolver -->
<bean class="org.jasig.cas.authentication.principal
.HttpBasedServiceCredentialsToPrincipalResolver" />
<bean class="org.jasig.cas.authentication.principal
.CredentialsToLDAPAttributePrincipalResolver">
<property name="credentialsToPrincipalResolver">
<bean class="org.jasig.cas.authentication.principal
.UsernamePasswordCredentialsToPrincipalResolver"/>
</property>
<property name="filter" value="(uid=%u)"/>
<property name="principalAttributeName" value="uid"/>
<property name="searchBase" value="ou=Users"/>
```

```
<property name="contextSource" ref="contextSource"/>
<property name="attributeRepository" ref="attributeRepository"/>
</bean>
</list>
</property>
```

You'll notice that, as with the Spring Security LDAP configuration, much of the same behavior exists in CAS with principals being searched on property matches below a subtree of the directory, based on a DN.

Note that we haven't yet configured the bean with the ID `attributeRepository` ourselves, which should refer to an implementation of `org.jasig.services.persondir.IPersonAttributeDao`. CAS ships with a default configuration that includes a simple implementation of this interface, `org.jasig.services.persondir.support.StubPersonAttributeDao`, which will be sufficient until we configure LDAP-based attributes in a later exercise.

> Your code should look like `chapter10.05-calendar` and `chapter10.05-cas-server`.

So, now we've configured basic LDAP authentication in CAS. At this point, you should be able to restart CAS, start JBCP calendar (if it's not already running), and authenticate it using `admin1@example.com/admin` or `user1@example.com/user1`. Go ahead and try it to see that it works. If it does not work, try checking the logs and comparing your configuration with the sample configuration.

As discussed in Chapter 5, *Authentication with Spring Data*, you may encounter issues starting the application, whether or not the temporary directory named `apacheds-spring-security` still exists. If the application appears to not exist, check the logs and see if the `apacheds-spring-security` directory needs to be removed.

Getting the UserDetails object from a CAS assertion

Up until this point, we have been authenticating with CAS by obtaining the roles from our `InMemoryUserDetailsManager` object. However, we can create the `UserDetails` object from the CAS assertion just as we did with OAuth2. The first step is to configure the CAS server to return the additional attributes.

Returning LDAP attributes in the CAS response

We know that CAS can return the username in the CAS response, but it can also return arbitrary attributes in the CAS response. Let's see how we can update the CAS server to return additional attributes. Again, all of the changes in this section are in the CAS server and not in the calendar application.

Mapping LDAP attributes to CAS attributes

The first step requires us to map LDAP attributes to attributes in the CAS assertion (including the `role` attribute, which we're expecting to contain the user's `GrantedAuthority`).

We'll add another bit of configuration to the CAS `deployerConfigContext.xml` file. This new bit of configuration is required to instruct CAS as to how to map attributes from the CAS `Principal` object to the CAS `IPersonAttributes` object, which will ultimately be serialized as part of ticket validation. This bean configuration should replace the bean of the same name—which is `attributeRepository`—as follows:

```
//cas-server/src/main/webapp/WEB-INF/deployerConfigContext.xml

<bean id="attributeRepository" class="org.jasig.services.persondir
.support.ldap.LdapPersonAttributeDao">
<property name="contextSource" ref="contextSource"/>
<property name="requireAllQueryAttributes" value="true"/>
<property name="baseDN" value="ou=Users"/>
<property name="queryAttributeMapping">
<map>
 <entry key="username" value="uid"/>
</map>
 </property>
<property name="resultAttributeMapping">
<map>
<entry key="cn" value="FullName"/>
<entry key="sn" value="LastName"/>
<entry key="description" value="role"/>
</map>
</property>
</bean>
```

The functionality behind the scenes here is definitely confusing—essentially, the purpose of this class is to map `Principal` back to the LDAP directory. (This is the `queryAttributeMapping` property mapping the `username` field of `Principal` to the `uid` attribute in the LDAP query.) The provided `baseDN` Java Bean property is searched using the LDAP query (`uid=user1@example.com`), and attributes are read from the matching entry. The attributes are mapped back to `Principal` using the key/value pairs in the `resultAttributeMapping` property. We recognize that LDAP's `cn` and `sn` attributes are being mapped to meaningful names, and the `description` attribute is being mapped to the role that will be used for determining the authorization of our user.

Part of the complexity comes from the fact that a portion of this functionality is wrapped up in a separate project called `Person Directory` (`http://www.ja-sig.org/wiki/display/PD/Home`), which is intended to aggregate multiple sources of information about a person into a single view. The design of `Person Directory` is such that it is not directly tied to the CAS server and can be reused as part of other applications. The downside of this design choice is that it makes some aspects of CAS configuration more complex than it initially seems should be required.

Troubleshooting LDAP attribute mapping in CAS

We would love to set up the same type of query in LDAP as we used with Spring Security LDAP in Chapter 6, *LDAP Directory Services*, to be able to map `Principal` to a full LDAP-distinguished name, and then to use that DN to look up group membership by matching on the basis of the `uniqueMember` attribute of a `groupOfUniqueNames` entry. Unfortunately, the CAS LDAP code doesn't have this flexibility yet, leading to the conclusion that more advanced LDAP mapping will require extensions to base classes in CAS.

Authorizing CAS services to access custom attributes

Next, we will need to authorize any CAS service over HTTPS to access these attributes. To do this, we can update `RegisteredServiceImpl`, which has the description `Only Allows HTTPS URLs` in `InMemoryServiceRegistryDaoImpl`, as follows:

```
//cas-server/src/main/webapp/WEB-INF/deployerConfigContext.xml

<bean class="org.jasig.cas.services.RegisteredServiceImpl">
  <property name="id" value="1" />
  <property name="name" value="HTTPS" />
  <property name="description" value="Only Allows HTTPS Urls" />
  <property name="serviceId" value="https://**" />
  <property name="evaluationOrder" value="10000002" />
  <property name="allowedAttributes">
  <list>
    <value>FullName</value>
    <value>LastName</value>
    <value>role</value>
 </list>
</property>
</bean>
```

Acquiring a UserDetails from CAS

When we first set up CAS integration with Spring Security, we configured `UserDetailsByNameServiceWrapper`, which simply translated the username presented to CAS into a `UserDetails` object from `UserDetailsService`, which we had referenced (in our case, it was `InMemoryUserDetailsManager`). Now that CAS is referencing the LDAP server, we can set up `LdapUserDetailsService`, as we discussed at the tail end of `Chapter 6`, *LDAP Directory Services*, and things will work just fine. Note that we have switched back to modifying the calendar application and not the CAS server.

The GrantedAuthorityFromAssertionAttributesUser object

Now that we have modified the CAS server to return custom attributes, we'll experiment with another capability of the Spring Security CAS integration—the ability to populate `UserDetails` from the CAS assertion itself! This is actually as simple as switching the `AuthenticationUserDetailsService` implementation to the `o.s.s.cas.userdetails.GrantedAuthorityFromAssertionAttributesUserDetailsService` object, whose job it is to read the CAS assertion, look for a certain attribute, and map the value of that attribute directly to the `GrantedAuthority` object for the user. Let's assume that there is an attribute entitled role that will be returned with the assertion. We'll simply configure a new `authenticationUserDetailsService` bean (be sure to replace the previously defined `authenticationUserDetailsService` bean) in the `CaseConfig.xml` file:

```
//src/main/java/com/packtpub/springsecurity/configuration/CasConfig.java

    @Bean
    public AuthenticationUserDetailsService userDetailsService(){
        GrantedAuthorityFromAssertionAttributesUserDetailsService uds
        = new GrantedAuthorityFromAssertionAttributesUserDetailsService(
        new String[]{"role"}
    );
     return uds;
    }
```

You will also want to remove the `userDetailsService` bean from our `SecurityConfig.java` file, since it is no longer needed.

Alternative ticket authentication using SAML 1.1

Security Assertion Markup Language (SAML) is a standard, cross-platform protocol for identify verification using structured XML assertions. SAML is supported by a wide variety of products, including CAS (in fact, we will look at support for SAML within Spring Security itself in a later chapter).

While the standard CAS protocol can be extended to return attributes, the SAML security assertion XML dialect solves some of the issues with attribute passing, using the CAS response protocol that we previously described. Happily, switching between CAS ticket validation and SAML ticket validation is as simple as changing the `TicketValidator` implementation configured in `CasSecurity.java`. Modify `ticketValidator`, as follows:

```
//src/main/java/com/packtpub/springsecurity/configuration/CasConfig.java

    @Bean
    public Saml11TicketValidator ticketValidator(){
      return new Saml11TicketValidator(casServer);
    }
```

You will notice that there is no longer a reference to the PGT URL. This is because the `Saml11TicketValidator` object does not support PGT. While both could exist, we opt to remove any references to the proxy ticket authentication, since we will no longer be using proxy ticket authentication. If you do not want to remove it from this exercise, don't worry; it won't prevent our application from running so long as your `ticketValidator` bean ID looks similar to the previous code snippet.

In general, it's recommended that SAML ticket validation be used over CAS 2.0 ticket validation, as it adds more non-repudiation features, including `timestamp` validation, and solves the attribute problem in a standard way.

Restart the CAS server and JBCP calendar application. You can then visit `https://localhost:8443` and see that our calendar application can obtain `UserDetails` from the CAS response.

Your code should now look like `chapter10.06-calendar` and `chapter10.06-cas-server`.

How is attribute retrieval useful?

Remember that CAS provides a layer of abstraction for our application, removing the ability for our application to directly access the user repository, and instead forcing all such access to be performed through CAS as a proxy.

This is extremely powerful! It means that our application no longer cares what kind of repository the users are stored in, nor does it have to worry about the details of how to access them—this simply confirms that authentication with CAS is sufficient to prove that a user should be able to access our application. For system administrators, this means that should an LDAP server be renamed, moved, or otherwise adjusted, they only need to reconfigure it in a single location—CAS. Centralizing access through CAS allows for a high level of flexibility and adaptability in the overall security architecture of the organization.

This story to the usefulness of attribute retrieval from CAS; now all applications authenticated through CAS have the same view of a user and can consistently display information across any CAS-enabled environment.

Be aware that, once authenticated, Spring Security CAS does not require the CAS server, unless the user is required to reauthenticate. This means that attributes and other user information stored locally in the application in the user's `Authentication` object may become stale over time, and possibly out of sync with the source CAS server. Take care to set session timeouts appropriately to avoid this potential issue!

Additional CAS capabilities

CAS offers additional advanced configuration capabilities outside of those that are exposed through the Spring Security CAS wrappers. Some of these include the following capabilities:

- Providing transparent single sign-on for users who are accessing multiple CAS-secured applications within a configurable time window on the CAS server. Applications can force users to authenticate to CAS by setting the `renew` property to `true` on `TicketValidator`; you may want to conditionally set this property in custom code in the event where the user is attempting to access a highly secured area of the application.
- The RESTful API for obtaining service tickets.
- JA-SIG's CAS server can also act as an OAuth2 server. If you think about it, this makes sense, since CAS is very similar to OAuth2.
- Providing OAuth support for the CAS server so that it can obtain access tokens to a delegate OAuth provider (that is, Google), or so that the CAS server can be the OAuth server itself.

We'd encourage you to explore the full capabilities of the CAS client and server as well as ask questions to the helpful folks in the JA-SIG community forums!

Summary

In this chapter, we learned about the CAS single sign-on portal and how it can be integrated with Spring Security, and we also covered the CAS architecture and communication paths between actors in a CAS-enabled environment. We also saw the benefits of CAS-enabled applications for application developers and system administrators. We also learned about configuring JBCP calendar to interact with a basic CAS installation. We also covered the use of CAS's single logout support.

We also saw how proxy ticket authentication works and how to leverage it to authenticate stateless services.
We also covered tasks of updating CAS to interact with LDAP, and sharing LDAP data with our CAS-enabled application. We even learned about implementing attribute exchange with the industry standard SAML protocol.

We hope this chapter was an interesting introduction to the world of single sign-on. There are many other single sign-on systems in the marketplace, mostly commercial, but CAS is definitely one of the leaders of the open source SSO world, and an excellent platform to build out SSO capability in any organization.

In the next chapter, we'll learn more about Spring Security authorization.

11
Fine-Grained Access Control

In this chapter, we will first examine two ways to implement fine-grained authorization—authorization that may affect portions of a page of the application. Next, we will look at Spring Security's approach to securing the business tier through method annotation and the use of interface-based proxies to accomplish AOP. Then, we will review an interesting capability of annotation-based security that allows for role-based filtering on collections of data. Last, we will look at how class-based proxies differ from interface-based proxies.

During the course of this chapter, we'll cover the following topics:

- Configuring and experimenting with different methods of performing in-page authorization checks on content, given the security context of a user request
- Performing configuration and code annotation to make caller preauthorization a key part of our application's business-tier security
- Several alternative approaches to implement method-level security, and reviewing the pros and cons of each type
- Implementing data-based filters on collections and arrays using method-level annotations
- Implementing method-level security on our Spring MVC controllers to avoid configuring `antMatcher()` methods and `<intercept-url>` elements

Gradle dependencies

There are a number of optional dependencies that may be required, depending on what features you decide to use. Many of these dependencies are commented as Spring Boot includes them already in the starter parent. You will find that our `build.gradle` file already includes all of the following dependencies:

```
//build.gradle
// Required for JSR-250 based security:
// JSR-250 Annotations

compile ('javax.annotation:javax.annotation-api:1.3')

// Already provided by Spring Boot
// compile('cglib:cglib-nodep')
// Already provided by Spring Boot
// Required for protect-pointcut
// compile('org.aspectj:aspectjweaver')
```

Integrating Spring Expression Language (SpEL)

Spring Security leverages **Spring Expression Language (SpEL)** integration in order to easily articulate various authorization requirements. If you recall, we have already looked at the use of SpEL in Chapter 2, *Getting Started with Spring Security*, when we defined our `antMatcher()` method:

```
.antMatchers("/events/").hasRole("ADMIN")
```

Spring Security provides an `o.s.s.access.expression.SecurityExpressionRoot` object that provides the methods and objects available for use, in order to make an access control decision. For example, one of the methods available to use is `hasRole` method, which accepts a string. This corresponds to the value of the access attribute (in the preceding code snippet). In fact, there are a number of other expressions available, as shown in the following table:

Expression	Description
`hasRole(String role)` `hasAuthority(String role)`	Returns `true` if the current user has the specified authority.
`hasAnyRole(String... role)` `hasAnyAuthority(String... authority)`	Returns `true` if the current user has any of the specified authorities.

`principal`	Allows access to the current `Authentication` object's principal attribute. As discussed in `Chapter 3`, *Custom Authentication*, this will often be an instance of `UserDetails`.
`authentication`	Obtains the current `Authentication` object from the `SecurityContext` interface returned by the `getContext()` method of the `SecurityContextHolder` class.
`permitAll`	Always returns `true`.
`denyAll`	Always returns `false`.
`isAnonymous()`	Returns true if the current principal is anonymous (is not authenticated).
`isRememberMe()`	Returns `true` if the current principal was authenticated using the remember-me feature.
`isAuthenticated()`	Returns `true` if the user is not an anonymous user (that is, they are authenticated).
`isFullyAuthenticated()`	Returns `true` if the user is authenticated through a means other than remember me.
`hasPermission(Object target, Object permission)`	Returns `true` if the user has permission to access the specified object for the given permission.
`hasPermission( String targetId, String targetType, Object permission)`	Returns `true` if the user has permission to access the specified identifier for a given type and permission.

We have provided some examples of using these SpEL expressions in the following code snippet. Keep in mind that we will go into more detail throughout this and the next chapter:

```
// allow users with ROLE_ADMIN

hasRole('ADMIN')

// allow users that do not have the ROLE_ADMIN

 !hasRole('ADMIN')

// allow users that have ROLE_ADMIN or ROLE_ROOT and
// did not use the remember me feature to login
```

```
fullyAuthenticated() and hasAnyRole('ADMIN','ROOT')

// allow if Authentication.getName() equals admin

authentication.name == 'admin'
```

The WebSecurityExpressionRoot class

The `o.s.s.web.access.expression.WebSecurityExpressionRoot` class makes a few additional properties available to us. These properties, along with the standard properties already mentioned, are made available in the access attribute of the `antMatchers()` method and in the JSP/Thymeleaf `access` attribute of the `<sec:authorize>` tag, as we will discuss shortly:

Expression	Description
`request`	The current `HttpServletRequest` method.
`hasIpAddress(String... ipAddress)`	Returns `true` if the current IP address matches the `ipAddress` value. This can be an exact IP address or the IP address/network mask.

Using the request attribute

The `request` attribute is fairly self-explanatory, but we have provided a few examples in the following code. Remember, any of these examples could be placed in the `antMatchers()` method's access attribute or the `<sec:authorize>` element's access attribute:

```
// allows only HTTP GETrequest.method == 'GET'
// allow anyone to perform a GET, but
// other methods require ROLE_ADMIN

request.method == 'GET' ? permitAll : hasRole('ADMIN')
```

Using the hasIpAddress method

The `hasIpAddress` method is not quite as clear-cut as the `request` attribute. The `hasIpAddress` will easily match an exact IP address; for example, the following code would allow access if the current user's IP address was `192.168.1.93`:

```
hasIpAddress('192.168.1.93')
```

However, this is not all that useful. Instead, we can define the following code, which would also match our IP address and any other IP address in our subnet:

```
hasIpAddress('192.168.1.0/24')
```

The question is: how is this calculated? The key is to understand how to calculate the network address and its mask. To learn how to do this, we can take a look at a concrete example. We launch `ifconfig` from our Linux Terminal to view our network information (Windows users can use enter `ipconfig /all` into the Command Prompt):

```
$ ifconfig
wlan0     Link encap:Ethernet HWaddr a0:88:b4:8b:26:64
inet addr:192.168.1.93 Bcast:192.168.1.255 Mask:255.255.255.0
```

Take a look at the following diagram:

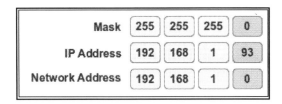

We can see that the first three octets of our mask are **255**. This means that the first three octets of our **IP Address** belong to the network address. In our calculation, this means that the remaining octets are **0**:

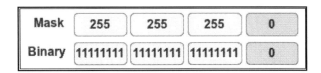

We can then calculate the mask by first transforming each octet into a binary number, and then count how many ones there are. In our instance, we get `24`.

This means our IP address will match `192.168.1.0/24`. A good site for additional information on netmasks is Cisco's documentation, available at `http://www.cisco.com/c/en/us/support/docs/ip/routing-information-protocol-rip/13788-3.html`.

The MethodSecurityExpressionRoot class

Method SpEL expressions also provide a few additional properties that can be used through the `o.s.s.access.expression.method.MethodSecurityExpressionRoot` class:

Expression	Description
`target`	Refers to `this` or the current object being secured.
`returnObject`	Refers to the object returned by the annotated method.
`filterObject`	Can be used on a collection or array in conjunction with `@PreFilter` or `@PostFilter`, to only include the elements that match the expression. The `filterObject` object represents the loop variable of the collection or array.
`#<methodArg>`	Any argument to a method can be referenced by prefixing the argument name with `#`. For example, a method argument named `id` can be referred to using `#id`.

If the description of these expressions appears a bit brief, don't worry; we'll work through a number of examples later in this chapter.

We hope that you have a decent grasp of the power of Spring Security's SpEL support. To learn more about SpEL, refer to the Spring reference documentation at `https://docs.spring.io/spring/docs/current/spring-framework-reference/html/expressions.html`.

Page-level authorization

Page-level authorization refers to the availability of application features based on the context of a particular user's request. Unlike coarse-grained authorization that we explored in Chapter 2, *Getting Started with Spring Security*, fine-grained authorization typically refers to the selective availability of the portions of a page, rather than restricting access to a page entirely. Most real-world applications will spend a considerable amount of time on the details of fine-grained authorization planning.

Spring Security provides us with the following three methods of selective display functionality:

- Spring Security JSP tag libraries allow conditional access declarations to be placed within a page declaration itself, using the standard JSP tag library syntax.
- Thymeleaf Spring Security tag libraries allow conditional access declarations to be placed within a page declaration itself, using the standard Thymeleaf tag library syntax.
- Checking user authorization in an MVC application's controller layer allows the controller to make an access decision and bind the results of the decision to the model data provided to the view. This approach relies on standard JSTL conditional page rendering and data binding, and is slightly more complicated than Spring Security tag libraries; however, it is more in line with the standard web application MVC logical design.

Any of these approaches are perfectly valid when developing fine-grained authorization models for a web application. Let's explore how each approach is implemented through a JBCP calendar use case.

Conditional rendering with the Thymeleaf Spring Security tag library

The most common functionality used in the Thymeleaf Spring Security tag library is to conditionally render portions of the page based on authorization rules. This is done with the `< sec:authorize*>` tag that functions similarly to the `<if>` tag in the core JSTL library, in that the tag's body will render depending on the conditions provided in the tag attributes. We have already seen a very brief demonstration of how the Spring Security tag library can be used to restrict the viewing of content if the user is not logged in.

Conditional rendering based on URL access rules

The Spring Security tag library provides functionality to render content based on the existing URL authorization rules that are already defined in the security configuration file. This is done via the use of the `authorizeRequests()` method and the `antMatchers()` method.

If there are multiple HTTP elements, the `authorizeRequests()` method uses the currently matched HTTP element's rules.

For example, we could ensure that the **All Events** link is displayed only when appropriate, that is, for users who are administrators—recall that the access rules we've previously defined are as follows:

```
.antMatchers("/events/").hasRole("ADMIN")
```

Update the `header.html` file to utilize this information and conditionally render the link to the **All Events** page:

```
//src/main/resources/templates/fragments/header.html

<html xmlns:th="http://www.thymeleaf.org"
xmlns:sec="http://www.thymeleaf.org/thymeleaf-extras-springsecurity
4">
...
<li sec:authorize-url="/events/">
<a id="navEventsLink" th:href="@{/events/}">All Events</a></li>
```

This will ensure that the content of the tag is not displayed unless the user has sufficient privileges to access the stated URL. It is possible to further qualify the authorization check using the HTTP method, by including the method attribute before the URL, as follows:

```
<li sec:authorize-url="GET /events/">
<a id="navEventsLink" th:href="@{/events/}">All Events</a></li>
```

Using the `authorize-url` attribute to define authorization checks on blocks of code is convenient because it abstracts the knowledge of the actual authorization checks from your pages and keeps it in your security configuration file.

Be aware that the HTTP method should match the case specified in your security `antMatchers()` method, otherwise they may not match as you expect. Also, note that the URL should always be relative to the web application context root (as your URL access rules are).

For many purposes, the use of the `<sec>` tag's `authorize-url` attribute will suffice to correctly display link- or action-related content only when the user is allowed to see it. Remember that the tag need not only surround a link; it could even surround a whole form if the user doesn't have permission to submit it.

Conditional rendering using SpEL

An additional, more flexible method of controlling the display of JSP content is available when the `<sec>` tag is used in conjunction with a SpEL expression. Let's review what we learned in `Chapter 2`, *Getting Started with Spring Security*. We could hide the **My Events** link from any unauthenticated users by changing our `header.html` file, as follows:

```
//src/main/resources/templates/fragments/header.html

<li sec:authorize="isAuthenticated()">
<a id="navMyEventsLink" th:href="@{/events/my}">My Events</a></li>
```

The SpEL evaluation is performed by the same code behind the scenes as the expressions utilized in the `antMatchers()` method access declaration rules (assuming the expressions have been configured). Hence, the same set of built-in functions and properties are accessible from the expressions built using the `<sec>` tag.

Both of these methods of utilizing the `<sec>` tag provide powerful, fine-grained control over the display of page content based on security authorization rules.

Go ahead and start up the JBCP calendar application. Visit `https://localhost:8443` and log in with the user `user1@example.com` and the password `user1`. You will observe that the **My Events** link is displayed, but the **All Events** link is hidden. Log out and log in as the user `admin1@example.com` with the password `admin1`. Now both links are visible.

> You should start with the code from `chapter11.01-calendar`.

Using controller logic to conditionally render content

In this section, we will demonstrate how we can use Java-based code to determine if we should render some content. We can choose to only show the **Create Event** link on the **Welcome** page to users who have a username that contains `user`. This will hide the **Create Event** link on the **Welcome** page from users who are not logged in as administrators.

The welcome controller from the sample code for this chapter has been updated to populate the model with an attribute named `showCreateLink`, derived from the method name, as follows:

```
//src/main/java/com/packtpub/springsecurity/web/controllers/WelcomeControll
er.java

    @ModelAttribute ("showCreateLink")
    public boolean showCreateLink(Authentication authentication) {
      return authentication != null &&
      authentication.getName().contains("user");
    }
```

You may notice that Spring MVC can automatically obtain the `Authentication` object for us. This is because Spring Security maps our current `Authentication` object to the `HttpServletRequest.getPrincipal()` method. Since Spring MVC will automatically resolve any object of the `java.security.Principal` type to the value of `HttpServletRequest.getPrincipal()`, specifying `Authentication` as an argument to our controller is an easy way to access the current `Authentication` object. We could also decouple the code from Spring Security by specifying an argument of the `Principal` type instead. However, we chose `Authentication` in this scenario to help demonstrate how everything connects.

If we were working in another framework that did not know how to do this, we could obtain the `Authentication` object using the `SecurityContextHolder` class, as we did in Chapter 3, *Custom Authentication*. Also note that if we were not using Spring MVC, we could just set the `HttpServletRequest` attribute directly rather than populating it on the model. The attribute that we populated on the request would then be available to our JSP, just as it is when using a `ModelAndView` object with Spring MVC.

Next, we will need to use the `HttpServletRequest` attribute in our `index.html` file to determine if we should display the **Create Event** link. Update `index.html`, as follows:

```
//src/main/resources/templates/header.html

<li th:if="${showCreateLink}"><a id="navCreateEventLink"
th:href="@{events/form}">...</li>
```

Now, start the application, log in using admin1@example.com as the username and admin1 as the password, and visit the **All Events** page. You should no longer see the **Create Events** link in the main navigation (although it will still be present on the page).

Your code should look like this: `chapter11.02-calendar`.

The WebInvocationPrivilegeEvaluator class

There may be times when an application will not be written using JSPs and will need to be able to determine access based upon a URL, as we did with `<... sec:authorize-url="/events/">`. This can be done by using the `o.s.s.web.access.WebInvocationPrivilegeEvaluator` interface, which is the same interface that backs the JSP tag library. In the following code snippet, we demonstrate its use by populating our model with an attribute named `showAdminLink`. We are able to obtain `WebInvocationPrivilegeEvaluator` using the `@Autowired` annotation:

```
//src/main/java/com/packtpub/springsecurity/web/controllers/WelcomeControll
er.java

    @ModelAttribute ("showAdminLink")
    public boolean showAdminLink(Authentication authentication) {
        return webInvocationPrivilegeEvaluator.
        isAllowed("/admin/", authentication);
    }
```

If the framework you are using is not being managed by Spring, `@Autowire` will not be able to provide you with `WebInvocationPrivilegeEvaluator`. Instead, you can use Spring's `org.springframework.web.context.WebApplicationContextUtils` interface to obtain an instance of `WebInvocationPrivilegeEvaluator`, as follows:

```
        ApplicationContext context = WebApplicationContextUtils
         .getRequiredWebApplicationContext(servletContext);
        WebInvocationPrivilegeEvaluator privEvaluator =
        context.getBean(WebInvocationPrivilegeEvaluator.class)
```

To try it out, go ahead and update `index.html` to use the `showAdminLink` request attribute, as follows:

```
        //src/main/resources/templates/header.html

        <li th:if="${showAdminLink}">
         <a id="h2Link" th:href="@{admin/h2/}" target="_blank">
         H2 Database Console</a>
         ...
        </li>
```

Restart the application and view the **Welcome** page before you have logged in. The H2 link should not be visible. Log in as `admin1@example.com/admin1`, and you should see it.

 Your code should look like `chapter11.03-calendar`.

What is the best way to configure in-page authorization?

Major advances in the Thymeleaf Spring Security `<sec>` tag in Spring Security 4 removed many of the concerns about the use of this tag in previous versions of the library. In many cases, the use of the `authorize-url` attribute of the tag can appropriately isolate the code from changes in authorization rules. You should use the `authorize-url` attribute of the tag in the following scenarios:

- The tag is preventing display functionality that can be clearly identified by a single URL
- The contents of the tag can be unambiguously isolated to a single URL

Unfortunately, in a typical application, the likelihood that you will be able to use the `authorize-url` attribute of the tag frequently is somewhat low. The reality is that applications are usually much more complex than this, and require more involved logic when deciding to render portions of a page.

It's tempting to use the Thymeleaf Spring Security tag library to declare bits of rendered pages as off-limits based on security criteria in other methods. However, there are a number of reasons why (in many cases) this isn't a great idea, as follows:

- Complex conditions beyond role membership are not supported by the tag library. For example, if our application incorporated customized attributes on the `UserDetails` implementation, IP filters, geolocation, and so on, none of these would be supported by the standard `<sec>` tag.
- These could, however, conceivably be supported by the custom tags or using SpEL expressions. Even in this case, the page is more likely to be directly tied to business logic rather than what is typically encouraged.

- The `<sec>` tag must be referenced on every page that it's used in. This leads to potential inconsistencies between the rulesets that are intended to be common, but may be spread across different physical pages. A good object-oriented system design would suggest that conditional rule evaluations be located in only one place, and logically referred to from where they should be applied.
- It is possible (and we illustrate this using our common header page include) to encapsulate and reuse portions of pages to reduce the occurrence of this type of problem, but it is virtually impossible to eliminate in a complex application.
- There is no way to validate the correctness of rules stated at compile time. Whereas compile-time constants can be used in typical Java-based, object-oriented systems, the tag library requires (in typical use) hardcoded role names where a simple typo might go undetected for some time.
- To be fair, such typos could be caught easily by comprehensive functional tests on the running application, but they are far easier to test using a standard Java component unit testing techniques.
- We can see that, although the **template-based** approach for conditional content rendering is convenient, there are some significant downsides.

All of these issues can be solved by the use of code in controllers that can be used to push data into the application view model. Additionally, performing advanced authorization determinations in code allows for the benefits of reuse, compile-time checks, and proper logical separation of the model, view, and controller.

Method-level security

Our primary focus up to this point in the book has been on securing the web-facing portion of the JBCP calendar application; however, in real-world planning of secured systems, equal attention should be paid to securing the service methods that allow users access to the most critical part of any system—its data.

Why we secure in layers?

Let's take a minute to see why it is important to secure our methods, even though we have already secured our URLs. Start the JBCP calendar application up. Log in using `user1@example.com` as the username and `user1` as the password, and visit the **All Events** page. You will see the custom **Access Denied** page. Now, add `.json` to the end of the URL in the browser so that the URL is now `https://localhost:8443/events/.json`. You will now see a JSON response with the same data as the **HTML All Events** page. This data should only be visible to an administrator, but we have bypassed it by finding a URL that was not configured properly.

We can also view the details of an event that we do not own and are not invited to. Change `.json` with `102` so that the URL is now `https://localhost:8443/events/102`. You will now see a **Lunch** event that is not listed on your **My Events** page. This should not be visible to us because we are not an administrator and this is not our event.

As you can see, our URL rules are not quite strong enough to entirely secure our application. These exploits do not even need to take advantage of more complex problems, such as differences in how containers handle URL normalization. In short, there are often ways to bypass URL-based security. Let's see how adding a security layer to our business tier can help with our new security vulnerability.

Securing the business tier

Spring Security has the ability to add a layer of authorization (or authorization-based data pruning) to the invocation of any Spring-managed bean in your application. While many developers focus on web-tier security, business-tier security is arguably just as important, as a malicious user may be able to penetrate the security of your web tier or access services exposed through a non-UI frontend, such as a web service.

Let's examine the following logical diagram to see why we're interested in applying a secondary layer of security:

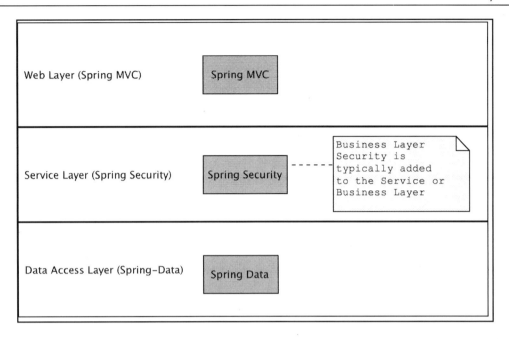

Spring Security has the following two main techniques for securing methods:

- **Preauthorization**: This technique ensures that certain constraints are satisfied prior to the execution of a method that is being allowed, for example, if a user has a particular GrantedAuthority, such as ROLE_ADMIN. Failure to satisfy the declared constraints means that the method call will fail.
- **Postauthorization**: This technique ensures that the calling principal still satisfies declared constraints after the method returns. This is rarely used but can provide an extra layer of security around some complex, interconnected business tier methods.

The preauthorization and postauthorization techniques provide formalized support for what are generally called preconditions and postconditions in a classic, object-oriented design. Preconditions and postconditions allow a developer to declare through runtime checks that certain constraints around a method's execution must always hold true. In the case of security preauthorization and postauthorization, the business tier developer makes a conscious decision about the security profile of particular methods by encoding expected runtime conditions as part of an interface or class API declaration. As you may imagine, this requires a great deal of forethought to avoid unintended consequences!

Adding the @PreAuthorize method annotation

Our first design decision will be to augment method security at the business tier by ensuring that a user must be logged in as an ADMIN user before he/she is allowed to access the getEvents() method. This is done with a simple annotation added to the method in the service interface definition, as follows:

```
import org.springframework.security.access.prepost.PreAuthorize;
...
public interface CalendarService {
  ...
 @PreAuthorize("hasRole('ADMIN')")
  List<Event> getEvents();
}
```

This is all that is required to ensure that anyone invoking our getEvents() method is an administrator. Spring Security will use a runtime **Aspect Oriented Programming (AOP)** pointcut to execute BeforeAdvice on the method, and throw o.s.s.access.AccessDeniedException if the security constraints aren't met.

Instructing Spring Security to use method annotations

We'll also need to make a one-time change to SecurityConfig.java, where we've got the rest of our Spring Security configuration. Simply add the following annotation to the class declaration:

```
//src/main/java/com/packtpub/springsecurity/configuration/SecurityC
onfig.java

@Configuration
@EnableWebSecurity
@EnableGlobalMethodSecurity(prePostEnabled = true)
public class SecurityConfig extends WebSecurityConfigurerAdapter {
```

Validating method security

Don't believe it was that easy? Log in with user1@example.com as the username and user1 as the password, and try accessing https://localhost:8443/events/.json. You should see the **Access Denied** page now.

Your code should look like `chapter11.04-calendar`.

If you look at the Tomcat console, you'll see a very long stack trace, starting with the following output:

```
DEBUG ExceptionTranslationFilter - Access is denied
(user is not anonymous); delegating to AccessDeniedHandler
org.s.s.access.AccessDeniedException: Access is denied
at org.s.s.access.vote.AffirmativeBased.decide
at org.s.s.access.intercept.AbstractSecurityInterceptor.
beforeInvocation
at org.s.s.access.intercept.aopalliance.
MethodSecurityInterceptor.invoke
...
at $Proxy16.getEvents
at com.packtpub.springsecurity.web.controllers.EventsController.events
```

Based on the **Access Denied** page, and the stack trace clearly pointing to the `getEvents` method invocation, we can see that the user was appropriately denied access to the business method because it lacked the `GrantedAuthority` of `ROLE_ADMIN`. If you run the same with the username `admin1@example.com` and the password `admin1`, you will discover that access will be granted.

Isn't it amazing that with a simple declaration in our interface, we're able to ensure that the method in question is secure? But how does AOP work?

Interface-based proxies

In the given example from the previous section, Spring Security used an interface-based proxy to secure our `getEvents` method. Let's take a look at the simplified pseudocode of what happened to understand how this works:

```
DefaultCalendarService originalService = context.getBean
(CalendarService.class)
CalendarService secureService = new CalendarService() {
 ... other methods just delegate to originalService ...
   public List<Event> getEvents() {
     if(!permitted(originalService.getEvents)) {
       throw AccessDeniedException()
       }
```

```
              return originalCalendarService.getEvents()
          }
      };
```

You can see that Spring creates the original `CalendarService` just as it normally does. However, it instructs our code to use another implementation of `CalendarService` that performs a security check before returning the result of the original method. The secure implementation can be created with no prior knowledge of our interface because Spring uses Java's `java.lang.reflect.Proxy` APIs to dynamically create new implementations of the interface. Note that the object returned is no longer an instance of `DefaultCalendarService`, since it is a new implementation of `CalendarService`, that is, it is an anonymous implementation of `CalendarService`. This means that we must program against an interface in order to use the secure implementation, otherwise, a `ClassCastException` exception will occur. To learn more about Spring AOP, refer to the Spring reference documentation at `http://static.springsource.org/spring/docs/current/spring-framework-reference/html/aop.html#aop-introduction-proxies`.

In addition to the `@PreAuthorize` annotation, there are several other ways of declaring security preauthorization requirements on methods. We can examine these different ways of securing methods and then evaluate their pros and cons in different circumstances.

JSR-250 compliant standardized rules

JSR-250 Common Annotations for the Java platform defines a series of annotations, some that are security-related, which are intended to be portable across JSR-250 compliant runtime environments. The Spring Framework became compliant with JSR-250 as part of the Spring 2.x release, including the Spring Security framework.

While JSR-250 annotations are not as expressive as Spring native annotations, they have the benefit that the declarations they provide are compatible across implementing Java EE application servers such as Glassfish or service-oriented runtime frameworks such as **Apache Tuscany**. Depending on your application's needs and requirements for portability, you may decide that the trade-off of reduced specificity is worth the portability of the code.

To implement the rule we specified in the first example, we make a few changes by performing the following steps:

1. First, we need to update our `SecurityConfig` file to use the JSR-250 annotations:

    ```
    //src/main/java/com/packtpub/springsecurity/configuration/
    SecurityConfig.java

    @Configuration
    @EnableWebSecurity
    @EnableGlobalMethodSecurity(jsr250Enabled = true)
    public class SecurityConfig extends WebSecurityConfigurerAdapter {
    ```

2. Lastly, the `@PreAuthorize` annotation needs to change to the `@RolesAllowed` annotation. As we might anticipate, the `@RolesAllowed` annotation does not support SpEL expressions, so we edit `CalendarService` as follows:

    ```
    @RolesAllowed("ROLE_ADMIN")
    List<Event> getEvents();
    ```

3. Restart the application, log in as `user1@example.com/user1`, and try to access `http://localhost:8080/events/.json`. You should see the **Access Denied** page again.

> Your code should look like this: `chapter11.05-calendar`.

Note that it's also possible to provide a list of allowed `GrantedAuthority` names using the standard Java 5 String array annotation syntax:

```
@RolesAllowed({"ROLE_USER","ROLE_ADMIN"})
List<Event> getEvents();
```

There are also two additional annotations specified by JSR-250, namely @PermitAll and @DenyAll, which function as you might expect, permitting and denying all requests to the method in question.

Annotations at the class level

Be aware that method-level security annotations can be applied at the class level as well! Method-level annotations, if supplied, will always override annotations specified at the class level. This can be helpful if your business needs to dictate the specification of security policies for an entire class. Take care to use this functionality in conjunction with good comments and coding standards, so that developers are very clear about the security characteristics of the class and its methods.

Method security using Spring's @Secured annotation

Spring itself provides a simpler annotation style that is similar to the JSR-250 @RolesAllowed annotation. The @Secured annotation is functionally and syntactically the same as @RolesAllowed. The only notable differences are that it does not require the external dependency, cannot be processed by other frameworks, and the processing of these annotations must be explicitly enabled with another attribute on the @EnableGlobalMethodSecurity annotation:

```
//src/main/java/com/packtpub/springsecurity/configuration/SecurityConfig.java

@EnableWebSecurity(debug = true)
@EnableGlobalMethodSecurity(securedEnabled=true)
public class SecurityConfig extends WebSecurityConfigurerAdapter {
```

As @Secured functions in the same way as the JSR standard @RolesAllowed annotation, there's no real compelling reason to use it in new code, but you may run across it in older Spring code.

Method security rules incorporating method parameters

Logically, writing rules that refer to method parameters in their constraints seem sensible for certain types of operations. For example, it might make sense for us to restrict the `findForUser(int userId)` method to meet the following constraints:

- The `userId` argument must be equal to the current user's ID
- The user must be an administrator (in this case, it is valid for the user to see any event)

While it's easy to see how we could alter the rule to restrict the method invocation only to administrators, it's not clear how we would determine if the user is attempting to change their own password.

Fortunately, SpEL binding, used by the Spring Security method annotations, supports more sophisticated expressions, including expressions that incorporate method parameters. You will also want to ensure that you have enabled pre- and post-annotations in the `SecurityConfig` file, as follows:

```
//src/main/java/com/packtpub/springsecurity/configuration/SecurityConfig.ja
va

@Configuration
@EnableWebSecurity
@EnableGlobalMethodSecurity(prePostEnabled = true)
public class SecurityConfig extends WebSecurityConfigurerAdapter {
Lastly, we can update our CalendarService interface as follows:
@PreAuthorize("hasRole('ADMIN') or principal.id == #userId")
List<Event> findForUser(int userId);
```

You can see here that we've augmented the SpEL directive we used in the first exercise with a check against the ID of the principal and against the `userId` method parameter (`#userId`, the method parameter name, is prefixed with a # symbol). The fact that this powerful feature of method parameter binding is available should get your creative juices flowing and allow you to secure method invocations with a very precise set of logical rules.

Our principal is currently an instance of `CalendarUser` due to the custom authentication setup from `Chapter 3`, *Custom Authentication*. This means that the principal has all of the properties that our `CalendarUser` application has on it. If we had not done this customization, only the properties of the `UserDetails` object would be available.

SpEL variables are referenced with the hash (#) prefix. One important note is that in order for method argument names to be available at runtime, debugging symbol table information must be retained after compilation. Common methods to retain the debugging symbol table information are listed as follows:

- If you are using the `javac` compiler, you will need to include the `-g` flag when building your classes
- When using the `<javac>` task in Ant, add the attribute `debug="true"`
- In Gradle, ensure to add `--debug` when running the main method, or the `bootRun` task
- In Maven, ensure the `maven.compiler.debug=true` property (the default is `true`)

Consult your compiler, build tool, or IDE documentation for assistance on configuring this same setting in your environment.

Start up your application and try logging in with `user1@example.com` as the username and `user1` as the password. On the **Welcome** page, request the **My Events** (`email=admin1@example.com`) link to see an **Access Denied** page. Try again with **My Events** (`email=user1@example.com`) to see it work. Note that the displayed user on the **My Events** page matches the currently logged-in user. Now, try the same steps and log in as `admin1@example.com/admin1`. You will be able to see both pages since you are logged in as a user with the `ROLE_ADMIN` permission.

Your code should look like `chapter11.06-calendar`.

Method security rules incorporating returned values

Just as we were able to leverage the parameters to the method, we can also leverage the returned value of the method call. Let's update the `getEvent` method to meet the following constraints on the returned value:

- The attendee's ID must be the current user's ID
- The owner'sID must be the current user's ID
- The user must be an administrator (in this case, it is valid for the user to see any event)

Add the following code to the `CalendarService` interface:

```
@PostAuthorize("hasRole('ROLE_ADMIN') or " + "principal.username ==
returnObject.owner.email or " +
"principal.username == returnObject.attendee.email")
Event getEvent(int eventId);
```

Now, try logging in with the username `user1@example.com` and the password `user1`. Next, try accessing the **Lunch** event using the link on the **Welcome** page. You should now see the **Access Denied** page. If you log in using the username `user2@example.com` and the password `user2`, the event will display as expected since `user2@example.com` is the attendee at the **Lunch** event.

Your code should look like `chapter11.07-calendar`.

Securing method data using role-based filtering

The two final Spring Security-dependent annotations are `@PreFilter` and `@PostFilter`, which are used to apply security-based filtering rules to collections or arrays (with `@PostFilter` only). This type of functionality is referred to as security trimming or security pruning and involves using the security credentials of `principal` at runtime to selectively remove members from a set of objects. As you might expect, this filtering is performed using SpEL expression notation within the annotation declaration.

We'll work through an example with JBCP calendar, as we want to filter the `getEvents` method to only return the events that this user is allowed to see. In order to do this, we remove any existing security annotations and add the `@PostFilter` annotation to our `CalendarService` interface, as follows:

```
@PostFilter("principal.id == filterObject.owner.id or " +
"principal.id == filterObject.attendee.id")
List<Event> getEvents();
```

 Your code should look like this: `chapter11.08-calendar`.

Remove the `antMatchers()` method, restricting access to `/events/`URL so that we can test our annotation. Start up the application and view the **All Events** page when logged in with the username `user1@example.com` and password `user1`. You will observe that only the events that are associated with our user are displayed.

With `filterObject` acting as the loop variable that refers to the current event, Spring Security will iterate over the `List<Event>` returned by our service and modify it to only contain the `Event` objects that match our SpEL expression.

In general, the `@PostFilter` method behaves in the following way. For brevity, we refer to the collection as the method return value, but be aware that `@PostFilter` works with either collection or array method return types.

The `filterObject` object is rebound to the SpEL context for each element in the collection. This means that if your method is returning a collection with 100 elements, the SpEL expression will be evaluated for each.

The SpEL expression must return a Boolean value. If the expression evaluates to true, the object will remain in the collection, while if the expression evaluates to false, the object will be removed.

In most cases, you'll find that collection post filtering saves you from the complexity of writing boilerplate code that you would likely be writing anyway. Take care that you understand how `@PostFilter` works conceptually; unlike `@PreAuthorize`, `@PostFilter` specifies method behavior and not a precondition. Some object-oriented purists may argue that `@PostFilter` isn't appropriate for inclusion as a method annotation, and such filtering should instead be handled through code in a method implementation.

Safety of collection filtering
Be aware that the actual collection returned from your method will be modified! In some cases, this isn't desirable behavior, so you should ensure that your method returns a collection that can be safely modified. This is especially important if the returned collection is an ORM-bound one, as post-filter modifications could inadvertently be persisted to the ORM data store!

Spring Security also offers functionality to prefilter method parameters that are collections; let's try implementing that now.

Prefiltering collections with @PreFilter

The @PreFilter annotation can be applied to a method to filter collection elements that are passed into a method based on the current security context. Functionally, once it has a reference to a collection, this annotation behaves exactly the same as the @PostFilter annotation, with a couple of exceptions, as follows:

- The @PreFilter annotation supports only collection arguments and does not support array arguments.
- The @PreFilter annotation takes an additional, optional filterTarget attribute which is used to specifically identify the method parameter and filter it when the annotated method has more than one argument.
- As with @PostFilter, keep in mind that the original collection passed to the method is permanently modified. This may not be desirable behavior, so ensure that callers know that the collection's security may be trimmed after the method is invoked!

Imagine if we had a save method that accepted a collection of event objects, and we wanted to only allow the saving of events that were owned by the currently logged in user. We could do this as follows:

```
@PreFilter("principal.id == filterObject.owner.id")
void save(Set<Event> events);
```

Much like our @PostFilter method, this annotation causes Spring Security to iterate over each event with the loop variable filterObject. It then compares the current user's ID against the event owner's ID. If they match, the event is retained. If they do not match, the result is discarded.

Comparing method authorization types

The following quick reference chart may assist you in selecting a type of method authorization check to use:

Method authorization type	Specified as	JSR standard	Allows SpEL expressions
@PreAuthorize @PostAuthorize	Annotation	No	Yes
@RolesAllowed, @PermitAll, @DenyAll	Annotation	Yes	No
@Secure	Annotation	No	No
protect-pointcut	XML	No	No

Most Java 5 consumers of Spring Security will probably opt to use the JSR-250 annotations for maximum compatibility and reuse their business classes (and relevant constraints) across an IT organization. Where needed, these basic declarations can be replaced with the annotations that tie the code to the Spring Security implementation itself.

If you are using Spring Security in an environment that doesn't support annotations (Java 1.4 or previous), unfortunately, your choices are somewhat limited to method security enforcement. Even in this situation, the use of AOP provides a reasonably rich environment in which we can develop basic security declarations.

Practical considerations for annotation-based security

One thing to consider is that when returning a collection of real-world applications, there is likely to be some sort of paging. This means that our @PreFilter and @PostFilter annotations cannot be used as the sole means of selecting which objects to return. Instead, we need to ensure that our queries only select the data that the user is allowed to access. This means that the security annotations become redundant checks. However, it is important to remember our lesson at the beginning of this chapter; we want to secure layers in case one layer is able to be bypassed.

Summary

In this chapter, we have covered most of the remaining areas in standard Spring Security implementations that deal with authorization. We've learned enough to take a thorough pass through the JBCP calendar application and verify that proper authorization checks are in place in all tiers of the application, to ensure that malicious users cannot manipulate or access data to which they do not have access.

We developed two techniques for micro-authorization, namely filtering out in-page content based on authorization or other security criteria using the Thymeleaf Spring Security tag library and Spring MVC controller data binding. We also explored several methods of securing business functions and data in the business tier of our application and supporting a rich, declarative security model that was tightly integrated with the code. We also learned how to secure our Spring MVC controllers and the differences between interface and class proxy objects

At this point, we've wrapped up coverage of much of the important Spring Security functionality that you're likely to encounter in most standard, secure web application development scenarios.

In the next chapter, we will discuss the ACL (domain object model) module of Spring Security. This will allow us to explicitly declare authorization, rather than relying on existing data.

12
Access Control Lists

In this chapter, we will address the complex topic of **access control lists** (**ACL**), which can provide a rich model of domain object instance-level authorization. Spring Security ships with a robust, but complicated, access control list module that can serve the needs of small to medium-sized implementations reasonably well.

In this chapter, we'll cover the following topics:

- Understanding the conceptual model of ACL
- Reviewing the terminology and application of ACL concepts in the Spring Security ACL module
- Building and reviewing the database schema required to support Spring ACL
- Configuring JBCP calendar to use ACL secured business methods via annotations and Spring beans
- Performing advanced configuration, including customized ACL permissions, ACL-enabled JSP tag checks and method security, mutable ACLs, and smart caching
- Examining architectural considerations and planning scenarios for ACL deployment

The conceptual module of ACL

The final piece of the non-web tier security puzzle is security at the business object level, applied at or below the business tier. Security at this level is implemented using a technique known as ACL, or ACLs. Summing up the objective of ACLs in a single sentence—ACLs allow specification of a set of group permissions based on the unique combination of a group, business object, and logical operation.

For example, an ACL declaration for JBCP calendar might declare that a given user has to write access to his or her own event. This can be shown as follows:

Username	Group	Object	Permissions
mick		event_01	read, write
	ROLE_USER	event_123	read
	ANONYMOUS	Any event	none

You can see that this ACL is eminently readable by a human—mick has read and write access to his own event (event_01); other registered users can read the events of mick, but anonymous users cannot. This type of rule matrix is, in a nutshell, what ACL attempts to synthesize about a secured system and its business data into a combination of code, access checking, and metadata. Most true ACL-enabled systems have extremely complex ACL lists, and may conceivably have millions of entries across the entire system. Although this sounds frighteningly complex, proper up-front reasoning and implementation with a capable security library can make ACL management quite feasible.

If you use a Microsoft Windows or Unix/Linux-based computer, you experience the magic of ACLs every single day. Most modern computer operating systems use ACL directives as part of their file storage systems, allowing permission granting based on a combination of a user or group, file or directory, and permission. In Microsoft Windows, you can view some of the ACL capabilities of a file by right-clicking on a file and examining its security properties (**Properties** | **Security**), as shown in the following screenshot:

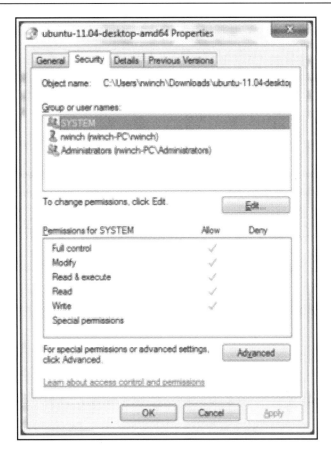

You will be able to see that the combinations of inputs to the ACL are visible and intuitive as you navigate through the various groups or users and permissions.

Access control lists in Spring Security

Spring Security supports ACL-driven authorization checks against access to individual domain objects by individual users of the secured system. Much as in the OS filesystem example, it is possible to use the Spring Security ACL components to build logical tree structures of both business objects and groups or principals. The intersection of permissions (inherited or explicit) on both the requestor and the requestee is used to determine allowed access.

It's quite common for users approaching the ACL capability of Spring Security to be overwhelmed by its complexity, combined with a relative dearth of documentation and examples. This is compounded by the fact that setting up the ACL infrastructure can be quite complicated, with many interdependencies and reliance on bean-based configuration mechanisms, which are quite unlike much of the rest of Spring Security (as you'll see in a moment when we set up the initial configuration).

The Spring Security ACL module was written to be a reasonable baseline, but users intending to build extensively on the functionality will likely run into a series of frustrating limitations and design choices, which have gone (for the most part) uncorrected as they were first introduced in the early days of Spring Security. Don't let these limitations discourage you! The ACL module is a powerful way to embed rich access controls in your application, and further scrutinize and secure user actions and data.

Before we dig into configuring Spring Security ACL support, we need to review some key terminology and concepts.

The main unit of secured actor identity in the Spring ACL system is the **Security Identity** (**SID**). The SID is a logical construct that can be used to abstract the identity of either an individual principal or a group (GrantedAuthority). The SIDs object defined by the ACL data model you construct are used as the basis for explicit and derived access control rules, when determining the allowed level of access for a particular principal.

If SIDs are used to define actors in the ACL system, the opposite half of the security equation is the definition of the secured objects themselves. The identification of individual secured objects is called (unsurprisingly) an object identity. The default Spring ACL implementation of an object identity requires ACL rules to be defined at the individual object instance level, which means, if desired, every object in the system can have an individual access rule.

Individual access rules are known as **Access Control Entries** (**ACEs**). An ACE is the combination of the following factors:

- The SID for the actor to which the rule applies
- The object identity to which the rule applies
- The permission that should be applied to the given SID and the stated object identity
- Whether or not the stated permission should be allowed or denied for the given SID and object identity

The purpose of the Spring ACL system as a whole is to evaluate each secured method invocation and determine whether the object or objects being acted on in the method should be allowed as per the applicable ACEs. Applicable ACEs are evaluated at runtime, based on the caller and the objects in play.

Spring Security ACL is flexible in its implementation. Although the majority of this chapter details the out-of-the-box functionality of the Spring Security ACL module, keep in mind, however, that many of the rules indicated represent default implementations, which in many cases can be overridden based on more complex requirements.

Spring Security uses helpful value objects to represent the data associated with each of these conceptual entities. These are listed in the following table:

ACL conceptual object	Java object
SID	`o.s.s.acls.model.Sid`
Object identity	`o.s.s.acls.model.ObjectIdentity`
ACL	`o.s.s.acls.model.Acl`
ACE	`o.s.s.acls.model.AccessControlEntry`

Let's work through the process of enabling Spring Security ACL components for a simple demonstration in the JBCP calendar application.

Basic configuration of Spring Security ACL support

Although we hinted previously that configuring ACL support in Spring Security requires bean-based configuration (which it does), you can use ACL support while retaining the simpler security XML namespace configuration if you choose. In the remaining examples in this chapter, we will be focusing on Java-based configuration.

Gradle dependencies

As with most of the chapters, we will need to add some dependencies in order to use the functionality in this chapter. A list of the dependencies we have added with comments about when they are needed can be checked as follows:

```
build.gradle
dependencies {
   // ACL
   compile('org.springframework.security:spring-security-acl')
   compile('net.sf.ehcache:ehcache')
   ...
}
```

Defining a simple target scenario

Our simple target scenario is to grant `user2@example.com` read access to only the birthday party event. All other users will not have any access to any events. You will observe that this differs from our other examples, since `user2@example.com` is not otherwise associated with the birthday party event.

Although there are several ways to set up ACL checking, our preference is to follow the annotation-based approach that we used in this chapter's method-level annotations. This nicely abstracts the use of ACLs away from the actual interface declarations and allows for replacement (if you want) of the role declarations with something other than ACLs at a later date (should you so choose).

We'll add an annotation to the `CalendarService.getEvents` method, which filters each event based upon the current user's permission to the event:

```
src/main/java/com/packtpub/springsecurity/service/CalendarService.java
@PostFilter("hasPermission(filterObject, 'read')")
List<Event> getEvents();
```

 You should be starting with `chapter12.00-calendar`.

Adding ACL tables to the H2 database

The first thing we'll need to do is add the required tables and data to support persistent ACL entries in our in-memory H2 database. To do this, we'll add a new SQL DDL file and the corresponding data to our embedded-database declaration in `schema.sql`. We will break down each of these files later in the chapter.

We have included the following `schema.sql` file with this chapter's source code, which is based upon the schema files included in the Spring Security reference's Appendix, *Additional Reference Material*:

```
src/main/resources/schema.sql
-- ACL Schema --
create table acl_sid (
id bigint generated by default as identity(start with 100) not
    null primary key,
principal boolean not null,
sid varchar_ignorecase(100) not null,
constraint uk_acl_sid unique(sid,principal) );

create table acl_class (
id bigint generated by default as identity(start with 100) not
    null primary key,
class varchar_ignorecase(500) not null,
constraint uk_acl_class unique(class) );

create table acl_object_identity (
id bigint generated by default as identity(start with 100) not
    null primary key,
object_id_class bigint not null,
object_id_identity bigint not null,
parent_object bigint,
owner_sid bigint not null,
entries_inheriting boolean not null,
constraint uk_acl_objid
    unique(object_id_class,object_id_identity),
constraint fk_acl_obj_parent foreign
    key(parent_object)references acl_object_identity(id),
constraint fk_acl_obj_class foreign
    key(object_id_class)references acl_class(id),
constraint fk_acl_obj_owner foreign key(owner_sid)references
    acl_sid(id) );

create table acl_entry (
id bigint generated by default as identity(start with 100) not
    null primary key,
acl_object_identity bigint not null,
```

```
ace_order int not null,
sid bigint not null,
mask integer not null,
granting boolean not null,
audit_success boolean not null,
audit_failure boolean not null,
constraint uk_acl_entry unique(acl_object_identity,ace_order),
constraint fk_acl_entry_obj_id foreign key(acl_object_identity)
references acl_object_identity(id),
constraint fk_acl_entry_sid foreign key(sid) references
    acl_sid(id) );
```

The preceding code will result in the following database schema:

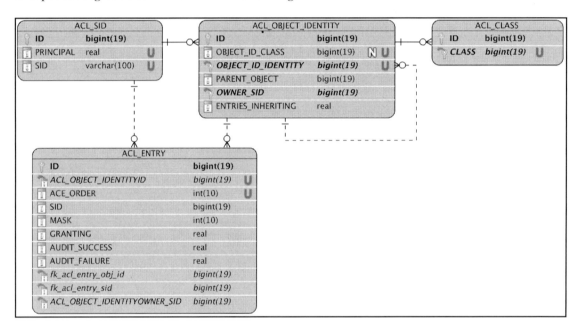

You can see how the concepts of `SIDs`, `OBJECT_IDENTITY`, and ACEs map directly to the database schema. Conceptually, this is convenient, as we can map our mental model of the ACL system and how it is enforced directly to the database.

If you've cross-referenced this with the H2 database schema supplied with the Spring Security documentation, you'll note that we've made a few tweaks that commonly bite users. These are as follows:

- Change the ACL_CLASS.CLASS column to 500 characters, from the default value of 100. Some long, fully qualified class names don't fit in 100 characters.
- Name the foreign keys with something meaningful so that failures are more easily diagnosed.

If you are using another database, such as Oracle, you'll have to translate the DDL into DDL and data types specific to your database.

Once we configure the remainder of the ACL system, we'll return to the database to set up some basic ACEs to prove the ACL functionality in its most primitive form.

Configuring SecurityExpressionHandler

We'll need to configure <global-method-security> to enable annotations (where we'll annotate based on the expected ACL privilege), and reference a custom access decision manager.

We will also need to provide an o.s.s.access.expression.SecurityExpressionHandler implementation that is aware of how to evaluate permissions. Update your SecurityConfig.java configuration, as follows:

```
src/main/java/com/packtpub/springsecurity/configuration/SecurityConfig.java
@EnableGlobalMethodSecurity(prePostEnabled = true)
@Import(AclConfig.class)
public class SecurityConfig extends WebSecurityConfigurerAdapter {
```

This is a bean reference to the DefaultMethodSecurityExpressionHandler object that we have defined in AclConfig.java file for you, as follows:

```
src/main/java/com/packtpub/springsecurity/configuration/AclConfig.java
@Bean
public DefaultMethodSecurityExpressionHandler expressionHandler(){
    DefaultMethodSecurityExpressionHandler dmseh =
    new DefaultMethodSecurityExpressionHandler();
  dmseh.setPermissionEvaluator(permissionEvaluator());
    dmseh.setPermissionCacheOptimizer(permissionCacheOptimizer());
    return dmseh;
}
```

With even a relatively straightforward ACL configuration, as we have in our scenario, there are a number of required dependencies to set up. As we mentioned previously, the Spring Security ACL module comes out of the box with a number of components that you can assemble to provide a decent set of ACL capabilities. Note that all of the components that we'll reference in the following diagram are part of the framework:

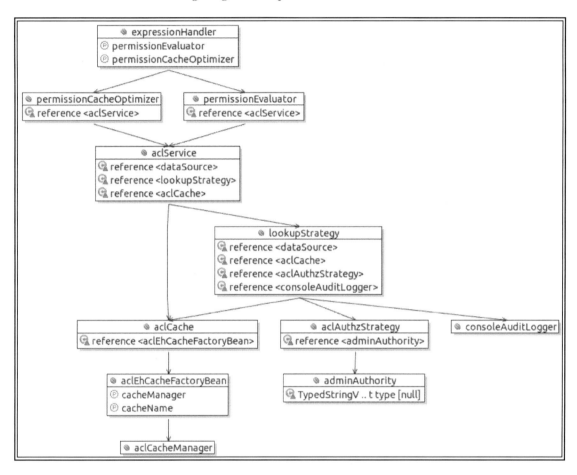

The AclPermissionCacheOptimizer object

The `DefaultMethodSecurityExpressionHandler` object has two dependencies. The `AclPermissionCacheOptimizer` object is used to prime the cache with all of the ACLs for a collection of objects in a single JDBC select statement. The relatively simple configuration included with this chapter can be checked, as follows:

```
src/main/java/com/packtpub/springsecurity/configuration/AclConfig.java
@Bean
public AclPermissionCacheOptimizer permissionCacheOptimizer(){
    return new AclPermissionCacheOptimizer(aclService());
}
```

Optimizing AclPermission Cache

The `DefaultMethodSecurityExpressionHandler` object then delegates to a `PermissionEvalulator` instance. For the purposes of this chapter, we are using ACLs so that the bean we will use `AclPermissionEvaluator`, which will read the ACLs that we define in our database. You can view the provided configuration for `permissionEvaluator`, as follows:

```
src/main/java/com/packtpub/springsecurity/configuration/AclConfig.java
@Bean
public AclPermissionEvaluator permissionEvaluator(){
    return new AclPermissionEvaluator(aclService());
}
```

The JdbcMutableAclService object

At this point, we have seen a reference to `th` with the `aclService` ID twice. The `aclService` ID resolves to an implementation of `o.s.s.acls.model.AclService` that is responsible (through delegation) for translating information about the object being secured by ACLs into expected ACEs:

```
src/main/java/com/packtpub/springsecurity/configuration/AclConfig.java
@Autowired
private DataSource dataSource;
@Bean
public JdbcMutableAclService aclService(){
```

```
            return new JdbcMutableAclService(dataSource,
                                    lookupStrategy(),
                                    aclCache());
    }
```

We'll use o.s.s.acls.jdbc.JdbcMutableAclService, which is the default implementation of o.s.s.acls.model.AclService. This implementation comes out of the box and is ready to use the schema that we defined in the last step of this exercise. The JdbcMutableAclService object will additionally use recursive SQL and post-processing to understand object and SID hierarchies and ensure that representations of these hierarchies are passed back to AclPermissionEvaluator.

The BasicLookupStrategy class

The JdbcMutableAclService class uses the same JDBC dataSource instance that we've defined with the embedded database declaration, and it also delegates to an implementation of o.s.s.acls.jdbc.LookupStrategy, which is solely responsible for actually making database queries and resolving requests for ACLs. The only LookupStrategy implementation supplied with Spring Security is o.s.s.acls.jdbc.BasicLookupStrategy, and is defined as follows:

```
src/main/java/com/packtpub/springsecurity/configuration/AclConfig.j
ava
@Bean
public LookupStrategy lookupStrategy(){
    return new BasicLookupStrategy(
            dataSource,
            aclCache(),
            aclAuthorizationStrategy(),
            consoleAuditLogger());
    }
```

Now, BasicLookupStrategy is a relatively complex beast. Remember that its purpose is to translate a list of the ObjectIdentity declarations to be protected into the actual, applicable ACE list from the database. As ObjectIdentity declarations can be recursive, this proves to be quite a challenging problem, and a system which is likely to experience heavy use should consider the SQL that's generated for performance impact on the database.

Querying with the lowest common denominator

Be aware that `BasicLookupStrategy` is intended to be compatible with all databases by strictly sticking with standard ANSI SQL syntax, notably `left [outer] joins`. Some older databases (notably, **Oracle8i**) did not support this join syntax, so ensure that you verify that the syntax and structure of SQL is compatible with your particular database!

There are also most certainly more efficient database-dependent methods of performing hierarchical queries using non-standard SQL, for example, Oracle's `CONNECT BY` statement and the **Common Table Expression** (**CTE**) capability of many other databases, including PostgreSQL and Microsoft SQL Server.

Much as you learned in the example in `Chapter 4`, *JDBC-Based Authentication*, using a custom schema for the `JdbcDaoImpl` implementation of the `UserDetailsService` properties are exposed to allow for configuration of the SQL utilized by `BasicLookupStrategy`. Consult the Javadoc and the source code itself to see how they are used so that they can be correctly applied to your custom schema.

We can see that `LookupStrategy` requires a reference to the same JDBC `dataSource` instance that AclService utilizes. The other three references bring us almost to the end of the dependency chain.

EhCacheBasedAclCache

The `o.s.s.acls.model.AclCache` interface declares an interface for a caching `ObjectIdentity` to ACL mappings, to prevent redundant (and expensive) database lookups. Spring Security ships with only one implementation of `AclCache`, using the third-party library `Ehcache`.

`Ehcache` is an open source, memory and disk-based caching library that is widely used in many open source and commercial Java products. As mentioned earlier in the chapter, Spring Security ships with a default implementation of ACL caching, which relies on the availability of a configured `Ehcache` instance, which it uses to store ACL information in preference to reading ACLs from the database.

While deep configuration of `Ehcache` is not something we want to cover in this section, we'll cover how Spring ACL uses the cache and walk you through a basic default configuration.

Setting up Ehcache is simple—we'll simply declare
o.s.s.acls.domain.EhCacheBasedAclCache along with its two dependent beans from
Spring Core that manage Ehcache instantiation and expose several helpful configuration
properties. Like our other beans, we have already provided the following configuration in
AclConfig.java:

```
src/main/java/com/packtpub/springsecurity/configuration/AclConfig.java
@Bean
public EhCacheBasedAclCache aclCache(){
    return new EhCacheBasedAclCache(ehcache(),
            permissionGrantingStrategy(),
            aclAuthorizationStrategy()
            );
}

@Bean
public PermissionGrantingStrategy permissionGrantingStrategy(){
    return new DefaultPermissionGrantingStrategy(consoleAuditLogger());
}

@Bean
public Ehcache ehcache(){
    EhCacheFactoryBean cacheFactoryBean = new EhCacheFactoryBean();
    cacheFactoryBean.setCacheManager(cacheManager());
    cacheFactoryBean.setCacheName("aclCache");
    cacheFactoryBean.setMaxBytesLocalHeap("1M");
    cacheFactoryBean.setMaxEntriesLocalHeap(0L);
    cacheFactoryBean.afterPropertiesSet();
    return cacheFactoryBean.getObject();
}

@Bean
public CacheManager cacheManager(){
    EhCacheManagerFactoryBean cacheManager = new
EhCacheManagerFactoryBean();
    cacheManager.setAcceptExisting(true);
cacheManager.setCacheManagerName(CacheManager.getInstance().getName());
    cacheManager.afterPropertiesSet();
return cacheManager.getObject();
}
```

The ConsoleAuditLogger class

The next simple dependency hanging off of `o.s.s.acls.jdbc.BasicLookupStrategy` is an implementation of the `o.s.s.acls.domain.AuditLogger` interface, which is used by the `BasicLookupStrategy` class to audit ACL and ACE lookups. Similar to the `AclCache` interface, only one implementation is supplied with Spring Security that simply logs to the console. We'll configure it with another one-line bean declaration:

```
src/main/java/com/packtpub/springsecurity/configuration/AclConfig.j
ava
@Bean
public ConsoleAuditLogger consoleAuditLogger(){
    return new ConsoleAuditLogger();
}
```

The AclAuthorizationStrategyImpl interface

The final dependency to resolve is to an implementation of the `o.s.s.acls.domain.AclAuthorizationStrategy` interface, which actually has no immediate responsibility at all during the load of the ACL from the database. Instead, the implementation of this interface is responsible for determining whether a runtime change to an ACL or ACE is allowed, based on the type of change. We'll explain more on this later when we cover mutable ACLs, as the logical flow is both somewhat complicated and not pertinent to getting our initial configuration complete. The final configuration requirements are as follows:

```
src/main/java/com/packtpub/springsecurity/configuration/AclConfig.j
ava
@Bean
public AclAuthorizationStrategy aclAuthorizationStrategy() {
    return new AclAuthorizationStrategyImpl(
            new SimpleGrantedAuthority("ROLE_ADMINISTRATOR")
    );
}
```

You might wonder what the reference to the bean with ID `adminAuthority` is for—`AclAuthorizationStrategyImpl` provides the ability to specify `GrantedAuthority` that is required to allow specific operations at runtime on mutable ACLs. We'll cover these later in this chapter.

Lastly, we need to update our `SecurityConfig.java` file to load our `AclConfig.java` file, as follows:

```
src/main/java/com/packtpub/springsecurity/configuration/SecurityCon
fig.java
@Import(AclConfig.class)
public class SecurityConfig extends WebSecurityConfigurerAdapter {
```

We're finally done with the basic configuration of an out-of-the-box Spring Security ACL implementation. The next and final step requires that we insert a simple ACL and ACE into the H2 database and test it out!

Creating a simple ACL entry

Recall that our very simple scenario is to only allow `user2@example.com` access to the birthday party event and ensure that no other events are accessible. You may find it helpful to refer back several pages to the database schema diagram to follow which data we are inserting and why.

We have already included a file named `data.sql` in the sample application. All of the SQL explained in this section will be from the file—you may feel free to experiment and add more test cases based on the sample SQL we've provided—in fact, we'd encourage that you experiment with sample data!

Let's take a look at the following steps for creating a simple ACL entry:

1. First, we'll need to populate the `ACL_CLASS` table with any or all of the domain object classes, which may have ACL rules—in the case of our example, this is simply our `Event` class:

   ```
   src/main/resources/data.sql
   insert into acl_class (id, class) values (10,
   'com.packtpub.springsecurity.domain.Event');
   ```

   We chose to use primary keys that are between 10 to 19 for the `ACL_CLASS` table, 20 to 29 for the `ACL_SID` table, and so on. This will help to make it easier to understand which data associates to which table. Note that our `Event` table starts with a primary key of 100. These conveniences are done for example purposes and are not suggested for production purposes.

2. Next, the `ACL_SID` table is seeded with `SID`s that will be associated with the `ACE`s. Remember that `SID`s can either be roles or users—we'll populate the roles and `user2@example.com` here.

3. While the `SID` object for roles is straightforward, the `SID` object for a user is not quite as clear-cut. For our purposes, the username is used for the `SID`. To learn more about how the `SID`s are resolved for roles and users, refer to `o.s.s.acls.domain.SidRetrievalStrategyImpl`. If the defaults do not meet your needs, a custom `o.s.s.acls.model.SidRetrievalStrategy` default can be injected into `AclPermissionCacheOptimizer` and `AclPermissionEvaluator`. We will not need this sort of customization for our example, but it is good to know that it is available if necessary:

```
src/main/resources/data.sql
insert into acl_sid (id, principal, sid) values (20, true,
'user2@example.com');
insert into acl_sid (id, principal, sid) values (21, false,
'ROLE_USER');
insert into acl_sid (id, principal, sid) values (22, false,
'ROLE_ADMIN');
```

The table where things start getting complicated is the `ACL_OBJECT_IDENTITY` table that is used to declare individual domain object instances, their parent (if any), and owning `SID`. For example, this table represents the `Event` objects that we are securing. We'll insert a row with the following properties:

- Domain object of type `Event` that is a foreign key, `10`, to our `ACL_CLASS` table via the `OBJECT_ID_CLASS` column.
- Domain object primary key of `100` (the `OBJECT_ID_IDENTITY` column). This is a foreign key (although not enforced with a database constraint) to our `Event` object.
- Owner `SID` of `user2@example.com`, which is a foreign key, `20`, to `ACL_SID` via the `OWNER_SID` column.

The SQL to represent our events with IDs of `100` (birthday event), `101`, and `102` is as follows:

```
src/main/resources/data.sql
insert into acl_object_identity(id,object_id_identity,object_id_class,
parent_object,owner_sid,entries_inheriting)
values (30, 100, 10, null, 20, false);
insert into acl_object_identity(id,object_id_identity,object_id_class,
parent_object,owner_sid,entries_inheriting)
values (31, 101, 10, null, 21, false);
```

```
insert into acl_object_identity(id,object_id_identity,object_id_class,
parent_object,owner_sid,entries_inheriting)
values (32, 102, 10, null, 21, false);
```

Keep in mind that the owning SID could also represent a role—both types of rules function equally well as far as the ACL system is concerned.

Finally, we'll add an ACE-related to this object instance, which declares that user2@example.com is allowed read access to the birthday event:

```
src/main/resources/data.sql
insert into acl_entry
(acl_object_identity, ace_order, sid, mask, granting, audit_success,
audit_failure) values(30, 1, 20, 1, true, true, true);
```

The MASK column here represents a bitmask, which is used to grant permission assigned to the stated SID on the object in question. We'll explain the details of this later in this chapter—unfortunately, it doesn't tend to be as useful as it may sound.

Now, we can start the application and run through our sample scenario. Try logging in with user2@example.com/user2 and accessing the **All Events** page. You will see that only the birthday event is listed. When logged in with admin1@example.com/admin1 and viewing the **All Events** page, no events will be displayed. However, if we navigated directly to an event, it would not be protected. Can you figure out how to secure direct access to an event based on what you learned in this chapter?

If you have not figured it out yet, you can secure direct access to an event by making the following update to CalendarService, as follows:

```
src/main/java/com/packtpub/springsecurity/service/CalendarService.java
@PostAuthorize("hasPermission(filterObject, 'read') " +
"or hasPermission(filterObject, 'admin_read')")
Event getEvent(int eventId);
```

We now have a basic working setup of ACL-based security (albeit, a very simple scenario). Let's move on to some more explanation about concepts we saw during this walkthrough, and then review a couple of considerations in a typical Spring ACL implementation that you should consider before using it.

Your code should look like `chapter12.01-calendar`.

It is worth noting that we have not created new ACL entries when we create events. Thus, in the current state, if you create an event, you will receive an error similar to the following:

```
Exception during execution of Spring Security
application! Unable to find ACL information for object
identity
org.springframework.security.acls.domain.ObjectIdentityIm
pl[Type: com.packtpub.springsecurity.domain.Event;
Identifier: 103].
```

Advanced ACL topics

Some high-level topics that we skimmed over during the configuration of our ACL environment had to do with ACE permissions and the use of the `GrantedAuthority` indicators to assist the ACL environment in determining whether certain types of runtime changes to ACLs were allowed. Now that we have a working environment, we'll review these more advanced topics.

How permissions work

Permissions are no more than single logical identifiers represented by bits in an integer. An access control entry grants permissions to `SIDs` based on the bitmask, which comprises the logical AND of all permissions applicable to that access control entry.

The default permission implementation, `o.s.s.acls.domain.BasePermission`, defines a series of integer values representing common ACL authorization verbs. These integer values correspond to single bits set in an integer, so a value of `BasePermission`, `WRITE`, with integer value 1 has a bitwise value of 21 or 2.

These are illustrated in the following diagram:

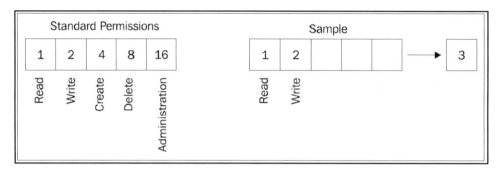

We can see that the **Sample** permission bitmask would have an integer value of **3**, due to the application of both the **Read** and **Write** permissions to the permission value. All of the standard integer single permission values shown in the preceding diagram are defined in the BasePermission object as static constants.

The logical constants that are included in BasePermission are just a sensible baseline of commonly used permissions in ACE, and have no semantic meaning within the Spring Security framework. It's quite common for very complex ACL implementations to invent their own custom permissions, augmenting best practice examples with domain- or business-dependent ones.

One issue that often confuses users is how the bitmasks are used in practice, given that many databases either do not support bitwise logic or do not support it in a scalable way. Spring ACL intends to solve this problem by putting more of the load of calculating appropriate permissions related to bitmasks on the application rather than on the database.

It's important to review the resolution process, where we see how AclPermissionEvaluator resolves permissions declared on the method itself (in our example, with the @PostFilter annotation) to real ACL permissions.

The following diagram illustrates the process that Spring ACL performs to evaluate the declared permission against the relevant ACEs for the requesting principal:

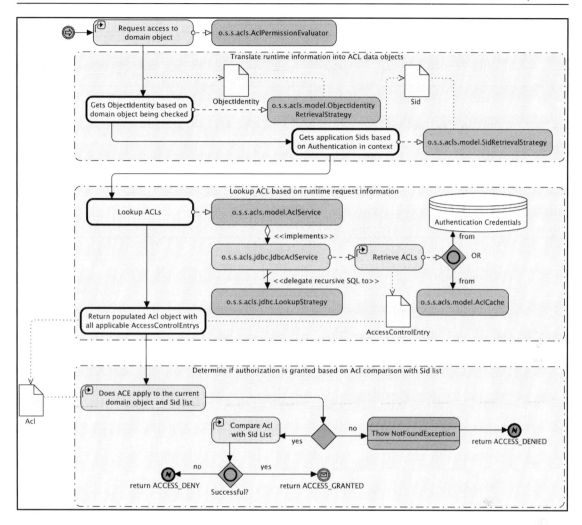

We see that `AclPermissionEvaluator` relies on classes implementing two interfaces, `o.s.s.acls.model.ObjectIdentityRetrievalStrategy` and `o.s.s.acls.model.SidRetrievalStrategy`, to retrieve `ObjectIdentity` and `SIDs` appropriate for the authorization check. The important thing to note about these strategies is how the default implementation classes actually determine the `ObjectIdentity` and `SIDs` objects to return, based on the context of the authorization check.

The ObjectIdentity object has two properties, type and identifier, that are derived from the object being checked at runtime, and used to declare ACE entries. The default ObjectIdentityRetrievalStrategy interface uses the fully-qualified class name to populate the type property. The identifier property is populated with the result of a method with the signature Serializable getId(), invoked on the actual object instance.

As your object isn't required to implement an interface to be compatible with ACL checks, the requirement to implement a method with a specific signature can be surprising for developers implementing Spring Security ACL. Plan ahead and ensure that your domain objects contain this method! You may also implement your own ObjectIdentityRetrievalStrategy class (or subclass the out-of-the-box implementation) to call a method of your choice. The name and type signature of the method is, unfortunately, not configurable.

Unfortunately, the actual implementation of AclImpl directly compares the permission specified in our SpEL expression specified in our @PostFilter annotation, and the permission stored on the ACE in the database, without using bitwise logic. The Spring Security community is in debate about whether this is unintentional or working as intended, but regardless, you will need to take care when declaring a user with a combination of permissions, as either AclEntryVoter must be configured with all combinations of permission, or the ACEs need to ignore the fact that the permission field is intended to store multiple values and instead store a single permission per ACE.

If you want to verify this with our simple scenario, change the READ permission we granted to the user2@example.com SID to the bitmask combination of Read and Write, which translates to a value of 3. This would be updated in the data.sql file, as follows:

```
src/main/resources/data.sql
insert into acl_entry
(acl_object_identity, ace_order, sid, mask, granting,
audit_success, audit_failure) values(30, 1, 20, 3, true, true, true);
```

 Your code should look like chapter12.02-calendar.

The custom ACL permission declaration

As stated in the earlier discussion on permission declarations, permissions are nothing but logical names for integer bit values. As such, it's possible to extend the o.s.s.acls.domain.BasePermission class and declare your own permissions. We'll cover a very straightforward scenario here, where we create a new ACL permission called ADMIN_READ. This is a permission that will be granted only to administrative users and will be assigned to protect resources that only administrators could read. Although a contrived example for the JBCP calendar application, this type of use of custom permissions occurs quite often in situations dealing with personally identifiable information (for example, social security number, and so on—recall that we covered PII in Chapter 1, *Anatomy of an Unsafe Application*).

Let's get started making the changes required to support this by performing the following steps:

1. The first step is to extend the BasePermission class with our own com.packtpub.springsecurity.acls.domain.CustomPermission class, as follows:

   ```
   package com.packtpub.springsecurity.acls.domain;
   public class CustomPermission extends BasePermission {
       public static final Permission ADMIN_READ = new
       CustomPermission(1 << 5, 'M'); // 32
       public CustomPermission(int mask, char code) {
           super(mask, code);
       }
   }
   ```

2. Next, we will need to configure the o.s.s.acls.domain.PermissionFactory default implementation, o.s.s.acls.domain.DefaultPermissionFactory, to register our custom permission logical value. The role of PermissionFactory is to resolve permission bitmasks into logical permission values (which can be referenced by the constant value, or by name, such as ADMIN_READ, in other areas of the application). The PermissionFactory instance requires that any custom permission is registered with it for proper lookup. We have included the following configuration that registers our CustomPermission class, as follows:

   ```
   src/main/java/com/packtpub/springsecurity/configuration/
   AclConfig.java
   @Bean
   public DefaultPermissionFactory permissionFactory(){
     return new DefaultPermissionFactory(CustomPermission.class);
   }
   ```

3. Next, we will need to override the default `PermissionFactory` instance for our `BasicLookupStrategy` and `AclPermissionEvaluator` interfaces with the customized `DefaultPermissionFactory` interface. Make the following updates to your `security-acl.xml` file:

```
src/main/java/com/packtpub/springsecurity/configuration/AclConf
ig.java
@Bean
public AclPermissionEvaluator permissionEvaluator(){
    AclPermissionEvaluator pe = new
AclPermissionEvaluator(aclService());
    pe.setPermissionFactory(permissionFactory());
    return pe;
}
@Bean
public LookupStrategy lookupStrategy(){
    BasicLookupStrategy ls = new BasicLookupStrategy(
                                      dataSource,
                                      aclCache(),
aclAuthorizationStrategy(),
                                      consoleAuditLogger());
    ls.setPermissionFactory(permissionFactory());
    return ls;
}
```

4. We also need to add the SQL query to utilize the new permission to grant access to the conference call (`acl_object_identity` ID of `31`) event to `admin1@example.com`. Make the following updates to `data.sql`:

```
src/main/resources/data.sql
insert into acl_sid (id, principal, sid) values (23, true,
'admin1@example.com');
insert into acl_entry (acl_object_identity, ace_order, sid,
mask, granting, audit_success, audit_failure)
values(31, 1, 23, 32, true, true, true);
```

We can see that the new integer bitmask value of 32 has been referenced in the ACE data. This intentionally corresponds to our new ADMIN_READ ACL permission, as defined in Java code. The conference call event is referenced by its primary key (stored in the `object_id_identity` column) value of 31, in the ACL_OBJECT_IDENTITY table.

5. The last step is to update our `CalendarService's` `getEvents()` method to utilize our new permission, as follows:

```
@PostFilter("hasPermission(filterObject, 'read') " + "or
hasPermission(filterObject, 'admin_read')")
List<Event> getEvents();
```

With all of these configurations in place, we can start up the site again and test out the custom ACL permission. Based on the sample data we have configured, here is what should happen when the various available users click on categories:

Username/password	Birthday party event	Conference call event	Other events
`user2@example.com/user2`	Allowed via READ	Denied	Denied
`admin1@example.com/admin1`	Denied	Allowed via ADMIN_READ	Denied
`user1@example.com/user1`	Denied	Denied	Denied

We can see that even with the use of our simple cases, we've now been able to extend the Spring ACL functionality in a very limited way to illustrate the power of this fine-grained access control system.

Your code should look like `chapter12.03-calendar`.

Enabling ACL permission evaluation

We saw in `Chapter 2`, *Getting Started with Spring Security*, that the Spring Security JSP tag library offers functionality to expose authentication-related data to the user and to restrict what the user can see based on a variety of rules. So far in this book, we have used the Thymeleaf Security tag libraries that are built on top of Spring Security.

The very same tag library can also interact with an ACL-enabled system right out of the box! From our simple experiments, we have configured a simple ACL authorization scenario around the first two categories in the list on the home page. Let's take a look at the following steps and learn how to enable ACL permission evaluation in our Thymeleaf pages:

1. First, we will need to remove our `@PostFilter` annotation from the `getEvents()` method in our `CalendarService` interface in order to give our JSP tag library a chance to filter out the events that are not allowed for display. Go ahead and remove `@PostFilter` now, as follows:

   ```
   src/main/java/com/packtpub/springsecurity/service/
   CalendarService.java
   List<Event> getEvents();
   ```

2. Now that we have removed `@PostFilter`, we can utilize the `<sec:authorize-acl>` tag to hide the events that the user doesn't actually have access to. Refer to the table in the preceding section as a refresher of the access rules we've configured up to this point!

3. We'll wrap the display of each event with the `<sec:authorize-acl>` tag, declaring the list of permissions to check on the object to be displayed:

   ```
   src/main/resources/templates/events/list.html
   <tr th:each="event : ${events}"
      sec:authorize-acl="${event} :: '1,32'">
      <td th:text="${#calendars.format(event.when,
      'yyyy-MM-dd HH:mm')}">today</td>
      <td th:text="${event.owner.name}"></td>
      <td th:text="${event.attendee.name}"> </td>
      <td><a th:href="@{'/events/{id}'(id=${event.id})}"
      th:text="${event.summary}"></a></td>
   </tr>
   ```

4. Think for a moment about what we want to occur here—we want the user to see only the items to which they actually have the READ or ADMIN_READ (our custom permission) access. However, to use the tag library, we need to use the permission mask, which can be referenced from the following table:

Name	Mask
READ	1
WRITE	2
ADMIN_READ	32

Behind the scenes, the tag implementation utilizes the same
`SidRetrievalStrategy` and `ObjectIdentityRetrievalStrategy` interfaces
discussed earlier in this chapter. So, the computation of access checking follows
the same workflow as it does with ACL-enabled voting on method security. As
we will see in a moment, the tag implementation will also use the same
`PermissionEvaluator`.

We have already configured our `GlobalMethodSecurityConfiguration`
configuration with an `expressionHandler` element that references
`DefaultMethodSecurityExpressionHandler`. The
`DefaultMethodSecurityExpressionHandler` implementation is aware of our
`AclPermissionEvaluator` interface, but we must also make Spring Security's
web tier aware of `AclPermissionEvalulator`. If you think about it, this
symmetry makes sense, since securing methods and HTTP requests are protecting
two very different resources. Fortunately, Spring Security's abstractions make this
rather simple.

5. Add a `DefaultWebSecurityExpressionHandler` handler that references the
   bean with the ID as `permissionEvaluator` that we have already defined:

```
src/main/java/com/packtpub/springsecurity/configuration/
AclConfig.java
@Bean
public DefaultWebSecurityExpressionHandler webExpressionHandler(){
    return new DefaultWebSecurityExpressionHandler(){{
        setPermissionEvaluator(permissionEvaluator());
    }};
}
```

6. Now, update `SecurityConfig.java` to refer to our
   `webExpressionHandler` implementation, as follows:

```
src/main/java/com/packtpub/springsecurity/configuration/
SecurityConfig.java
@Autowired
private DefaultWebSecurityExpressionHandler webExpressionHandler;
@Override
protected void configure(HttpSecurity http) throws Exception {
    http.authorizeRequests()
      .expressionHandler(webExpressionHandler);
    ...
}
```

You can see how these steps are very similar to how we added support for permission handling to our method security. This time, it was a bit simpler, since we were able to reuse the same bean with ID as `PermissionEvaluator` that we already configured.

Start up our application and try accessing the **All Events** page as different users. You will find that the events that are not allowed for a user are now hidden using our tag library instead of the `@PostFilter` annotation. We are still aware that accessing an event directly would allow a user to see it. However, this could easily be added by combining what you learned in this chapter with what you learned about the `@PostAuthorize` annotation in this chapter.

 Your code should look like `chapter12.04-calendar`.

Mutable ACLs and authorization

Although the JBCP calendar application doesn't implement full user administration functionality, it's likely that your application will have common features, such as new user registration and administrative user maintenance. To this point, lack of these features—which we have worked around using SQL inserts at application startup—hasn't stopped us from demonstrating many of the features of Spring Security and Spring ACL.

However, the proper handling of runtime changes to declared ACLs, or the addition or removal of users in the system, is critical to maintaining the consistency and security of the ACL-based authorization environment. Spring ACL solves this issue through the concept of the mutable ACL (`o.s.s.acls.model.MutableAcl`).

Extending the standard ACL interface, the `MutableAcl` interface allows for runtime manipulation of ACL fields in order to change the in-memory representation of a particular ACL. This additional functionality includes the ability to create, update, or delete ACEs, change ACL ownership, and other useful functions.

We might expect, then, that the Spring ACL module would come out of the box with a way to persist runtime ACL changes to the JDBC datastore, and indeed it does. The `o.s.s.acls.jdbc.JdbcMutableAclService` class may be used to create, update, and delete the `MutableAcl` instances in the database, as well as to do general maintenance on the other supporting tables for ACLs (handling `SID`s, `ObjectIdentity`, and domain object class names).

Recall from earlier in the chapter that the `AclAuthorizationStrategyImpl` class allows us to specify the administrative role for actions on mutable ACLs. These are supplied to the constructor as part of the bean configuration. The constructor arguments and their meaning are as follows:

Arg #	What it does?
1	Indicates the authority that a principal is required to have in order to take ownership of an ACL-protected object at runtime
2	Indicates the authority that a principal is required to have in order to change the auditing of an ACL-protected object at runtime
3	Indicates the authority that a principal is required to have in order to make any other kind of change (create, update, and delete) to an ACL-protected object at runtime

It may be confusing that we only specified a single constructor argument when there are three arguments listed. The AclAuthorizationStrategyImpl class can also accept a single `GrantedAuthority`, which will then be used for all three arguments. This is convenient if we want the same `GrantedAuthority` to be used for all of the operations.

The JdbcMutableAclService interface contains a number of methods used to manipulate ACL and ACE data at runtime. While the methods themselves are fairly understandable (`createAcl`, `updateAcl`, and `deleteAcl`), the correct way to configure and use `JdbcMutableAclService` is often difficult for even advanced Spring Security users.

Let's modify `CalendarService` to create a new ACL for newly created events.

Adding ACLs to newly created events

Currently, if a user creates a new event, it will not be visible to the user in the **All Events** view, since we are using the `<sec:authorize-acl>` tag to only display event objects that the user has access to. Let's update our `DefaultCalendarService` interface so that when a user creates a new event, they are granted read access to that event and it will be displayed for them on the **All Events** page.

Let's take a look at the following steps to add ACLs to newly created events:

1. The first step is to update our constructor to accept `MutableAclService` and `UserContext`:

```
src/main/java/com/packtpub/springsecurity/service/
DefaultCalendarService.java
public class DefaultCalendarService implements CalendarService {
    ...
    private final MutableAclService aclService;
    private final UserContext userContext;
    @Autowired
    public DefaultCalendarService(EventDao eventDao,
    CalendarUserDao userDao, CalendarUserRepository userRepository,
    PasswordEncoder passwordEncoder, MutableAclService aclService,
    UserContext userContext) {
        ...
        this.aclService = aclService;
        this.userContext = userContext;
    }
```

2. Then, we need to update our `createEvent` method to also create an ACL for the current user. Make the following changes:

```
src/main/java/com/packtpub/springsecurity/service/
DefaultCalendarService.java
@Transactional
public int createEvent(Event event) {
    int result = eventDao.createEvent(event);
    event.setId(result);
    // Add new ACL Entry:
    MutableAcl acl = aclService.createAcl
    (new ObjectIdentityImpl(event));
    PrincipalSid sid = new PrincipalSid(
            userContext.getCurrentUser().getEmail());
    acl.setOwner(sid);
    acl.insertAce(0, BasePermission.READ, sid, true);
    aclService.updateAcl(acl);
    return result;
}
```

3. The `JdbcMutableAclService` interface uses the current user as the default owner for the created `MutableAcl` interface. We chose to explicitly set the owner again to demonstrate how this can be overridden.

4. We then add a new ACE and save our ACL. That's all there is to it.

5. Start the application and log in with user1@example.com/user1.

6. Visit the **All Events** page and see that there are no events currently listed. Then, create a new event and it will be displayed the next time you visit the **All Events** page. If you log in as any other user, the event will not be visible on the **All Events** page. However, it will potentially be visible to the user, since we have not applied security to other pages. Again, we encourage you to attempt to secure these pages on your own.

Your code should look like chapter12.05-calendar.

Considerations for a typical ACL deployment

Actually deploying Spring ACL in a true business application tends to be quite involved. We wrap up coverage of Spring ACL with some considerations that arise in most Spring ACL implementation scenarios.

ACL scalability and performance modeling

For small and medium-sized applications, the addition of ACLs is quite manageable, and while it adds overhead to database storage and runtime performance, the impact is not likely to be significant. However, depending on the granularity with which ACLs and ACEs are modeled, the numbers of database rows in a medium- to the large-sized application can be truly staggering and can task even the most seasoned database administrator.

Let's assume we were to extend ACLs to cover an extended version of the JBCP calendar application. Let's assume that users can manage accounts, post pictures to events, and administer (add/remove users) from an event. We'll model the data as follows:

- All users have accounts.
- 10% of users are able to administer an event. The average number of events that a user can administer will be two.
- Events will be secured (read-only) per customer, but also need to be accessible (read/write) by administrators.

- 10 percent of all customers will be allowed to post pictures. The average number of posts per user will be 20.
- Posted pictures will be secured (read-write) per user, as well as administrators. Posted pictures will be read-only for all other users.

Given what we know about the ACL system, we know that the database tables have the following scalability attributes:

Table	Scales with data	Scalability notes
ACL_CLASS	No	One row is required per domain class.
ACL_SID	Yes (users)	One row is required per role (GrantedAuthority). One row is required for each user account (if individual domain objects are secured per user).
ACL_OBJECT_IDENTITY	Yes (domain class instances per class)	One row is required per instance of a secured domain object.
ACL_ENTRY	Yes (domain object instances individual ACE entries)	One row is required per ACE; may require multiple rows for a single domain object.

We can see that ACL_CLASS doesn't really have scalability concerns (most systems will have fewer than 1,000 domain classes). The ACL_SID table will scale linearly based on the number of users in the system. This is probably not a matter of concern because other user-related tables will scale in this fashion as well (user account, and so on).

The two tables of concern are ACL_OBJECT_IDENTITY and ACL_ENTRY. If we model the estimated rows required to model an order for an individual customer, we come up with the following estimates:

Table	ACL data per event	ACL data per picture post
ACL_OBJECT_IDENTITY	One row is required for a single event.	One row is required for a single post.

ACL_ENTRY	Three rows—one row is required for read access by the owner (the user `SID`), two rows are required (one for read access, one for write access) for the administrative group `SID`.	Four rows—one row is required for read access by the user group `SID`, one row is required for write access by the owner, two rows are required for the administrative group `SID` (as with events)

We can then take the usage assumptions from the previous page and calculate the following ACL scalability matrix as follows:

Table/Object	Scale factor	Estimates (Low)	Estimates (High)
Users		10,000	1,000,000
Events	# Users * 0.1 * 2	2,000	200,000
Picture Posts	# Users * 0.1 * 20	20,000	2,000,000
ACL_SID	# Users	10,000	1,000,000
ACL_OBJECT_IDENTITY	# Events + # Picture Posts	220,000	2,200,000
ACL_ENTRY	(# Events * 3) + (# Picture Posts * 4)	86,000	8,600,000

From these projections based on only a subset of the business objects likely to be involved and secured in a typical ACL implementation, you can see that the number of database rows devoted to storing ACL information is likely to grow linearly (or faster) in relation to your actual business data. Especially in large system planning, forecasting the amount of ACL data that you are likely to use is extremely important. It is not uncommon for very complex systems to have hundreds of millions of rows related to ACL storage.

Do not discount custom development costs

Utilizing a Spring ACL-secured environment often requires significant development work above and beyond the configuration steps we've described to this point. Our sample configuration scenario has the following limitations:

- No facility is provided for responding to the manipulation modification of events or modification of permissions

- Not all of the application is using permissions. For example, the **My Events** page and directly navigating to an event are both not secured

The application does not effectively use ACL hierarchies. These limitations would significantly impact the functionality were we to roll out ACL security to the whole site. This is why it is critical that when planning Spring ACL rollout across an application, you must carefully review all of the places where the domain data is manipulated and ensure that these locations correctly update ACL and ACE rules, and invalidate caches. Typically, the securing of methods and data takes place at the service or business application layer, and the hooks required to maintain ACLs and ACEs occur at the data access layer.

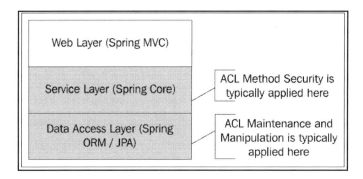

If you are dealing with a reasonably standard application architecture, with proper isolation and encapsulation of functionality, it's likely that there's an easily identified central location for these changes. On the other hand, if you're dealing with an architecture that has devolved (or was never designed well in the first place), then adding ACL functionality and supporting hooks in data manipulation code can prove to be very difficult.

As previously hinted, it's important to keep in mind that the Spring ACL architecture hasn't changed significantly since the days of Acegi 1.x. During that time, many users have attempted to implement it, and have logged and documented several important restrictions, many of which are captured in the Spring Security JIRA repository (`http://jira.springframework.org/`). Issue `SEC-479` functions as a useful entry point for some of the key limitations, many of which remain unaddressed with Spring Security 3, and (if they are applicable to your situation) can require significant custom coding to work around.

The following are some of the most important and commonly encountered issues:

- The ACL infrastructure requires a numeric primary key. For applications that use a GUID or UUID primary key (which occurs more frequently due to more efficient support in modern databases), this can be a significant limitation.
- At the time of writing this, the JIRA issue, SEC-1140, documents the issue that the default ACL implementation does not correctly compare permission bitmasks using bitwise operators. We covered this earlier in the section on permissions.
- Several inconsistencies exist between the method of configuring Spring ACL and the rest of Spring Security. In general, it is likely that you will run into areas where class delegates or properties are not exposed through DI, necessitating an override and rewrite strategy that can be time consuming and expensive to maintain.
- The permission bitmask is implemented as an integer, and thus has 32 possible bits. It's somewhat common to expand the default bit assignments to indicate permissions on individual object properties (for example, assigning a bit to read the social security number of an employee). Complex deployments may have well over 32 properties per domain object, in which case the only alternative would be to remodel your domain objects around this limitation.

Depending on your specific application's requirements, it is likely that you will encounter additional issues, especially with regards to the number of classes requiring change when implementing certain types of customizations.

Should I use Spring Security ACL?

Just like the details of applying Spring Security as a whole are highly business dependent, so is the application of Spring ACL support. In fact, this tends to be even more true of ACL support due to its tight coupling to business methods and domain objects. We hope that this guide to Spring ACL explained the important high-level and low-level configurations and concepts required to analyze Spring ACL for use in your application and can assist you in determining and matching its capabilities to real-world use.

Summary

In this chapter, we focused on security based on ACL and the specific details of how this type of security is implemented by the Spring ACL module.

We reviewed the basic concept of ACL, and many reasons why they can be very effective solutions to authorization. Also, you learned the key concepts related to the Spring ACL implementation, including ACEs, SIDs, and object identity. We examined the database schema and logical design required to support a hierarchical ACL system. We configured all the required Spring beans to enable the Spring ACL module and enhanced one of the service interfaces to use annotated method authorization. We then tied the existing users in our database, and business objects used by the site itself, into a sample set of ACE declarations and supporting data. We reviewed the concepts around Spring ACL permission handling. We expanded our knowledge of the Spring Security Thymeleaf tag library and SpEL expression language (for method security) to utilize ACL checks. We discussed the mutable ACL concept and reviewed the basic configuration and custom coding required in a mutable ACL environment. We developed a custom ACL permission and configured the application to demonstrate its effectiveness. We configured and analyzed the use of the `Ehcache` cache manager to reduce the database impact of Spring ACL. We analyzed the impact and design considerations of using the Spring ACL system in a complex business application.

This wraps up our discussion about Spring Security ACLs. In the next chapter, we'll dig a bit further into how Spring Security works.

13
Custom Authorization

In this chapter, we will write some custom implementations for Spring Security's key authorization APIs. Once we have done this, we will use the understanding of the custom implementations to understand how Spring Security's authorization architecture works.

Throughout this chapter, we will cover the following topics:

- Gaining an understanding of how authorization works
- Writing a custom `SecurityMetaDataSource` backed by a database instead of `antMatchers()` methods
- Creating a custom SpEL expression
- Implementing a custom `PermissionEvaluator` object that allows our permissions to be encapsulated

Authorizing the requests

As in the authentication process, Spring Security provides an `o.s.s.web.access.intercept.FilterSecurityInterceptor` servlet filter, which is responsible for coming up with a decision as to whether a particular request will be accepted or denied. At the point the filter is invoked, the principal has already been authenticated, so the system knows that a valid user has logged in; remember that we implemented the `List<GrantedAuthority> getAuthorities()` method, which returns a list of authorities for the principal, in Chapter 3, Custom Authentication. In general, the authorization process will use the information from this method (defined by the `Authentication` interface) to determine, for a particular request, whether or not the request should be allowed.

Remember that authorization is a binary decision—a user either has access to a secured resource or he does not. There is no ambiguity when it comes to authorization.

A Smart object-oriented design is pervasive within the Spring Security framework, and authorization decision management is no exception.

In Spring Security, the `o.s.s.access.AccessDecisionManager` interface specifies two simple and logical methods that fit sensibly into the processing decision flow of requests, as follows:

- `Supports`: This logical operation actually comprises two methods that allow the `AccessDecisionManager` implementation to report whether or not it supports the current request.
- `Decide`: This allows the `AccessDecisionManager` implementation to verify, based on the request context and security configuration, whether or not access should be allowed and the request accepted. The `Decide` method actually has no return value, and instead reports the denial of a request by throwing an exception to indicate rejection.

Specific types of exceptions can further dictate the action to be taken by the application to resolve authorization decisions. The `o.s.s.access.AccessDeniedException` interface is the most common exception thrown in the area of authorization and merits special handling by the filter chain.

The implementation of `AccessDecisionManager` is completely configurable using standard Spring bean binding and references. The default `AccessDecisionManager` implementation provides an access granting mechanism based on `AccessDecisionVoter` and votes aggregation.

A voter is an actor in the authorization sequence whose job is to evaluate any or all of the following things:

- The context of the request for a secured resource (such as a URL requesting an IP address)
- The credentials (if any) presented by the user
- The secured resource being accessed
- The configuration parameters of the system, and the resource itself

The `AccessDecisionManager` implementation is also responsible for passing the access declaration (referred to in the code as implementations of the `o.s.s.access.ConfigAttribute` interface) of the resource being requested to the voter. In the case of web URLs, the voter will have information about the access declaration of the resource. If we look at our very basic configuration file's URL intercept declaration, we'll see `ROLE_USER` being declared as the access configuration for the resource the user is trying to access, as follows:

```
.antMatchers("/**").hasRole("USER");
```

Based on the voter's knowledge, it will decide whether the user should have access to the resource or not. Spring Security allows the voter to make one of three decisions, whose logical definition is mapped to constants in the interface, as shown in the following table:

Decision type	Description
Grant (ACCESS_GRANTED)	The voter recommends giving access to the resource.
Deny (ACCESS_DENIED)	The voter recommends denying access to the resource.
Abstain (ACCESS_ABSTAIN)	The voter abstains (does not make a decision) on access to the resource. This may happen for a number of reasons, such as follows: • The voter doesn't have conclusive information • The voter can't decide on a request of this type

As you may have guessed from the design of access decision-related objects and interfaces, this portion of Spring Security has been designed so that it can be applied to authentication and access control scenarios that aren't exclusively in the web domain. We'll encounter voters and access decision managers when we look at method-level security later in this chapter.

When we put this all together, the overall flow of the default authorization check for web requests is similar to the following diagram:

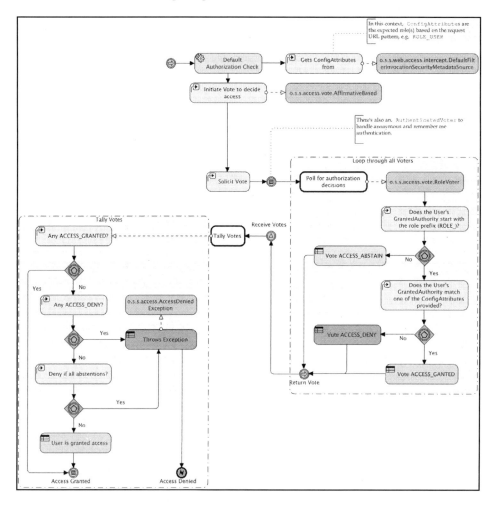

We can see that the abstraction of `ConfigAttribute` allows for data to be passed from the configuration declarations (retained in the `o.s.s.web.access.intercept.DefaultFilterinvocationSecurityMetadataSourc e` interface) to the voter responsible for acting on `ConfigAttribute` without any intervening classes needing to understand the contents of `ConfigAttribute`. This separation of concerns provides a solid foundation for building new types of security declarations (such as the declarations we will see within method security) while utilizing the same access decision pattern.

Configuration of access decision aggregation

Spring Security does actually allow for the configuration of `AccessDecisionManager` in the security namespace. The `access-decision-manager-ref` attribute on the `<http>` element allows you to specify a Spring bean reference to an implementation of `AccessDecisionManager`. Spring Security ships with three implementations of this interface, all in the `o.s.s.access.vote` package as follows:

Class name	Description
`AffirmativeBased`	If any voter grants access, access is immediately granted, regardless of previous denials.
`ConsensusBased`	The majority vote (grant or deny) governs the decision of `AccessDecisionManager`. Tie-breaking and the handling of empty votes (containing only abstentions) is configurable.
`UnanimousBased`	All voters must grant access, otherwise, access is denied.

Configuring a UnanimousBased access decision manager

If we want to modify our application to use the access decision manager, we require two modifications. In order to do this, we add the `accessDecisionManager` entry to the `http` element in our `SecurityConfig.java` file, as follows:

```
//src/main/java/com/packtpub/springsecurity/configuration/
SecurityConfig.java

http.authorizeRequests()
    .anyRequest()
    .authenticated()
    .accessDecisionManager(accessDecisionManager());
```

This is a standard Spring bean reference, so this should correspond to the `id` attribute of a bean. We could then define the `UnanimousBased` bean, as shown in the following code snippet. Note that we will not actually utilize this configuration in our exercises:

```
//src/main/java/com/packtpub/springsecurity/configuration/SecurityC
onfig.java

@Bean
public AccessDecisionManager accessDecisionManager() {
```

```
List<AccessDecisionVoter<? extends Object>> decisionVoters
    = Arrays.asList(
    new AuthenticatedVoter(),
    new RoleVoter(),
    new WebExpressionVoter()
);

return new UnanimousBased(decisionVoters);
}
```

You may be wondering what the `decisionVoters` property is about. This property is auto-configured until we declare our own `AccessDecisionManager`. The default `AccessDecisionManager` class requires us to declare the list of voters who are consulted to make authentication decisions. The two voters listed here are the defaults supplied by the security namespace configuration.

Spring Security doesn't come with a wide variety of voters, but it would be trivial to implement a new one. As we will see later in the chapter, in most situations, creating a custom voter is not necessary, since this can typically be implemented using custom expressions or even a custom `o.s.s.access.PermissionEvaluator`.

The two voter implementations that we reference here are the following:

Class name	Description	Example
`o.s.s.access.vote.RoleVoter`	Checks that the user has the matching declared role. Expects the attribute to define a comma-delimited list of names. The prefix is expected, but optionally configurable.	`access="ROLE_USER,ROLE_ADMIN"`
`o.s.s.access.vote.AuthenticatedVoter`	Supports special declarations allowing wildcard matches: • `IS_AUTHENTICATED_FULLY` allows access if a fresh username and password are supplied. • `IS_AUTHENTICATED_REMEMBERED` allows access if the user has authenticated with the remember-me functionality. • `IS_AUTHENTICATED_ANONYMOUSLY` allows access if the user is anonymous	`access="IS_AUTHENTICATED_ANONYMOUSLY"`

Expression-based request authorization

As you might expect, SpEL handling is supplied by a different `Voter` implementation, `o.s.s.web.access.expression.WebExpressionVoter`, which understands how to evaluate the SpEL expressions. The `WebExpressionVoter` class relies on an implementation of the `SecurityExpressionHandler` interface for this purpose. The `SecurityExpressionHandler` interface is responsible both for evaluating the expressions and for supplying the security-specific methods that are referenced in the expressions. The default implementation of this interface exposes methods defined in the `o.s.s.web.access.expression.WebSecurityExpressionRoot` class.

The flow and relationship between these classes are shown in the following diagram:

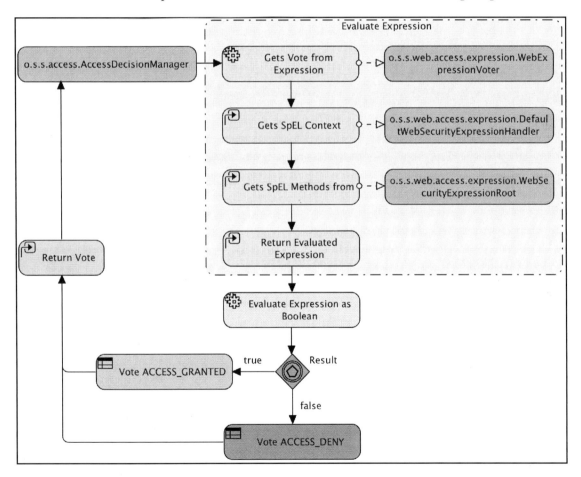

Now that we know how to request authorization works, let's solidify our understanding by making a few custom implementations of some key interfaces.

Customizing request authorization

The real power of Spring Security's authorization is demonstrated by how adaptable it is to custom requirements. Let's explore a few scenarios that will help reinforce our understanding of the overall architecture.

Dynamically defining access control to URLs

Spring Security provides several methods for mapping ConfigAttribute objects to a resource. For example, the antMatchers() method ensures it is simple for developers to restrict access to specific HTTP requests in their web application. Behind the scenes, an implementation of o.s.s.acess.SecurityMetadataSource is populated with these mappings and queried to determine what is required in order to be authorized to make any given HTTP request.

While the antMatchers() method is very simple, there may be times that it would be desirable to provide a custom mechanism for determining the URL mappings. An example of this might be if an application needs to be able to dynamically provide the access control rules. Let's demonstrate what it would take to move our URL authorization configuration into a database.

Configuring the RequestConfigMappingService

The first step is to be able to obtain the necessary information from the database. This will replace the logic that reads in the antMatchers() methods from our security bean configuration. In order to do this, the chapter's sample code contains JpaRequestConfigMappingService, which will obtain a mapping of an ant pattern and an expression from the database represented as RequestConfigMapping. The rather simple implementation is as follows:

```
//
src/main/java/com/packtpub/springsecurity/web/access/intercept/
    JpaRequestConfigMappingService.java

@Repository("requestConfigMappingService")
public class JpaRequestConfigMappingService
implements RequestConfigMappingService {
```

```
        @Autowired
    private SecurityFilterMetadataRepository
securityFilterMetadataRepository;


    @Autowired
    public JpaRequestConfigMappingService(
            SecurityFilterMetadataRepository sfmr
    ) {
        this.securityFilterMetadataRepository = sfmr;
    }


    @Override
    public List<RequestConfigMapping> getRequestConfigMappings() {
        List<RequestConfigMapping> rcm =
            securityFilterMetadataRepository
                .findAll()
                .stream()
                .sorted((m1, m2) -> {
                return m1.getSortOrder() - m2.getSortOrder()
                })
                .map(md -> {
                    return new RequestConfigMapping(
                            new AntPathRequestMatcher
                            (md.getAntPattern()),
                            new SecurityConfig
                            (md.getExpression())));
                }).collect(toList());
        return rcm;
    }
}
```

It is important to notice that, just as with the antMatchers() methods, order matters. Therefore, we ensure the results are sorted by the sort_order column. The service creates an AntRequestMatcher and associates it to SecurityConfig, an instance of ConfigAttribute. This will provide a mapping of the HTTP request to ConfigAttribute objects that can be used by Spring Security to secure our URLs.

We need to create a domain object to use for JPA to map to as follows:

```
//
src/main/java/com/packtpub/springsecurity/domain/SecurityFilterMeta
data.java

@Entity
@Table(name = "security_filtermetadata")
```

```java
public class SecurityFilterMetadata implements Serializable {


    @Id
    @GeneratedValue(strategy = GenerationType.AUTO)
    private Integer id;
    private String antPattern;
    private String expression;
    private Integer sortOrder;


... setters / getters ...
}
```

Finally, we need to create a Spring Data repository object as follows:

```java
// src/main/java/com/packtpub/springsecurity/repository/
SecurityFilterMetadataRepository.java

public interface SecurityFilterMetadataRepository
extends JpaRepository<SecurityFilterMetadata, Integer> {}
```

In order for the new service to work, we will need to initialize our database with the schema and the access control mappings. Just as with the service implementation, our schema is rather straightforward:

```sql
// src/main/resources/schema.sql

...
create table security_filtermetadata (
 id           INTEGER GENERATED BY DEFAULT AS IDENTITY,
 ant_pattern VARCHAR(1024) NOT NULL unique,
 expression VARCHAR(1024) NOT NULL,
 sort_order INTEGER NOT NULL,
 PRIMARY KEY (id)
);
```

We can then use the same `antMatchers()` mappings from our `SecurityConfig.java` file to produce the `schema.sql` file:

```sql
// src/main/resources/data.sql

-- Security Filter Metadata --

insert into
security_filtermetadata(id,ant_pattern,expression,sort_order)
values (110, '/admin/h2/**','permitAll',10);
```

```
insert into
security_filtermetadata(id,ant_pattern,expression,sort_order)
values (115, '/','permitAll',15);

insert into
security_filtermetadata(id,ant_pattern,expression,sort_order)
values (120, '/login/*','permitAll',20);

insert into
security_filtermetadata(id,ant_pattern,expression,sort_order)
values (140, '/logout','permitAll',30);

insert into
security_filtermetadata(id,ant_pattern,expression,sort_order)
values (130, '/signup/*','permitAll',40);

insert into
security_filtermetadata(id,ant_pattern,expression,sort_order)
values (150, '/errors/**','permitAll',50);

insert into
security_filtermetadata(id,ant_pattern,expression,sort_order)
values (160, '/admin/**','hasRole("ADMIN")',60);

insert into
security_filtermetadata(id,ant_pattern,expression,sort_order)
values (160, '/events/','hasRole("ADMIN")',60);

insert into
security_filtermetadata(id,ant_pattern,expression,sort_order)
values (170, '/**','hasRole("USER")',70);
```

At this point, your code should be starting with `chapter13.00-calendar`.

Custom SecurityMetadataSource implementation

In order for Spring Security to be aware of our URL mappings, we need to provide a custom `FilterInvocationSecurityMetadataSource` implementation. The `FilterInvocationSecurityMetadataSource` package extends the `SecurityMetadataSource` interface which, given a particular HTTP request, is what provides Spring Security with the information necessary for determining if access should be granted. Let's take a look at how we can utilize our `RequestConfigMappingService` interface to implement a `SecurityMetadataSource` interface:

```
//src/main/java/com/packtpub/springsecurity/web/access/intercept/
FilterInvocationServiceSecurityMetadataSource.java

@Component("filterInvocationServiceSecurityMetadataSource")
public class FilterInvocationServiceSecurityMetadataSource implements
FilterInvocationSecurityMetadataSource, InitializingBean{
    ... constructor and member variables omitted ...


  public Collection<ConfigAttribute> getAllConfigAttributes() {
      return this.delegate.getAllConfigAttributes();
  }


  public Collection<ConfigAttribute> getAttributes(Object object) {
      return this.delegate.getAttributes(object);
  }


  public boolean supports(Class<?> clazz) {
      return this.delegate.supports(clazz);
  }


  public void afterPropertiesSet() throws Exception {
  List<RequestConfigMapping> requestConfigMappings =
  requestConfigMappingService.getRequestConfigMappings();
  LinkedHashMap requestMap = new
  LinkedHashMap(requestConfigMappings.size());
  for(RequestConfigMapping requestConfigMapping
  requestConfigMappings) {
      RequestMatcher matcher =
          requestConfigMapping.getMatcher();
      Collection<ConfigAttribute> attributes =
              requestConfigMapping.getAttributes();
```

```
            requestMap.put(matcher,attributes);
        }
            this.delegate =
            new
            ExpressionBasedFilterInvocationSecurityMetadataSource
            (requestMap,expressionHandler);
        }
    }
```

We are able to use our `RequestConfigMappingService` interface to create a map of `RequestMatcher` objects that map to `ConfigAttribute` objects. We then delegate to an instance of `ExpressionBasedFilterInvocationSecurityMetadataSource` to do all the work. For simplicity, the current implementation would require restarting the application to pick up changes. However, with a few minor changes, we could avoid this inconvenience.

Registering a custom SecurityMetadataSource

Now, all that is left is for us to configure `FilterInvocationServiceSecurityMetadataSource`. The only problem is that Spring Security does not support configuring a custom `FilterInvocationServiceSecurityMetadataSource` interface directly. This is not too difficult, so we will register this `SecurityMetadataSource` with our `FilterSecurityInterceptor` in our `SecurityConfig` file:

```
// src/main/java/com/packtpub/springsecurity/configuration/
SecurityConfig.java

@Override
public void configure(final WebSecurity web) throws Exception {
    ...
    final HttpSecurity http = getHttp();
    web.postBuildAction(() -> {
    FilterSecurityInterceptor fsi = http.getSharedObject
    (FilterSecurityInterceptor.class);
    fsi.setSecurityMetadataSource(metadataSource);
    web.securityInterceptor(fsi);
    });
}
```

This sets up our custom `SecurityMetadataSource` interface with the `FilterSecurityInterceptor` object as the default metadata source.

Removing our antMatchers() method

Now that the database is being used to map our security configuration, we can remove the `antMatchers()` method from our `SecurityConfig.java` file. Go ahead and remove them, so that the configuration looks similar to the following code snippet:

```
// src/main/java/com/packtpub/springsecurity/configuration/
SecurityConfig.java

@Override
protected void configure(HttpSecurity http) throws Exception {


// No interceptor methods
// http.authorizeRequests()
//      .antMatchers("/").permitAll()
   ...


http.formLogin()
    ...


http.logout()
    ...
```

 If you use even one `http antMatchers` expression, then the custom expression handler will not be invoked.

You should now be able to start the application and test to ensure that our URLs are secured as they should be. Our users will not notice a difference, but we know that our URL mappings are persisted in a database now.

 Your code should now look like `chapter13.01-calendar`.

Creating a custom expression

The `o.s.s.access.expression.SecurityExpresssionHandler` interface is how Spring Security abstracts how the Spring expressions are created and initialized. Just as with the `SecurityMetadataSource` interface, there is an implementation for creating expressions for web requests and creating expressions for securing methods. In this section, we will explore how we can easily add new expressions.

Configuring a custom SecurityExpressionRoot

Let's assume that we want to support a custom web expression named `isLocal` that will return `true` if the host is localhost and false otherwise. This new method could be used to provide additional security for our SQL console by ensuring that it is only accessed from the same machine that the web application is deployed from.

This is an artificial example that does not add any security benefits since the host comes from the headers of the HTTP request. This means a malicious user could inject a header stating the host is localhost even if they are requesting to an external domain.

All of the expressions that we have seen are available because the `SecurityExpressionHandler` interface makes them available via an instance of `o.s.s.access.expression.SecurityExpressionRoot`. If you open this object, you will find the methods and properties we use in Spring expressions (that is, `hasRole`, `hasPermission`, and so on), which are common in both web and method security. A subclass provides the methods that are specific to web and method expressions. For example, `o.s.s.web.access.expression.WebSecurityExpressionRoot` provides the `hasIpAddress` method for web requests.

To create a custom web `SecurityExpressionhandler`, we will first need to create a subclass of `WebSecurityExpressionRoot` that defines our `isLocal` method as follows:

```
//src/main/java/com/packtpub/springsecurity/web/access/expression/
CustomWebSecurityExpressionRoot.java

public class CustomWebSecurityExpressionRoot extends
 WebSecurityExpressionRoot {

  public CustomWebSecurityExpressionRoot(Authentication a,
  FilterInvocation fi) {
   super(a, fi);
   }
```

```
public boolean isLocal() {
    return "localhost".equals(request.getServerName());
}
}
```

 It is important to note that getServerName() returns the value that is provided in the Host header value. This means that a malicious user can inject a different value into the header to bypass constraints. However, most application servers and proxies can enforce the value of the Host header. Please read the appropriate documentation before leveraging such an approach to ensure that malicious users do not inject a Host header value to bypass such a constraint.

Configuring a custom SecurityExpressionHandler

In order for our new method to become available, we need to create a custom SecurityExpressionHandler interface that utilizes our new root object. This is as simple as extending WebSecurityExpressionHandler, as follows:

```
//src/main/java/com/packtpub/springsecurity/web/access/expression/
CustomWebSecurityExpressionHandler.java

@Component
public class CustomWebSecurityExpressionHandler extends
        DefaultWebSecurityExpressionHandler {
    private final AuthenticationTrustResolver trustResolver =
    new AuthenticationTrustResolverImpl();

    protected SecurityExpressionOperations
    createSecurityExpressionRoot(Authentication authentication,
    FilterInvocation fi)
{
        WebSecurityExpressionRoot root = new
        CustomWebSecurityExpressionRoot(authentication, fi);
        root.setPermissionEvaluator(getPermissionEvaluator());
        root.setTrustResolver(trustResolver);
        root.setRoleHierarchy(getRoleHierarchy());
    return root;
    }
}
```

We perform the same steps that the superclass does, except that we use
`CustomWebSecurityExpressionRoot,` which contains the new method.
The `CustomWebSecurityExpressionRoot` becomes the root of our SpEL expression.

 For further details, refer to the SpEL documentation within the Spring
Reference at `http://static.springsource.org/spring/docs/current/`
`spring-framework-reference/html/expressions.html.`

Configuring and using CustomWebSecurityExpressionHandler

Let's take a look at the following steps to configure
`CustomWebSecurityExpressionHandler:`

1. We now need to configure `CustomWebSecurityExpressionHandler.`
   Fortunately, this can be done easily using the Spring Security namespace
   configuration support. Add the following configuration to the
   `SecurityConfig.java` file:

   ```
   // src/main/java/com/packtpub/springsecurity/configuration/
   SecurityConfig.java

   http.authorizeRequests()
       .expressionHandler(customWebSecurityExpressionHandler);
   ```

2. Now, let's update our initialization SQL query to use the new expression. Update
   the `data.sql` file so that it requires the user to be `ROLE_ADMIN` and requested
   from the local machine. You will notice that we are able to write local instead of
   `isLocal`, since SpEL supports Java Bean conventions:

   ```
   // src/main/resources/data.sql

   insert into
   security_filtermetadata(id,ant_pattern,expression,sort_order)
       values (160, '/admin/**','local and hasRole("ADMIN")',60);
   ```

3. Restart the application and access the H2 console using
   `localhost:8443/admin/h2` and `admin1@example.com/admin1` to see the
   admin console. If the H2 console is accessed using `127.0.0.1:8443/admin/h2`
   and `admin1@example.com admin1`, the access denied page will be displayed.

Your code should look like `chapter13.02-calendar`.

Alternative to a CustomWebSecurityExpressionHandler

Another way to use a custom expression instead of using a
`CustomWebSecurityExpressionHandler` interface is to add a `@Component` web, as
follows:

```java
// src/main/java/com/packtpub/springsecurity/web/access/expression/
CustomWebExpression.java

@Component
  public class CustomWebExpression {
    public boolean isLocal(Authentication authentication,
                    HttpServletRequest request) {
    return "localhost".equals(request.getServerName());
  }
}
```

Now, let's update our initialization SQL query to use the new expression. You will notice
that we are able to reference the `@Component` directly since SpEL supports Java Bean
conventions:

```sql
// src/main/resources/data.sql

insert into security_filtermetadata(id,ant_pattern,expression,sort_order)
values (160, '/admin/**','@customWebExpression.isLocal(authentication,
request) and hasRole("ADMIN")',60);
```

How does method security work?

The access decision mechanism for method security—whether or not a given request is allowed—is conceptually the same as the access decision logic for web request access. `AccessDecisionManager` polls a set of `AccessDecisionVoters`, each of which can provide a decision to grant or deny access, or abstain from voting. The specific implementation of `AccessDecisionManager` aggregates the voter decisions and arrives at an overall decision to allow for the method invocation.

Web request access decision making is less complicated, due to the fact that the availability of servlet filters makes interception (and summary rejection) of securable requests relatively straightforward. As method invocation can happen from anywhere, including areas of code that are not directly configured by Spring Security, Spring Security designers chose to use a Spring-managed AOP approach to recognize, evaluate, and secure method invocations.

The following high-level flow illustrates the main players involved in authorization decisions for method invocation:

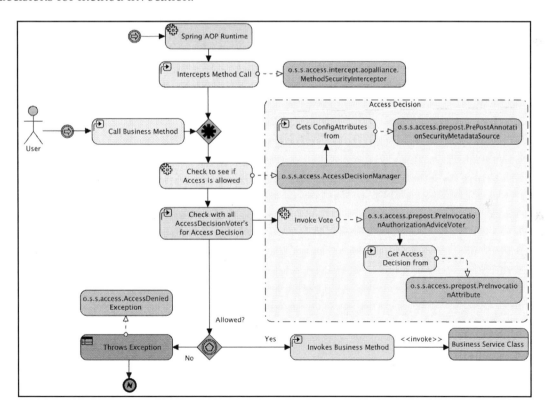

We can see that Spring Security's
`o.s.s.access.intercept.aopalliance.MethodSecurityInterceptor` is invoked by
the standard Spring AOP runtime to intercept method calls of interest. From here, the logic
of whether or not to allow a method call is relatively straightforward, as per the previous
flow diagram.

At this point, we might wonder about the performance of the method security feature.
Obviously, `MethodSecurityInterceptor` can't be invoked for every method call in the
application—so how do annotations on methods or classes result in AOP interception?

First of all, AOP proxying isn't invoked for all Spring-managed beans by default. Instead, if
`@EnableGlobalMethodSecurity` is defined in the Spring Security configuration, a
standard Spring AOP `o.s.beans.factory.config.BeanPostProcessor` will be
registered that will introspect the AOP configuration to see if any AOP advisors indicate
that proxying (and the interception) is required. This workflow is standard Spring AOP
handling (known as AOP auto-proxying), and doesn't inherently have any functionality
specific to Spring Security. All registered `BeanPostProcessor` run upon initialization of
the spring `ApplicationContext`, after all, Spring bean configurations have occurred.

The AOP auto-proxy functionality queries all registered `PointcutAdvisor` to see if there
are AOP pointcuts that resolve method invocations that should have AOP advice applied.
Spring Security implements the
`o.s.s.access.intercept.aopalliance.MethodSecurityMetadataSourceAdvisor`
class, which examines any and all configured method security and sets up appropriate AOP
interception. Take note that only interfaces or classes with declared method security rules
will be proxied for AOP!

Be aware that it is strongly encouraged to declare AOP rules (and other
security annotations) on interfaces, and not on implementation classes.
The use of classes, while available using CGLIB proxying with Spring,
may unexpectedly change the behavior of your application, and is
generally less semantically correct than security declarations (through
AOP) on interfaces. `MethodSecurityMetadataSourceAdvisor`
delegates the decision to affect methods with the AOP advice to an
`o.s.s.access.method.MethodSecurityMetadataSource` instance.
The different forms of method security annotation each have their own
`MethodSecurityMetadataSource` implementation, which is used to
introspect each method and class in turn and add AOP advice to be
executed at runtime.

The following diagram illustrates how this process occurs:

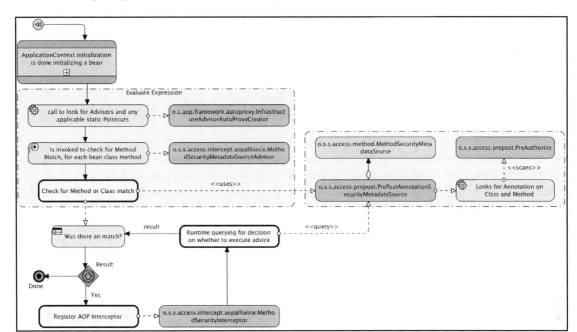

Depending on the number of Spring beans configured in your application, and the number of secured method annotations you have, adding method security proxying may increase the time required to initialize your ApplicationContext. Once your Spring context is initialized, however, there is a negligible performance impact on individual proxied beans.

Now that we have an understanding of how we can use AOP to apply Spring Security, let's strengthen our grasp of Spring Security authorization by creating a custom `PermissionEvaluator`.

Creating a custom PermissionEvaluator

In the previous chapter, we demonstrated that we could use Spring Security's built-in PermissionEvaluator implementation, AclPermissionEvaluator, to restrict access to our application. While powerful, this can often be more complicated than necessary. We have also discovered how SpEL can formulate complex expressions that are able to secure our application. While simple, one of the downsides of using complex expressions is that the logic is not centralized. Fortunately, we can easily create a custom PermissionEvaluator that is able to centralize our authorization logic and still avoid the complexity of using ACLs.

CalendarPermissionEvaluator

A simplified version of our custom PermissionEvaluator that does not contain any validation can be seen as follows:

```
//src/main/java/com/packtpub/springsecurity/access/CalendarPermissionEvalua
tor.java

public final class CalendarPermissionEvaluator implements
PermissionEvaluator {
    private final EventDao eventDao;

    public CalendarPermissionEvaluator(EventDao eventDao) {
        this.eventDao = eventDao;
    }

    public boolean hasPermission(Authentication authentication, Object
    targetDomainObject, Object permission) {
        // should do instanceof check since could be any domain object
        return hasPermission(authentication, (Event) targetDomainObject,
permission);
    }

    public boolean hasPermission(Authentication authentication,
    Serializable targetId, String targetType,
        Object permission) {
        // missing validation and checking of the targetType
        Event event = eventDao.getEvent((Integer)targetId);
        return hasPermission(authentication, event, permission);
    }
```

```java
private boolean hasPermission(Authentication authentication,
Event event, Object permission) {
    if(event == null) {
        return true;
    }
    String currentUserEmail = authentication.getName();
    String ownerEmail = extractEmail(event.getOwner());
    if("write".equals(permission)) {
        return currentUserEmail.equals(ownerEmail);
    } else if("read".equals(permission)) {
        String attendeeEmail =
        extractEmail(event.getAttendee());
        return currentUserEmail.equals(attendeeEmail) ||
        currentUserEmail.equals(ownerEmail);
    }
    throw new IllegalArgumentException("permission
    "+permission+" is not supported.");
}


private String extractEmail(CalendarUser user) {
    if(user == null) {
        return null;
    }
    return user.getEmail();
}
}
```

The logic is fairly similar to the Spring expressions that we have already used, except that it differentiates read and write access. If the current user's username matches the owner's email of the `Event` object, then both read and write access is granted. If the current user's email matches the attendee's email, then read access is granted. Otherwise, access is denied.

 It should be noted that a single `PermissionEvaluator` is used for every domain object. So, in a real-world situation, we must perform `instanceof` checks first. For example, if we were also securing our `CalendarUser` objects, these could be passed into this same instance. For a full example of these minor changes, refer to the sample code included in the book.

Configuring CalendarPermissionEvaluator

We can then leverage the `CustomAuthorizationConfig.java` configuration that is provided with this chapter to provide an `ExpressionHandler` that uses our `CalendarPermissionEvaluator`, like so:

```
//src/main/java/com/packtpub/springsecurity/configuration/
CustomAuthorizationConfig.java


@Bean
public DefaultMethodSecurityExpressionHandler
defaultExpressionHandler(EventDao eventDao){
    DefaultMethodSecurityExpressionHandler deh = new
DefaultMethodSecurityExpressionHandler();
    deh.setPermissionEvaluator(
            new CalendarPermissionEvaluator(eventDao));
    return deh;
}
```

The configuration should look similar to the configuration from Chapter 12, *Access Control Lists*, except that we now use our `CalendarPermissionEvalulator` class instead of `AclPermissionEvaluator`.

Next, we inform Spring Security to use our customized `ExpressionHandler` by adding the following configuration to `SecurityConfig.java`.

```
//src/main/java/com/packtpub/springsecurity/configuration/SecurityConfig.ja
va
    http.authorizeRequests().expressionHandler
    (customWebSecurityExpressionHandler);
```

In the configuration, we ensure that `prePostEnabled` is enabled and point the configuration to our `ExpressionHandler` definition. Once again, the configuration should look very similar to our configuration from Chapter 11, *Fine-Grained Access Control*.

Securing our CalendarService

Lastly, we can secure our `CalendarService getEvent(int eventId)` method with a `@PostAuthorize` annotation. You will notice that this step is exactly the same as what we did in `Chapter 1`, *Anatomy of an Unsafe Application*, and we have only changed the implementation of `PermissionEvaluator`:

```
//src/main/java/com/packtpub/springsecurity/service/CalendarService.java

@PostAuthorize("hasPermission(returnObject,'read')")
Event getEvent(int eventId);
```

If you have not done so already, restart the application, log in as username/password `admin1@example.com`/`admin1`, and visit the Conference Call event (`events/101`) using the link on the Welcome page. The access denied page will be displayed. However, we would, like `ROLE_ADMIN` users, to be able to access all events.

Benefits of a custom PermissionEvaluator

With only a single method being protected, it would be trivial to update the annotation to check if the user has the role of `ROLE_ADMIN` or has permission. However, if we had protected all of our service methods that use an event, it would have become quite cumbersome. Instead, we could just update our `CalendarPermissionEvaluator`. Make the following changes:

```
private boolean hasPermission(Authentication authentication, Event
event, Object permission) {
    if(event == null) {
        return true;
    }
    GrantedAuthority adminRole =
            new SimpleGrantedAuthority("ROLE_ADMIN");
    if(authentication.getAuthorities().contains(adminRole)) {
        return true;
    }
    ...
}
```

Now, restart the application and repeat the previous exercise. This time, the Conference Call event will display successfully. You can see that the ability to encapsulate our authorization logic can be extremely beneficial. However, sometimes it may be useful to extend the expressions themselves.

Your code should look like `chapter13.03-calendar`.

Summary

After reading this chapter, you should have a firm understanding of how Spring Security authorization works for HTTP requests and methods. With this knowledge, and the provided concrete examples, you should also know how to extend authorization to meet your needs. Specifically, in this chapter, we covered the Spring Security authorization architecture for both HTTP requests and methods. We also demonstrated how to configure secured URLs from a database.

We also saw how to create a custom `PermissionEvaluator` object and custom Spring Security expression.

In the next chapter, we will explore how Spring Security performs session management. We will also gain an understanding of how it can be used to restrict access to our application.

14
Session Management

This chapter discusses Spring Security's session management functionality. It starts off with an example of how Spring Security defends against session fixation. We will then discuss how concurrency control can be leveraged to restrict access to software licensed on a per-user basis. We will also see how session management can be leveraged for administrative functions. Last, we will explore how `HttpSession` is used in Spring Security and how we can control its creation.

The following is a list of topics that will be covered in this chapter:

- Session management/session fixation
- Concurrency control
- Managing logged in users
- How `HttpSession` is used in Spring Security and how to control creation
- How to use the `DebugFilter` class to discover where `HttpSession` was created

Configuring session fixation protection

As we are using the security namespace style of configuration, session fixation protection is already configured on our behalf. If we wanted to explicitly configure it to mirror the default settings, we would do the following:

```
http.sessionManagement()
.sessionFixation().migrateSession();
```

Session fixation protection is a feature of the framework that you most likely won't even notice unless you try to act as a malicious user. We'll show you how to simulate a session-stealing attack; before we do, it's important to understand what session fixation does and the type of attack it prevents.

Understanding session fixation attacks

Session fixation is a type of attack whereby a malicious user attempts to steal the session of an unauthenticated user of your system. This can be done by using a variety of techniques that result in the attacker obtaining the unique session identifier of the user (for example, JSESSIONID). If the attacker creates a cookie or a URL parameter with the user's JSESSIONID identifier in it, they can access the user's session.

Although this is obviously a problem, typically, if a user is unauthenticated, they haven't entered any sensitive information. This becomes a more critical problem if the same session identifier continues to be used after a user has been authenticated. If the same identifier is used after authentication, the attacker may now gain access to the authenticated user's session without even having to know their username or password!

 At this point, you may scoff in disbelief and think this is extremely unlikely to happen in the real world. In fact, session-stealing attacks happen frequently. We would suggest that you spend some time reading the very informative articles and case studies on the subject, published by the **Open Web Application Security Project (OWASP)** organization (http://www.owasp.org/). Specifically, you will want to read the OWASP top 10 lists. Attackers and malicious users are real, and they can do very real damage to your users, your application, or your company if you don't understand the techniques that they commonly use and know how to avoid them.

The following diagram illustrates how a session fixation attack works:

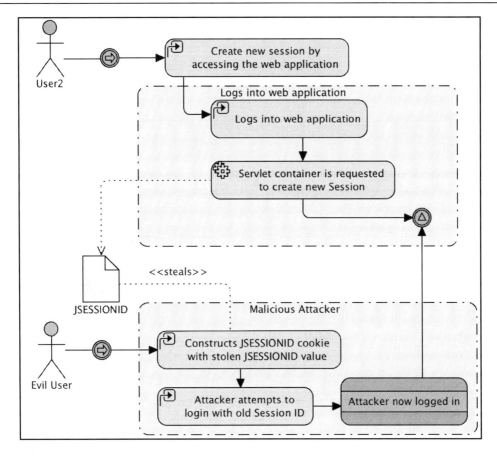

Now that we have seen how an attack like this works, we'll see what Spring Security can do to prevent it.

Preventing session fixation attacks with Spring Security

If we can prevent the same session that the user had prior to authentication from being used after authentication, we can effectively render the attacker's knowledge of the session ID useless. Spring Security session fixation protection solves this problem by explicitly creating a new session when a user is authenticated and invalidating their old session.

Let's take a look at the following diagram:

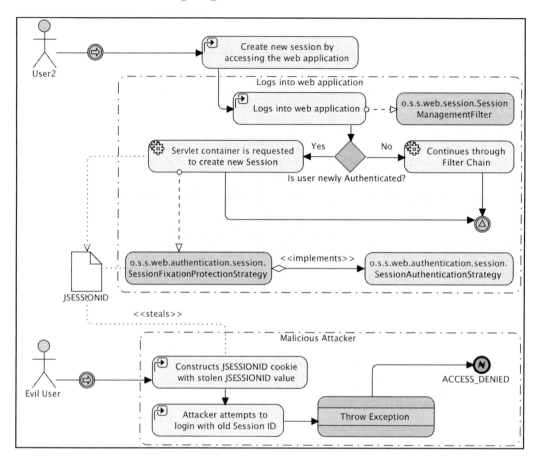

We can see that a new filter, `o.s.s.web.session.SessionManagementFilter`, is responsible for evaluating if a particular user is newly authenticated. If the user is newly authenticated, a configured `o.s.s.web.authentication.session.SessionAuthenticationStrategy` interface determines what to do.

`o.s.s.web.authentication.session.SessionFixationProtectionStrategy` will create a new session (if the user already had one), and copy the contents of the existing session to the new one. That's pretty much it—seems simple. However, as we can see in the preceding diagram, it effectively prevents the malicious user from reusing the session ID after the unknown user is authenticated.

Simulating a session fixation attack

At this point, you may want to see what's involved in simulating a session fixation attack:

1. You'll first need to disable session fixation protection in the `SecurityConfig.java` file by adding the `sessionManagement()` method as a child of the `http` element.

    You should start with the code from `chapter14.00-calendar`.

    Let's take a look at the following code snippet:

    ```
    //src/main/java/com/packtpub/springsecurity/configuration/
    SecurityConfig.java

    http.sessionManagement().sessionFixation().none();
    ```

    Your code should now look like `chapter14.01-calendar`.

2. Next, you'll need to open two browsers. We'll initiate the session in Google Chrome, steal it from there, and our attacker will log in using the stolen session in Firefox. We will use the Google Chrome and the Firefox web developer add-on in order to view and manipulate cookies. The Firefox web developer add-on can be downloaded from `https://addons.mozilla.org/en-US/firefox/addon/web-developer/`. Google Chrome's web developer tools are built-in.
3. Open the JBCP calendar home page in Google Chrome.

4. Next, from the main menu, navigate to **Edit** | **Preferences** | **Under the Hood**. In the **Privacy** category, press the **Content Settings...** button. Next, in **Cookies Settings**, press the **All Cookies and Site Data...** button. Finally, enter `localhost` into the **Search** field, as follows:

5. Select the JSESSIONID cookie, copy the value of **Content** to the clipboard, and log in to the JBCP calendar application. If you repeat the **View Cookie Information** command, you'll see that JSESSIONID did not change after you logged in, making you vulnerable to a session fixation attack!

6. In Firefox, open the JBCP calendar website. You will have been assigned a session cookie, which you can view by using *Ctrl + F2* to open the bottom **Cookie** console. Then type in `cookie list [enter]` to bring up cookies for the current page.

7. To complete our hack, we'll click on the **Edit Cookie** option and paste in the JSESSIONID cookie that we copied to the clipboard from Google Chrome, as shown in the following screenshot:

8. Keep in mind that newer versions of Firefox include web developer tools, too. However, you will need to ensure that you are using the extension and not the built-in one, as it provides additional capabilities.

Our session fixation hack is complete! If you now reload the page in Firefox, you will see that you are logged in as the same user who was logged in using Google Chrome, but without the knowledge of the username and password. Are you scared of malicious users yet?

Now, re-enable session fixation protection and try this exercise again. You'll see that, in this case, the JSESSIONID changes after the user logs in. Based on our understanding of how session fixation attacks occur, this means that we have reduced the likelihood of an unsuspecting user falling victim to this type of attack. Excellent job!

Cautious developers should note that there are many methods of stealing session cookies, some of which—such as XSS—may make even session fixation protected sites vulnerable. Please consult the OWASP site for additional resources on preventing these types of attacks.

Comparing the session-fixation-protection options

The `session-fixation-protection` attribute has the following three options that allow you to alter its behavior, as follows:

Attribute value	Description
`none()`	This option disables session fixation protection and (unless other `sessionManagement()` attributes are non-default) does not configure `SessionManagementFilter`.
`migrateSession()`	When the user is authenticated and a new session is allocated, it ensures that all attributes of the old session are moved to the new session.
`newSession()`	When the user is authenticated, a new session is created and no attributes from the old (unauthenticated) session will be migrated.

In most cases, the default behavior of `migrateSession()` will be appropriate for sites that wish to retain important attributes of the user's session (such as click interest and shopping carts) after the user has been authenticated.

Restricting the number of concurrent sessions per user

In the software industry, software is often sold on a per-user basis. This means that, as software developers, we have an interest in ensuring that only a single session per user exists, to combat the sharing of accounts. Spring Security's concurrent session control ensures that a single user cannot have more than a fixed number of active sessions simultaneously (typically one). Ensuring that this maximum limit is enforced involves several components working in tandem to accurately track changes in user session activity.

Let's configure the feature, review how it works, and then test it out!

Configuring concurrent session control

Now that we have understood the different components involved in concurrent session control, setting it up should make much more sense. Let's take a look at the following steps to configure concurrent session control:

1. Firstly, you update your `security.xml` file as follows:

```
// src/main/java/com/packtpub/springsecurity/configuration/
SecurityConfig.java

http.sessionManagement().maximumSessions(1)
```

2. Next, we need to enable `o.s.s.web.session.HttpSessionEventPublisher` in the `SecurityConfig.java` deployment descriptor, so that the servlet container will notify Spring Security (through `HttpSessionEventPublisher`) of session life cycle events, as follows:

```
// src/main/java/com/packtpub/springsecurity/configuration/
SecurityConfig.java

@Bean
public HttpSessionEventPublisher httpSessionEventPublisher() {
    return new HttpSessionEventPublisher();
}
```

With these two configuration bits in place, concurrent session control will now be activated. Let's see what it actually does, and then we'll demonstrate how it can be tested.

Understanding concurrent session control

Concurrent session control uses `o.s.s.core.session.SessionRegistry` to maintain a list of active HTTP sessions and the authenticated users with which they are associated. As sessions are created and expired, the registry is updated in real time based on the session life cycle events published by `HttpSessionEventPublisher` to track the number of active sessions per authenticated user.

Refer to the following diagram:

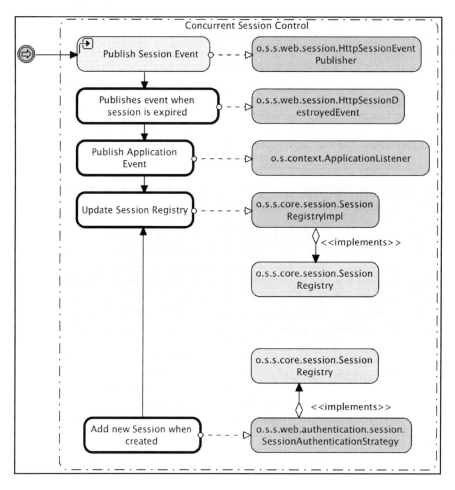

An extension of `SessionAuthenticationStrategy`, `o.s.s.web.authentication.session.ConcurrentSessionControlStrategy` is the method by which new sessions are tracked and the method by which concurrency control is actually enforced. Each time a user accesses the secured site, `SessionManagementFilter` is used to check the active session against `SessionRegistry`. If the user's active session isn't in the list of active sessions tracked in `SessionRegistry`, the least recently used session is immediately expired.

The secondary actor in the modified concurrent session control filter chain is
`o.s.s.web.session.ConcurrentSessionFilter`. This filter will recognize expired
sessions (typically, sessions that have been expired either by the servlet container or forcibly
by the `ConcurrentSessionControlStrategy` interface) and notify the user that their
session has expired.

Now that we have understood how concurrent session control works, it should be easy for
us to reproduce a scenario in which it is enforced.

> Your code should now look like `chapter14.02-calendar`.

Testing concurrent session control

As we did when verifying session fixation protection, we will need to access two web
browsers by performing the following steps:

1. In Google Chrome, log in to the site as `user1@example.com/user1`.
2. Now, in Firefox, log in to the site as the same user.
3. Finally, go back to Google Chrome and take any action. You will see a message
   indicating that your session has expired, as shown in the following screenshot:

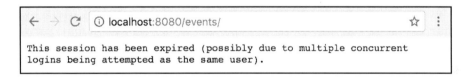

If you were using this application and received this message, you'd probably be confused.
This is because it's obviously not a friendly method of being notified that only a single user
can access the application at a time. However, it does illustrate that the session has been
forcibly expired by the software.

Concurrent session control tends to be a very difficult concept for new Spring Security users to grasp. Many users try to implement it without truly understanding how it works and what the benefits are. If you're trying to enable this powerful feature, and it doesn't seem to be working as you expect, make sure you have everything configured correctly and then review the theoretical explanations in this section—hopefully, they will help you understand what may be wrong!

When a session expiration event occurs, we should probably redirect the user to the login page and provide them with a message to indicate what went wrong.

Configuring expired session redirect

Fortunately, there is a simple method for directing users to a friendly page (typically the login page) when they are flagged by concurrent session control—simply specify the `expired-url` attribute and set it to a valid page in your application. Update your `security.xml` file as follows:

```
//src/main/java/com/packtpub/springsecurity/configuration/SecurityConfig.ja
va

    http.sessionManagement()
    .maximumSessions(1)
     .expiredUrl("/login/form?expired")
    ;
```

In the case of our application, this will redirect the user to the standard login form. We will then use the query parameter to display a friendly message indicating that we determined that they had multiple active sessions, and should log in again. Update your `login.html` page to use this parameter to display our message:

```
//src/main/resources/templates/login.html

...
<div th:if="${param.expired != null}" class="alert alert-success">
<strong>Session Expired</strong>
<span>You have been forcibly logged out due to multiplesessions
on the same account (only one activesession per user is allowed).</span>
</div>
<label for="username">Username</label>
```

Go ahead and give it a try by logging in as the user `admin1@example.com/admin1` using both Google Chrome and Firefox. This time, you should see a login page with a custom error message.

Your code should now look like `chapter14.03-calendar`.

Common problems with concurrency control

There are a few common reasons that logging in with the same user does not trigger a logout event. The first occurs when using custom `UserDetails` (as we did in *Chapter 3, Custom Authentication*) while the equals and `hashCode` methods are not properly implemented. This occurs because the default `SessionRegistry` implementation uses an in-memory map to store `UserDetails`. In order to resolve this, you must ensure that you have properly implemented the `hashCode` and equals methods.

The second problem occurs when restarting the application container while the user sessions are persisted to a disk. When the container has started back up, the users who were already logged in with a valid session are logged in. However, the in-memory map of `SessionRegistry` that is used to determine if the user is already logged in will be empty. This means that Spring Security will report that the user is not logged in, even though the user is. To solve this problem, either a custom `SessionRegistry` is required along with disabling session persistence within the container, or you must implement a container-specific way to ensure that the persisted sessions get populated into the in-memory map at startup.

Yet another reason is that at the time of writing, concurrency control is not implemented for the remember-me feature. If users are authenticated with remember-me, that concurrency control is not enforced. There is a JIRA to implement this feature, so refer to it for any updates if your application requires both remember-me and concurrency control: `https://jira.springsource.org/browse/SEC-2028`

The last common reason we will cover is that concurrency control will not work in a clustered environment with the default `SessionRegistry` implementation. As mentioned previously, the default implementation uses an in-memory map. This means that if `user1` logs in to application server A, the fact that they are logged in will be associated with that server. Thus, if `user1` then authenticates to Application Server B, the previously associated authentication will be unknown to application server B.

Preventing authentication instead of forcing logout

Spring Security can also prevent a user from being able to log in to the application if the user already has a session. This means that instead of forcing the original user to be logged out, Spring Security will prevent the second user from being able to log in. The configuration changes can be seen as follows:

```
//src/main/java/com/packtpub/springsecurity/configuration/SecurityConfig.java

http.sessionManagement()
.maximumSessions(1)
.expiredUrl("/login/form?expired")
 .maxSessionsPreventsLogin(true);
```

Make the updates and log in to the calendar application with Google Chrome. Now, attempt to log in to the calendar application with Firefox using the same user. You should see our custom error message from our `login.html` file.

> Your code should now look like `chapter14.04-calendar`.

There is a disadvantage to this approach that may not be apparent without some thought. Try closing Google Chrome without logging out and then opening it up again. Now, attempt to log in to the application again. You will observe that you are unable to log in. This is because when the browser is closed, the `JSESSIONID` cookie is deleted. However, the application is not aware of this, so the user is still considered authenticated. You can think of this as a kind of memory leak, since `HttpSession` still exists but there is no pointer to it (the `JSESSIONID` cookie is gone). It is not until the session times out that our user will be able to authenticate again. Thankfully, once the session times out, our `SessionEventPublisher` interface will remove the user from our `SessionRegistry` interface. What we can take away from this is that if a user forgets to log out and closes the browser, they will not be able to log in to the application until the session times out.

Just as in `Chapter 7`, *Remember-Me Services*, this experiment may not work if the browser decides to remember a session even after the browser is closed. Typically, this will happen if a plugin or the browser is configured to restore sessions. In this event, you might want to delete the `JSESSIONID` cookie manually to simulate the browser being closed.

Other benefits of concurrent session control

Another benefit of concurrent session control is that `SessionRegistry` exists to track active (and, optionally, expired) sessions. This means that we can get runtime information about what user activity exists in our system (for authenticated users, at least) by performing the following steps:

1. You can even do this if you don't want to enable concurrent session control. Simply set `maximumSessions` to −1, and session tracking will remain enabled, even though no maximum will be enforced. Instead, we will use the explicit bean configuration provided in the `SessionConfig.java` file of this chapter, as follows:

    ```
    //src/main/java/com/packtpub/springsecurity/configuration/
    SessionConfig.java

    @Bean
    public SessionRegistry sessionRegistry(){
      return new SessionRegistryImpl();
    }
    ```

2. We have already added the import of the `SessionConfig.java` file to the `SecurityConfig.java` file. So, all that we need to do is reference the custom configuration in our `SecurityConfig.java` file. Go ahead and replace the current `sessionManagement` and `maximumSessions` configurations with the following code snippet:

    ```
    //src/main/java/com/packtpub/springsecurity/configuration/
    SecurityConfig.java

    http.sessionManagement()
    .maximumSessions(-1)
    .sessionRegistry(sessionRegistry)
    .expiredUrl("/login/form?expired")
    .maxSessionsPreventsLogin(true);
    ```

Your code should now look like `chapter14.05-calendar`.

Now, our application will allow an unlimited number of authentications for the same user. However, we can use `SessionRegistry` to forcibly log out the users. Let's see how we can use this information to enhance the security of our users.

Displaying active sessions for a user

You've probably seen how many websites allow a user to view and forcibly log out sessions for their account. We can easily use this forcible logout functionality to do the same. We have already provided `UserSessionController`, which obtains the active sessions for the currently logged in user. You can see the implementation as follows:

```
//src/main/java/com/packtpub/springsecurity/web/controllers/
UserSessionController.java

@Controller
public class UserSessionController {
 private final SessionRegistry sessionRegistry;
@Autowired
 public UserSessionController(SessionRegistry sessionRegistry) {
   this.sessionRegistry = sessionRegistry;
}
  @GetMapping("/user/sessions/")
public String sessions(Authentication authentication, ModelMap model) {
List<SessionInformation> sessions = sessionRegistry.getAllSessions
(authentication.getPrincipal(), false);
model.put("sessions", sessions);
  return "user/sessions";
 }
  @DeleteMapping(value="/user/sessions/{sessionId}")
 public String removeSession(@PathVariable String sessionId,
  RedirectAttributes redirectAttrs) {
SessionInformation sessionInformation = sessionRegistry.
getSessionInformation(sessionId);
if(sessionInformation != null) {
  sessionInformation.expireNow();
 }
```

```
redirectAttrs.addFlashAttribute("message", "Session was removed");
return "redirect:/user/sessions/";
}
}
```

Our sessions method will use Spring MVC to automatically obtain the current Spring Security `Authentication`. If we were not using Spring MVC, we could also get the current `Authentication` from `SecurityContextHolder`, as discussed in *Chapter 3, Custom Authentication*. The principal is then used to obtain all the `SessionInformation` objects for the current user. The information is easily displayed by iterating over the `SessionInformation` objects in our `sessions.html` file, as follows:

```
//src/main/resources/templates/sessions.html

...
<tr th:each="session : ${sessions}">
<td th:text="${#calendars.format(session.lastRequest, 'yyyy-MM-dd
HH:mm')}">
</td>
<td th:text="${session.sessionId}"></td>
<td>
<form action="#"
th:action="@{'/user/sessions/{id}'(id=${session.sessionId})}"
th:method="delete" cssClass="form-horizontal">
<input type="submit" value="Delete" class="btn"/>
</form>
</td>
</tr>
...
```

You can now safely start the JBCP calendar application and log in to it using `user1@example.com/user1` in Google Chrome. Now, log in using Firefox and click on the `user1@example.com` link in the upper-right corner. You will then see both sessions listed on the display as shown in the following screenshot:

While in Firefox, click on the **Delete** button for the first session. This sends the request to our `deleteSession` method of `UserSessionsController`. This indicates that the session should be terminated. Now, navigate to any page within Google Chrome. You will see the custom message saying the session has been forcibly terminated. While the message could use updating, we see that this is a nice feature for users to terminate other active sessions.

Other possible uses include allowing an administrator to list and manage all active sessions, displaying the number of active users on the site, or even extending the information to include things like an IP address or location information.

How Spring Security uses the HttpSession method?

We have already discussed how Spring Security uses `SecurityContextHolder` to determine the currently logged in user. However, we have not explained how `SecurityContextHolder` gets automatically populated by Spring Security. The secret to this lies in the `o.s.s.web.context.SecurityContextPersistenceFilter` filter and the `o.s.s.web.context.SecurityContextRepository` interface. Let's take a look at the following diagram:

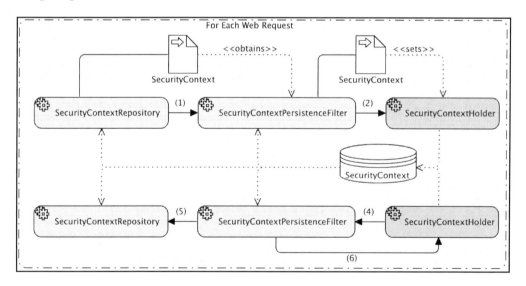

Here is an explanation for each step shown in the preceding diagram:

1. At the beginning of each web request, `SecurityContextPersistenceFilter` is responsible for obtaining the current `SecurityContext` implementation using `SecurityContextRepository`.

2. Immediately afterwards, it sets `SecurityContext` on `SecurityContextHolder`.

3. For the remainder of the web request, `SecurityContext` is available via `SecurityContextHolder`. For example, if a Spring MVC controller or `CalendarService` wanted to access `SecurityContext`, it could use `SecurityContextHolder` to access it.

4. Then, at the end of each request, `SecurityContextPersistenceFilter` gets the `SecurityContext` from `SecurityContextHolder`.

5. Immediately afterwards, `SecurityContextPersistenceFilter` saves `SecurityContext` in `SecurityContextRepository`. This ensures that if `SecurityContext` is updated at any point during the web requests (that is, when a user creates a new account, as done in Chapter 3, *Custom Authentication*) `SecurityContext` is saved.

6. Lastly, `SecurityContextPersistenceFilter` clears `SecurityContextHolder`.

The question that now arises is how is this related to `HttpSession`? This is all tied together by the default `SecurityContextRepository` implementation, which uses `HttpSession`.

The HttpSessionSecurityContextRepository interface

The default implementation of `SecurityContextRepository`, `o.s.s.web.context.HttpSessionSecurityContextRepository`, uses `HttpSession` to retrieve and store the current `SecurityContext` implementation. There are no other `SecurityContextRepository` implementations provided out of the box. However, since the usage of `HttpSession` is abstracted behind the `SecurityContextRepository` interface, we could easily write our own implementation if we desired.

Configuring how Spring Security uses HttpSession

Spring Security has the ability to configure when the session is created by Spring Security. This can be done with the `http` element's `create-session` attribute. A summary of the options can be seen in the following table:

Attribute value	Description
`ifRequired`	Spring Security will create a session only if one is required (default value).
`always`	Spring Security will proactively create a session if one does not exist.
`never`	Spring Security will never create a session, but will make use of one if the application does create it. This means if there is a `HttpSession` method, `SecurityContext` will be persisted or retrieve from it.
`stateless`	Spring Security will not create a session and will ignore the session for obtaining a Spring `Authentication`. In such instances, `NullSecurityContextRepository` is used, which will always state that the current `SecurityContext` is `null`.

In practice, controlling session creation can be more difficult than it first appears. This is because the attributes only control a subset of Spring Security's usage of `HttpSession`. It does not apply to any other components, such as JSPs, in the application. To help figure out when the `HttpSession` method was created, we can add Spring Security's `DebugFilter`.

Debugging with Spring Security's DebugFilter

Let's take a look at the following steps and learn about how to debug with `DebugFilter` of Spring Security:

1. Update your `SecurityConfig.java` file to have a session policy of NEVER. Also, add the `debug` flag to `true` on the `@EnableWebSecurity` annotation, so that we can track when the session was created. The updates can be seen as follows:

```
//src/main/java/com/packtpub/springsecurity/configuration/
SecurityConfig.java

@Configuration
@Enable WebSecurity(debug = true)
```

```
public class SecurityConfig extends WebSecurityConfigurerAdapter {
    ...
    http.sessionManagement()
    .sessionCreationPolicy(SessionCreationPolicy.NEVER);
```

2. When you start up the application, you should see something similar to the following code written to standard output. If you have not already, ensure that you have logging enabled across all levels of the Spring Security debugger category:

```
********************************************************************
*
            **********        Security debugging is enabled.
**************
            **********    This may include sensitive information.
**************
            **********       Do not use in a production system!
**************
********************************************************************
*
```

3. Now, clear out your cookies (this can be done in Firefox with *Shift + Ctrl + Delete*), start up the application, and navigate directly to http://localhost:8080. When we look at the cookies, as we did earlier in the chapter, we can see that JSESSIONID is created even though we stated that Spring Security should never create HttpSession. Look at the logs again, and you will see a call stack of the code that created HttpSession as follows:

```
*********************************************************
2017-07-25 18:02:31.802 INFO 71368 --- [nio-8080-exec-1]
Spring Security Debugger              :
*********************************************************
New HTTP session created: 2A708D1C3AAD508160E6189B69D716DB
```

4. In this instance, our JSP page is responsible for creating the new HttpSession method. In fact, all JSPs will create a new HttpSession method by default unless you include the following code at the top of each JSP:

```
<%@ page session="false" %>
```

There are a number of other uses for DebugFilter, which we encourage you to explore on your own, for example, determining when a request will match a particular URL, which Spring Security filters are being invoked, and so on.

Summary

After reading this chapter, you should be familiar with how Spring Security manages sessions and protects against session fixation attacks. We also know how to use Spring Security's concurrency control to prevent the same user from being authenticated multiple times.

We also explored the utilization of concurrency control to allow a user to terminate sessions associated with their account. Also, we saw how to configure Spring Security's creation of sessions. We also covered how to use Spring Security's `DebugFilter` filter to troubleshoot issues related to Spring.

We also learned about security, including determining when a `HttpSession` method was created and what caused it to be created.

This concludes our discussion about Spring Security's session management. In the next chapter, we will discuss some specifics about integrating Spring Security with other frameworks.

15
Additional Spring Security Features

In this chapter, we will explore several additional Spring Security features that we have not covered so far in this book, including the following topics:

- **Cross-Site Scripting (XSS)**
- **Cross-Site Request Forgery (CSRF)**
- Synchronizer tokens
- **Clickjacking**

We will understand how to include various HTTP headers to protect against common security vulnerabilities, using the following methods:

- Cache-Control
- Content-Type Options
- **HTTP Strict Transport Security (HSTS)**
- X-Frame-Options
- X-XSS-Protection

Before you read this chapter, you should already have an understanding of how Spring Security works. This means you should already be able to set up authentication and authorization in a simple web application. If you are unable to do this, you will want to ensure you have read up to Chapter 3, *Custom Authentication*, before proceeding with this chapter. If you keep the basic concepts of Spring Security in mind and you understand the framework you are integrating with, then integrating with other frameworks is fairly straightforward.

Security vulnerabilities

In the age of the internet, there is a multitude of possible vulnerabilities that can be exploited. A great resource to learn more about web-based vulnerabilities is **The Open Web Application Security Project (OWASP)**, which is located at `https://www.owasp.org`.

In addition to being a great resource to understand various vulnerabilities, OWASP categorizes the top 10 vulnerabilities based on industry trends.

Cross-Site Scripting

XSS attacks involve malicious scripts that have been injected into a trusted site.

XSS attacks occur when an attacker exploits a given web application that is allowing unventilated input to be sent into the site generally in the form of browser-based scripts, which are then executed by a different user of the website.

There are many forms that attackers can exploit, based on validated or unencoded information provided to websites.

At the core of this issue is expecting a user to trust the site's information that is being sent. The end user's browser has no way to know that the script should not be trusted because there has been an implicit trust of the website they're browsing. Because it thinks the script came from a trusted source, the malicious script can access any cookies, session tokens, or other sensitive information retained by the browser and used with that website.

XSS can be described by the following sequence diagram:

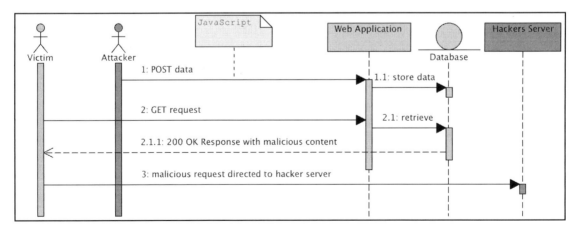

Cross-Site Request Forgery

CSRF is an attack that tricks the victim into submitting a malicious request. This type of attack inherits or hijacks the identity and privileges of the victim and performs unauthorized functions and access on the victim's behalf.

For web applications, most browsers automatically include credentials associated with the site, which includes a user session, cookie, IP address, Windows domain credentials, and so forth.

So, if a user is currently authenticated on a site, that given site will have no way to distinguish between the forged request sent by the victim and a legitimate court request.

CSRF attacks target functionality that causes a state change on the server, such as changing the victim's email address or password, or engaging in a financial transaction.

This forces the victim to retrieve data that doesn't benefit an attacker because the attacker does not receive the response; the victim does. Thus, CSRF attacks target state-changing requests.

The following sequence diagram details how a CSRF attack would occur:

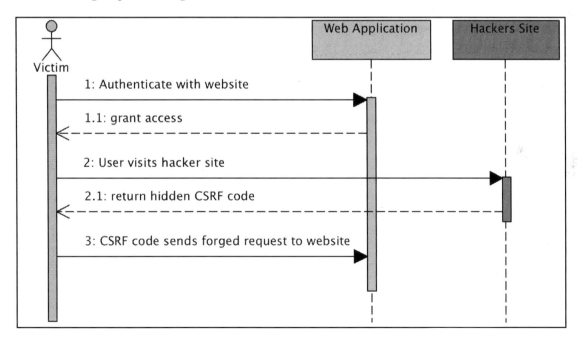

There are several different design measures that may be taken to attempt to prevent CSRF, however, measures such as secret cookies, HTTP POST requests, multistep transactions, URL rewriting, and HTTPS, in no way prevent this type of attack.

 OWASP's top 10 security vulnerabilities list details CSRF as the eighth most common attack at `https://www.owasp.org/index.php/Cross-Site_Request_Forgery_(CSRF)`.

Synchronizer tokens

A solution to this is to use the synchronizer token pattern. This solution is to ensure that each request requires, in addition to our session cookie, a randomly generated token as an HTTP parameter. When a request is submitted, the server must look up the expected value for the parameter and compare it to the actual value in the request. If the values do not match, the request should fail.

 The *Cross-Site Request Forgery (CSRF) Prevention Cheat Sheet* recommends the synchronizer token pattern as a viable solution for CSRF attacks: `https://www.owasp.org/index.php/Cross-Site_Request_Forgery_(CSRF)_Prevention_Cheat_Sheet#General_Recommendation:_Synchronizer_Token_Pattern`

Relaxing the expectation is to only require the token for each HTTP request that updates state. This can be safely done since the same origin policy ensures the evil site cannot read the response. Additionally, we do not want to include the random token in HTTP GET, as this can cause the tokens to be leaked.

Let's take a look at how our example would change. Assume the randomly generated token is present in an HTTP parameter named `_csrf`. For example, the request to transfer money would look like as follows:

```
POST /transfer HTTP/1.1
Host: bank.example.com
Cookie: JSESSIONID=randomid; Domain=bank.example.com; Secure;
HttpOnly
Content-Type: application/x-www-form-urlencoded
amount=100.00&routingNumber=1234&account=9876&_csrf=<secure-random
token>
```

You will notice that we added the _csrf parameter with a random value. Now, the malicious website will not be able to guess the correct value for the _csrf parameter (which must be explicitly provided on the malicious website) and the transfer will fail when the server compares the actual token to the expected token.

The following diagram shows a standard use case for a synchronizer token pattern:

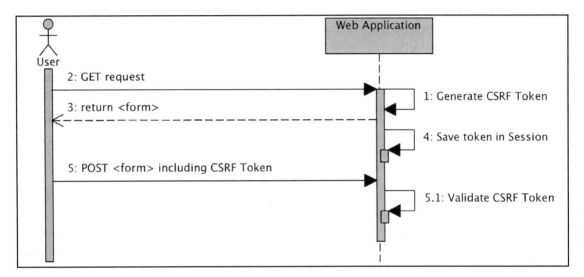

Synchronizer token support in Spring Security

Spring Security provides synchronizer token support that is turned on by default. You might have noticed from the previous chapters that in our SecurityConfig.java file, we have disabled CSRF protection, as shown in the following code snippet:

```
//src/main/java/com/packtpub/springsecurity/configuration/SecurityC
onfig.java

protected void configure(HttpSecurity http) throws Exception {
...
// CSRF protection is enabled by default.
http.csrf().disable();
...
}
```

Up to this point in the book, we have disabled synchronizer token protection so we could focus on other security concerns.

If we start the application at this point, we can run through the security and there will be no synchronizer token support added to any of the pages.

 You should start with the code from `chapter16.00-calendar`.

When to use CSRF protection

It is recommended you use CSRF protection for any request that could be processed by a browser or by normal users. If you are only creating a service that is used by non-browser clients, you will most likely want to disable CSRF protection.

CSRF protection and JSON

A common question is: do I need to protect JSON requests made by JavaScript? The short answer is, it depends. However, you must be very careful, as there are CSRF exploits that can impact JSON requests. For example, a malicious user can create a CSRF with JSON using the following form:

```
<form action="https://example.com/secureTransaction" method="post"
enctype="text/plain">
<input name='{"amount":100,"routingNumber":"maliciousRoutingNumber",
"account":"evilsAccountNumber", "ignore_me":"' value='test"}'
type='hidden'>
<input type="submit" value="Win Money!"/>
</form>This will produce the following JSON structure{ "amount":
100,"routingNumber": "maliciousRoutingNumber","account":
"maliciousAccountNumber","ignore_me": "=test"
}
```

If an application were not validating the Content-Type method, then it would be exposed to this exploit. Depending on the setup, a Spring MVC application that validates the Content-Type method could still be exploited by updating the URL suffix to end with `.json`, as shown in the following code:

```
<form action="https://example.com/secureTransaction.json" method="post"
enctype="text/plain">
<input name='{"amount":100,"routingNumber":"maliciousRoutingNumber",
"account":"maliciousAccountNumber", "ignore_me":"' value='test"}'
type='hidden'>
<input type="submit" value="Win Money!"/>
</form>
```

CSRF and stateless browser applications

What if your application is stateless? That doesn't necessarily mean you are protected. In fact, if a user does not need to perform any actions in the web browser for a given request, they are likely still vulnerable to CSRF attacks.

For example, consider an application using a custom cookie that contains all of the states within it for authentication instead of the `JSESSIONID` cookie. When the CSRF attack happens, the custom cookie will be sent with the request in the same manner that the `JSESSIONID` cookie was sent in our previous example.

Users using basic authentication are also vulnerable to CSRF attacks, since the browser will automatically include the username and password in any requests, in the same manner, that the `JSESSIONID` cookie was sent in our previous example.

Using Spring Security CSRF protection

So, what are the steps necessary to use Spring Security to protect our site against CSRF attacks? The steps for using Spring Security's CSRF protection are as follows:

1. Use proper HTTP verbs.
2. Configure CSRF protection.
3. Include the CSRF token.

Using proper HTTP verbs

The first step to protecting against CSRF attacks is to ensure your website uses proper HTTP verbs. Specifically, before Spring Security's CSRF support can be of use, you need to be certain that your application is using PATCH, POST, PUT, and/or DELETE for anything that modifies state.

This is not a limitation of Spring Security's support, but instead a general requirement for proper CSRF prevention. The reason is that including private information in an HTTP GET method can cause the information to be leaked.

Refer to *RFC 2616, Section 15.1.3, Encoding Sensitive Information in URI's* for general guidance on using POST instead of GET for sensitive information (https://www.w3.org/Protocols/rfc2616/rfc2616-sec15.html#sec15.1.3).

Configuring CSRF protection

The next step is to include Spring Security's CSRF protection within your application. Some frameworks handle invalid CSRF tokens by invaliding the user's session, but this causes its own problems. Instead, by default, Spring Security's CSRF protection will produce HTTP 403 access denied. This can be customized by configuring AccessDeniedHandler to process InvalidCsrfTokenException differently.

For passivity reasons, if you are using the XML configuration, CSRF protection must be explicitly enabled using the <csrf> element. Refer to the <csrf> element's documentation for additional customizations.

SEC-2347 is logged to ensure Spring Security 4.x's XML namespace configuration will enable CSRF protection by default (https://github.com/spring-projects/spring-security/issues/2574).

Default CSRF support

CSRF protection is enabled by default with Java configuration. Refer to the Javadoc of csrf() for additional customizations regarding how CSRF protection is configured.

Just to be verbose in this configuration, we are going to add the CSRS method to our SecurityConfig.java file as follows:

```
//src/main/java/com/packtpub/springsecurity/configuration/SecurityConfig.java
    @Override
```

```
public void configure(HttpSecurity http) throws Exception {
    http.csrf();
}
```

Including the CSRF token in the <Form> submissions

The last step is to ensure that you include the CSRF token in all PATCH, POST, PUT, and DELETE methods. One way to approach this is to use the _csrf request attribute to obtain the current CsrfToken token. An example of doing this with a JSP is shown as follows:

```
<c:url var="logoutUrl" value="/logout"/>
<form action="${logoutUrl}" method="post">
  <input type="submit" value="Log out" />
  <input type="hidden"name="${_csrf.parameterName}"
value="${_csrf.token}"/>
</form>
```

Including the CSRF token using the Spring Security JSP tag library

If CSRF protection is enabled, this tag inserts a hidden form field with the correct name and value for the CSRF protection token. If CSRF protection is not enabled, this tag has no output.

Normally, Spring Security automatically inserts a CSRF form field for any <form:form> tags you use, but if for some reason you cannot use <form:form>, csrfInput is a handy replacement.

You should place this tag within an HTML <form></form> block, where you would normally place other input fields. Do not place this tag within a Spring <form:form></form:form> block. Spring Security handles Spring forms automatically as follows:

```
<form method="post" action="/logout">
  <sec:csrfInput />
  ...
</form>
```

Default CSRF token support

If you are using the Spring MVC `<form:form>` tag, or Thymeleaf 2.1+, and you replace `@EnableWebSecurity` with `@EnableWebMvcSecurity`, the `CsrfToken` token is automatically included for you (using the `CsrfRequestDataValue` token we have been processing).

So, for this book, we have been using Thymeleaf for all of our web pages. Thymeleaf has CSRF support enabled by default if we enable CSRF support in Spring Security.

 You should start with the code from `chapter16.01-calendar`.

If we start up the JBCP calendar application and navigate to the login page at `https://localhost:8443/login.html`, we can view the generated source for the `login.html` page, as follows:

```
<form method="POST" action="/login" ...>
    ...
    <input type="hidden" name="_csrf"
value="e86c9744-5b7d-4d5f-81d5-450463222908">
    </form>
```

Ajax and JSON requests

If you are using JSON, then it is not possible to submit the CSRF token within an HTTP parameter. Instead, you can submit the token within a HTTP header. A typical pattern would be to include the CSRF token within your `<meta>` HTML tags. An example with a JSP is as follows:

```
<html>
    <head>
        <meta name="_csrf" content="${_csrf.token}"/>
        <!-- default header name is X-CSRF-TOKEN -->
        <meta name="_csrf_header" content="${_csrf.headerName}"/>
        ...
    </head>
    ...
```

Instead of manually creating the meta tags, you can use the simpler `csrfMetaTags` tag from the Spring Security JSP tag library.

The csrfMetaTags tag

If CSRF protection is enabled, this tag inserts meta tags containing the CSRF protection token form field, header names, and CSRF protection token value. These meta tags are useful for employing CSRF protection within JavaScript in your applications.

You should place the `csrfMetaTags` tag within an HTML `<head></head>` block, where you would normally place other meta tags. Once you use this tag, you can access the form field name, header name, and token value easily using JavaScript, as follows:

```html
<html>
  <head>
      ...
      <sec:csrfMetaTags />
      <script type="text/javascript" language="javascript">
          var csrfParameter =
$("meta[name='_csrf_parameter']").attr("content");
          var csrfHeader =
$("meta[name='_csrf_header']").attr("content");
          var csrfToken = $("meta[name='_csrf']").attr("content");
          ...
      <script>
  </head>
  ...
```

If CSRF protection is not enabled, `csrfMetaTags` outputs nothing.

jQuery usage

You can then include the token within all of your Ajax requests. If you were using jQuery, this could be done with the following code snippet:

```javascript
$(function () {
var token = $("meta[name='_csrf']").attr("content");
var header = $("meta[name='_csrf_header']").attr("content");
$(document).ajaxSend(function(e, xhr, options) {
   xhr.setRequestHeader(header, token);
});
});
```

Using the cujoJS's rest.js module

As an alternative to jQuery, we recommend using the `rest.js` module of cujoJS. The `rest.js` module provides advanced support for working with HTTP requests and responses in RESTful ways. A core capability is the ability to contextualize the HTTP client, adding behavior as needed by chaining interceptors onto the client, as follows:

```
var client = rest.chain(csrf, {
token: $("meta[name='_csrf']").attr("content"),
name: $("meta[name='_csrf_header']").attr("content")
});
```

The configured client can be shared with any component of the application that needs to make a request to the CSRF protected resource. One significant difference between `rest.js` and jQuery is that the only requests made with the configured client will contain the CSRF token, versus in jQuery, where all requests will include the token. The ability to determine which requests receive the token helps guard against leaking the CSRF token to a third-party.

 Please refer to the `rest.js` reference documentation for more information on `rest.js`
(`https://github.com/cujojs/rest/tree/master/docs`).

CSRF caveats

There are a few caveats when implementing CSRF in Spring Security that you need to be aware of.

Timeouts

One issue is that the expected CSRF token is stored in the `HttpSession` method, so as soon as the `HttpSession` method expires, your configured `AccessDeniedHandler` handler will receive `InvalidCsrfTokenException`. If you are using the default `AccessDeniedHandler` handler, the browser will get an HTTP 403 and display a poor error message.

You might ask why the expected `CsrfToken` token isn't stored in a cookie. This is because there are known exploits in which headers (specifying the cookies) can be set by another domain.

 This is the same reason Ruby on Rails no longer skips CSRF checks when the header X-Requested-With is present (`http://weblog.rubyonrails.org/2011/2/8/csrf-protection-bypass-in-ruby-on-rails/`).

The *Web Application Security Consortium* (`http://www.webappsec.org`) has a detailed thread on using CSRF and an HTTP 307 redirect to perform exploit CSRF cookies.

 See this `www.webappsec.org` thread for details on how to perform the exploit at `http://lists.webappsec.org/pipermail/websecurity_lists.webappsec.org/2011-February/007533.html`.

Another disadvantage is that by removing the state (the timeout), you lose the ability to forcibly terminate the token if something is compromised.

A simple way to mitigate an active user experiencing a timeout is to have some JavaScript that lets the user know their session is about to expire. The user can click a button to continue and refresh the session.

Alternatively, specifying a custom `AccessDeniedHandler` handler allows you to process `InvalidCsrfTokenException` any way you like, as we can see in the following code:

```
//src/main/java/com/packtpub/springsecurity/configuration/SecurityConfig.java

@Override
public void configure(HttpSecurity http) throws Exception {
    http.exceptionHandling()
            .accessDeniedHandler(accessDeniedHandler);
}
@Bean
public CustomAccessDeniedHandler accessDeniedHandler(){
    return new CustomAccessDeniedHandler();
}
```

Logging in

In order to protect against forged login requests, the login form should be protected against CSRF attacks, too. Since the `CsrfToken` token is stored in `HttpSession`, this means an `HttpSession` mehthod will be created as soon as the `CsrfToken` attribute is accessed. While this sounds bad in a RESTful/stateless architecture, the reality is that the state is necessary to implement practical security. Without the state, we have nothing we can do if a token is compromised. Practically speaking, the CSRF token is quite small in size and should have a negligible impact on our architecture.

 An attacker may forge a request to log the victim into a target website using the attacker's credentials; this is known as login CSRF (`https://en.wikipedia.org/wiki/Cross-site_request_forgery#Forging_login_requests`).

Logging out

Adding CSRF will update the `LogoutFilter` filter to only use HTTP `POST`. This ensures that logging out requires a CSRF token and that a malicious user cannot forcibly log out your users.

One approach is to use a `<form>` tag for logout. If you want an HTML link, you can use JavaScript to have the link perform an HTTP `POST` (which can be in a hidden form). For browsers with JavaScript disabled, you can optionally have the link take the user to a logout confirmation page that will perform the HTTP `POST`.

If you want to use HTTP `GET` with logout, you can do so, but remember, this is generally not recommended. For example, the following Java configuration will perform logout when the logout URL pattern is requested with any HTTP method:

```
//src/main/java/com/packtpub/springsecurity/configuration/SecurityConfig.java

@Override
protected void configure(HttpSecurity http) throws Exception {
    http.logout()
        .logoutRequestMatcher(
            new AntPathRequestMatcher("/logout"));
}
```

Security HTTP response headers

The following sections discuss Spring Security's support for adding various security headers to the response.

Default security headers

Spring Security allows users to easily inject default security headers to assist in protecting their application. The following is a list of the current default security headers provided by Spring Security:

- Cache-Control
- Content-Type Options
- HTTP Strict Transport Security
- X-Frame-Options
- X-XSS-Protection

While each of these headers is considered best practice, it should be noted that not all clients utilize these headers, so additional testing is encouraged. For passivity reasons, if you are using Spring Security's XML namespace support, you must explicitly enable the security headers. All of the default headers can be easily added using the <headers> element with no child elements.

SEC-2348 is logged to ensure Spring Security 4.x's XML namespace configuration will enable Security headers by default (https://github.com/spring-projects/spring-security/issues/2575).

If you are using Spring Security's Java configuration, all of the default security headers are added by default. They can be disabled using Java configuration, as follows:

```
//src/main/java/com/packtpub/springsecurity/configuration/SecurityConfig.java

@Override
protected void configure(HttpSecurity http) throws Exception {
    http.headers().disable();
}
```

The following code adds the security headers to the response. This is activated by default when using the default constructor of `WebSecurityConfigurerAdapter`. Accepting the default provided by `WebSecurityConfigurerAdapter`, or only invoking the `headers()` method without invoking additional methods, is the equivalent of the following code snippet:

```
@Override
protected void configure(HttpSecurity http) throws Exception {
    http
        .headers()
            .contentTypeOptions()
            .and()
            .xssProtection()
            .and()
            .cacheControl()
            .and()
            .httpStrictTransportSecurity()
            .and()
            .frameOptions()
            .and()
        ...;
}
```

As soon as you specify any headers that should be included, then only those headers will be included. For example, the following configuration will include support for X-Frame-Options only:

```
@Override
protected void configure(HttpSecurity http) throws Exception {
    ...
    http.headers().frameOptions();
}
```

Cache-Control

In the past, Spring Security required you to provide your own `Cache-Control` method for your web application. This seemed reasonable at the time, but browser caches have evolved to include caches for secure connections as well. This means that a user may view an authenticated page, log out, and then a malicious user can use the browser history to view the cached page.

To help mitigate this, Spring Security has added `Cache-Control` support, which will insert the following headers into your response:

```
Cache-Control: no-cache, no-store, max-age=0, must-revalidate
Pragma: no-cache
Expires: 0
```

Simply adding the `headers()` method with no child elements will automatically add `Cache-Control` and quite a few other protection options. However, if you only want `Cache-Control`, you can enable this feature using Spring Security's Java Configuration with the `cacheControl()` method, as follows:

```
@Override
protected void configure(HttpSecurity http) throws Exception {
    http.headers()
        .cacheControl();
}
```

If you want to cache specific responses, your application can selectively invoke `HttpServletResponse.setHeader(String,String)` to override the header set by Spring Security. This is useful to ensure things such as CSS, JavaScript, and images are properly cached.

When using Spring Web MVC, this is typically done within your configuration. For example, the following configuration will ensure that the cache headers are set for all of your resources:

```
@EnableWebMvc
public class WebMvcConfiguration
extends WebMvcConfigurerAdapter {
    @Override
    public void addResourceHandlers(
                    ResourceHandlerRegistry registry) {
        registry
            .addResourceHandler("/resources/**")
            .addResourceLocations("/resources/")
            .setCachePeriod(3_155_6926);
    }
    // ...
}
```

Content-Type Options

Historically, browsers, including Internet Explorer, would try to guess the content type of a request using content sniffing. This allowed browsers to improve the user experience by guessing the content type of resources that had not specified the content type. For example, if a browser encountered a JavaScript file that did not have the content type specified, it would be able to guess the content type and then execute it.

 There are many additional things one should do, such as only displaying the document in a distinct domain, ensuring the Content-Type header is set, sanitizing the document, and so on, when allowing content to be uploaded. However, these measures are out of the scope of what Spring Security provides. It is also important to point out that when disabling content sniffing, you must specify the content type in order for things to work properly.

The problem with content sniffing is that this allows malicious users to use polyglots (a file that is valid as multiple content types) to execute XSS attacks. For example, some sites may allow users to submit a valid postscript document to a website and view it. A malicious user might create a postscript document that is also a valid JavaScript file and execute an XSS attack with it (`http://webblaze.cs.berkeley.edu/papers/barth-caballero-song.pdf`).

Content sniffing can be disabled by adding the following header to our response:

```
X-Content-Type-Options: nosniff
```

Just as with the `Cache-Control` element, the `nosniff` directive is added by default when using the `headers()` method with no child elements. The X-Content-Type-Options header is added by default within the Spring Security Java configuration. If you want more control over the headers, you can explicitly specify the content type options with the following code:

```
@Override
protected void configure(HttpSecurity http) throws Exception {
    http.headers()
        .contentTypeOptions();
}
```

HTTP Strict Transport Security

When you type in your bank's website, do you enter mybank.example.com, or do you enter https://mybank.example.com? If you omit the HTTPS protocol, you are potentially vulnerable to man in the middle attacks. Even if the website performs a redirect to https://**my**bank.example.com, a malicious user could intercept the initial HTTP request and manipulate the response (redirect to https://**mi**bank.example.com and steal their credentials).

Many users omit the HTTPS protocol, and this is why HSTS was created.

In accordance with *RFC6797*, the HSTS header is only injected into HTTPS responses. In order for the browser to acknowledge the header, the browser must first trust the CA that signed the SSL certificate used to make the connection, not just the SSL certificate (https://tools.ietf.org/html/rfc6797).

Once mybank.example.com is added as an HSTS host, a browser can know beforehand that any request to mybank.example.com should be interpreted as https://mybank.example.com. This greatly reduces the possibility of a man in the middle attack occurring.

One way for a site to be marked as an HSTS host is to have the host preloaded into the browser. Another is to add the Strict-Transport-Security header to the response. For example, the following would instruct the browser to treat the domain as an HSTS host for a year (there are approximately 31,536,000 seconds in a year):

```
Strict-Transport-Security: max-age=31536000 ; includeSubDomains
```

The optional includeSubDomains directive instructs Spring Security that subdomains (such as secure.mybank.example.com) should also be treated as an HSTS domain.

As with the other headers, Spring Security adds the previous header to the response when the headers() method is specified with no child elements, but it is automatically added when you are using Java configuration. You can also only use HSTS headers with the hsts() method, as shown in the following code:

```
@Override
protected void configure(HttpSecurity http) throws Exception {
    http.headers()
        .hsts();
}
```

X-Frame-Options

Allowing your website to be added to a frame can be a security issue. For example, using clever CSS styling, users could be tricked into clicking on something that they did not intend to.

View a Clickjacking video demo here at `https://www.youtube.com/watch?v=3mk0RySeNsU`.

For example, a user that is logged in to their bank might click a button that grants access to other users. This sort of attack is known as Clickjacking.

Read more about Clickjacking at `https://www.owasp.org/index.php/Clickjacking`.

Another modern approach to dealing with Clickjacking is using a content security policy. Spring Security does not provide support for this as the specification has not been released, and it is quite a bit more complicated. However, you could use the static headers feature to implement this. To stay up to date on this issue and to see how you can implement it with Spring Security, refer to *SEC-2117* at `https://github.com/spring-projects/spring-security/issues/2342`.

There are a number of ways to mitigate Clickjacking attacks. For example, to protect legacy browsers from Clickjacking attacks, you can use frame-breaking code. While not perfect, a frame-breaking code is the best you can do for legacy browsers.

A more modern approach to address Clickjacking is to use the X-Frame-Options header, as follows:

```
X-Frame-Options: DENY
```

The `X-Frame-Options` response header instructs the browser to prevent any site with this header in the response from being rendered within a frame. As with the other response headers, this is automatically included when the `headers()` method is specified with no child elements. You can also explicitly specify the frame-options element to control which headers are added to the response, as follows:

```
@Override
protected void configure(HttpSecurity http) throws Exception {
   http.headers()
       .frameOptions();
}
```

If you want to change the value for the X-Frame-Options header, then you can use a `XFrameOptionsHeaderWriter` instance.

Some browsers have built-in support for filtering out reflected XSS attacks. This is by no means foolproof, but it does assist with XSS protection.

Filtering is typically enabled by default, so adding the header just ensures it is enabled and instructs the browser as to what to do when an XSS attack is detected. For example, the filter might try to change the content in the least invasive way to still render everything. At times, this type of replacement can become an XSS vulnerability in itself. Instead, it is best to block the content, rather than attempt to fix it. To do this, we can add the following header:

```
X-XSS-Protection: 1; mode=block
```

This header is included by default when the `headers()` method is specified with no child elements. We can explicitly state it using the `xssProtection` element, as follows:

```
@Override
protected void configure(HttpSecurity http) throws Exception {
    http.headers()
        .xssProtection();
}
```

Custom Headers

Spring Security has mechanisms to make it convenient to add more common security headers to your application. However, it also provides hooks to enable the adding of custom headers.

Static headers

There may be times you wish to inject custom security headers into your application that are not supported out of the box. For example, perhaps you wish to have early support for a content security policy in order to ensure that resources are only loaded from the same origin. Since support for a content security policy has not been finalized, browsers use one of two common extension headers to implement the feature. This means we will need to inject the policy twice. An example of the headers can be seen in the following code snippet:

```
X-Content-Security-Policy: default-src 'self'
X-WebKit-CSP: default-src 'self'
```

When using Java configuration, these headers can be added to the response using the `header()` method, as follows:

```
@Override
protected void configure(HttpSecurity http) throws Exception {
    http.headers()
        .addHeaderWriter(
          new StaticHeadersWriter(
              "X-Content-Security-Policy",
              "default-src 'self'"))
        .addHeaderWriter(
            new StaticHeadersWriter(
              "X-WebKit-CSP",
              "default-src 'self'"));
}
```

The HeadersWriter instance

When the namespace or Java configuration does not support the headers you want, you can create a custom `HeadersWriter` instance or even provide a custom implementation of `HeadersWriter`.

Let's take a look at an example of using a custom instance of `XFrameOptionsHeaderWriter`. Perhaps you want to allow the framing of content for the same origin. This is easily supported by setting the policy attribute to `SAMEORIGIN`, but let's take a look at a more explicit example using the `ref` attribute, as shown in the following code snippet:

```
@Override
protected void configure(HttpSecurity http) throws Exception {
    http.headers()
        .addHeaderWriter(
            new XFrameOptionsHeaderWriter(
                XFrameOptionsMode.SAMEORIGIN));
}
```

The DelegatingRequestMatcherHeaderWriter class

At times, you may want to only write a header for certain requests. For example, perhaps you want to only protect your login page from being framed. You could use the DelegatingRequestMatcherHeaderWriter class to do so. When using Java configuration, this can be done with the following code:

```java
@Override
protected void configure(HttpSecurity http) throws Exception {
    DelegatingRequestMatcherHeaderWriter headerWriter =
        new DelegatingRequestMatcherHeaderWriter(
            new AntPathRequestMatcher("/login"),
            new XFrameOptionsHeaderWriter());
    http.headers()
        .addHeaderWriter(headerWriter);
}
```

Summary

In this chapter, we covered several security vulnerabilities, as well employing Spring Security to circumvent those vulnerabilities. After reading this chapter, you should understand the threat of CSRF and use of the synchronizer tokens to prevent CSRF.

You should also know how to include various HTTP headers to protect against common security vulnerabilities using the Cache-Control, Content-Type Options, HSTS, X-Frame-Options, and X-XSS-Protection methods.

In the next chapter, we will discuss how to migrate from Spring Security 3.x to Spring Security 4.2.

16
Migration to Spring Security 4.2

In this final chapter, we will review information relating to common migration issues when moving from Spring Security 3 to Spring Security 4.2. We'll spend much more time discussing the differences between Spring Security 3 and Spring Security 4, because this is what most users will struggle with. This is due to the fact that the updates from Spring Security 3 to Spring Security 4.2 contain a lot of non-passive refactoring.

At the end of the chapter, we will also highlight some of the new features that can be found in Spring Security 4.2. However, we do not explicitly cover changes from Spring Security 3 to Spring Security 4.2. This is because by explaining the differences between Spring Security 3 and Spring Security 4, users should be able to update to Spring Security 4.2 with ease since the changes to Spring Security 4.2 are passive.

During the course of this chapter, we will cover the following topics:

- Reviewing important enhancements in Spring Security 4.2.
- Understanding configuration changes required in your existing Spring version.
- Reviewing Security 3 applications when moving them to Spring Security 4.2.
- Illustrating the overall movement of important classes and packages in Spring Security 4.
- Highlighting some of the new features found in Spring Security 4.2. Once you have completed the review of this chapter, you will be in a good position to migrate an existing application from Spring Security 3 to Spring Security 4.2.
- Migrating from Spring Security 3.

You may be planning to migrate an existing application to Spring Security 4.2, or you may be trying to add functionality to a Spring Security 3 application and are looking for guidance in the pages of this book. We'll try to address both of your concerns in this chapter.

First, we'll run through the important differences between Spring Security 3 and 4.2—both in terms of features and configuration. Second, we'll provide some guidance on mapping configuration or class name changes. This will better enable you to translate the examples in the book from Spring Security 4.2 back to Spring Security 3 (where applicable).

A very important migration note is that Spring Security 3+ mandates a migration to Spring Framework 4 and Java 5 (1.5) or greater. Be aware that in many cases, migrating these other components may have a greater impact on your application than the upgrade of Spring Security!

Introduction

As exploits against applications evolve, so must Spring Security. In a major release version, the Spring Security team took the opportunity to make some non-passive changes that focused on the following things:

- Ensuring Spring Security is more secure by default (`https://www.owasp.org/index.php/Establish_secure_defaults`)
- Minimizing information leakage (`https://www.owasp.org/index.php/Information_Leakage`)
- Removing deprecated APIs

A complete list of non-passive changes between 3.x and 4.x can be found in JIRA at `https://jira.spring.io/browse/SEC-2916?jql=project%20%3D%20SEC%20AND%20fixVersion%20in%20(4.0.0%2C%204.0.0.M1%2C%204.0.0.M2%2C%204.0.0.RC1%2C%204.0.0.RC2)%20AND%20labels%20%3D%20passivity`.

Sample migration

The Spring Security team has created a sample project illustrating all of the changes when migrating from 3.x to 4.x and has made the project available on GitHub.

The sample includes both XML and JavaConfig examples and can be found at `https://github.com/spring-projects/spring-security-migrate-3-to-4/`.

Enhancements in Spring Security 4.2

There are quite a few notable changes in Spring Security 4.2, and this release also brings early support for Spring Framework 5. You can find the changelogs for 4.2.0.M1, 4.2.0.RC1, and 4.2.0.RELEASE, which covers over 80 issues. The community contributed the overwhelming majority of these features.

Significant enhancements in Spring Security 4.2, improved since Spring Security 3 include the following features and their support numbers:

Web improvements:

The following items are related to Spring Security's interaction with Web-based applications:

- **#3812**: Jackson support
- **#4116**: Referrer policy
- **#3938**: Added HTTP response splitting prevention
- **#3949**: Added bean reference support to `@AuthenticationPrincipal`
- **#3978**: Support for Standford WebAuth and Shibboleth using the newly added `RequestAttributeAuthenticationFilter`
- **#4076**: Document proxy server configuration
- **#3795**: `ConcurrentSessionFilter` supports `InvalidSessionStrategy`
- **#3904**: Added `CompositeLogoutHandler`

Spring Security Configuration improvements:

The following items are related to the configuration of Spring Security:

- **#3956**: Central configuration of the default role prefix. See the issue for details
- **#4102**: Custom default configuration in `WebSecurityConfigurerAdapter`
- **#3899**: `concurrency-control@max-sessions` supports unlimited sessions.
- **#4097**: `intercept-url@request-matcher-ref` adds more powerful request matching support to the XML namespace
- **#3990**: Support for constructing `RoleHierarchy` from Map (such as YML).
- **#4062**: Custom `cookiePath` to `CookieCsrfTokenRepository`.

- **#3794**: Allowing the configuration of `InvalidSessionStrategy` on `SessionManagementConfigurer`
- **#4020**: Fixing exposed beans for `defaultMethodExpressionHandler` can prevent Method Security

Miscellaneous changes in Spring Security 4.x

The following items are miscellaneous changes that are worth noting as many of them might impact upgrading to Spring Security 4.x:

- **#4080**: Spring 5 support
- **#4095** - Added `UserBuilder`
- **#4018**: Fixes after `csrf()` is invoked, future `MockMvc` invocations use original `CsrfTokenRepository`
- General dependency version updates

Note that the listed numbers refer to the GitHub pull requests or issues.

Other, more innocuous changes, encompassed a general restructuring and cleaning up of the code base and the configuration of the framework so that the overall structure and usage makes much more sense. The authors of Spring Security have added extensibility where none previously existed, especially in the areas of login and URL redirection.

If you are already working in a Spring Security 3 environment, you may not find compelling reasons to upgrade if you aren't pushing the boundaries of the framework. However, if you have found limitations in the available extension points, code structure, or configurability of Spring Security 3, you'll welcome many of the minor changes that we discuss in detail in the remainder of this chapter.

Changes to configuration in Spring Security 4

Many of the changes in Spring Security 4 will be visible in the namespace style of configuration in XML-based configuration. We will be covering mostly Java-based configuration in this chapter, but will also note some notable XML-based changes. Although this chapter cannot cover all of the minor changes in detail, we'll try to cover those changes that will be most likely to affect you as you move to Spring Security 4.

Deprecations

A number of deprecations were removed in Spring Security 4 to clean up clutter.

The following is the final commit for the XML and JavaConfig deprecations, which contained 177 changed files with 537 additions and 5,023 deletions: `https://github.com/spring-projects/spring-security/commit/6e204fff72b80196a83245cbc3bd0cd401feda00`.

If you are using the XML namespace or Java-based configuration, there are many instances where you will be shielded from deprecation. If you (or a non-spring library you use) do not use an API directly, then you will not be impacted. You can easily search your workspace to find these listed deprecations.

The spring-security-core deprecations

This section described all of the deprecated APIs within the `spring-security-core` module.

org.springframework.security.access.SecurityConfig

The `SecurityConfig.createSingleAttributeList(String)` interface was removed in favor of using `SecurityConfig.createList(String... )`. This means that if you have something like as follows:

```
List<ConfigAttribute> attrs = SecurityConfig.createSingleAttributeList
    ("ROLE_USER");
```

It will need to be replaced with the following code:

```
List<ConfigAttribute> attrs = SecurityConfig.createList("ROLE_USER");
```

UserDetailsServiceWrapper

`UserDetailsServiceWrapper` was deprecated in favor of using `RoleHierarchyAuthoritiesMapper`. For example, you may have something like as follows:

```
@Bean
public AuthenticationManager
authenticationManager(List<AuthenticationProvider> providers) {
```

```
        return new ProviderManager(providers);
}
@Bean
public AuthenticationProvider
authenticationProvider(UserDetailsServiceWrapper
userDetailsService) {
        DaoAuthenticationProvider provider = new
DaoAuthenticationProvider();
        provider.setUserDetailsService(userDetailsService);
        return provider;
}
@Bean
public UserDetailsServiceWrapper
userDetailsServiceWrapper(RoleHierarchy roleHierarchy) {
        UserDetailsServiceWrapper wrapper = new
UserDetailsServiceWrapper();
        wrapper.setRoleHierarchy(roleHierarchy);
        wrapper.setUserDetailsService(userDetailsService());
        return wrapper;
}
```

It will need to be replaced to something like this:

```
@Bean
public AuthenticationManager
authenticationManager(List<AuthenticationProvider> providers) {
        return new ProviderManager(providers);
}
@Bean
public AuthenticationProvider
authenticationProvider(UserDetailsService userDetailsService,
GrantedAuthoritiesMapper authoritiesMapper) {
        DaoAuthenticationProvider provider = new
DaoAuthenticationProvider();
        provider.setUserDetailsService(userDetailsService);
        provider.setAuthoritiesMapper(authoritiesMapper);
        return provider;
}
@Bean
public RoleHierarchyAuthoritiesMapper
roleHierarchyAuthoritiesMapper(RoleHierarchy roleHierarchy) {
        return new RoleHierarchyAuthoritiesMapper(roleHierarchy);
}
```

UserDetailsWrapper

`UserDetailsWrapper` was deprecated in favor of using `RoleHierarchyAuthoritiesMapper`. Typically it users would not use the `UserDetailsWrapper` class directly. However, if they are, they can use `RoleHierarchyAuthoritiesMapper`, for example, the following code may be present:

```
UserDetailsWrapper authenticate = new UserDetailsWrapper
(userDetails, roleHiearchy);
```

If so, then it needs to be replaced by the following code snippet:

```
Collection<GrantedAuthority> allAuthorities = roleHiearchy.
getReachableGrantedAuthorities(userDetails.getAuthorities());
UserDetails authenticate = new User(userDetails.getUsername(),
userDetails.getPassword(), allAuthorities);
```

AbstractAccessDecisionManager

The default constructor for `AbstractAccessDecisionManager` has been deprecated along with the `setDecisionVoters` method. Naturally, this impacts the `AffirmativeBased`, `ConsensusBased`, and `UnanimousBased` subclasses. For example, you may be using the following code snippet:

```
AffirmativeBased adm = new AffirmativeBased();
adm.setDecisionVoters(voters);
```

If so, it needs to be migrated to the following code snippet:

```
AffirmativeBased adm = new AffirmativeBased(voters);
```

AuthenticationException

The constructor that accepts `extraInformation` within `AuthenticationException` was removed to prevent the accidental leaking of the `UserDetails` object. Specifically, we removed the following code:

```
public AccountExpiredException(String msg, Object extraInformation) {
  ...
}
```

This impacts the subclasses AccountStatusException, AccountExpiredException, BadCredentialsException, CredentialsExpiredException, DisabledException, LockedException, and UsernameNotFoundException. If you are using any of these constructors, simply remove the additional argument. For example, the following code snippet is changed:

```
new LockedException("Message", userDetails);
```

The preceding code snippet should be changed to the following code snippet:

```
new LockedException("Message");
```

AnonymousAuthenticationProvider

The AnonymousAuthenticationProvider default constructor and the setKey method were deprecated in favor of using the constructor injection. For example, you may have the following code snippet:

```
AnonymousAuthenticationProvider provider = new
AnonymousAuthenticationProvider();
provider.setKey(key);
```

The preceding code snippet should be changed to the following code:

```
AnonymousAuthenticationProvider provider = new
AnonymousAuthenticationProvider(key);
```

AuthenticationDetailsSourceImpl

The AuthenticationDetailsSourceImpl class was deprecated in favor of writing a custom AuthenticationDetailsSource. For example, you may have the following:

```
AuthenticationDetailsSourceImpl source = new
AuthenticationDetailsSourceImpl();
source.setClazz(CustomWebAuthenticationDetails.class);
```

You should implement the `AuthenticationDetailsSource` class directly to return the `CustomSource` object:

```
public class CustomWebAuthenticationDetailsSource implements
AuthenticationDetailsSource<HttpServletRequest,
WebAuthenticationDetails> {
      public WebAuthenticationDetails
buildDetails(HttpServletRequest context) {
            return new CustomWebAuthenticationDetails(context);
      }
}
```

ProviderManager

The `ProviderManager` class has removed the deprecated default constructor and the corresponding setter methods in favor of using constructor injection. It has also removed the `clearExtraInformation` property, since the `AuthenticationException` exception had the extra information property removed.

For example, you may have something like the following:

```
ProviderManager provider = new ProviderManager();
provider.setParent(parent);
provider.setProviders(providers);
provider.setClearExtraInformation(true);
```

If so, the preceding code should be changed to the following code:

```
ProviderManager provider = new ProviderManager(providers, parent);
```

The `clearExtraInformation` property was removed since the `AuthenticationException` exception had the extra information property removed. There is no replacement for this.

RememberMeAuthenticationProvider

The `RememberMeAuthenticationProvider` class had the default constructor and the `setKey` method removed in favor of the constructor injection. For example, take a look at the following code:

```
RememberMeAuthenticationProvider provider = new
RememberMeAuthenticationProvider();
provider.setKey(key);
```

The preceding code snippet should be migrated to the following:

```
RememberMeAuthenticationProvider provider = new
RememberMeAuthenticationProvider(key);
```

GrantedAuthorityImpl

GrantedAuthorityImpl was removed in favor of SimpleGrantedAuthority, or implementing your own GrantAuthority object. For example:

```
new GrantedAuthorityImpl(role);
```

This should be replaced with the following:

```
new SimpleGrantedAuthority(role);
```

InMemoryDaoImpl

InMemoryDaoImpl was replaced in favor of InMemoryUserDetailsManager. For example:

```
InMemoryDaoImpl uds = new InMemoryDaoImpl();
uds.setUserProperties(properties);
```

This should be replaced with:

```
InMemoryUserDetailsManager uds = new
InMemoryUserDetailsManager(properties);
spring-security-web
```

The spring-security-web deprecations

This section described all of the deprecated APIs within the spring-security-web module.

FilterChainProxy

FilterChainProxy removed the setFilterChainMap method in favor of constructor injection. For example, you may have the following:

```
FilterChainProxy filter = new FilterChainProxy();
filter.setFilterChainMap(filterChainMap);
```

It should be replaced with:

```
FilterChainProxy filter = new
FilterChainProxy(securityFilterChains);
```

FilterChainProxy also removed getFilterChainMap in favor of using getFilterChains, for example:

```
FilterChainProxy securityFilterChain = ...
Map<RequestMatcher,List<Filter>> mappings =
securityFilterChain.getFilterChainMap();
for(Map.Entry<RequestMatcher, List<Filter>> entry :
mappings.entrySet()) {
        RequestMatcher matcher = entry.getKey();
        boolean matches = matcher.matches(request);
        List<Filter> filters = entry.getValue();
    }
```

This should be replaced with the following code:

```
FilterChainProxy securityFilterChain = ...
List<SecurityFilterChain> mappings =
securityFilterChain.getFilterChains();
for(SecurityFilterChain entry : mappings) {
        boolean matches = entry.matches(request);
        List<Filter> filters = entry.getFilters();
    }
```

ExceptionTranslationFilter

The default constructor for ExceptionTranslationFilter and the setAuthenticationEntryPoint method was removed in favor of using the constructor injection:

```
ExceptionTranslationFilter filter = new
ExceptionTranslationFilter();
filter.setAuthenticationEntryPoint(entryPoint);
filter.setRequestCache(requestCache);
```

This can be replaced with the following code:

```
ExceptionTranslationFilter filter = new
ExceptionTranslationFilter(entryPoint, requestCache);
```

AbstractAuthenticationProcessingFilter

The `AbstractAuthenticationProcessingFilter` class had its `successfulAuthentication(HttpServletRequest,HttpServletResponse,Authentication)` method removed. So, your application may override the following method:

```
protected void successfulAuthentication(HttpServletRequest request,
    HttpServletResponse response, Authentication authResult) throws
IOException,
    ServletException {
    }
```

It should be replaced with the following code:

```
protected void successfulAuthentication(HttpServletRequest request,
    HttpServletResponse response, FilterChain chain, Authentication
    authResult) throws IOException, ServletException {
    }
```

AnonymousAuthenticationFilter

The `AnonymousAuthenticationFilter` class had the default constructor and the `setKey` and `setPrincipal` methods removed in favor of the constructor injection. For example, take a look at the following code snippet:

```
AnonymousAuthenticationFilter filter = new
AnonymousAuthenticationFilter();
filter.setKey(key);
filter.setUserAttribute(attrs);
```

This should be replaced with the following code:

```
AnonymousAuthenticationFilter filter = new
AnonymousAuthenticationFilter(key,attrs.getPassword(),
attrs.getAuthorities());
```

LoginUrlAuthenticationEntryPoint

The `LoginUrlAuthenticationEntryPoint` default constructor and the `setLoginFormUrl` method was removed in favor of the constructor injection. For example:

```
LoginUrlAuthenticationEntryPoint entryPoint = new
LoginUrlAuthenticationEntryPoint();
entryPoint.setLoginFormUrl("/login");
```

This should be replaced with the following code:

```
LoginUrlAuthenticationEntryPoint entryPoint = new
LoginUrlAuthenticationEntryPoint(loginFormUrl);
```

PreAuthenticatedGrantedAuthoritiesUserDetailsService

The `PreAuthenticatedGrantedAuthoritiesUserDetailsService` interface removed `createuserDetails` in favor of `createUserDetails`.

The new method has a correction in the case (U instead of u).

This means that if you have a subclass of the `PreAuthenticatedGrantedAuthoritiesUserDetailsService` class that overrides the `createuserDetails`, `SubclassPreAuthenticatedGrantedAuthoritiesUserDetailsService` extends `PreAuthenticatedGrantedAuthoritiesUserDetailsService`.

```
{
    @Override
    protected UserDetails createuserDetails(Authentication token,
            Collection<? extends GrantedAuthority> authorities) {
        // customize
    }
}
```

It should be changed to override `createUserDetails`:

```
public class SubclassPreAuthenticatedGrantedAuthoritiesUserDetailsService
extends PreAuthenticatedGrantedAuthoritiesUserDetailsService {
    @Override
    protected UserDetails createUserDetails(Authentication token,
            Collection<? extends GrantedAuthority> authorities) {
        // customize
    }
}
```

AbstractRememberMeServices

`AbstractRememberMeServices` and its subclasses
`PersistentTokenBasedRememberMeServices` and `TokenBasedRememberMeServices`
removed the default constructor, the `setKey`, and the `setUserDetailsService` methods
in favor of constructor injection.

PersistentTokenBasedRememberMeServices

The changes to the `AbstractRememberMeServices` and its subclasses had a usage similar
to the following example:

```
PersistentTokenBasedRememberMeServices services = new
PersistentTokenBasedRememberMeServices();
services.setKey(key);
services.setUserDetailsService(userDetailsService);
services.setTokenRepository(tokenRepository);
```

But the implementation usage should now be replaced with:

```
PersistentTokenBasedRememberMeServices services = new
PersistentTokenBasedRememberMeServices(key, userDetailsService,
tokenRepository);
```

RememberMeAuthenticationFilter

The `RememberMeAuthenticationFilter` default constructor, the
`setAuthenticationManager`, and `setRememberMeServices` methods were removed in
favor of the constructor injection, like so:

```
RememberMeAuthenticationFilter filter = new
RememberMeAuthenticationFilter();
filter.setAuthenticationManager(authenticationManager);
filter.setRememberMeServices(rememberMeServices);
```

This should be replaced with:

```
RememberMeAuthenticationFilter filter = new
RememberMeAuthenticationFilter(authenticationManager,rememberMeServices);
```

TokenBasedRememberMeServices

`AbstractRememberMeServices` and its subclasses
`PersistentTokenBasedRememberMeServices` and `TokenBasedRememberMeServices`
removed the default constructor, the `setKey`, and the `setUserDetailsService` methods
in favor of the constructor injection. For example:

```
TokenBasedRememberMeServices services = new TokenBasedRememberMeServices();
services.setKey(key);
services.setUserDetailsService(userDetailsService);
```

This should be replaced with:

```
TokenBasedRememberMeServices services = new
TokenBasedRememberMeServices(key, userDetailsService);
```

ConcurrentSessionControlStrategy

`ConcurrentSessionControlStrategy` was replaced with
`ConcurrentSessionControlAuthenticationStrategy`. Previously,
`ConcurrentSessionControlStrategy` could not be decoupled from
`SessionFixationProtectionStrategy`. Now it is completely decoupled. For example:

```
ConcurrentSessionControlStrategy strategy = new
ConcurrentSessionControlStrategy(sessionRegistry);
```

This can be replaced with:

```
List<SessionAuthenticationStrategy> delegates = new
ArrayList<SessionAuthenticationStrategy>();
delegates.add(new
ConcurrentSessionControlAuthenticationStrategy(sessionRegistry));
delegates.add(new SessionFixationProtectionStrategy());
delegates.add(new RegisterSessionAuthenticationStrategy(sessionRegistry));
CompositeSessionAuthenticationStrategy strategy = new
CompositeSessionAuthenticationStrategy(delegates);
```

SessionFixationProtectionStrategy

SessionFixationProtectionStrategy removed the setRetainedAttributes method in favor of users subclassing SessionFixationProtectionStrategy and overriding the extractAttributes method. Look at the following code:

```
SessionFixationProtectionStrategy strategy = new
SessionFixationProtectionStrategy();
strategy.setRetainedAttributes(attrsToRetain);
```

It should be replaced with:

```
public class AttrsSessionFixationProtectionStrategy extends
SessionFixationProtectionStrategy {
    private final Collection<String> attrsToRetain;
    public AttrsSessionFixationProtectionStrategy(
            Collection<String> attrsToRetain) {
        this.attrsToRetain = attrsToRetain;
    }
    @Override
    protected Map<String, Object> extractAttributes(HttpSession session)
{
        Map<String,Object> attrs = new HashMap<String, Object>();
        for(String attr : attrsToRetain) {
            attrs.put(attr, session.getAttribute(attr));
        }
        return attrs;
    }
}
SessionFixationProtectionStrategy strategy = new
AttrsSessionFixationProtectionStrategy(attrsToRetain);
```

BasicAuthenticationFilter

The `BasicAuthenticationFilter` default constructor, the
`setAuthenticationManager`, and the `setRememberMeServices` methods were removed
in favor of the constructor injection:

```
BasicAuthenticationFilter filter = new BasicAuthenticationFilter();
filter.setAuthenticationManager(authenticationManager);
filter.setAuthenticationEntryPoint(entryPoint);
filter.setIgnoreFailure(true);
```

This should be replaced with:

```
BasicAuthenticationFilter filter = new
BasicAuthenticationFilter(authenticationManager, entryPoint);
```

Using this constructor automatically sets `ignoreFalure` to `true`.

SecurityContextPersistenceFilter

`SecurityContextPersistenceFilter` removed the `setSecurityContextRepository`
in favor of the constructor injection. For example:

```
SecurityContextPersistenceFilter filter = new
SecurityContextPersistenceFilter();
filter.setSecurityContextRepository(securityContextRepository);
```

This should be replaced with:

```
SecurityContextPersistenceFilter filter = new
SecurityContextPersistenceFilter(securityContextRepository);
```

RequestCacheAwareFilter

`RequestCacheAwareFilter` removed the `setRequestCache` in favor of the constructor
injection. For example:

```
RequestCacheAwareFilter filter = new RequestCacheAwareFilter();
filter.setRequestCache(requestCache);
```

This should be replaced with:

```
RequestCacheAwareFilter filter = new RequestCacheAwareFilter(requestCache);
```

ConcurrentSessionFilter

`ConcurrentSessionFilter` removed the default constructor, the `setExpiredUrl`, and the `setSessionRegistry` methods in favor of the constructor injection. For example:

```
ConcurrentSessionFilter filter = new ConcurrentSessionFilter();
filter.setSessionRegistry(sessionRegistry);
filter.setExpiredUrl("/expired");
```

This should be replaced with:

```
ConcurrentSessionFilter filter = new
ConcurrentSessionFilter(sessionRegistry,"/expired");
```

SessionManagementFilter

`SessionManagementFilter` removed the `setSessionAuthenticationStrategy` method in favor of the constructor injection. For example:

```
SessionManagementFilter filter = new
SessionManagementFilter(securityContextRepository);
filter.setSessionAuthenticationStrategy(sessionAuthenticationStrategy);
```

This should be replaced with:

```
SessionManagementFilter filter = new
SessionManagementFilter(securityContextRepository,
sessionAuthenticationStrategy);
```

RequestMatcher

The `RequestMatcher` and its implementations have moved from the `org.springframework.security.web.util` package to `org.springframework.security.web.util.matcher`. Specifically:

```
org.springframework.security.web.util.RequestMatcher
org.springframework.security.web.util.matcher.RequestMatcher
org.springframework.security.web.util.AntPathRequestMatcher
→org.springframework.security.web.util.matcher.AntPathRequestMatcher
org.springframework.security.web.util.AnyRequestMatcher
```

```
org.springframework.security.web.util.matcher.AnyRequestMatcher.INSTANCE
org.springframework.security.web.util.ELRequestMatcher
org.springframework.security.web.util.matcher.ELRequestMatcher
org.springframework.security.web.util.IpAddressMatcher
org.springframework.security.web.util.matcher.IpAddressMatcher
org.springframework.security.web.util.RequestMatcherEditor
org.springframework.security.web.util.matcher.RequestMatcherEditor
org.springframework.security.web.util.RegexRequestMatcher
org.springframework.security.web.util.matcher.RegexRequestMatcher
```

WebSecurityExpressionHandler

WebSecurityExpressionHandler was removed in favor of using
SecurityExpressionHandler<FilterInvocation>.

This means you may have the following:

```
WebSecurityExpressionHandler handler = ...
```

This needs to be updated to:

```
SecurityExpressionHandler<FilterInvocation> handler = ...
```

You can implement WebSecurityExpressionHandler like so:

```
public class CustomWebSecurityExpressionHandler implements
WebSecurityExpressionHandler {
    ...
}
```

Then it must be updated to:

```
public class CustomWebSecurityExpressionHandler implements
SecurityExpressionHandler<FilterInvocation> {
    ...
}
```

@AuthenticationPrincipal

`org.springframework.security.web.bind.annotation.AuthenticationPrincipal` has been deprecated in favor of
`org.springframework.security.core.annotation.AuthenticationPrincipal`.
For example:

```
import
org.springframework.security.web.bind.annotation.AuthenticationPrincipal;
// ...

@RequestMapping("/messages/inbox")
public ModelAndView findMessagesForUser(@AuthenticationPrincipal CustomUser
customUser) {
      // .. find messages for this user and return them ...
}
```

This should be replaced with:

```
import
org.springframework.security.core.annotation.AuthenticationPrincipal;
// ...

@RequestMapping("/messages/inbox")
public ModelAndView findMessagesForUser(@AuthenticationPrincipal CustomUser
customUser) {
      // .. find messages for this user and return them ...
}
```

Migrating default filter URLs

A number of servlet filters had their default URLs switched to help guard against information leakage.

There were many URLs that were changed and the following commit contains 125 changed files with 8,122 additions and 395 deletions: `https://github.com/spring-projects/spring-security/commit/c67ff42b8abe124b7956896c78e9aac896fd79d9`.

JAAS

Unfortunately, we did not have space to discuss Spring Security's JAAS integration. However, there is a JAAS sample application included in the Spring Security samples at `https://docs.spring.io/spring-security/site/docs/current/reference/htmlsingle/#jaas-sample`. In fact, there is also excellent documentation about JAAS integration, available in the Spring Security reference at `https://docs.spring.io/spring-security/site/docs/current/reference/htmlsingle/#jaas`. When looking at the JAAS reference documentation, you will notice that, from Spring Security 4.2 onwards, support was added for using JAAS login modules with arbitrary JAAS configuration implementations. Spring Security 4.2 also added the `jaas-api-provision` attribute to the `<http>` element, which ensures that the JAAS Subject is populated for applications that may also rely on the JAAS Subject.

Summary

This chapter reviewed the major and minor changes that you will find when upgrading an existing Spring Security 3 project to Spring Security 4.2. In this chapter, we have reviewed the significant enhancements to the framework that are likely to motivate an upgrade. We also examined upgrade requirements, dependencies and common types of code, and configuration changes that will prevent applications from working post-upgrade. We also covered investigation (at a high level) of the overall code-reorganization changes that the Spring Security authors made as part of codebase restructuring.

If this is the first chapter you've read, we hope that you return to the rest of the book and use this chapter as a guide to allow your upgrade to Spring Security 4.2 to proceed as smoothly as possible!

17
Microservice Security with OAuth 2 and JSON Web Tokens

In this chapter, we will take a look at microservices-based architectures and look at how OAuth 2 with **JSON Web Tokens (JWT)** plays a role in securing microservices in a Spring-based application.

The following is a list of topics that will be covered in this chapter:

- The general difference between monolithic applications and microservices
- Comparing **service-oriented architectures (SOA)** with microservices
- The conceptual architecture of OAuth 2 and how it provides your services with trustworthy client access
- Types of OAuth 2 access tokens
- Types of OAuth 2 grant types
- Examining JWT and their general structure
- Implementing a resource server and authentication server used to grant access rights to clients in order to access OAuth 2 resources
- Implementing a RESTful client to gain access to resources through an OAuth 2 grant flow

We have quite a few items to cover in this chapter, but before we dig into the details of how to start leveraging Spring Security to implement OAuth 2 and JWT, we first want to create a baseline of the calendar application that does not have Thymeleaf or any other browser-based user interface.

After removing all Thymeleaf configuration and resources, the various controllers have been converted to **JAX-RS REST** controllers.

You should start with the code from `chapter16.00-calendar`.

What are microservices?

Microservices are an architectural approach that allows the development of physically separated modular applications which are autonomous, enabling agility, rapid development, continuous deployment, and scaling.

An application is built as a set of services, similar to SOA, such that services communicate through standard APIs, for example, JSON or XML, and this allows the aggregation of language-agnostic services. Basically, a service can be written in the best language for the task the service is being created for.

Each service runs in its own process and is location neutral, thus it can be located anywhere on the access network.

Monoliths

The microservices approach is the opposite of the traditional monolithic software approach, which consists of tightly integrated modules that ship infrequently and have to scale as a single unit. Traditional Java EE applications and the JBCP calendar application in this book are examples of monolithic applications. Take a look at the following diagram which depicts the monolithic architecture:

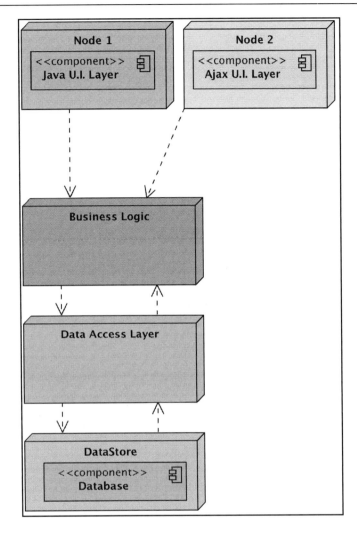

Although the monolithic approach fits well for some organizations and some applications, microservices is becoming popular with companies that need more options for agility and scalability in their ecosystem.

Microservices

A microservice architecture is a collection of small discrete services where each service implements a specific business capability. These services run their own process and communicate via an HTTP API usually using a RESTful service approach. These services are created to serve only one specific business function, such as user management, administrative roles, an e-commerce cart, a search engine, social media integration, and many others. Take a look at the following diagram which depicts the microservices architecture:

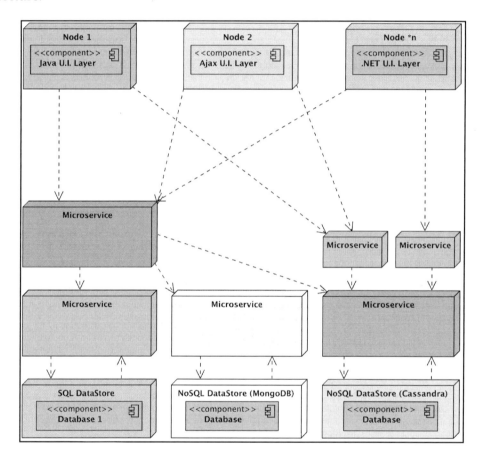

Each service can be deployed, upgraded, scaled, restarted, and removed independently of other services in the application and other systems in the enterprise.

Because each service is created independently of the other, they can each be written in different programming languages and use different data storage. Centralized service management is virtually non-existent and these services use lightweight HTTP, REST, or Thrift APIs for communicating among themselves.

 The **Apache Thrift** software framework can be downloaded from `https:/ /thrift.apache.org`. It is a framework for developing scalable cross-language services that combines a software stack with a code generation engine to build services that work efficiently and seamlessly between C++, Java, Python, PHP, Ruby, Erlang, Perl, Haskell, C#, Cocoa, JavaScript, Node.js, Smalltalk, and other languages.

Service-oriented architectures

You might be asking yourself, "Isn't this the same as SOA?" Not exactly, you could say microservices achieve what SOA promised in the first place.

An SOA is a style of software design where services are exposed to other components through a language-agnostic, communication protocol over a computer network.

The basic principle of SOA is to be independent of vendors, products, and technologies.

The definition of a service is a discrete unit of functionality that can be accessed remotely and acted upon and updated independently, such as retrieving a credit card statement online.

Although similar, SOA and microservices are still different types of architectures.

A typical SOA is often implemented inside deployment monoliths and is more platform driven, while microservices can be independently deployable and, therefore, offer more flexibility in all dimensions.

The key difference, of course, is the size; the word micro says it all. Microservices tend to be significantly smaller than regular SOA services. As Martin Fowler said:

"We should think about SOA as a superset of microservices."

—*Martin Fowler*

Microservice security

Microservices can provide great flexibility but also introduce challenges that must be addressed.

Service communication

Monolithic applications use in-memory communication between processes, while microservices communicate over the network. The move to network communication raises issues of not only speed but also security.

Tight coupling

Microservices use many datastores rather than a few. This creates the opportunity for implicit service contracts between microservices and services that are tightly coupled.

Technical complexity

Microservices can create additional complexity, which can create security gaps. If the team does not have the correct experience, then managing these complexities can quickly become unmanageable.

The OAuth 2 specification

There is sometimes a misconception that OAuth 2 is an evolution from OAuth 1, but it is a completely different approach. OAuth1 specification requires signatures, so you would have to use cryptographic algorithms to create generate and validate those signatures that are no longer required for OAuth 2. The OAuth 2 encryption is now handled by TLS, which is required.

OAuth 2 *RFC-6749, The OAuth 2.0 Authorization Framework* (https://
tools.ietf.org/html/rfc6749):
*The OAuth 2.0 authorization framework enables a third-party application to
obtain limited access to an HTTP service, either on behalf of a resource owner by
orchestrating an approval interaction between the resource owner and the HTTP
service, or by allowing the third-party application to obtain access on its own
behalf.*

This specification replaces and makes obsolate the OAuth 1.0 protocol
described in *RFC 5849, The OAuth 1.0 Protocol* (https://tools.ietf.org/
html/rfc5849).

To properly understand how to utilize OAuth 2, we need to identify certain roles and the
collaboration between these roles. Let's define each of the roles that are participating in the
OAuth 2 authorization process:

- **Resource owner:** The resource owner is the entity capable of granting access to a
  protected resource that is located on a resource server
- **Authorization server:** The authorization server is a centralized security gateway
  for issuing access tokens to the client after successfully authenticating the
  resource owner and obtaining authorization
- **Resource server:** The resource server is the server hosting the protected resources
  and is capable of dissecting and responding to protected resource requests using
  the OAuth 2 access token
- **Microservice client:** The client is the application making resource requests that
  are protected on behalf of the resource owner, but with their authorization

Access tokens

An OAuth 2 access token, commonly referred to as access_token in code samples,
represents a credential that can be used by a client to access an API.

Access token

An access token usually has a limited lifetime and is used to enable the client to access
protected resources when including this token in the HTTP request header for each request.

Refresh token

A refresh token has a longer lifetime and is used to get a new access token once the access token has expired, but without the need to send credentials to the server again.

Grant types

Grant types are methods that a client can use to gain an access token that represents the permissions granted. There are different grant types that allow different types of access based on the needs of your application. Each grant type can support a different OAuth 2 flow without worrying about the technical aspects of the implementation.

Authorization code

The authorization code grant type, defined in *RFC 6749, Section 4.1* (`https://tools.ietf.org/html/rfc6749`), is a redirection-based flow where the browser receives an authorization code from anauthorization server and sends this to the client. The client will then interact with the authorization server and exchange the authorization code for `access_token` and, optionally, `id_token` and `refresh_token`. The client can now use this `access_token` to call the protected resource on behalf of the user.

Implicit

The implicit grant type, defined in *RFC 6749, Section 4.1* (`https://tools.ietf.org/html/rfc6749`), is similar to the authorization code grant type, but the client application receives `access_token` directly, without the need for `authorization_code`. This happens because the client application, which is usually a JavaScript application running within a browser and is less trusted than a client application running on the server, cannot be trusted with `client_secret` (which is required in the authorization code grant type). The implicit grant type does not send a refresh token to the application due to limited trust.

Password credentials

The resource owner password grant type, defined in *RFC 6749, Section 4.3* (`https://tools.ietf.org/html/rfc6749`), can be used directly as an authorization grant to obtain `access_token` and, optionally, `refresh_token`. This grant is used when there is a high degree of trust between the user and the client and when other authorization grant flows are not available. This grant type eliminates the need for the client to store the user credentials by exchanging the credentials with a long-lived `access_token` or `refresh_token`.

Client credentials

The Client Credentials Grant's, defined in *RFC 6749, Section 4.4* (`https://tools.ietf.org/html/rfc6749#section-4.4`), is for a non-interactive client (CLI), a daemon, or another service running. The client can directly ask the authorization server for `access_token` by using client-provided credentials (client id and client secret) to authenticate.

JSON Web Tokens

JWT is an open standard, *RFC 7519* (`https://tools.ietf.org/html/rfc7519`) that defines a compact and self-contained format for securely transmitting information between parties in the form of a JSON object. This information can be verified and trusted because it is digitally signed. JWTs can be signed using a secret (with the **hash-based message authentication code (HMAC) algorithm**) or a public/private key pair using the **Rivest–Shamir–Adleman (RSA)** encryption algorithm.

> JWT *RFC- 7519* (`https://tools.ietf.org/html/ rfc7519`):
> *JSON Web Token (JWT) is a compact, URL-safe means of representing claims to be transferred between two parties. The claims in a JWT are encoded as a JSON object that is used as the payload of a JSON Web Signature (JWS) structure or as the plaintext of a JSON Web Encryption (JWE) structure, enabling the claims to be digitally signed or integrity protected with a Message Authentication Code (MAC) and/or encrypted.*

JWT is used to carry information related to the identity and characteristics (claims) of the client bearing the token. JWT is a container and is signed by the server in order to avoid client tampering. This token is created during the authentication process and is verified by the authorization server before any processing. It is used by a resource server to allow a client to present a token representing its "identity card" to the resource server, and allows the resource server to verify the validity and integrity of the token in a stateless, secure manner.

Token structure

The structure of a JWT adheres to the following three-part structure including a header, payload, and signature:

```
[Base64Encoded(HEADER)] . [Base64Encoded (PAYLOAD)] .
[encoded(SIGNATURE)]
```

Encoded JWT

The following code snippet is the complete encoded `access_token` that is returned based on the client request:

```
eyJhbGciOiJSUzI1NiIsInR5cCI6IkpXVCJ9.eyJleHAiOjE1MDk2MTA2ODks
InVzZXJfbmFtZSI6InVzZXIxQGV4YW1wbGUuY29tIiwiYXV0aG9yaXRpZXMiOlsi
Uk9MRV9VU0VSIl0sImp0aSI6Ijc1NTRhZGM4LTBhMjItNDBhYS05YjQ5LTU4MTU2N
DBhNDUzNyIsImNsaWVudF9pZCI6Im9hdXRoQ2xpZW50MSIsInNjb3BlIjpb
Im9wZW5pZCJdfQ.iM5BqXj70ET1e5uc5UKgws1QGDv6NNZ4iVEHimsp1Pnx6WXuFwtpHQoerH_F
-

pTkbldmYWOwLC8NBDHElLeDi1VPFCt7xuf5Wb1VHe-uwslupz3maHsgdQNGcjQwIy7_U-
SQr0wmjcc5Mc_1BWOq3-pJ65bFV1v2mjIo3R1TAKgIZ091WG0e8DiZ5AQase
Yy43ofUWrJEXok7kUWDpnSezV96PDiG56kpyjF3x1VRKPOrm8CZuylC57wclk-
BjSdEenN_905sC0UpMNtuk9ENkVMOpa9_Redw356qLrRTYgKA-qpRFUpC-3g5
CXhCDwDQM3jyPvYXg4ZW3cibG-yRw
```

Header

The encoded header for our `access_token` JWT is **base64** encoded, as shown in the following code:

```
eyJhbGciOiJSUzI1NiIsInR5cCI6IkpXVCJ9
```

By decoding the encoded header, we have the following payload:

```
{
  "alg": "RS256",
   "typ": "JWT"
}
```

Payload

The encoded payload for our `access_token` JWT is base64 encoded, as shown here:

```
eyJleHAiOjE1MDk2MTA2ODksInVzZXJfbmFtZSI6InVzZXIxQGV4YW1wbGUuY29
tIiwiYXV0aG9yaXRpZXMiOlsiUk9MRV9VU0VSIl0sImp0aSI6Ijc1NTR
hZGM4LTBhMjItNDBhYS05YjQ5LTU4MTU2NDBhNDUzNyIsImNsaWVudF9pZCI6I
m9hdXRoQ2xpZW50MSIsInNjb3BlIjpbIm9wZW5pZCJdfQ
```

By decoding the encoded payload, we have the following payload claims:

```
{
  "exp": 1509610689,
  "jti": "7554adc8-0a22-40aa-9b49-5815640a4537",
  "client_id": "oauthClient1",
  "authorities": [
    "ROLE_USER"
   ],
    "scope": [
    "openid"
   ],
  "user_name": "user1@example.com"
}
```

Signature

The encoded payload for our `access_token` has been encoded with a private key by the authorization server, as seen in the following code:

```
iM5BqXj70ET1e5uc5UKgws1QGDv6NNZ4iVEHimsp1Pnx6WXuFwtpHQoerH_F-
pTkbldmYWOwLC8NBDHElLeDi1VPFCt7xuf5Wb1VHe-uwslupz3maHsgdQNGcjQwIy7_U-
SQr0wmjcc5Mc_1BWOq3-
pJ65bFV1v2mjIo3R1TAKgIZ091WG0e8DiZ5AQaseYy43ofUWrJEXok7kUWDpn
SezV96PDiG56kpyjF3x1VRKPOrm8CZuylC57wclk-
BjSdEenN_905sC0UpMNtuk9ENkVMOpa9_Redw356qLrRTYgKA-qpRFUp
C-3g5CXhCDwDQM3jyPvYXg4ZW3cibG-yRw
```

The following is pseudo code for the creation of a JWT signature:

```
var encodedString = base64UrlEncode(header) + ".";
encodedString += base64UrlEncode(payload);
var privateKey = "[-----PRIVATE KEY-----]";
var signature = SHA256withRSA(encodedString, privateKey);
var JWT = encodedString + "." + base64UrlEncode(signature);
```

OAuth 2 support in Spring Security

The Spring Security OAuth project provides support for using Spring Security with OAuth 2 authorization using the standard Spring Framework and Spring Security programming models and configuration idioms.

Resource owner

The resource owner can be one or multiple sources, and in the context of the JBCP calendar, it is going to have the calendar application as the resource owner. The JBCP calendar will not have any specific configuration that is needed to denote its ownership aside from configuring the resource server.

Resource server

The `@EnableResourceServer` annotation denotes the intention for the containing application to enable a Spring Security filter that authenticates requests via an incoming OAuth2 token:

```
//src/main/java/com/packtpub/springsecurity/configuration/
OAuth2ResourceServerConfig.java

@EnableResourceServer
public class OAuth2ResourceServerConfig
extends ResourceServerConfigurerAdapter {...}
```

The `@EnableResourceServer` annotation denotes the intention for the containing application to enable an `OAuth2AuthenticationProcessingFilter` filter that authenticates requests via an incoming OAuth 2 token. The `OAuth2AuthenticationProcessingFilter` filter requires web security to be enabled using the `@EnableWebSecurity` annotation somewhere in the application. The `@EnableResourceServer` annotation registers a custom `WebSecurityConfigurerAdapter` class with a hardcoded `@Order` of 3. It is currently not possible to change the order of this `WebSecurityConfigurerAdapter` class due to technical limitations in the Spring Framework. To deal with this limitation, it is advised not to use other security adapters with the order of 3, and Spring Security will complain in the event that you do set one in the same order:

```
//o.s.s.OAuth
2.config.annotation.web.configuration.ResourceServerConfiguration.class

    @Configuration
    public class ResourceServerConfiguration
        extends WebSecurityConfigurerAdapter implements Ordered {
          private int order = 3;
            ...
        }
```

Authorization server

To enable the authorization server capability, we include the `@EnableAuthorizationServer` annotation in our configuration. The addition of this annotation will put an `o.s.s.OAuth 2.provider.endpoint.AuthorizationEndpoint` interface and an `o.s.s.OAuth 2.provider.endpoint.TokenEndpoint` interface into context. The developer will be responsible for securing the `AuthorizationEndpoint` (/oauth/authorize) with the `@EnableWebSecurity` configuration. The `TokenEndpoint` (/oauth/token) will be automatically secured using HTTP basic authentication based on the OAuth 2 client credentials:

```
//src/main/java/com/packtpub/springsecurity/configuration/
OAuth2AuthorizationServerConfig.java

@Configuration
@EnableAuthorizationServer
public class OAuth 2AuthorizationServerConfig {...}
```

RSA JWT access token converter keypair

In order to create a secure JWT encoded signature, we will create a custom RSA `keystore` that we will use to create a custom `o.s.s.OAuth 2.provider.token.storeJwtAccessTokenConverter` interface:

```
$ keytool -genkey -alias jbcpOAuth 2client -keyalg RSA \
-storetype PKCS12 -keystore jwtConverterStore.p12 \
-storepass changeit \
-dname "CN=jwtAdmin1@example.com,OU=JBCP Calendar,O=JBCP,L=Park
City,S=Utah,C=US"
```

This will create a `PKCS12` certificate called `jwtConverterStore.p12`, which needs to be copied into the `./src/main/resources/key` directory.

OAuth 2 resource configuration properties

We want to externalize the properties required to configure our JWT resources by providing `keyPair` attributes, including `keystore`, `alias`, and `storePassword` for our generated certificate, as you can see in our `application.yml` file, `src/main/resources/application.yml`:

```
# OAuth 2 Configuration:
security:
OAuth 2:
   # Resource Config:
   resource:
     jwt:
       keyPair:
         keystore: keys/jwtConverterStore.p12
         alias: jbcpOAuth 2client
         storePassword: changeit
```

OAuth 2 client configuration properties

We need to configure the client details for the client authentication, grants, and OAuth 2 scopes, as you can see in the `application.yml` file, `src/main/resources/application.yml`:

```
# OAuth 2 Configuration:
security:
OAuth 2:
   # Client Config:
```

```
client:
   # Basic Authentication credentials for OAuth 2
   clientId: oauthClient1
   clientSecret: oauthClient1Password
   authorizedGrantTypes: password, refresh_token
   scope: openid
```

JWT access token converter

The final step for creating JWT tokens is creating a custom `JwtAccessTokenConverter` that will use the generated RSA certificate for our JWT signatures. To do this, we need to pull our keyPair configuration and configure a custom `JwtAccessTokenConverter` as seen in the OAuth2AuthorizationServerConfig.java file:

```java
//src/main/java/com/packtpub/springsecurity/configuration/
OAuth2AuthorizationServerConfig.java

public class OAuth2AuthorizationServerConfig {
    @Value("${security.OAuth 2.resource.jwt.keyPair.keystore}")
    private String keystore;
    @Value("${security.OAuth 2.resource.jwt.keyPair.alias}")
    private String keyPairAlias;
  @Value("${security.OAuth 2.resource.jwt.keyPair.storePassword}")
    private String keyStorePass;
    @Bean
    public JwtAccessTokenConverter jwtAccessTokenConverter() {
        JwtAccessTokenConverter converter = new
        JwtAccessTokenConverter();
        KeyPair keyPair = new KeyStoreKeyFactory
        (new ClassPathResource(keystore),
        keyStorePass.toCharArray() ).getKeyPair(keyPairAlias);
        converter.setKeyPair(keyPair);
        return converter;
    }
}
```

The UserDetailsService object

We will use `CalendarUser` credentials to assign an authorized `GrantedAuthority` to the client. In order to do this, we must either configure our `CalendarUserDetailsService` class or qualify it with the name `userDetailsService`, as you can see in the following `CalendarUserDetailsService.java` file:

```
//src/main/java/com/packtpub/springsecurity/core/userdetails/
CalendarUserDetailsService.java

@Component("userDetailsService")
public class CalendarUserDetailsService
implements UserDetailsService {...}
```

Another alternative to defining a custom name for our `@Component` annotation is to define an `@Bean` declaration, which we can accomplish using the following entry in our `SecurityConfig.java` file:

```
//src/main/java/com/packtpub/springsecurity/configuration/SecurityConfig.ja
va

@Bean
public CalendarUserDetailsService userDetailsService
(CalendarUserDao calendarUserDao) {
    return new CalendarUserDetailsService(calendarUserDao);
}
```

Running the OAuth 2 server application

At this point, we can start the application and we will be ready to send OAuth 2 requests.

 At this point, your code should look like this: `chapter16.01-calendar`.

Server requests

We can test the application with either a command-line tool such as `cURL` or `HTTPie`, or you could also use a REST client plugin such as Postman to send requests to the server.

`HTTPie`: a CLI, cURL-like tool for humans, `HTTPie` (pronounced aitch-tee-tee-pie) is a command-line HTTP client. Its goal is to make CLI interaction with web services as human-friendly as possible. It provides a simple HTTP command that allows for sending arbitrary HTTP requests using a simple and natural syntax, and displays colorized output. `HTTPie` can be used for testing, debugging, and generally interacting with HTTP servers (https://httpie.org).

Token requests

When we make the initial token request, we should get a successful response similar to the following:

```
$ http -a oauthClient1:oauthClient1Password -f POST
localhost:8080/oauth/token
grant_type=password username=user1@example.com password=user1
HTTP/1.1 200
Cache-Control: no-cache, no-store, max-age=0, must-revalidate
Cache-Control: no-store
Content-Type: application/json;charset=UTF-8
Date: Thu, 09 Nov 2017 20:29:26 GMT
Expires: 0
Pragma: no-cache
Pragma: no-cache
Transfer-Encoding: chunked
X-Application-Context: application:default
X-Content-Type-Options: nosniff
X-Frame-Options: DENY
X-XSS-Protection: 1; mode=block
{
"access_token": "eyJhbGciOiJSUzI1NiIsInR5cCI6IkpXVCJ9.eyJleHAiOjE1MT
AzMDI1NjYsInVzZXJfbmFtZSI6InVzZXIxQGV4YW1wbGUuY29tIiwiYXV0aG9yaXRp
ZXMiOlsiUk9MRV9VU0VSIl0sImp0aSI6ImYzNzYzMWI4LWI0OGEtNG
Y1MC1iNGQyLTVlNDk1NTRmYzZjZSIsImNsaWVudF9pZCI6Im9hdXRo
Q2xpZW50MSIsInNjb3BlIjpbIm9wZW5pZCJdfQ.d5I2ZFX9ia_43eeD5X3JO6i_uF1Zw-
SaZ1CWbphQlYI3oCq6Xr9Yna5fvvosOZoWjb8pyo03EPVCig3mobhO6AF
18802XOlBRx3qb0FGmHZzDoPw3naTDHlhE97ctlIFIcuJVqi34T60cvii
uXmcE1tJ-H6-7AB04-wZl_WaucoO8-K39GvPyVabWBfSpfv0nbhh_XMNiB
PnN8u5mqSKI9xGjYhjxXspRyy--
zXx50Nqj1aYzxexy8Scawrtt2F87o1IesOodoPEQGTgVVieIilplwkMLhMvJfxhyMOt
ohR63XOGBSI4dDz58z3zOlk9P3k2Uq5FmkqwNNkduKceSw","expires_in": 43199,
"jti": "f37631b8-b48a-4f50-b4d2-5e49554fc6ce","refresh_token":
"eyJhbGciOiJSUzI1NiIsInR5cCI6IkpXVCJ9.eyJ1c2VyX25hbWUiOiJ1c2VyM
UBleGFtcGxlLmNvbSIsInNjb3BlIjpbIm9wZW5pZCJdLCJhdGkiOiJmMzc2MzF
iOC1iNDhhLTRmNTAtYjRkMi01ZTQ5NTU0ZmM2Y2UiLCJleHAiOjE1MTI4NTEzNjYs
```

```
ImF1dGhvcml0aWVzIjpbIlJPTEVfVVNFUiJdLCJqdGkiOiJjODM2OGI4NS0xNTk5L
TQ0NTgtODQ2Mi1iNGFhNDg1OGIzY2IiLCJjbGllbnRfaWQiOiJvYXV0aENsaWVudDEifQ.
RZJ2GbEvcmFbZ3SVHmtFnSF_O2kv-
TmN56tddW2GkG0gIRr612nN5DVlfWDKorrftmmm64x8bxuV2CcFx8Rm4SSWuoYv
j4oxMXZzANqXWLwj6Bei4z5uvuu00g6PtJvy5Twjt7GWCvEF82PBoQL-
bTM3RNSKmPnYPBwOGaRFTiSTdKsHCcbrg-
H84quRKCjXTl7Q6l8ZUxAf1eqWlOYEhRiGHtoULzdOvL1_W0OoWrQds1EN5g
AuoTTSI3SFLnEE2MYu6cNznJFgTqmVs1hYmX1hiXUhmCq9nwYpWei-
bu0MaXCa9LRjDRl9E6v86vWJiBVzd9qQilwTM2KIvgiG7w", "scope": "openid",
"token_type": "bearer"
}
```

Specifically, we have been granted an access token that can be used in subsequent requests. The following is the `access_token` that will be used as our bearer:

```
eyJhbGciOiJSUzI1NiIsInR5cCI6IkpXVCJ9.eyJleHAiOjE1MTAzMDI1
NjYsInVzZXJfbmFtZSI6InVzZXIxQGV4YW1wbGUuY29tIiwiYXV0aG9yaXRpZXM
iOlsiUk9MRV9VU0VSIl0sImp0aSI6ImYzNzYzMWI4LWI0OGEtNGY1MC1iNGQyL
TVlNDk1NTRmYzZjZSIsImNsaWVudF9pZCI6Im9hdXRoQ2xpZW50MSIsInNjb
3BlIjpbIm9wZW5pZCJdfQ.d5I2ZFX9ia_43eeD5X3JO6i_uF1Zw-
SaZ1CWbphQlYI3oCq6Xr9Yna5fvvosOZoWjb8pyo03EPVCig3mobhO6AF18802XO
lBRx3qb0FGmHZzDoPw3naTDHlhE97ctlIFIcuJVqi34T60cviiuXmcE1tJ-H6-7AB04-
wZl_WaucoO8-
K39GvPyVabWBfSpfv0nbhh_XMNiBPnN8u5mqSKI9xGjYhjxXspRyy--
zXx50Nqj1aYzxexy8Scawrtt2F87o1IesOodoPEQGTgVVieIilplwkMLhMvJfxhyMOto
hR63XOGBSI4dDz58z3zOlk9P3k2Uq5FmkqwNNkduKceSw
```

Now we will take the `access_token` and use that token to initiate additional requests to the server with the following format:

```
$ http localhost:8080/ "Authorization: Bearer [access_token]"
```

When adding the `access_token` we received in the first request, we should get the following request:

```
$ http localhost:8080/ 'Authorization: Bearer
eyJhbGciOiJSUzI1NiIsInR5cCI6IkpXVCJ9.eyJleHAiOjE1MTAzMD
I1NjYsInVzZXJfbmFtZSI6InVzZXIxQGV4YW1wbGUuY29tIiwiYXV0aG9yaXRp
ZXMiOlsiUk9MRV9VU0VSIl0sImp0aSI6ImYzNzYzMWI4LWI0OGEtNGY1MC1iNGQyLT
VlNDk1NTRmYzZjZSIsImNsaWVudF9pZCI6Im9hdXRoQ2xpZW50MSIsInNjb3BlIjpb
Im9wZW5pZCJdfQ.d5I2ZFX9ia_43eeD5X3JO6i_uF1Zw-
SaZ1CWbphQlYI3oCq6Xr9Yna5fvvosOZoWjb8pyo03EPVCig3mobhO6AF18802XOl
BRx3qb0FGmHZzDoPw3naTDHlhE97ctlIFIcuJVqi34T60cviiuXmcE1tJ-H6-7AB04-
wZl_WaucoO8-
K39GvPyVabWBfSpfv0nbhh_XMNiBPnN8u5mqSKI9xGjYhjxXspRyy--
zXx50Nqj1aYzxexy8Scawrtt2F87o1IesOodoPEQGTgVVieIilplwkMLhMvJf
xhyMOtohR63XOGBSI4dDz58z3zOlk9P3k2Uq5FmkqwNNkduKceSw'
HTTP/1.1 200
```

```
Cache-Control: no-cache, no-store, max-age=0, must-revalidate
Content-Length: 55
Content-Type: text/plain;charset=UTF-8
Date: Thu, 09 Nov 2017 20:44:00 GMT
Expires: 0
Pragma: no-cache
X-Application-Context: application:default
X-Content-Type-Options: nosniff
X-Frame-Options: DENY
X-XSS-Protection: 1; mode=block
```

{'message': 'welcome to the JBCP Calendar Application'}

We can continue to make subsequent requests with the same access_token, such as retrieving the events for the current user:

```
$ http localhost:8080/events/my 'Authorization: Bearer
eyJhbGciOiJSUzI1NiIsInR5cCI6IkpXVCJ9.eyJleHAiOjE1MTAzMDI1NjYsI
nVzZXJfbmFtZSI6InVzZXIxQGV4YW1wbGUuY29tIiwiYXV0aG9yaXRpZXMiOlsiU
k9MRV9VU0VSIl0sImp0aSI6ImYzNzYzMWI4LWI0OGEtNGY1MC1iNGQyLTVlNDk1NT
RmYzZjZSIsImNsaWVudF9pZCI6Im9hdXRoQ2xpZW50MSIsInNjb3BlIjpbIm9wZW5pZ
CJdfQ.d5I2ZFX9ia_43eeD5X3JO6i_uF1Zw-
SaZ1CWbphQlYI3oCq6Xr9Yna5fvvosOZoWjb8pyo03EPVCig3mobhO6AF18802XO
lBRx3qb0FGmHZzDoPw3naTDHlhE97ctlIFIcuJVqi34T60cviiuXmcE1tJ-H6-7AB04-
wZl_WaucoO8-
K39GvPyVabWBfSpfv0nbhh_XMNiBPnN8u5mqSKI9xGjYhjxXspRyy--
zXx50Nqj1aYzxexy8Scawrtt2F87o1IesOodoPEQGTgVVieIilplwkMLhMvJfxhyMOtohR63
XOGBSI4dDz58z3zOlk9F3k2Uq5FmkqwNNkduKceSw'
HTTP/1.1 200
Cache-Control: no-cache, no-store, max-age=0, must-revalidate
Content-Type: application/json;charset=UTF-8
Date: Thu, 09 Nov 2017 20:57:17 GMT
Expires: 0
Pragma: no-cache
Transfer-Encoding: chunked
X-Application-Context: application:default
X-Content-Type-Options: nosniff
X-Frame-Options: DENY
X-XSS-Protection: 1; mode=block
{
    "currentUser": [
        {
            "description": "This is going to be a great birthday",
            "id": 100,
            "summary": "Birthday Party",
```

```
        "when": 1499135400000
    }
  ]
}
```

Now that we have our OAuth 2 server ready to issue `access_tokens` for clients, we now can create a microservices client to interact with our system.

Microservices client

We start our new client application by enabling this application as an OAuth 2 client with the addition of the `@EnableOAuth2Client` annotation. The addition of the `@EnableOAuth2Client` annotation will allow this application to retrieve and use authorization code grants from one or more OAuth2 authorization server. Client applications that use client credential grants do not need `AccessTokenRequest` or the scoped `RestOperations` (the state is global for the applications), but they should still use the filter to trigger `OAuth2RestOperations` to obtain a token when necessary. Applications that use password grants need to set the authentication properties in `OAuth2ProtectedResourceDetails` before using the `RestOperations` method, which we will configure shortly. Let's take a look at the following steps and see how it is done:

1. We need to set up a few properties that will be used to configure the client, as shown in the following `JavaConfig.java` file:

```java
//src/main/java/com/packtpub/springsecurity/configuration/JavaConfig.java

@Configuration
@EnableOAuth 2Client
public class JavaConfig {
    @Value("${oauth.token.uri}")
    private String tokenUri;
    @Value("${oauth.resource.id}")
    private String resourceId;
    @Value("${oauth.resource.client.id}")
    private String resourceClientId;
    @Value("${oauth.resource.client.secret}")
    private String resourceClientSecret;
    @Value("${oauth.resource.user.id}")
    private String resourceUserId;
    @Value("${oauth.resource.user.password}")
    private String resourceUserPassword;
    @Autowired
    private DataSource dataSource;
```

```
    . . .
}
```

2. In addition to several standard properties we need to execute the OAuth 2 RESTful operations, we also need to create a `dataSource` to hold `oauth_client_token` that will be retrieved upon the initial request, then used in subsequent operations for a given resource. Now let's create `ClientTokenServices` for managing `oauth_client_token`, as shown in the following `JavaConfig.java` file:

```
//src/main/java/com/packtpub/springsecurity/configuration/JavaC
onfig.java

@Bean
public ClientTokenServices clientTokenServices() {
  return new JdbcClientTokenServices(dataSource);
}
```

3. Now we create the `OAuth2RestTemplate` that will manage the OAuth2 communication. We will start by creating a `ResourceOwnerPasswordResourceDetails` to hold the resource connection details, then construct an `OAuth2RestTemplate` to be used as an `OAuth2RestOperations` for the client request:

```
//src/main/java/com/packtpub/springsecurity/configuration/J
avaConfig.java

@Bean
public OAuth2RestOperationsOAuth2RestOperations() {
    ResourceOwnerPasswordResourceDetails resource =
                    new
ResourceOwnerPasswordResourceDetails();
    resource.setAccessTokenUri(tokenUri);
    resource.setId(resourceId);
    resource.setClientId(resourceClientId);
    resource.setClientSecret(resourceClientSecret);
    resource.setGrantType("password");
    resource.setScope(Arrays.asList("openid"));
    resource.setUsername(resourceUserId);
    resource.setPassword(resourceUserPassword);
    return new OAuth 2RestTemplate(resource);
}
```

Configuring the OAuth 2 client

Now that we have enabled our @EnableOAuth2Client annotation and set up a
ResourceOwnerPasswordResourceDetails object, we need to configure the properties
used to connect to the resource server and authentication server:

```
//src/main/resources/application.yml

oauth:
url: ${OAUTH_URL:http://localhost:8080}
token:
   uri: ${OAUTH_URL:http://localhost:8080}/oauth/token
resource:
   id: microservice-test
   # Client BASIC Authentication for Authentication Server
   client:
     id: ${OAUTH_CLIENT_ID:oauthClient1}
     secret: ${OAUTH_CLIENT_SECRET:oauthClient1Password}
   # Resource Password Credentials
   user:
     id: ${OAUTH_USER_ID:user1@example.com}
     password: ${OAUTH_USER_PASSWORD:user1}
```

We now have the pieces in place and can start making requests with the
OAuth2RestOperations object. We will start by creating RestController to pull remote
details and display them as a result of RESTful requests, as shown in our
OAuth2EnabledEventsController.java file:

```
//src/main/java/com/packtpub/springsecurity/web/controllers/
OAuth2EnabledEventsController.java

@RestController
public class OAuth2EnabledEventsController {
   @Autowired
   private OAuth2RestOperations template;
   @Value("${base.url:http://localhost:8888}")
   private String baseUrl;
   @Value("${oauth.url:http://localhost:8080}")
   private String baseOauthUrl;
   @GetMapping("/events/my")
  public String eventsMy() {
     @SuppressWarnings("unchecked")
     String result = template.getForObject(baseOauthUrl+"/events/my",
     String.class);
     return result;
   }
}
```

We now should have the same codebase for a client application.

 Your code should look like `chapter16.01-calendar-client`.

We need to ensure that the `chapter16.01-calendar` application is running and ready to take OAuth 2 requests from clients. We can then start the `chapter16.01-calendar-client` application, which will expose several RESTful endpoints, including one to access the configured user events located at `/events/my` on the remote resource, and will return the following result by running `http://localhost:8888/events/my`:

```
{
 "currentUser": [
{
  "id": 100,
  "summary": "Birthday Party",
  "description": "This is going to be a great birthday",
  "when": 1499135400000
}
 ]
 }
```

Summary

In this chapter, you learned the general difference between monolithic applications and microservices and compared SOA with microservices. You also learned the conceptual architecture of OAuth 2 and how it provides your services with trustworthy client access, and learned about the types of OAuth 2 access tokens and the types of OAuth 2 grant types.

We examined the JWT and their general structure, implemented a resource server and authentication server used to grant access rights to clients in order to access OAuth 2 resources, and implemented a RESTful client to gain access to resources through an OAuth 2 grant flow.

Additional Reference Material

In this appendix, we will cover some reference material that we feel is helpful (and largely undocumented) but too comprehensive to insert in the chapters.

Getting started with the JBCP calendar sample code

As we described in Chapter 1, *Anatomy of an Unsafe Application*, we have assumed, that you have installed a JDK. You can download a JDK from Oracle's website http://www.oracle.com/technetwork/java/javase/downloads/index.html. You will need to have JDK 8 installed in order run the code samples. The codebase uses many JDK 8 features that are not compatible with JDK 7, and there has not been an attempt to sort out various JDK 9 issues with the IDEs as well as project dependencies.

Gradle Build Tool

All of the code in this book has been built using the Gradle Build Tool and is organized in a chapter-by-chapter multimodule build. You can find instructions and options for getting Gradle locally at https://gradle.org/install/.

A local installation of Gradle is not required as the root of the source code already has the Gradle wrapper installed. The Gradle wrapper can be installed in any submodule. You can find additional information about the Gradle wrapper at https://docs.gradle.org/current/userguide/gradle_wrapper.html.

Downloading the example code

You can download the example code files for all Packt books you have purchased from your account at http://www.packtpub.com. If you purchased this book from elsewhere, you can visit http://www.packtpub.com/support and register to have the files emailed directly to you.

Gradle IDE plugins

The codebase has been configured with the IntelliJ and Eclipse IDE plugin. This means Gradle can create all of the necessary IDE project files instead of manually importing the codebase, although you are not forced to use these plugins.

To use these plugins, open a Terminal or Command Prompt window to the root of the codebase. To execute the plugin, issue the following command on OSX or Linux:

```
$ ./gradlew idea
```

After running this task, there will be several IDEA project files in each directory, as shown in the following screenshot:

```
-rw-r--r--   1 mickknutson  staff   3.0K Nov 16 15:56 gradle.properties
-rwxr-xr-x   1 mickknutson  staff   5.2K Nov  3 09:18 gradlew*
-rwxr-xr-x@  1 mickknutson  staff   2.2K Nov  3 09:18 gradlew.bat*
-rw-r--r--   1 mickknutson  staff   644B Nov 17 12:14 jbcpcalendar.iml
-rw-r--r--   1 mickknutson  staff    23K Nov 17 12:14 jbcpcalendar.ipr
-rw-r--r--   1 mickknutson  staff   9.1K Nov 17 12:14 jbcpcalendar.iws
-rw-r--r--   1 mickknutson  staff   7.2K Nov 17 12:14 settings.gradle
```

If you are on a Windows machine, you will issue the following command:

```
C:\jbcdcalendar> gradlew.bat idea
```

The previous examples execute the `gradlew` script, which is the Gradle wrapper, and then give the command for the IDE files to create. IntelliJ project files are created with the `idea` task, and STS or any Eclipse-based IDE's project files are created with the eclipse task.

After running the Eclipse task, there will be several Eclipse project files and directories in each directory:

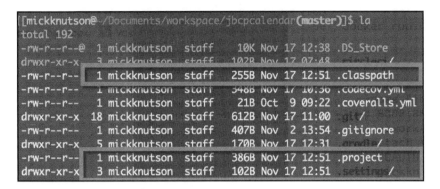

IntelliJ IDEA

Most of the diagrams used in this book were taken from IntelliJ IDEA from Jet Brains (https://www.jetbrains.com/idea/). IDEA has a wonderful support for multimodule Gradle builds.

IDEA will allow you to import an existing project, or you can simply open the `build.gradle` file from the root of the source code base and IDEA will create the necessary project files for you.

Once you have created the IDEA project files with the Gradle `idea` task, you can import the entire project using the **Import Project** option, as shown in the following screenshot:

Then, you will be prompted to select various options for how IDEA will execute this Gradle build, as shown in the following screenshot:

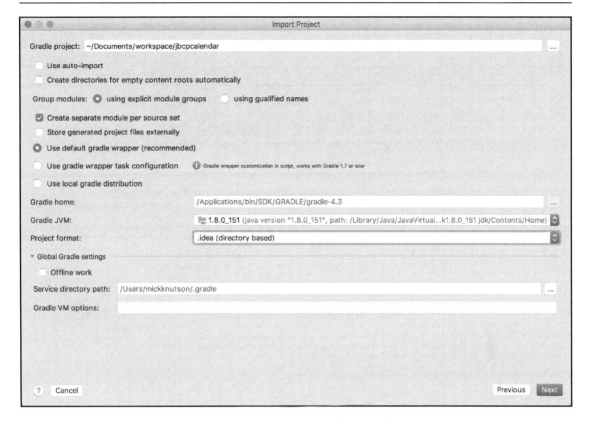

A special note for IDEA importing of Gradle projects

In the previous listing, you will notice that there is an option to use Gradle wrapper task configuration, versus the option that was selected, which is to use the default Gradle wrapper (recommended) option. The only difference is the use of the Gradle wrapper task configuration option, which will create a Gradle wrapper instance in each and every project directory. This will be helpful if you want to execute build commands on a Terminal or command line and not have to install a local version of Gradle. Otherwise, IDEA handles the Gradle wrapper calls for all projects.

Once the project is imported, you will be able to work with any of the chapters, and the layout will look as shown in the following screenshot:

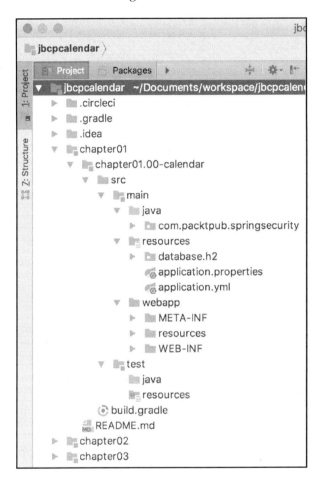

Spring Tool Suite or Eclipse

If using STS, we assume that you have access to **Spring Tool Suite (STS)** 3.9.1. You can download STS from `https://spring.io/tools/sts`. STS version 3.9.1 is based on Eclipse Oxygen 1a (4.7.1a) and you can find more information about the Oxygen release at `https:/ /www.eclipse.org/ide/`.

Creating a new workspace

It is best to create a fresh workspace in order to minimize discrepancies with your environment, which can be done by performing the following steps:

1. When you first open STS, it will prompt you for the workspace location. If you were previously using STS, you may need to go to **File | Switch Workspace | Other** to create a new workspace. We recommend entering a workspace location that does not contain any spaces. For example, take a look at the following screenshot:

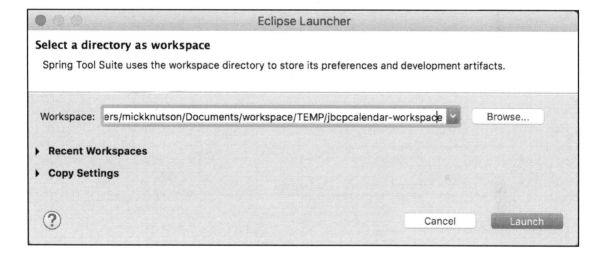

2. Once you have created a new workspace, you will want to exit the welcome screen by clicking on the close button on the **Welcome** tab, as shown in the following screenshot:

A sample code structure

The sample code is structured in a `.zip` file and contains folders of a multimodule Gradle project. Each folder is named `chapterNN`, where `NN` is the chapter number. Each `chapterNN` folder has additional folders containing each milestone project with the format `chapterNN.mm-calendar`, where `NN` is the chapter number and `mm` is the milestone within that chapter. For simplicity, we recommend that you extract the source to a path that does not contain any spaces. Each milestone is a checkpoint within the chapter and allows you to easily compare your code with the book's code. For example, `chapter02.03-calendar` contains the milestone number `03` within `Chapter 2`, *Getting Started with Spring Security*, of the calendar application. The location of the preceding project would be `~/jbcpcalendar/chapter02/chapter02.03-calendar`.

Chapter 1, *Anatomy of an Unsafe Application*, and Chapter 2, *Getting Started with Spring Security*, have been created as Spring IO projects, not using Spring Boot as a project base. Chapter 3, *Custom Authentication*, converted the calendar project to a Spring Boot codebase, and in Chapter 5, *Authentication with Spring Data*, JDBC was replaced with Spring Data as the persistence mechanism.

In order to keep each chapter as independent as possible, most chapters in the book are built off of Chapter 9, *Opening up to OpenID*, or Chapter 15, *Additional Spring Security Features*. This means that, in most cases, you can read through Chapter 9, *Opening up to OpenID*, and then skip around to the other parts of the book. However, this also means that it is important to start each chapter with the chapter's milestone 00 source code rather than continuing to work on the code from the previous chapter. This ensures that your code starts in the same place that the chapter does.

While you can get through the entire book without performing any of the steps, we recommend starting each chapter with milestone 00 and implementing the steps in the book. This will ensure that you get the most out of the book. You can use the milestone versions to copy large portions of code or to compare your code if you run into problems.

Importing the samples

Before we can import this Gradle project into Eclipse, you must install a Gradle plugin from the Eclipse marketplace. There are only two options at the time of writing this book. One is the Gradle IDE pack (http://marketplace.eclipse.org/content/gradle-ide-pack), but this project is not being maintained, and if you do install this plugin, Eclipse will warn you and suggest that you migrate to the **Buildship Gradle Integration** plugin (http://marketplace.eclipse.org/content/buildship-gradle-integration). Once installed, you will have an option to import an existing Gradle project.

Starting with our fresh workspace, perform the following steps:

1. Go to **File** | **Import** and select **Existing Gradle Project**, as shown in the following screenshot:

2. Click on **Next >**, as shown in the following screenshot:

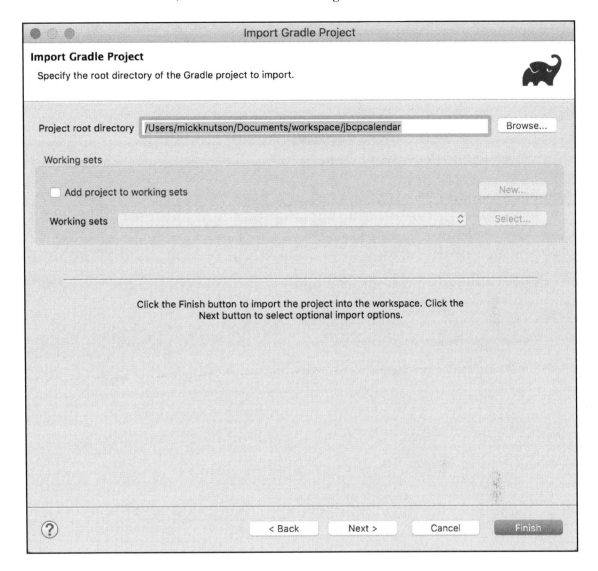

3. Click on **Next >** as shown in the following screenshot:

Make sure that you keep the defaults unless you want to use a local installation of Gradle.

4. Browse to the location you exported the code to and select the parent folder of the code. You will see all of the projects listed. You can select the projects you are interested in or leave all of the projects selected. If you decide to import all of the projects, you can easily focus on the current chapter since the naming conventions will ensure that the projects are sorted in the order that they are presented in the book:

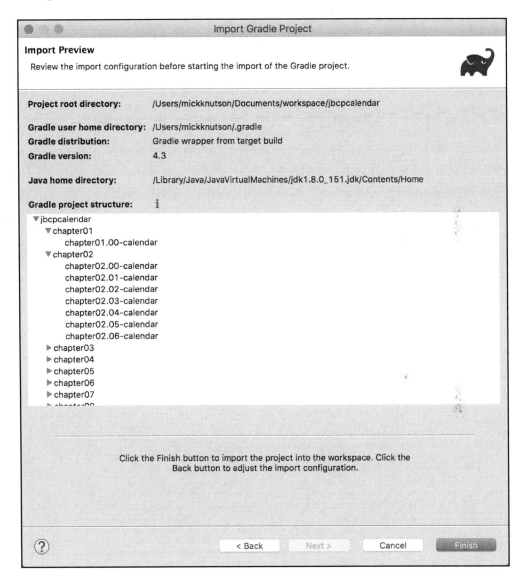

5. Click on **Finish**. All of the selected projects will be imported. If you have not used Gradle frequently, it will take a while to download your dependencies.

 An internet connection is required to download the dependencies.

Updated instructions for running the projects will be found in the README.md files in each section. This ensures that, as updates are made to STS, the code can still be built and run with the latest tools.

Running the samples

There are a few things that are necessary in order to run the sample applications within IDEA or STS. In all of the projects, a Tomcat plugin has been configured in Gradle to run the embedded instance to help you get started faster.

Starting the samples within IDEA

Running milestone projects can be done by creating a Run/Debug Configuration entry for each project.

Starting with our fresh workspace, perform the following steps:

1. Go to **File** | **Run** and select **Edit Configurations...**, as shown in the following screenshot:

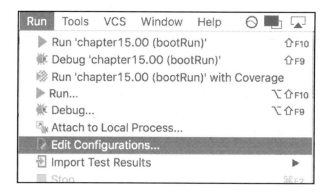

2. You will be presented with options to add new configurations. Select the plus (+) sign in the upper-left corner to choose a new Gradle configuration, as shown in the following screenshot:

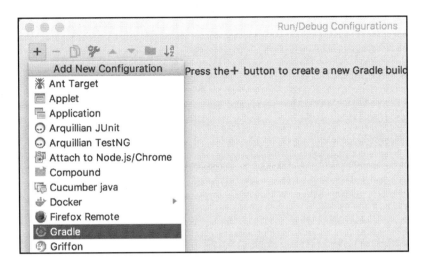

3. Now, you can give it a name like `chapter15.00 (bootRun)` and select the actual milestone directory for this configuration. Finally, enter `bootRun` under the **Tasks** option to execute, as shown in the following screenshot:

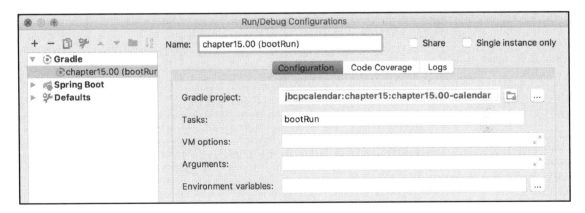

4. Select the configuration you want to execute; click on the green run button or use the *Shift + F10* key, as shown in the following screenshot:

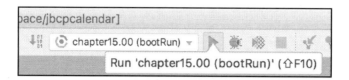

Gradle tasks

In `Chapter 1`, *Anatomy of an Unsafe Application*, and `Chapter 2`, *Getting Started with Spring Security*, the Gradle task to run the project will be *tomcatRun*. For the rest of the chapters in the book, Spring Boot has been used, and the Gradle task to start the project will be `bootRun`.

Starting the samples within STS

In STS, a run configuration is also created and the same information needs to be included for each milestone project to run, as depicted in the following screenshot:

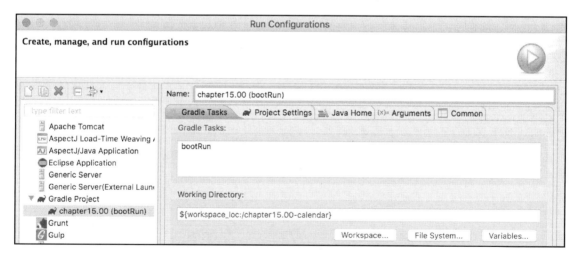

Using HTTPS within STS

Some of the chapters' sample code (that is, Chapter 8, *Client Certificate Authentication with TLS*, Chapter 9, *Opening up to OAuth2*, and Chapter 10, *Single Sign-On with the Central Authentication Service*) requires the use of HTTPS in order for the sample code to work.

All of the projects have been configured to run HTTPS; most of the configuration is managed in properties or YAM files.

Now, when you run the sample code on the embedded Tomcat server from Gradle, you can connect to http://localhost:8080 or to https://localhost:8443.

HTTPS setup in Tomcat

In this section, we outline how to set up HTTPS in Tomcat to provide TLS to our application. All of the included projects are running in an embedded Tomcat instance, but we will cover the certificate creation process as well as some tips for running these applications in a standalone Tomcat instance.

Generating a server certificate

If you do not already have a certificate, you must first generate one. If you wish, you can skip this step and use the tomcat.keystore file, which contains a certificate that is located in the etc directory in the book's sample source. Enter the following command lines at the Command Prompt:

```
$ keytool -genkey -alias jbcpcalendar -keypass changeit -keyalg RSA \
-keystore tomcat.keystore
Enter keystore password: changeit
Re-enter new password: changeitWhat is your first and last name? [Unknown]:
localhost
What is the name of your organizational unit? [Unknown]: JBCP Calendar
What is the name of your organization? [Unknown]: JBCP
What is the name of your City or Locality? [Unknown]: Anywhere
What is the name of your State or Province? [Unknown]: UT
What is the two-letter country code for this unit? [Unknown]: US
Is CN=localhost, OU=JBCP Calendar, O=JBCP, L=Anywhere, ST=UT, C=US correct?
[no]: yes
```

Most of the values are self-explanatory, but you will want to ensure that the answer to "What is your first and last name?" is the host that you will be accessing your web application from. This is necessary to ensure that the SSL handshake will succeed.

You should now have a file in the current directory named `tomcat.keystore`. You can view its contents using the following command from within the same directory:

```
$ keytool -list -v -keystore tomcat.keystore
Enter keystore password: changeit
Keystore type: JKS
Keystore provider: SUN
...
Alias name: jbcpcalendar
...
Owner: CN=localhost, OU=JBCP Calendar, O=JBCP, L=Anywhere, ST=UT, C=US
Issuer: CN=localhost, OU=JBCP Calendar, O=JBCP, L=Anywhere, ST=UT, C=US
```

As you may have guessed, it is insecure to use `changeit` as a password, as this is the default password used with many JDK implementations. In a production environment, you should use a secure password rather than something as simple as `changeit`.

For additional information about the `keytool` command, refer to the documentation found on Oracle's website at `https://docs.oracle.com/javase/9/tools/keytool.htm`. If you are having issues, you might also find the *CAS SSL Troubleshooting and Reference Guide* helpful (`https://apereo.github.io/cas/5.1.x/installation/Troubleshooting-Guide.html`).

Configuring Tomcat connector to use SSL

In this section, we will discuss how to configure a Tomcat 8.5 connector to SSL by performing the following steps:

1. Open the `server.xml` file that was included with the download of Tomcat 8.5. You can find this in the `conf` directory of your Tomcat server's home directory. Find the following entry in your `server.xml` file:

```
<!--
<Connector port="8443" protocol="HTTP/1.1" SSLEnabled="true"
maxThreads="150"
    scheme="https" secure="true" clientAuth="false" sslProtocol="TLS" />
```

2. Uncomment the connector and modify the value of the `keystoreFile` attribute to be the location of the keystore from the previous section. Also, ensure that you update the value of the `keystorePass` attribute to be the password used when generating the keystore. An example is shown in the following code snippet, but ensure that you update the values of both `keystoreFile` and `keystorePass`:

```
<Connector port="8443" protocol="HTTP/1.1" SSLEnabled="true"
maxThreads="150"
   scheme="https" secure="true" clientAuth="false" sslProtocol="TLS"
   keystoreFile="/home/mickknutson/packt/etc/tomcat.keystore"
   keystorePass="changeit"/>
```

3. You should now be able to start Tomcat and access it at `https://locahost:8443/`. For more information on configuring SSL on Tomcat, refer to the *SSL Configuration How-To* at `http://tomcat.apache.org/tomcat-8.5-doc/ssl-howto.html`.

Basic Tomcat SSL termination guide

This section is intended to help set up Tomcat to use SSL when using an SSL termination. The idea is that an external entity, such as a load balancer, manages the SSL connection instead of Tomcat. This means that the connection from the client (that is, the web browser) to the load balancer is over HTTPS and is secured. The connection from the load balancer to Tomcat is over HTTP and insecure. For this sort of setup to provide any layer of security, the connection from the load balancer to Tomcat should be over a private network.

The problem this setup causes is that Tomcat will now believe that the client is using HTTP and thus redirects will be sent as though there is an HTTP connection. To get around this, you can modify the configuration to instruct Tomcat that it is behind a proxy server.

The following example is a complete connector that will be used for Tomcat deployments that employ client certificate authentication:

```
//server.xml

<Connector
scheme="https"
secure="true"
proxyPort="443"
proxyHost="example.com"
port="8443"
protocol="HTTP/1.1"
```

```
        redirectPort="443"
        maxThreads="750"
        connectionTimeout="20000" />
```

The `server.xml` file can be found at `TOMCAT_HOME/conf/server.xml`. If you are interacting with Tomcat using Eclipse or Spring Tool Suite, you will find a project named `Servers` that contains the `server.xml` file. For example, if you are using Tomcat 8.5, the path in your Eclipse workspace might look similar to `/Servers/Tomcat v8.5 Server` at `localhost-config/server.xml`.

Note that there is no reference to a `keystore` because Tomcat does not manage the SSL connection. This setup will override the `HttpServletRequest` object to believe that the connection is HTTPS so that redirects are performed correctly. However, it will continue to accept HTTP connections. If the client can make an HTTP connection as well, a separate connector can be created—one that does not include the HTTPS setup. The proxy server can then send requests to the appropriate connector depending on whether the original request was HTTP or HTTPS.

For more information, refer to the *Tomcat Proxy How To* documentation at `http://tomcat.apache.org/tomcat-8.5-doc/proxy-howto.html`. If you are working with a different application, you can refer to their documentation for working with proxy servers.

Supplementary materials

This section contains a listing of additional resources to technologies and concepts that are used throughout the book:

- **Java Development Kit Downloads**: Refer to `http://www.oracle.com/technetwork/java/javase/downloads/index.html` for downloading the JDK.
- **MVC Architecture**: Refer to `https://en.wikipedia.org/wiki/Model%E2%80%93view%E2%80%93controller`.
- **Spring Security site**: Refer to `https://projects.spring.io/spring-security/`. You can find links to the Spring Security Javadoc, downloads, source code, and reference from at this link.
- **Spring Framework:** Refer to `https://projects.spring.io/spring-framework/`. You can find links to the Spring Framework Javadoc, downloads, source code, and reference from this link.
- **Spring Boot:** Refer to `https://projects.spring.io/spring-boot/`. You can find links to the Spring Boot Javadoc, downloads, source code, and reference from this link.

- **Spring Data:** Refer to `https://projects.spring.io/spring-data/`. You can find links to the Spring Data Javadoc, downloads, source code, and reference from this link. In this book, we covered three of the sub-projects of Spring-Data, including Spring Data Rest (`https://projects.spring.io/spring-data-rest/`), Spring Data JPA (`https://projects.spring.io/spring-data-jpa/`), and Spring Data MongoDB (`https://projects.spring.io/spring-data-mongodb/`).

- **Maven:** For more information about Maven, visit their site at `https://maven.apache.org`. For more information about Maven Transitive dependencies, refer to the *Introduction to the Dependency Mechanism* documentation at `https://maven.apache.org/guides/introduction/introduction-to-dependency-mechanism.html#Transitive_Dependencies`.

- **Building with Gradle:** Spring Security builds with Gradle (`https://gradle.org`) instead of using Maven. You can refer to the samples, for examples of how to build with Gradle at `https://docs.spring.io/spring-security/site/docs/4.2.x/reference/html/sample-apps.html`.

- **Object-relational mapping (ORM):** You can find more general information on Wikipedia at `https://en.wikipedia.org/wiki/Object-relational_mapping`. If you want more hands-on instruction, you may also be interested in the Hibernate (a common Java ORM Framework) documentation at `http://www.hibernate.org/`.

- **Undertow:** Undertow is a lightweight flexible performant web server written in Java, providing both blocking and non-blocking APIs based on NIO. There has been some work in the chapters to offer Undertow as an alternative to Tomcat. You can find more general information at `http://undertow.io/`.

The following are UI technologies:

- **JSP:** You can find more information about JSPs on Oracle's site at `https://javaee.github.io/tutorial/overview008.html#BNACM`.

- **Thymeleaf:** It is a modern, tempting framework that provides an excellent alternative to JSPs. An additional benefit is that it provides support for both Spring and Spring Security out of the box. You can find more information about Thymeleaf at `http://www.thymeleaf.org`.

Index